A Prescription for Life

Studying the Writings of Luke

Volume 2

The Acts of the Apostles

Whit Longcore

ISBN: 979-8-9881328-3-7

Printed in the United States of America

Acknowledgements

I want to thank all who have supported me.

My readers, who make the publishing of my studies well worth the effort.

My incredible editing team:
Frederick Foote
Melissa Kranzo
Pamela Anderson
Kathi Dunlap
My father, Wayne Longcore
And my mother, Mary Longcore

You have dedicated untold hours to help me with this publication, finding and helping me eliminate many goofs along the way.

My wife, Jenn, and son, Weylin. You have graciously and patiently supported me throughout the several hundred hours required to bring this study to print. You've sacrificed quality time for the cause, picked me up when I've fallen, and encouraged me when it all seemed futile.

Most importantly, my God, who pulled me out of the muck and mire for a greater purpose, The Lord, who gives me strength, and His Spirit which implants these words which I could not write alone.
None of this is possible without You, O Lord.

The Acts of

Jesus Christ,

through

the Apostles

Day 1

Just the Beginning

"The former treatise have I made, O Theophilus, concerning all that Jesus *began* both to do and teach," - Acts 1:1 MEV

As we've seen throughout the study of Luke's Gospel, that word "began" is a recurring theme in the physician's treatises, and I believe there's a very specific reason that God inspired such. The work of God is bigger than we can comprehend. It is more extensive than any book could cover. It is as John closed out His Gospel, "I suppose not even the world itself could contain the books that would be written." (John 21:25 MEV)

In Genesis, we saw what He by Whom all things were created *began* to do from nothingness. In Exodus, we saw what the Son of David *began* to do for and through His people, Israel. In Leviticus, we saw what the Eternal Judge *began* to do with the Law. In 1 and 2 Samuel, we saw what the King of Kings *began* to do with the governments of the world. In Song of Songs, we saw the way our Bridegroom *began* to love His Church. In the prophets, we saw the way the Faithful and True *began* to tell of all that would come.

In the Gospels, we saw the way the Son of Man *began* to teach and do His redeeming work. In the Epistles, we saw the way the Wonderful Counselor *began* to purify His bride. In Revelation, we saw the way the Alpha and Omega will *begin* to fulfill His promise of eternal life. Here in Acts, we will see the way the Light of the World *began* to shine further and further, starting with the very ones who crucified Him in Jerusalem, and spreading His rays of hope out to all the world. But it was all just a beginning. It was all a testimony of the Lord Jesus Christ who returns yet in glory, with eyes like fire.

"If the theme of the story be what Christ did, then the book is not the 'Acts of the Apostles,' but the 'Acts of Jesus Christ' through His servants. He, and He alone, is the Actor; and the men who appear in it are but instruments in His hands, He alone being the mover of the pawns on the board." - Charles Ellicott

The finished work of Christ on the cross is just that: finished, completed, sealed, everlasting. But the work of Christ in the hearts of His elect goes on until the Day we are resurrected in His glory. Up until that last moment, it's only just begun. Luke lays this out, beginning His second book with what Christ, "began both to do and teach," and ending with an ending that is not really an ending at all. Luke seemingly never concludes his narrative; He merely stops writing, for there is no conclusion until Christ returns.

"The theme is the work of Christ through the ages, of which each successive depository of His energies can do but a small portion, and must leave that portion unfinished; the book does not so much end as stop. It is a fragment, because the work of which it tells is not yet a whole." - Ellicott

Christ deposited his evangelistic energies on Peter and the other apostles, on Stephen, on Paul, on Luke, on Timothy, on Irenaeus, on Tertullian, on Henry, on Luther, on Spurgeon, on your grandmother, and if you have indeed received the down payment of the promise - the Holy Spirit - He deposits those energies on you. We can only do small things for the grand picture of God's work, and only do them by His Acts, but in that grand picture, each of us plays a role. All of *His*-story testifies that it's not *all* of His story. God works in and through His people, and will continue the work He began in you until the day of Christ Jesus.

Each of our lives, as servants of the Most High, could be missed in a blink of an eye in the grand scale of Christ's work. If I hear a supposed servant of Christ claim, "look what I have done for the kingdom, and how many I've brought to Christ," red flags go up all around. No amount of service to God can be to our credit. It is all His work. If you receive a crown on that day, I assure you, it will be cast at the feet of our Christ! How easily though we look here on earth at the servants and think highly of them.

Can I ask you a favor? If you enjoy or benefit from the work God does through me, please place the credit where it is due. Don't think highly of me, or any man, for service to God. Rather, think highly of the God who takes broken men like me and does better spiritual things with our broken flesh. "For from Him and through Him and to Him are all things. To Him be glory forever. Amen" (Romans 11:36 MEV)

Day 2

Infallible Proof

"to whom He presented Himself alive after His passion by many infallible proofs, appearing to them for forty days, and speaking concerning the kingdom of God." - Acts 1:3 MEV

Infallible is a pretty clear and precise word, but it doesn't do justice to the Greek word that we see here translated as "infallible proofs." The word doesn't have an English equivalent. Luke is the only writer of scripture to use it, and only here. Other Greek authors did utilize this word though, and it was always used to signify evidences that were definitive and undeniable. What Luke tells us here is that in His many varied appearances, the Risen Lord gave every proof that would dispel any doubt.

We have in scripture, at least 13 different appearances recorded over this 40-day period. Appearances to Mary, to 10 of the 11, to all 11, to two other disciples, to 500 witnesses, and more. Appearances at night, and day; while walking an open road, and while hiding behind locked doors; in the immediacy of their sorrow and fear, and well after the shock had worn off. What Luke tells us is that his careful investigation revealed that all who claimed to see him were absolutely convinced of what they saw, and their stories stood against inspection beyond a shadow of a doubt.

In the presence of many witnesses, Jesus had turned water into wine, purified the leper, caused the blind to see, fed 5000 men (plus women and children) with only five loaves and two small fishes, and resurrected the dead, but the absolute resurrection of His own broken body is the most captivating marvel of all. The resurrection of the Lord Jesus Christ is the defining point of all the Gospel. He who was dead now lives. Death had been defeated, and the Apostles had no room for doubt.

Why do you seek the living among the dead? Christ is risen, and with Him, every saint has the assurance of such resurrection. In glorified bodies, free of the corruption that has plagued us, we shall all be raised up again to live eternally in the wonderful presence of God.

"These forty days assure us of the narrow limits of the power of death. Love lives through death, memory lives through it. Christ has lived through it and comes up from the grave, serene and tender, with unruffled peace, with all the old tones of tenderness in the voice that said 'Mary!' So may we be sure that through death and after it we shall live and be ourselves. We, too, shall show ourselves alive after we have experienced the superficial change of death." - Alexander McLaren

What a gift this is. Brothers and sisters, the presence of many witnesses testified that without reasonable doubt Christ lives! The Holy Spirit testifies that all who truly believe on His name have the same promise. Fear neither man nor reaper.

Notes

Day 3

Wait Here

"Being assembled with them, He commanded them, 'Do not depart from Jerusalem, but wait for the promise of the Father, of which you have heard from Me. For John baptized with water, but you shall be baptized with the Holy Spirit not many days from now.' " - Acts 1:4-5 MEV

In studying this passage, I read one commentator after another, and the majority of their texts were little more than a debate over whether Christ "assembled with," or "dined with" them. Was this said at a meal, like so many other conversations Luke recorded, or was The Risen Savior of the world merely hanging around with the 11 and teaching them? What does it matter? Either way, we know He is giving them final instructions before His Ascension, and we also know, that after Jesus was resurrected, He asked them for food so He could eat.

How easily we miss the point... Almost across the board, in spending so many words on how a single word should be translated there weren't words left to point out God's glory in the instruction itself. Don't leave Jerusalem, wait for the Promise, sit down, fear not, be patient.

The implication here is that they need be told. Naturally, could we blame these men if they would have wanted to take their leave of the town stained with the blood of their Master? If the sheep, whose Shepherd had stepped between them and the wolves, would have sought to flee the city swarming with Pharisees, Sadducees, and Roman soldiers, can we be surprised? The Lord speaks clearly though, "It must begin here!"

In the city of David, which had enjoyed more of God's graces than any other, grace must begin here. In the city of promises, which had seen more fulfilled promises than any other and awaits many more yet to come, The Promise of promises must begin here. In the city named the Great Harlot, most offensive to God despite His long-suffering kindness, mercy must begin here. In the city more rotten with the hardened hearts of religious fruitlessness, the harvest must begin here. In the city stained with the blood of its Messiah, the washing of water by the word must begin here.

We've already discussed repeatedly how important it is to note that the gospel first began to be believed in the one place where it would be most easily disproven; Such a location is evidence that the miracle working teacher, Jesus of Nazareth, died on the cross, and that the body of Christ lay not in that grave, but was seen by many, alive again. But the fact that it began here gives us another truth we cannot afford to overlook. Absolutely no offense (bar one) can be too great for the mercy of God!

"God doesn't want me."

"The church would burn down if I walked in."

"I'm too far gone."

All these statements have one thing in common. They are lies the enemy uses to keep us from being reconciled to God in Christ. Think about it. The men of Jerusalem had just chanted "crucify, crucify," whipped Him, stripped Him, and spit on Him. These men tortured and murdered God! But it was these same men to whom the Lord Jesus Christ first sent His Apostles to preach the Good News of grace. What greater offense could you have done to think there's not room for you in Heaven? In light of this Awesome mercy, can you really believe the lie of Satan, that God doesn't love you?

Notes

Day 4

Our God, or THE God

"So when they had come together, they asked Him, 'Lord, will You at this time restore the kingdom to Israel?' " - Acts 1:6 MEV

Insert here an eye roll so extreme the eyeballs risk leaving their sockets. After all that had happened and had been spoken by their Lord, the apostles still hold firm to their notion that the Messiah was going to take an earthly throne; He would lead Israel out from under the thumb of the Romans and establish a rule which would restore Israel to the glory of the time of David and Solomon. Their question seemingly isn't even just will you, but rather, will you now? They were so convinced of their own belief the only question was when it would happen. Sound familiar?

"For the time will come when people will not endure sound doctrine, but they will gather to themselves teachers in accordance with their own desires, having itching ears, and they will turn their ears away from the truth and turn to myths." - 2 Timothy 4:3-4 MEV

The Apostles had an excuse. The Holy Spirit hadn't yet come down to teach and remind them of all that Christ said. On the other hand, they had the Messiah there correcting them in person every time they brought this up, but don't we have almost 1200 chapters of God's instruction here for our daily perusal?

Still, we can look around our world and see that the time has come. People flock, by the millions, to prosperity preachers, and others who espouse lies in the name of God. But that's not my concern today. These were the Apostles - Christ's most intimate friends. These were the men whom He had chosen to found His Church. These were the men the Lord had personally mentored and prepared. Yet their own notions still shaped their understanding of the Messiah.

If even the Apostles essentially forged a god of their own desires (for a time), shouldn't we also be wary of our own opinions? Once the Spirit of God came down upon them, their eyes were opened to the truth, but even so, there's an inherent danger in the spirit of men that we cannot afford to overlook.

Mankind has a natural tendency to look for evidences of our own desires. We want a god that will do X for us, and if we turn our heads at a funny angle, and squint our eyes, that passage of scripture gives the promise of X, direct from the mouth of God. Before we know it, our heads never stand straight, and the squint is our normal state.

The Holy Spirit is able to correct our posture, and open our eyes, but still, we must be aware. Many a man and woman follow a false god of their own creation. Ascribing the name of Christ to a false god does not bring the Holy Spirit on a "believer." How many of us let our desires, politics, lusts, and other worldly understanding shape our God?

Brothers and sisters, we must be very careful that we interpret scripture by scripture, not by our own perspectives. We must be very careful that we seek teachers who teach truth and sound doctrine, not teachers of our own desires and myths. We must be careful, but if we truly know Christ and have the Holy Spirit, we can be confident that God is faithful to exhort us to all holiness.

Notes

Day 5

Be My Witnesses

"He said to them, 'It is not for you to know the times or the dates, which the Father has fixed by His own authority. But you shall receive power when the Holy Spirit comes upon you. And you shall be My witnesses in Jerusalem, and in all Judea and Samaria, and to the ends of the earth.' " - Acts 1:7-8 MEV

Discussion and consideration of the end times is quite varied among the Church. Some look constantly for the next sign, eager for His return, while others intentionally turn a blind eye to the prophecies, focusing on the work here and now. On either side of these lay the extremes, and everywhere in between, the variations of balance. But I tend to think the balance is vital.

Christ here tells us that to know the days and times is not for us, but elsewhere he tells us we must "watch therefore... Be ready" (Matthew 24:42, 44 MEV). Paul tells the church at Thessaloniki "Concerning the times and the seasons, brothers, you have no need that I write to you" (1 Thessalonians 5:1 MEV), but he writes to Timothy that the power of the Holy Spirit, which had come down, gave testimony of the signs of the times.

"Now the Spirit clearly says that in the last times some will depart from the faith and pay attention to seducing spirits and doctrines of devils," - 1 Timothy 4:1 MEV

Brothers and sisters, let us watch with eager intent for the return of our King, keeping our lamps trimmed all night, for we "are not of the night nor of darkness" (1 Thess 5:5). But at the same time that we look ahead to more wonderful days, we must also live in the moment. I don't believe the Holy Spirit is going to lead me to spend every waking moment searching the news for end times prophecies fulfilled, while neglecting the great commission. I once did that, and I'll just lay this out there: that was before I came to truly know Christ, and definitively before the Holy Spirit came upon me.

Notice here, Christ doesn't rebuke the disciples for their desire that His kingdom should come soon, but He does correct their focus.

"But you shall receive power when the Holy Spirit comes upon you. And you shall be My witnesses in Jerusalem, and in all Judea and Samaria, and to the ends of the earth." - Acts 1:8 MEV

I do personally both believe and hope that Christ's return comes soon, but that merely makes the sharing of the Gospel, and the exhortation and encouragement of my brethren, all the more urgent.

"And let us consider how to stir up one another to love and good works, not neglecting to meet together, as is the habit of some, but encouraging one another, and all the more as you see the Day drawing near." - Hebrews 10:24-25 ESV

Oh, I do see the signs of the times, yes indeed; The Master returns soon. But all the more as the day approaches, "you shall be my witnesses... to the ends of the Earth."

Today's devotional could give the wrong impression though, and so it must be balanced with another truth. The fact of the matter is, we're not all called to the same ministry. We're not all appointed by the Spirit to pastoral ministry, children's ministry, worship ministry, prayer ministry, financial ministry, family ministry, or any other ministry. God has different work, and different gifts distributed differently to each of His children. The key there is that it's to "each" of His children. In Christ there is a calling upon the heart of every Christian to heed. The one thing each Christian's call has in common is to live life for Christ. Beyond that, the power of the Holy Spirit will lead us to, and strengthen us for the work prepared for us.

Whatever you do, be it declaring the Name in public, or sweeping the floor in the presence of only your children, do it all for the Lord Jesus Christ, and all the more as you see the day drawing near.

Day 6

Better That He Go

"When He had spoken these things, while they looked, He was taken up. And a cloud received Him from their sight. While they looked intently toward heaven as He ascended, suddenly two men stood by them in white garments. They said, 'Men of Galilee, why stand looking toward heaven? This same Jesus, who was taken up from you to heaven, will come in like manner as you saw Him go into heaven.' " - Acts 1:9-11 MEV

Jesus could have stayed, right then and there establishing the Kingdom on earth as the disciples had expected, but that wouldn't be the good work. Jesus could have, but then who would be our Intercessor in heaven? What the Holy Spirit would soon reveal to the Apostles is that this was all typified in Levitical law - foreshadowed, if you will. The High Priest of Israel would pass through the veil, and make intercession for Israel at the mercy seat.

Well, brothers and sisters, that temple veil was torn, and now our Eternal High Priest has entered up through the true veil, where His throne is eternal, and His intercession on our behalf is final. Hallelujah, He reigns! He could have stayed, but it wouldn't have ended in our salvation. I believe His Earthly ministry reveals it would have ended in continual rejection and persecution, requiring miracle after miracle, for all the ages. He could have stayed, but the truth is, that wasn't the plan for our salvation. In Christ's prayer, we see the truth that His earthly work was finished:

"I have glorified You on the earth. I have finished the work You have given Me to do. And now, O Father, glorify Me in Your own presence with the glory which I had with You before the world existed." - John 17:4-5 MEV

Indeed, Jesus' earthly work was fulfilled and now He was taken up and glorified in the presence of the Father forevermore, with the glory He had from before time began. If Christ had not ascended, the power of the Holy Spirit, which filled Him without measure would not have come down upon the elect. If Christ had not ascended... Actually, let's look at this through the lens of another foreshadowing.

When Elijah had finished the work God had ordained for him to do here on Earth, he was honored to be one of only two men other than Christ Himself, who was taken up to heaven alive. Similarly, his disciple witnessed the event. Remember how Elisha had asked for a double portion of the Spirit that was on Elijah? Elijah's response was that if Elisha saw him when he was taken up, it would happen.

Here at the beginning of Luke's second treatise the Apostles saw Christ taken, and as we move forward, we'll see a few examples of how that Spirit was poured out greatly upon them. In John 14, Jesus gives the promise of the Holy Spirit. Jesus tells them that He will intercede to the Father on their behalf, and the Father will send the Spirit. The Lord tells them they will do all He had done and greater, "because I am going to my Father" (John 14:12 MEV)! And go He did, even as they watched.

Rewind again to Elijah and Elisha, and we see the widow of Zarephath's last oil and grain not run out by the prophetic Spirit of God working through Elijah, in the same way we see another widow's last oil fill every jar that could be found, by that same Spirit working through Elisha. We see Elijah pray to God who raises the widow's son from the dead, and likewise we see Elisha pray to God who raises the Shunamite woman's son from the dead. When we read these histories, let's keep in mind it was all done to show what would come. The Spirit that was on Elijah was given to Elisha after watching his master taken up, and we see the same after the disciples watched the Master ascend into heaven.

When Jesus came, He performed many miracles, one of which was to literally feed 5000 with literal bread and fish. When He left, His Spirit descended on the Apostles, and they did far greater things. When we're told 3000 were added to their number that day, that was the Apostles distributing the Bread of Life to many a man, woman, and child. Of the 5000 Jesus fed, we can be sure many did not come to saving faith. But of the 3000 the Apostles fed, scripture defines for us the truth that they were added to the number of the elect that day.

Brothers and sisters, Jesus could have stayed, but it was better that He go. Even as the Apostles stared into the sky, wondering what was next, they couldn't have imagined how God's plan would unfold. The key is that in faith they trusted and followed the Lord, and by the Holy Spirit working the works prepared for them, the Church was formed. Let us do the same, living in utmost faith, even when we can't figure out what God is doing. Many things will come that will try to shake us, but take heart for Christ has overcome the world. He will come on the clouds again, but this time as the Judge.

Notes

Notes

Day 7

Wait For It

"Then they returned to Jerusalem from the Mount of Olives, which is a Sabbath day's walk from Jerusalem. When they had entered, they went up into the upper room, where they were staying: Peter, James, John, and Andrew; Philip and Thomas; Bartholomew and Matthew; James the son of Alphaeus and Simon the Zealot; and Judas the son of James. These all continued with one accord in prayer and supplication, with the women and Mary the mother of Jesus, and with His brothers." - Acts 1:12-14 MEV

I know in a week we haven't gotten very far, but there's just so very much here in these early verses for us to learn and grow from. What have we here is what "Jesus began both to do and teach," (Acts 1:1 MEV) from His heavenly throne. Over the next several months we will see signs and wonders and great speeches pour out of these followers of Christ, but here, before the coming of the Holy Spirit, all they could do was gather, pray, and seek to follow the scriptures.

"They were too feeble to act alone, and silence and retirement were all that He enjoined till they had been plunged into the fiery baptism which should quicken, strengthen, and transform them." - Alexander McLaren

Seeing the works of the Spirit in the apostles, and in Paul, some recognized the godhead, falsely assuming they were to be worshipped, but like the angels that presented themselves to prophets, the response came that "We are just servants; God alone is to be worshipped."

In the same manner, it is natural for us, as we read through Acts and the Epistles, to place these "great" patriarchs and matriarchs (notice “the women and Mary the mother of Jesus") of the faith on high pedestals. While they will indeed be honored among men and angels in heaven, and we must revere all that was taught through them, we must also keep the focus where it belongs. Just as, "without Him nothing was created that was created" (John 1:3 MEV), likewise, without His Spirit, nothing of the Church was done that was done... Before His Spirit fell upon them, all they had was to wait, gather, and pray.

God has a tendency to take people with no talent or inclination toward a task, then call and equip them to it, thereby making even their puny lives a testimony that it is all His work. Just as reckless Simon became the stoic apostle Peter, one of the sons of thunder became the Apostle of love, and Matthew the tax collector became the evangelist to the Jews.

I realized something the other day, and while it was an eye-opening moment of introspection for me, I believe it testifies to the extent of the power of God's Spirit to work in any man. When my wife and I first started hanging out, people asked her how we had a relationship because I never spoke. I was an extreme introvert, with no desire or skill for social interaction. Anything beyond a smile and a nod was reserved only for a few close friends. But one of the first services God called me to after coming to Christ was to socialize and make people feel welcome at church. Now, Jenn gets tired of waiting after church as I can't stop talking to people. That's not of me.

When I was in middle school, a man came around to all the band students before the semester to figure out what instruments suited us. After briefly running me through a handful of instruments, he told me I had no musical talent and handed me a pair of drumsticks. The next ministry God called me to was worship ministry, and not on drums. Years later I'd still say I have no musical talent, but God has carried me through weekend after weekend. That's not of me.

When I was in high school, mathematics and sciences were my thing, whereas English was the scar on my GPA. But for several years now, God has imprinted on my heart that I cannot fail to record my daily Bible study in these public devotionals. He has even nudged me to write a book (over and over again), until I finally broke down and did it. That's not of me.

A few months ago, I was asked if I would teach a Bible study in person, and I was terrified. I repeatedly spoke the words, "I'm a writer not a speaker." Introvert, remember? Even so, over the past month, God has faithfully carried my tongue through His service. That's not of me.

In response to everything I and the world have said about who I am, God has said, "So what? It's about who I AM." I can't help but fall in humbled helplessness before the glory of my Lord. From before I came to Christ and His Spirit came upon me, my constant prayer was that I could be of service to God (though I didn't yet understand who He was). That prayer has continued through the years, and He has shown Himself faithful. So, when I see these Apostles hiding in the upper chamber with nothing but prayer and supplication as they await the Holy Spirit, my heart is drawn to dwell on how it is all His work.

Men are nothing that they should be seen, but if we love Christ, and He lives in us, may people evermore see Christ's work in us! He has promised us His Holy Spirit, and He doesn't send us to work unless He equips us to complete it. Looking back at Christ's final words in Acts 1:4-8, McLaren points our eyes to this truth:

"Not a word does He say of their task of witnessing, till He has filled their hearts with the promise of the Spirit. He shows them the armour of power in which they are to be clothed, before He points them to the battlefield. Waiting times are not wasted times."

Notes

Notes

Day 8

We Are Your Temple

"In those days Peter stood up among the disciples (the number of people together was about a hundred and twenty), and said, 'Brothers, this Scripture had to be fulfilled, which the Holy Spirit previously spoke by the mouth of David concerning Judas, who became the guide to those who seized Jesus.'" - Acts 1:15-16 MEV

If you read with me through Luke's Gospel, you'll remember the Sanhedrin which condemned our Lord. We'll see them extensively as we venture further into the book of Acts, but I'd suggest that their authority had collapsed under the ruling thumb of Christ. To my knowledge, we don't see specific reference of this ruling body in Old Testament canonical scripture, but the rabbinical writings give us history as to when, why, and how this court originally convened.

At the return of the exiles from Babylon, we can read about the rebuilding of the temple in Ezra and Nehemiah, as well as the teaching of the scriptures, and the establishment of the doctrines and laws intended to protect Israel from falling back into the spiritual harlotry that had destroyed them. What the Holy Bible doesn't go into detail about is the group of men, appointed to leadership, called "the men of the great assembly." This was a group of prophets, scribes, and wise men, including Ezra, Nehemiah, Daniel, Mordecai, Haggai, Zechariah, and Malachi. No, scripture doesn't count them out, but they made up the majority of post exilic prophets.

But why is this relevant? Their number was a hundred and twenty. These were great men of God who set the stage for the coming of the Lord, and the salvation of Israel. Over the centuries, they evolved into the Sanhedrin, but even rabbinical literature attests that the greatness of this assembly lasted only through that first generation. By the time of Christ, it was merely a tradition of authority, and we see plenty of evidence it had been corrupted.

So, why is this relevant? The "men of the great assembly" convened at the rebuilding of the temple, to lay the groundwork for God's people to remember Him. But as Jesus Christ gave up the ghost on the cross, the temple veil was torn. That temple was no longer blessed with the Shekinah presence of God. Christ had fulfilled the need for the physical temple, and now as we move into the next chapter, we see the fulfillment of the promise that this same Shekinah came to rest on the assembly of these 120, by whom the groundwork of the Church would be laid. They were the first who could fall in humbled awe saying, "we are your temple." The first living stones.

Have you heard the phrase, "I only follow the words Jesus spoke," or some variation of that sentiment? This is the testimony of those who don't want the consequence of sin (spiritual death and hell), but don't actually want to be lifted out of that bondage to sin either. The calls to holiness which Christ spoke through His Apostles are an offense to those who love their sin, prompting a convenient attempt to discredit them.

Regardless of who these Apostles were, the fact of the matter is that Jesus is the incarnate Word of God. Everything from cover to cover in that Bible, was inspired by Him. But we find confirmation of that in these 120. These were the men, appointed and ordained to teach and remind the world about the Gospel of Jesus Christ. These were the men through whom God would first begin the work of purifying the bride which shall be presented spotless to the Son. To reject the words of the Apostles is to reject the words of the Spirit which spoke through them.

Notes

Day 9

"Suddenly a sound like a mighty rushing wind came from heaven, and it filled the whole house where they were sitting. There appeared to them tongues as of fire, being distributed and resting on each of them, and they were all filled with the Holy Spirit and began to speak in other tongues, as the Spirit enabled them to speak. Now dwelling in Jerusalem were Jews, devout men, from every nation under heaven. When this sound occurred, the crowd came together and were confounded, because each man heard them speaking in his own language." - Acts 2:2-6 MEV

The promise was fulfilled, and the power came upon not only the Apostles, but on each of them (the 120). Something I've never noticed before though, is how it is only a "sound *like* a mighty rushing wind." This is like a mighty wind, but there is no wind. Then the eyes are given a similar experience, as the Spirit comes like tongues of flame, but without the heat. There was no doubt this was something supernatural and unprecedented. So why did it happen at Pentecost? I'd suggest that there's a plethora of meaning.

Aside from the spiritual implications which we'll discuss in a moment, this was the feast to which travel was the safest, due to seasonal weather patterns. Thereby, though all able-bodied men were required to attend all three feasts, this feast would have had the greatest number of the people of Israel present in Jerusalem. There was no greater time than this to reveal the fulfillment of the Messiah's promise, and the beginning of His Church. The great crowd that came together, came from all nations and tongues, from the dispersion of the Jews. There were men. There were women. There were children. They all saw something fantastical.

What about those spiritual implications though? Pentecost means, literally, fifty. This was the feast of weeks, celebrated as the fulfillment of seven full weeks beyond Passover. It was the fiftieth day. Remember the risen Christ moved in and out from among them for 40, and now shortly after His Ascension, the Spirit fell on His disciples. Within this feast there is symbolism galore. The feast of weeks (Pentecost, Shavuot) was a festival to commemorate the giving of the law at mount Sinai.

First, at Passover, God had rescued Israel from bondage and slavery to Egypt through Moses, and then, at Shavuot, He came down to Moses and gave the Law by which they should live.

Likewise, first, at Passover, God had rescued the world from bondage and slavery to sin through Christ, and then at Pentecost, He came down to indwell His people, and gave the Law of the Spirit (see Romans 8).

There's a very significant pattern there. First comes salvation, and then, the law. Keeping the law was never the condition of salvation, it has always been the response to His salvation, from those who loved Him. I mentioned Romans 8. Did you take a moment to go read it? Will you now? I'll wait...

Did you see that? The law of the Spirit of life in Christ Jesus has set me free from the law of sin and death.

There's still more symbolism though. The 49 days between Passover and Pentecost was the counting of the days... Those were the days of the ripening of the wheat. We've just studied through Luke and if you came along for that ride, you may remember how frequently Jesus likened His followers to wheat. Now, as the wheat has ripened, Pentecost is a feast of harvest. It was when you would present the first fruits of the harvest as an offering to the Lord, and here, in the upper chamber, the 120 first fruits became an offering.

Even that though, is not the full extent of the symbolism here. Feast of weeks was the only one of these commanded feasts in which the bread was leavened. When we note that leaven always represented sin, we can see these two leavened loaves represented the sin of Israel, and the sin of the gentiles. Passover was unleavened bread, as the Lord Jesus Christ was our sinless sacrifice, but Pentecost was the outset of the ongoing work of sanctification - the bringing of those who love God into the conformity of Christ. Though the Spirit will continue this work of sanctification in us, we will still have sin - those leavened loaves - present until that wonderful day when we are resurrected in glorified bodies.

Of all the many ways that scripture perfectly ties together to tell the Good News, can you imagine what kind of intellect it must take for God to have organized it all, from before Adam even took that first bite? No. The fact of the matter is our greatest thinkers couldn't comprehend a minute portion of the great wisdom of God. If that doesn't humble you before the Lord, I'd suggest you may not even know Him. It can also give us courage though. As the Lord of Hosts lives, if God be for me, who can stand against me? He has formed all of human history to His plan. What could come against His good will for my salvation?

Notes

Notes

Day 10

Each In Our Own Native Language

"They were all amazed and marveled, saying to each other, 'Are not all these who are speaking Galileans? How is it that we hear, each in our own native language? Parthians, Medes and Elamites, residents of Mesopotamia, Judea and Cappadocia, Pontus and Asia, Phrygia and Pamphylia, Egypt and the regions of Libya near Cyrene, and visitors from Rome, both Jews and proselytes, Cretans and Arabs—we hear them speaking in our own languages the mighty works of God.' They were all amazed and perplexed, saying to each other, 'What does this mean?' " - Acts 2:7-12 MEV

I'll venture not to get into the debate about tongues as we move forward here, but that does not mean I can bypass what may have been one of the greatest acts recorded in this book of Acts. Imagine being a group of unlearned fishermen and the like, and being told your duty was to not only go tell the Good News to people of every nation and tribe and tongue, but also to make disciples of them. Such a charge requires extensive communication.

This may have been one of the greatest troubles of their minds for the 10 days they awaited the Holy Spirit. It's quite probable they discussed and debated how they would go about it. To learn one or two languages well enough to properly communicate the nuances of the faith would be a work of many years. Yet in but a moment it was, as we've discussed, all the work of God.

Were they surprised? Maybe, and maybe not. It was foretold, both in Old Testament prophecy (Isaiah 28:11), and by the Lord Jesus Christ. Even as He had told them to go into all the world and preach the Gospel, he also told them they will speak with new tongues (Mark 16:15). So, for those 10 days did they understand? We're not told one way or another, but now 120 men and women stood in the presence of people of all the nations and tongues, speaking the mighty works of God.

In the course of studying Acts, we'll see demons driven out, ailments healed, prison gates thrown open and far more, but the work of God to empower the disciples and Apostles of Christ to declare the Gospel to all the world is possibly the greatest of these. Even so, we should not wonder at the power that could do such a thing, for it was that same power which in a moment confused the languages in the first place.

"The Lord said, 'The people are one and they have one language, and this is only the beginning of what they will do; now nothing that they propose to do will be impossible for them. Come, let us go down and there confuse their language, so that they may not understand one another's speech.' " - Genesis 11:6-7

At the Tower of Babel, God did what must be done to lead to salvation in Christ, but now that He had come, His disciples had need to speak to all people. Notice though, in that passage above, what God said about a people unhindered by language. "Now nothing that they propose to do will be impossible for them." I can't help but wonder if that was a great comfort to the early Church, as they considered this particular gift of the Spirit. It is yet another reminder that nothing is impossible with God. If what a true believer proposes to do aligns with what God has prepared for them to do, it shall not fail. There's great confidence there, brothers and sisters.

Notes

Day 11

Respectfully But Firmly

"But Peter, standing up with the eleven, lifted up his voice and said to them, “Men of Judea and all you who dwell in Jerusalem, let this be known to you, and listen to my words. For these are not drunk, as you suppose, since it is the third hour of the day. But this is what was spoken by the prophet Joel:" - Acts 2:14-16 MEV

Look at Peter now. Simon was rash, and up 'til now his recorded words had been nothing more than brief and often erroneous discourse. Just a few weeks before, Simon had cowered in fear among these same people, claiming, "I do not know the man" (Matthew 26:72). But look at Peter now, as he stands up respectfully but firmly declaring, "let this be known to you and listen to my words." Peter's sermon is now extensive, filled with reason and scriptural evidence. He declares, "I can confidently speak to you... Therefore, let all the house of Israel know with certainty that God has made this Jesus, whom you crucified, both Lord and Messiah" (Acts 2:29, 36 CSB).

"If we were reading a fictitious history, we should rightly criticise the author for the want of consistency in his portraiture of the same character in the first and second volumes of his work. As it is, the inconsistency becomes almost an evidence of the truth of the narratives that contain it. The writer of a made-up-history, bent only upon reconciling the followers of Peter and of Paul, would have made the former more prominent in the Gospels or less prominent in the Acts." - C.J. Ellicott

The end of this chapter clarifies this is but a portion of what Peter spoke that day, saying, "with many other words he testified and exhorted" (vs 40 MEV). We can see from what Luke did record though, that Peter taught straight from the scriptures. His speech here is roughly 500 words and over 200 of them were taken from the word of God.

"Though Peter was filled with the Holy Ghost, and spake with tongues as the Spirit gave him utterance, yet he did not think to set aside the Scriptures. Christ's scholars never learn above their Bible; and the Spirit is given, not to do away the Scriptures, but to enable us to understand, approve, and obey them." - Henry

We see Peter speaks boldly and fearlessly, straight from the scriptures, but we can also note that he speaks unrestrained. The Spirit of God does not lead Peter to soft teaching, cushioning the blow so as not to offend anyone. This speech concludes with the declaration that "you crucified the Messiah."

"When they heard this, they were stung in the heart and said to Peter and to the rest of the apostles, 'Brothers, what shall we do?' Peter said to them, 'Repent and be baptized, every one of you, in the name of Jesus Christ for the forgiveness of sins, and you shall receive the gift of the Holy Spirit. For the promise is to you, and to your children, and to all who are far away, as many as the Lord our God will call.' " - Acts 2:37-39 MEV

After centuries upon centuries of following the example of the Apostles, we've suddenly decided that to share the Gospel, we must hold back from speaking the truth about sin for fear of offending anyone. Yet at the same time that the Church is shifting away from being clear about the uncomfortable truths, we're seeing the most rapid decline of faith our country has ever seen.

Notice by the Apostles words that "they were stung in the heart," and wanted the solution, which is Jesus Christ. That doesn't mean we must be mean about it. Oh, far from it. Peter speaks harsh truth, but he calls them to freedom. He calls them to Christ for forgiveness and the promise of the Holy Spirit. He also lives the example he later teaches:

"not paying back evil for evil or insult for insult but, on the contrary, giving a blessing, since you were called for this, so that you may inherit a blessing." - 1 Peter 3:9 CSB

These men of Judea accused them of drunkenness before the morning sacrifice on one of the holiest days of the year - quite an insult - but Peter stands up and shares with them the best news any man has ever heard, not repaying insult for insult; by the Spirit of God Peter gives them the greatest gift any man has ever received. That's a far cry from cutting off a servant's ear less than eight full weeks prior. Look what God has done!

Day 12

The Last Days

"But this is what was spoken by the prophet Joel: 'In the last days it shall be,' says God, 'that I will pour out My Spirit on all flesh; your sons and your daughters shall prophesy, your young men shall see visions, and your old men shall dream dreams. Even on My menservants and maidservants I will pour out My Spirit in those days; and they shall prophesy. And I will show wonders in heaven above and signs on the earth below: blood, and fire, and vapor of smoke. The sun shall be turned into darkness, and the moon into blood, before that great and glorious day of the Lord comes. And whoever calls on the name of the Lord shall be saved.' " - Acts 2:16-21 MEV

It must begin here... Here we are in Jerusalem, the 120 are speaking the good news in languages never learned - languages for every ear present - and Peter says this is the sign foretold that the last days are here. He doesn't quote Joel perfectly, either by the original Hebrew or Septuagint Greek, but by the Spirit of God, the Apostle distills the heart of the passage.

The heart? God gives extensive signs, both glorious and terrifying, as a call to repent. Look at the signs here "in the last days": The promise, "I will pour out My Spirit," began to be witnessed here as unlearned Galileans spoke in every language. But we know that the indwelling of the Holy Spirit has continued even 'til today. That's an important note when considering the phrase "the last days." It denotes the entirety of time from the resurrection of Christ to His second coming. This is the time in which men are called to salvation.

Remember, it must begin here, in Jerusalem. And it did, as they were given the signs of the Spirit, and they were given the "wonders in heaven above and signs on earth below." You may remember from earlier in our study, before the destruction of the City of David, history records a flaming sword seen in the sky above Jerusalem, a fiery comet pointing at the city for a year, the massively heavy temple gate opening on its own, a mysterious voice saying, "let us depart," and several notable earthquakes.

Long before permitting the Roman legions to destroy His city, God called His people back to Him.

That's a particular note about the nature of God that we would do well to remember. The long-suffering mercy of God is His common work. The Lord does not execute judgement hastily. His patience with us extends far beyond the grace any human judge would have. He gave Jerusalem 30 years of Apostolic Gospel ministry before executing His strange work. Mercy is God's nature; judgement is His strange work.

We should note though, that, there are more warnings in Peter's sermon here. Warnings that precede the "great and glorious day of the Lord." We're still in these last days, in which God calls all men to Him. Signs and wonders, plagues and fires will again call men to Christ even up until the Day when God executes His strange work. But what began in Jerusalem continues to all nations: the promise that "whoever calls on the name of the Lord shall be saved." Yes indeed, Peter preached hellfire, but it was to draw the eye to salvation in Jesus Christ.

Notes

Day 13

God's Plan – Our Act

"this Jesus, delivered up according to the definite plan and foreknowledge of God, you crucified and killed by the hands of lawless men." - Acts 2:23 ESV

The Church began on this sermon spoken through Peter, and in it were extensive truths - one of those being the coexistence of man's free will, and God's sovereign will. Let's break this down a little before looking at the whole of it.

"*This Jesus,*" the Christ (defined: anointed) to this work by God's grand plan. The King of kings for whom we've waited.

"*Delivered up,*" by Judas to the priests, the priests to the Sanhedrin, the Sanhedrin to Pilate, Pilate to Herod and back again, and Pilate to the will of the people. Handed over to death by men of the very world He came to save from death.

"*According to the definite plan and foreknowledge of God,*" who remains the victor through it all. Though all of this was done by men, it was the will of God that His Son should suffer and die for us, the innocent for the guilty; the sinless made judicially sin for us sinners, so that we could be made righteous and reconciled to God. The crucifixion of the Son of God was not God's defeat. Though you have seemingly triumphed over this One you accused of blasphemy, it was actually His triumph, as our God incarnate who came chiefly for this purpose - that He should die in our stead.

"*You crucified and killed by the hands of lawless men,*" for which you shall be held accountable, unless you seek the salvation of Christ. God's permission that you be allowed to commit the most heinous crime imaginable does not shift the guilt from you to Him. When the Righteous Judge returns and all is revealed, you will understand that such an argument would fall entirely flat. You'll dare not even mutter such accusation.

We must consider (to the best of our feeble ability) the full perspective if we want to ponder the relationship between man's sin and God's sovereignty. When God created the world, it was good. When Adam and Eve chose not to trust Him, sin and death entered that same world, and good became veiled from our sight. Yet as Peter points out, God already had foreknowledge of this fall - every stage of it from the forbidden fruit, to the chants of "Crucify," even up to that lustful glance you cast last week - and He had a definite plan to raise us back up. God was never the source of evil, but was always, as we shall see, the solution to it. I'll ask you to consider Charles Spurgeon's view of Peter's conviction for a moment:

"Surely Peter would have been a bad pleader to introduce into his argument anything that could be readily construed into an excuse for those he was accusing. But there is no real excuse in it; The free agency of humans is as true as the predestination of God. The two truths stand fast forever. It is the folly of people to imagine that these two disagree. If we do wrong, we are accountable for the wrong. And that there is a Providence who ordains everything, does not take away from any person the full responsibility for anything he or she does."

As the saying goes, God is good all the time, and all the time God is good. He is not the one to blame for suffering, murder, rape, theft, slavery, hatred, betrayal, sexual immorality, adultery, or any of our vast number of sins. No, He is the one we sinned against, yet who loved us and offered us redemption. Take it or not, but don't assume you'll receive any mercy if you don't accept the mercy that is offered freely in Christ. Don't assume you'll have any defense, unless the one and only Intercessor stands up in your defense claiming, "this debt is paid in full."

Notes

Day 14

"God raised up this Jesus, of which we all are witnesses. Therefore being exalted to the right hand of God, and having received from the Father the promise of the Holy Spirit, He has poured out this which you now see and hear." - Acts 2:32-33 MEV

If you've been studying along with us through Acts, you know that Peter has just (very loosely) quoted the prophet Joel, that God would pour out the Spirit upon His people, and all who call on the name of the Lord would be saved. Next, Peter quoted a Psalm of David, which prophesied that the Messiah would not be left in the grave to rot. Now, in the Apostle's first sermon, we see the connection.

I'm not a fan of paraphrased bibles, because they set themselves in the place of the Holy word of God, but sometimes a paraphrase can be useful for getting to the meaning of a passage, just as Peter did with Joel. Similarly, maybe a paraphrase of Peter's words could help make sense of what he's saying here:

We knew Jesus alive, we saw the Son of God dead, and we witnessed the Messiah resurrected. Now you see us, filled with the Holy Spirit of God, speaking His praises in every language known to man. According to the scriptures both you and I revere, this could only be possible if Jesus is the Christ, who was raised up in glory, set at the right hand of God, and given the promise of the Holy Spirit to pour out upon His followers. What you are seeing is the proof that this Jesus you killed is both the King of Kings and Lord of Lords. The Good News is that He has enough mercy, even for you, if you should just believe.

As we've already discovered, the fact that everyone in Jerusalem knew what had happened at Calvary and at the guarded grave was established. Peter need not defend their witness, but rather uses it to draw these men to the only reasonable conclusion, and Luke tells us, "They were stung in the heart." As the Spirit of God testified through this first hundred and twenty, that day 3,000 men and women felt the pull of His call; their hearts of stone were made flesh again, and they now knew their need of the Savior.

"When they heard this, they were stung in the heart and said to Peter and to the rest of the apostles, 'Brothers, what shall we do?' " - Acts 2:37 MEV

Evangelism indeed requires we point to the consequence of sin. Notice in verses 34-36, Peter doesn't stop with "sit at my right hand," referencing only the Lordship of Christ. He continues with the rest of the passage, "until I make your enemies your footstool," then declares in no uncertain terms that the house of Israel had made themselves enemies of God. Peter indeed pointed to their sin, but only so he could point them to salvation.

Yes, that's to salvation, not to works. These men and women responded, pleading, "what shall we do?" It is the natural response of a heart that truly sees Christ for the first time to seek this answer; "in light of this new information, what should I do?" Notice, though, Peter's response was not, "care for widows and orphans, tell the world about Jesus, exhort one another to holiness, give to the church, do this, do that, etc., etc., etc.

"Peter said to them, 'Repent and be baptized, every one of you, in the name of Jesus Christ for the forgiveness of sins, and you shall receive the gift of the Holy Spirit. For the promise is to you, and to your children, and to all who are far away, as many as the Lord our God will call.' " - Acts 2:38-39 MEV

What does Peter respond? "Repent and be baptized... in the name of Jesus Christ." That is, change your mind, both about who He is (already done as seen above), and from your love of sin toward love of God, then testify through baptism that you have died and been raised up new, in Jesus Christ. When Peter says "the forgiveness of sins," that's linked to the name of Jesus Christ, not to any works, and not even the baptism. After this repentant faith, Peter says, the Holy Spirit comes.

You'll quite often see calls to works in my devotionals, but these are not the Gospel call. They are merely the ongoing conviction of the Holy Spirit in my life, as God repairs this broken flesh. Works aren't our salvation. They are merely the changed heart's response to God's salvation; the ongoing work of the Holy Spirit within those who are in Christ. It is not the evangelist's job to call people to good works. The mission is to call people to Christ, after which the Holy Spirit draws redeemed hearts to those works through the Word of God.

Notes

Notes

Day 15

The Early Church

"So those who received his word were baptized, and there were added that day about three thousand souls. And they devoted themselves to the apostles' teaching and the fellowship, to the breaking of bread and the prayers." - Acts 2:41-42 ESV

"...about three thousand souls. And they..." In this last portion of chapter 2, Acts 2:42-47, we see a holy example of Church, but it's also a church in its infancy. At this point, the vast majority of this church knew nothing of Jesus Christ but the rumors. It has been suggested that even Peter's early teachings hadn't yet formed the full doctrine he and the others would later teach. I'm not sure we have any solid evidence for that case though, as it could just be the literary progression of Luke, as the beloved physician introduces his reader to the Truth. To what extent the Holy Spirit had yet revealed the depths of spiritual truth to Peter for teaching is not certain. Even so, I'd be hard pressed to not believe he experienced a lifetime of learning.

So, we have a church example. It lays out this wonderful ideal of Church. They "continued steadfastly" (as some versions translate "proskartereō") in the Apostles' teaching, in fellowship, in the breaking of bread, and in prayers.

In the teaching, these 3000 humbly sat to learn all they could about the Lord and His instructions. In fellowship, this new and enormous adopted family gathered in love and friendship, bearing one another's burdens and encouraging one another. In the breaking of bread, they shared both common meals (later named love feasts) and holy communion. In prayers, both private and corporate, this church interceded for all men constantly, as evidenced by the testimony, "the Lord added to the church daily those who were being saved" (Acts 2:47 MEV).

Yet this idyllic church example was still a church in its infancy. It hadn't yet faced the tougher questions that arise as fellowship meets earthly life, such as we see both later in the epistles and our personal experiences with Church. It hadn't yet come across casual professors and apostates;

These early Church men and women were steadfastly devoted, and neither scripture, nor history, give any evidence that a single one of these ever turned from the faith. It hadn't yet been challenged by the division of opposing viewpoints. It hadn't yet faced the suffering, death, and persecution that would soon scar their ranks. It hadn't yet, but by the time they testified to Luke, these children of God had been through the ringer, and still this is what they told him about those early days.

We have here, a great example for our churches to follow, but without the rest of the Church example, given through the Epistles and Christ's letters to the 7 churches in Revelation 2 and 3, we'll have to progress through all the false steps they did. Without utilizing the full example of scripture, we may not even find our churches fully guided and strengthened by the Holy Spirit. I'd suggest, though, that we should keep this ideal as our goal, in seeking to follow all Christ's instruction. The purity and simplicity of Christian Fellowship has, on Earth, never been finer than this early stage, unmarred by the world.

Before moving on though, the Spirit draws my eyes to a couple more points within this passage. "Mega-church" has become a bit of a dirty word in many circles of Christianity these days. Several large and heretical gatherings claiming His name while playing loosely with scripture have rather earned such disdain. Likewise, the damage done to so many individuals, as they are lost in the crowds, has built this terrible name.

But while the pitfalls that lay before a large fellowship are indeed a threat, the first recorded Christian Church is evidence that large numbers in a church aren't the evil we should be avoiding. Here we have 120, plus 3000, and more every day, and it's the Lord doing the work. How many of us who balk at the word "mega-church," also love the works of Charles Spurgeon? Have we considered that the prince of preachers often had far more than 10,000 in attendance for his sermons?

Moving ahead, let's move back to the beginning: "about 3000 souls, and they..." The Church is the collection of "they," but it is also made up of the individual souls. A body doesn't work properly when individual parts don't work together. My inner ear tells my brain how to balance, but my brain tells my big toes, my core, my arms, and more. If any of those parts isn't congruent to the body, my balance is off. When tempted to complain about the church - what it's doing, what it's not doing, etc. - you must realize that you are part of the church. In following that temptation, we are actually complaining about what we are not doing. The Church isn't just a group of staff members paid to serve us. We are all the church. "About three-thousand souls."

Oh Lord, I cannot wait to hear what that number is when you return! In the meantime, guide us in all truth how we can continue steadfastly, devoting ourselves to the Apostles' teaching, to fellowship, to the breaking of bread, and to prayers. Guide us in humility, and into the mindset of servants, saved by the King who came to serve.

Notes

Notes

Day 16

Christian Charity

"All who believed were together and had all things in common. They sold their property and goods and distributed them to all, according to their need." - Acts 2:44-45 MEV

As Marxist ideologies have risen, many have tried to support them by leveraging passages such as this one above, and the parallel found in chapter 4:32-37. The idea put forth suggests that these examples, and the Lord's instruction regarding treasures that don't fade, support socialist policies. It takes an unbelievable amount of cognitive dissonance for a Christian to make such connections though. There's a clear distinction between state mandated distribution of wealth and Christian charity. In Volume 1, the reader has just seen Jesus saying "render to Caesar what is Caesar's, and to God what is God's" (Luke 20:25 MEV)?

And yet, while these passages do not support the blasphemy that "Jesus would be a socialist," they do show an example of what Christian love inspires. First, let's clarify this community charity was given under no compulsion. Look ahead to the story of Ananias and Sapphira in chapter 5. What do we see said about personal property as Peter convicts Ananias?

"While it remained unsold, was it not your own? And when it was sold, was it not under your authority? Why have you conceived this deed in your heart? You did not lie to men, but to God." - Acts 5:4 MEV

The selling of property was willing charity, according to need, not a required condition of the fellowship. It was the expression of love, seeing brothers and sisters in dire need as worth more than earthly possessions. Remember that many of these thousands of believers were hundreds of miles from home. Not only were some of their rank poverty stricken, but some were without home or income as they stayed in Jerusalem to learn from the Apostles.

Rather than the imagery that all these men and women instantly sold everything and pooled their money, we see it's according to need. The imperfect tense, which Luke used when writing about the sale of land and goods, clarified this was an ongoing practice.

"And continuing daily with one mind in the temple, and breaking bread from house to house, they ate their food with gladness and simplicity of heart," - Acts 2:46 MEV

Do you know where the early church met? In the homes of believers. They were privately owned, but became an example that even private property can be used for the glory of God.

For a church to follow this example (continually selling off property) to the extreme, we would find a fellowship of pure poverty. Eventually, like the church at Jerusalem (see Acts 11:29), that church would run out of finances to leverage for the good of the Kingdom, and become dependent upon other churches.

Though the word of God does not espouse Marxist ideologies, it does teach self-denying charity. Charity that is discriminate - according to need - but charity that is sometimes beyond our comfort zone. How many times have we lamented that "I just don't have the funds to help," but spent a couple dollars a day or more on fancy drinks? How many of us have said, "I'd love to help, but I just don't have the money," then purchased the upgraded phone because we really wanted those extra features? I'm guilty. Too often, "the good I desire to do, I do not do, but the evil I do not want is what I do" (Romans 7:19 MEV).

Brothers and sisters, the Lord was clear that we'll have the poor with us for all time, but he also taught that the Christian response is self-sacrificing charity. We're no longer 3,000, but rather 2 billion strong. Imagine what we could do for the Kingdom of God on earth if each of us did just a little more.

Notes

Day 17

Better Than Gold

"A man lame from birth was being carried, whom people placed daily at the gate of the temple called Beautiful to ask alms from those who entered the temple. Seeing Peter and John about to go into the temple, he asked for alms. Peter, gazing at him with John, said, 'Look at us.' So he paid attention to them, expecting to receive something from them." - Acts 3:2-5 MEV

As we studied Luke's Gospel, I pointed the eye forward to this interaction, but now let's look a little closer. Luke has just told us the Lord worked "many wonders and signs... through the Apostles," yet of all the testimonies he heard, he deemed this specific one worth recording. Maybe due to the fulfillment of prophecy within, or maybe for the extremely public nature of it; Maybe because of the opportunity to preach the Gospel it opened for Peter, or maybe to stage the narrative for consequences it led to. Perhaps all of the above.

Yet for a moment I ask you to look out from the eyes of this lame man. His whole life, over 40 years, all he has known was the suffering of broken flesh. Every day he is carried to this same spot, parroting his plea at every passerby, for so long and with so little result that he hopelessly cast not a second glance at anyone. Day after day the lame beggar mechanically asks alms, hoping there's mercy enough that he could eat and live another day.

This lame beggar asks a coin or two from Peter and John, but then looks away for the next candidate. But Peter stops and says "Look at us." Finally, some hope, but what is it? It can't be good when Peter says, "silver and gold have I none," but then something intriguing is said: "I give you what I have." We have the luxury of reading ahead to see what that is, but it is uncertain what the beggar now expected. Was it, "Ok fine, I'll take whatever. Something is better than nothing I guess." Or possibly he recognized what Peter was truly implying: "What I have is better than silver and gold."

"They shall cast their silver in the streets, and their gold shall become abhorrent; their silver and their gold shall not be able to deliver them in the day of the wrath of the Lord; they shall not satisfy their souls, or fill their stomachs, for their iniquity has become a stumbling block." - Ezekiel 7:19 MEV

Through Ezekiel, the Lord told of the Day of wrath. We saw in His words that salvation in Jesus Christ is far greater than even the largest sum of silver and gold. Even enough silver to buy a loaf to eat would be a great distraction (let alone a poor consolation) from the true Bread of Life. But Peter doesn't have a dime to give; what he offers, "in the name of Jesus Christ of Nazareth" (Acts 3:6 MEV), is much better.

Can you blame this man for jumping around and praising God? Can you blame him for holding on to his new brothers? Can you blame him for walking with them? Yet do we sometimes?

A strangely enthusiastic Christian arrives in our fellowship acting differently than we're used to - maybe it's jumping and dancing around in worship, maybe hooting out "amens" at the sermon, maybe falling on the steps of the altar/stage in tears, or endless other ways people express their joy in the Lord that may be foreign to our normal experience - and maybe we keep our distance. Maybe we avoid eye contact or give sidelong glances. Maybe we talk behind their backs. Maybe we even go complain to leadership. Brothers and sisters, maybe they're not the ones in the wrong...

There are many ways that people express their worship, and likewise, many ways that people come to Christ. Look at chapter 2 and we see people come through the logic of apologetics. Look at the end of chapter 2 and we see more added daily through recognizing the people of Christ by their love. Look ahead to the rest of chapter as Peter speaks to those wondering about the lame man healed, and we see people come by conviction of sin and a call to repent. But look here, at the lame man healed, and we see a man come to Christ in the way of the Sermon on the Mount.

"Blessed are the poor in spirit, for theirs is the kingdom of heaven. Blessed are those who mourn, for they shall be comforted. Blessed are the meek, for they shall inherit the earth." - Matthew 5:3-5 MEV

Sometimes God's work to call a heart to redemption is done by unexpected blessing in the midst of hopelessness. Sometimes it's by comfort in a time of sorrow. Sometimes it is by peace in the midst of a battle. Sometimes it's a direct revelation from the Lord Himself. For each of us, the Father has a different path to find His Son, the Light. In that light, as the Holy Spirit has given each of us a different gift to serve the Kingdom, we can take heart that there is no comparison from one gift to another. Each and every one of us may be the tool God uses to call a soul to Christ in one way or another.

Look out from the eyes of the lame beggar. Do you see as you once did? I do. Do you see, as so many more still do, from the hopelessness of broken flesh? In that perspective, do you see yourself walking toward the gate called Beautiful, having no silver or gold? Will you give what you have?

Notes

Notes

Day 18

Not By Our Power

"When Peter saw it, he answered the people: 'Men of Israel, why do you marvel at this man? Or why do you stare at us, as if by our own power or piety we had made him walk?' " - Acts 3:12 MEV

Why do you marvel at this man? Talk about a rhetorical question! The man they've seen every day for probably 20 years or more, laying at the gate begging with useless, shriveled legs, is walking, jumping, dancing and praising God! Why wouldn't we marvel? Maybe as Peter asked this question and the next, he saw the state of the people he addressed.

These men of Israel had no cause to be so amazed at miracles. They claimed to serve the God of miracles, who had given Jerusalem, and the full family of the children of Israel, endless examples of his miraculous power. But even those fabulous occurrences, having been read in the histories, may seem a marvel when seen played out right in these people's presence. Yet lo, for three and a half years they had been blessed with miracle after miracle, performed in their presence - great and fabulous testimonies of the Christ. The very fact they now marveled revealed how fully these men had rejected Jesus, that now they marveled at a lesser thing as if they'd never seen anything like it.

Why do you marvel at this man, or why do you think it was our power by which it was done? Well, I'll tell you why: Because when the God you claim to serve, the God of Abraham, Isaac, and Jacob, raised up the Messiah, who we were promised, you denied Him and handed Him over to a gentile judge. You were so insistent on this rejection, you demanded a murderer be released so that Jesus would be put to death. "And you killed the Creator of Life, whom God has raised from the dead, of which we are witnesses." - Acts 3:15 MEV

Peter lays it out there that this was not done by his or John's power, but by the power of the very One who knit this man together in his mother's womb, and that One is Jesus Christ. He was dead by your hand but we testify to you that He is alive! Matthew Henry notes here, "Not unto us, O Lord, not unto us, but to thy name, give glory."

The Apostle makes it clear that this was no new religion they taught, but the fulfillment of what was spoken by the God who spoke to Moses on the mountain. But I ask you forgive me for shifting the focus here.

Do you think Peter shed a tear as the Spirit put these words in His mouth? "You denied the Holy and Righteous One." We like to think our pastors have it all together, but we forget they're teaching from what the Spirit has been speaking into their broken hearts. We look at all the pillars of our churches and as we see Christ shine through them, we tend to forget that they still struggle with the same trials and temptations as any other man. Yet here is Simon called Peter, preaching repentance, and his sermon exposes what was probably the greatest heartache of his life. "Before the rooster crows..."

We like to look at those upstanding members of our churches - you know the ones, the smiling faces serving every weekend - and we forget they still have weaknesses, doubts, struggles, and sorrows. They still need a shoulder to lean on sometimes. They still need someone to pray for them.

Oh Peter, I see you, preaching to those who "denied the Holy Spirit." I see you preaching about the work of Christ in the lame man who by faith in the Only Name was made strong, and I see you leaning into your faith for the strength that only the Lord can provide. I see you calling men to repentance so that their sins may be washed away, and I see you grasping the faith that your denial has been put away from God, as far as East is from the West.

Notes

Day 19

The Author of Life

"But you denied the Holy and Righteous One, and asked for a murderer to be granted to you, and you killed the Author of life, whom God raised from the dead. To this we are witnesses." - Acts 3:14-15 ESV

Depending upon what translation you read, you'll see a variety of words in this passage. It may be the Prince of life, the Creator of life, the Source of life, or as above, the Author of life. The most basic translation of the word used was prince - as in a military leader who is counted as the source of victory. "So the word comes to denote one who is the 'cause,' the 'author,'" (Albert Barnes).

It is the same word we see used of Christ in Hebrews 2:10, "the captain of their salvation." (KJV), and Hebrews 12:2, "the author and finisher of our faith" (MEV). As Charles Ellicott states, "The 'Prince of life,' the 'Captain of salvation,' is accordingly He who is the source from which life and salvation flow."

There are those who deny the deity of Christ (I know, for I once was one), and those who deny that the apostles and early church ever held Christ to be God. To them, as to a younger, more foolish me, it can rightly be said, "get behind me Satan!" All throughout the Bible we can see the Godhead proclaimed in our Christ. Looking back upon the original languages does not take away that truth, as if modern translators had twisted the word to their own perception.

No, Simon Peter, who walked with Jesus, indeed viewed the Messiah he knew as the Creator of life. To affirm such a thing was indeed a recognition that Jesus Christ is God, the source of all creation, First and Last.

Looking beyond that, we see how quite the antithesis was laid out here in Peter's words, "you demanded a murderer, and you killed the source of all life." In other words, you were offered he who took life, but you murdered He by whom all life was breathed.

Do we fully comprehend that when the apostles taught us how to make disciples, they didn't sugar coat the truth? Fire and brimstone is never pleasant to the lost soul, but the apostles knew it held a place in the salvation call. We cannot know our need for Christ if we can't see the end of the path we're on. It has worked to bring men and women to Christ's mercy for generations.

But now it's 2022 and we think we know better and have to curtail our preaching to not offend people? The Church survived and thrived for 1900 years, but our numbers have been dwindling since we became afraid of telling the truth about where those without Christ are headed. Maybe it proves that we're not as wise as we think.

"And now, brothers, I know that you acted in ignorance, as did also your rulers. But what God foretold by the mouth of all the prophets, that his Christ would suffer, he thus fulfilled. Repent therefore, and turn back, that your sins may be blotted out, that times of refreshing may come from the presence of the Lord, and that he may send the Christ appointed for you, Jesus," - Acts 3:17-20 ESV

Simon Peter may have thrown quite the fire and brimstone punch, but he balances it as well with the truth that God had already accounted for this transgression. It was part of His plan for our salvation all along. Now even those on whose account Christ was crucified are called to "repent, and turn back, that your sins may be blotted out."

Nave's topical bible defines repentance as, "a complete reversal of one's attitude, and values; a turning toward God."

Believe in God, change your mind about who He is, and what our own wills have led us to, and turn back to God. Salvation is a gift for any who would receive it.

Day 20

Truth and Mercy

“Now brothers, I know that you acted in ignorance, as did also your rulers. But what God foretold through all the prophets, that His Christ should suffer, He thus fulfilled. Therefore repent and be converted, that your sins may be wiped away, that times of refreshing may come from the presence of the Lord, and that He may send the One who previously was preached to you, Jesus Christ, whom the heavens must receive until the time of restoring what God spoke through all His holy prophets since the world began." - Acts 3:17-21 MEV

"You killed the Creator of Life," (vs 15) was a sharp sting, but Peter's intent was not to utterly cripple these "men of Israel" to whom he spoke. The sting to the heart would call nobody to life, if it was a stab through the heart. He says, "now brothers," implying that:

A) he's still a man like them, not holier than thou.
B) he still loves and cares for them who were his people
C) he has not turned away from them.

The Messiah's messenger hadn't disowned them and therein was revealed the truth that the Messiah hadn't disowned them. "You killed the Creator of Life," was extra spicy fire and brimstone, but what the Spirit led Peter to know and to apply, was that such preaching was incomplete and dangerous if it wasn't balanced with the mercy of an outstretched hand.

"You killed the Creator of Life," was certainly met by pained faces. As the realization dawned on some of these men that they had crucified their Messiah, I'd suggest to you that even though they had not yet felt the flames of wrath, even at this point the flames of guilt that flared up were charring them from the inside. But Peter's Gospel call wasn't about the condemnation. In opening their eyes to their surroundings (that is, the crime for which they'd be thrown in the lake of fire), Peter stands on the banks of salvation, reaching out two hands; one hand ready to pull the repentant sinner up on shore, and the other holding a wet cloth, ready to cool the burning flesh and soothe the soul.

"I know that you acted in ignorance." You've likely heard it said in regard to our human nations, "ignorance of the law is no excuse." The same is true in the judgement of God. This ignorance did not absolve them of the guilt; Only Christ, crucified and resurrected, could do this. Remember Jesus dying on the cross? What did He pray? "Father, forgive them, for they know not what they do" (Luke 23:34 MEV). If, due to ignorance, there were no guilt, there would be no need for that mercy prayer. Likewise Paul, in rehashing his past, recognizes the mercy shown his ignorant sin.

"I was previously a blasphemer, and a persecutor, and an insolent man. But I was shown mercy, because I did it ignorantly in unbelief." - 1 Timothy 1:13 MEV

But what Peter states here is that for those who now mourned their actions, endless mercy was available for the taking. If they had known Jesus was the Messiah, based upon the miracles of the Holy Spirit He performed, and crucified Him as a blasphemer anyway, they'd have committed the unforgivable sin of blaspheming the Holy Spirit. It is quite possible some did. But to these men, having not known what they were doing, Peter reveals the forgiveness that is in Christ.

"For God did not send His Son into the world to condemn the world, but that the world through Him might be saved. He who believes in Him is not condemned. But he who does not believe is condemned already, because he has not believed in the name of the only begotten Son of God." - John 3:17-18 MEV

The fire and brimstone we preach is not "holier than thou" condemnation. It is merely the revelation to every heart that without Christ we are all headed toward our just desserts. But it's not the full Gospel if we stop our preaching at hellfire. It's not the full Gospel if we don't continue, in love, preaching the unlimited mercy we can find by believing on the name of the Lord Jesus Christ. Peter preached the balance of truth and grace, and we see the result in the next chapter:

"But many of those who heard the word believed, and the number of the men grew to about five thousand." - Acts 4:4 MEV

Peter preached truth in love, and mercy dawned on many a soul.

Day 21

The Blessing of Repentance

"God, having raised up His Son Jesus, sent Him to you first, to bless you in turning every one of you from your iniquities." - Acts 3:26 MEV

Blessings. Mankind has a tendency to take a very wide approach to such a word - financial, material, relational, occupational, and more - but the ultimate blessing is restoration to fellowship with God. Through the salvation of faith in Christ and His finished, redemptive work, the new work of God begins here: "to bless you in turning every one of you from your iniquities."

Blessings can indeed come in many forms. There's a suggestion I've seen in social media recently that of all the mentions of blessings in the New Testament, not a single one relates to earthly blessings such as finances or material wealth. It's a nice thought, but does not hold up to the test of scripture. Paul tells the Romans that Macedonia and Achaia had sent money for the poor in Jerusalem, and that he couldn't come to Rome until he had delivered that blessing (Romans 15:25-28). Even so, follow that reading into the very next verse and we see confirmation that Gospel truths themselves are the primary blessings.

"There were people in Christ's lifetime who were all untouched by His teachings, but when they found that He gave bread miraculously they said, 'This is of a truth the Prophet! That's the prophet for my money; the Man that can make bread, and secure material well-being.' Have not certain modern views of Christ's work and mission a good deal in common with these vulgar old Jews-views which regard Him mainly as contributing to the material good, the social and economical well-being of the world?" - Alexander McLaren

God can and often does bless His children in other ways when such blessings would not interfere with their sanctification (among other things), yet we must stand firm on the truth that the primary blessing remains, "turning each of you from your sins." To the unbeliever, or even to the immature believer, repentance may not seem a blessing at all. "Men loved darkness rather than the light" (John 3:19 MEV). What you need to understand though, is that the sins mankind love not only come with eternal consequences - which as any procrastinator could tell you, belongs to the future me so "care I not" - but they also ruin true joy.

"Let none think that they can be happy by continuing in sin, when God declares that the blessing is in being turned from all iniquity." - Matthew Henry

The carnal amusements of sin are temporary at best, and as those pink clouds disperse, we certainly find ourselves one step further from true happiness. Every time we immerse ourselves in those sins, their pleasure is diminished from the previous indulgence. Sin becomes, like a chemical addiction, something we need stronger and stronger doses of to get the same high, until one day we need a near lethal dose just to drown the pain.

I mentioned unbelievers and immature believers, but don't think for a second that excludes you, my brothers and sisters. So, you've been a faithful Christian, zealous for his word for maybe 40 or more years. Guess what? There's still sin in that flesh of yours. Have you conveniently overlooked that sin which you hold most dear? Or maybe you've felt the sting of a sin that won't let go? Is it possible you're on the verge of giving up hope that you'll ever be freed from those chains? Cast such thoughts into the pit from whence they've come.

"Sin is that which we naturally cleave to, and the design of divine grace is, to turn us from it; nay, to turn us against it, that we may not only forsake it, but hate it, and strive against it. And the gospel has a direct tendency to produce this effect, not only as it requires us to turn, but as it promises us grace to enable us to do so. Therefore let us apply to Christ for this, and by the aid and right use of it, repent and be converted, and so do our part; because he is ready to do his, namely, to give the grace we need, and thereby to save us from our sins, and the consequences thereof, and to bless us effectually, abundantly, and for ever." - Joseph Benson

Our Christ is ultimately powerful and His work is to turn you from your sin. Yes, we're still in flesh, but when we live by the Spirit, His grace is sufficient. Yes, we will still fail, but the ongoing work of God in us will turn us back from the sin that so easily entangles. Stand firm on that Holy Name, for no deficiency is found in it.

Maybe you're on that path already. Great! Now take heed: Temptations are not done with you yet. Never let yourself be deceived that even the tiniest taste of what you once enjoyed won't hurt. No sin is harmless. Let iniquity not sink its barbs back into your flesh.

Wherever you're at in your walk, sing it with me:

I stand on the chain breaking,
Miracle making,
Powerful Name of Jesus;
On the body raising,
Prodigal saving,
Powerful Name of Jesus!
Hallelujah, I'm free!

- Phil Wickham: Where I'm Standing Now

Notes

Notes

Day 22

A Living Hope

"As they spoke to the people, the priests, the captain of the temple, and the Sadducees came upon them, being greatly troubled because they taught the people and preached through Jesus the resurrection from the dead." - Acts 4:1-2 MEV

Peter and John went up to the temple around 3PM, but now we're told evening has come (vs 3). We can note that the Pharisees are not found counted among those who came against them this time. In chapter 23, Paul will likewise be brought before the Sanhedrin, and there we'll see the confirmation that the doctrine of Resurrection in Christ is what truly offended the chief priests, the captain (essentially the captain of the temple guard), and the Sadducees. Just as it is said here, they were grieved because these men, witnessed to by the miracle God performed through them, preached the resurrection of Jesus Christ whom they'd crucified. Yet it was not only His resurrection that became the sore spot.

"knowing that He who raised the Lord Jesus will also raise us through Jesus and will present us with you." - 2 Corinthians 4:14 MEV

You may remember from our study in Luke, the Sadducees were those who believed and taught that there was no resurrection from the dead; this life was all there was. For the Apostles, therefore, to teach the resurrection from the dead through Jesus Christ would absolutely undermine any authority they held. Peter and John publicly taught, with the esteem of the people, that the Sadducees were not only half-w[h]its like me, they were complete idiots, or as Solomon would put it, fools. It made them very, ahem, sad you see...

Dad jokes aside, what we see is that the resurrection of Christ, the first born from the dead, is central to the gospel, but likewise is the truth that, if Jesus has been raised, then we who have died with Him will be raised with Him. Do you remember what Jesus told Martha? If not, see John 11:23-27.

"Now if Christ is preached that He rose from the dead, how can some of you say that there is no resurrection of the dead? If there is no resurrection of the dead, then Christ has not risen. If Christ has not risen, then our preaching is vain, and your faith is also vain." - 1 Corinthians 15:12-14 MEV

Just as Paul would tell the Sanhedrin at his trial, Peter and John now stood before them, "being judged for my hope in the resurrection of the dead"(Acts 23:6 MEV). Years after standing before this council, Peter begins his first Epistle on this same hope:

"Blessed be the God and Father of our Lord Jesus Christ, who according to His abundant mercy has given us a new birth into a living hope through the resurrection of Jesus Christ from the dead," - 1 Peter 1:3 MEV

For those of us who are in Christ, what a great living hope we have! This world and our flesh are corrupt, but at the resurrection, all things will be made new, and our flesh will be raised incorruptible. How many of us have had those "come quickly, Lord" moments of despair in the evil world we inhabit? We have this hope, in earthen vessels, that at just the right time, the King of Kings will indeed come, and we will be resurrected into the presence and image of His glory.

"But now is Christ risen from the dead and become the first fruits of those who have fallen asleep. For since death came by man, by man came also the resurrection of the dead. For as in Adam all die, even so in Christ shall all be made alive. But every man in his own order: Christ the first fruits; afterward, those who are Christ's at His coming." - 1 Corinthians 15:20-23 MEV

If any has read this far with me yet still hasn't given his or her life to Christ, I invite you today, come find the hope that we preach. The world we live in is a place of pain, sorrow, suffering, and injustice, but if you would just believe on the name and finished work of Jesus Christ, this world will not be your portion; It will become nothing more than a temporary mission field as we collectively await the glory that is yet to be revealed.

When Christ returns, those who know Him and are known by Him will find joy the likes of which we can only imagine, but those who have refused

His free gift of salvation will look back on this broken world as nothing compared to the judgement that then falls. There's no need to be among the latter on that day.

Notes

Notes

Day 23

God's Rebels

"And they seized them and put them in custody until the next day, for it was already evening. But many of those who heard the word believed, and the number of the men grew to about five thousand." - Acts 4:3-4 MEV

While I'm a big fan of the KJV, it seems here is one of those places where it may have skimmed the edge of the nail, rather than hitting it on the head. Most other translations accurately represent the specific "grew to," or "became" about 5,000 (which counts the previous 3,000), whereas King James just says "was about five thousand." Beyond that though, there's an interesting quirk here which we did not see in the 3,000. This is "the number of the men," about 5,000.

While such explosive growth is noteworthy of itself, it has been suggested there's more to this passage. Notice how this number is counted after "it was already evening." Among others, Charles Ellicott believed that this number was counted from those who, after hearing Peter and John preach, attended the evening's meeting of the Church. They broke bread together, possibly even taking communion together. If that's true, then Luke's witnesses likely remembered this number for its similarity to the Christ's miraculous feeding. The 5,000 men of the Church, plus women and children, now gathered to symbolically feed on the Bread of Life.

Within these two verses, though, we see the ancient roots of the proverb, "the blood of the martyrs is the seed of the Church." Throughout history, persecution has often, though not always, strengthened the resolve of those under the name of Christ, and drawn countless souls to this "underdog" religion; the one that sometimes calls its warriors to fight by dying without a raising a weapon. I can't help but notice the nature of mankind within that. We are inherently rebels.

In the garden of Eden, we rebelled against God. In the courts of Pharoah, we rebelled against God. From the foot of Mt Sinai, we rebelled against God. From King David's porch, we rebelled against God. From Jeroboam's new kingdom, we rebelled against God. From Jezreel we rebelled against

God. From the boat above a certain famous whale, we rebelled against God. On and on it goes, until from the steps of Pilate's court, we rebelled against God.

The nature of mankind is rebellion. What can be known in hindsight is that God always managed to work His plan through, and even by, our rebellions, both large and small. But now He takes that one step further, and calls the hearts of men to rebel against the god of this world. The harder Satan wrought upon the hearts of men to discredit, silence, and terminate with extreme prejudice the Church of our Lord, the more the rebellious hearts of men have been drawn to this persecuted Truth.

It's no wonder Americans are witnessing the death of faith in our nation. As a nation with centuries of religious freedoms and protections, Satan has schemed to not push back so hard against us. As can be expected, the rebellious heart of man still seeks a fight, and so the Lord's word is in the crosshairs again.

Brothers and sisters, this nature of mankind is something we must keep in mind as we seek to share the Gospel. The more strictly you push against something, the more people will push back. Ask any father of a dating age, teenage girl.

We can't take this to the extreme though, and just stop speaking out. If we sit on our haunches waiting for people to come, then our feet are not shod with the sandals of the readiness of the Gospel. Rather, it might be said our butts would be planted in the lazyboys of the apathy of the gospel. We are indeed here to declare the Truth of God, and to stand against the wiles of the enemy. We are here as warriors in a fight.

Where's the balance? I don't have the answer for you today, and I doubt there even is a one size fits all solution. We must approach this conundrum in the instruction of the Lord: "wise as serpents and harmless as doves."

For those of us in the USA, we find ourselves in an interesting time, where those who rebel against God are again taking control in our land. The enemy is again leading the hearts of wayward men (or whatever they call themselves these days) to silence and discredit the word of God. Maybe we are at a turning point wherein, if our resolve be strengthened in the face of the enemy's schemes, some of those previously undecided rebellious souls will choose a side.

So, where are the broad chested men of God? Where are the faithful women of God? Where are the rebels, who rebel not against God, but against Satan? Where are the rebels who will take on this guerilla warfare with me and speak Christ? Where are they who will obey the Commander of the armies of the Lord; They who will stand firm on these front lines, not to resist our fellow men, but to resist with our every breath the works of the father of lies? Where are those? Sit thou on the other side of this page?

Notes

Notes

Day 24

No Other Name

"Then Peter, filled with the Holy Spirit, said to them, 'Rulers of the people and elders of Israel: If we today are being examined concerning a good deed done to a crippled man, how this man has been healed, be it known to you all, and to all the people of Israel, that by the name of Jesus Christ of Nazareth, whom you crucified, whom God raised from the dead, by Him this man stands before you whole. He is "the stone you builders rejected, which has become the cornerstone." ' " - Acts 4:8-11 MEV

The Sanhedrin examined Peter and John concerning a good deed done to a lame man, but as we read Luke's historical account, we examine Peter and John concerning a good testimony spoken before human opponents. While these are two very different charges, and while we examine from two very different perspectives, the answer remains the same.

Be it known to you all that by the name of Jesus Christ of Nazareth who was crucified, raised from the dead, and taken up in glory, by Him this Cephas (translated: Peter) and John now stand before Caiaphas and another John and they speak.

Remember only two months earlier, as Simon Peter stood among this very court witnessing the trial of his Lord, he cowered in fear. The boldness of Peter and John which the rulers and elders and Scribes now saw (vs 13) was not of them. We can be sure, just as Peter's response is prefaced by "Peter, filled with the Holy Spirit, said," that this is the bold speech of God. These words are not to Peter's credit, and they come not from his years of education or faithfulness. They are the fulfillment of a promise: the prophetic truth which Jesus had spoken to them:

"But before all these things, they will seize you and persecute you, delivering you up to the synagogues and prisons, and you will be brought before kings and governors for My name's sake. It will turn out as a testimony for you. Therefore resolve in your hearts beforehand not to practice your defense. For I will give you a mouth and wisdom, which all your opponents will be able to neither refute nor resist. You will be betrayed by parents and brothers and relatives and friends. And they will put some of you to death. You will be hated by all men for My name's sake," - Luke 21:12-17 MEV

By the power of the Lord Jesus, Peter and John approached a lame (crippled) man, and healed him so that he walked, and jumped, and praised God. By His own power, that same Lord Jesus approached a lame (uneducated, sinful) man, and healed him so that he now stood in bold confidence, declaring the only Name by which we may be saved.

"There is no salvation in any other, for there is no other name under heaven given among men by which we must be saved." - Acts 4:12 MEV

Studies are showing that more and more people who identify themselves as Christians believe that there are many paths to heaven. More and more are accepting the enemy's lie that all religions point to the same God. What this says is that more and more have been treacherously deceived, both by the enemy, and their own hearts.

These are the core tenets of the Gospel of Jesus Christ brothers and sisters, and we cannot neglect these truths:

That Jesus Christ lived, the Son of God, who was with God and was God. That He was rejected and crucified unto death. That He was raised again, not as a ghost but alive in flesh. That He was taken up in glory to the glory He had with the Father from everlasting to everlasting. That by His name, and His name alone can we be saved from the death that sin has born in each and every one of us. That those whose iniquity is put away by the redemption of Jesus Christ will also be washed by the Spirit, freed from the bondage to sin. And that Jesus Christ returns soon, to resurrect His Bride, the Church, and reign over all creation.

For Satan to write lies upon the hearts of unbelievers is to be expected. But for these lies to penetrate those who claim to be Christians should cause such people to question their faithfulness to the One called Faithful and True. Do they know Him, and are they known by Him?

"When they saw the boldness of Peter and John and perceived that they were illiterate and uneducated men, they marveled. And they recognized that they had been with Jesus. But seeing the man who was healed standing with them, they had nothing to say against it." - Acts 4:13-14 MEV

Brothers and sisters, is there any here among us that wouldn't want to look back in the annals of time and see such a record? "They recognized that they had been with Jesus." Once we've received salvation in Christ, my fellow adopted sons and daughters of the Most High, there could be no higher goal than that we would so live in the Spirit that all the world would recognize that we have been with Jesus.

And so, we are called to live in the Spirit, not in flesh, because it is Christ who gives us a mouth and wisdom, that even our worst experiences will become a testimony for us; that is the testimony that, "there is no other name under heaven given among men by which we must be saved."

I leave you with one last thought: notice that it is not by which we *can* be saved. It is "by which we *must* be saved." This is a necessity that none will do well to neglect. If you don't yet know salvation in Christ, I beg you, seek the Son before wrath dawns. There's no need to suffer that wrath, but outside of faith in Christ, all will.

Notes

Notes

Day 25

We Cannot Help but Speak

"Then they called them and commanded them not to speak or teach at all in the name of Jesus. But Peter and John answered them, 'Whether it is right in the sight of God to listen to you more than to God, you judge. For we cannot help but declare what we have seen and heard.' " - Acts 4:18-20 MEV

The first of these three verses breaks my heart, the second encourages, and the last is felt deep within my soul. Let's start with the first.

"Then they called them and commanded them not to speak or teach at all in the name of Jesus." – Acts 4:18 MEV

Here is the same ruling council of 71 or 72 influential leaders before whom Jesus of Nazareth stood, falsely convicted. Many of these are the same men who bribed the soldiers to lie about the empty grave. Now they see miracles they cannot deny, and hear testimony they cannot refute. Even so, their hearts are so hardened, and their love of reputation and authority so full, they are only concerned that the Apostles should not spread the truth which convicts them.

What a sad truth it is when we see hearts that will be hardened to the end. Nothing is more distressing, for the soul that knows the joy of the Lord, than to dwell on the thought of so many who will utterly refuse this free gift. Some are people we naturally love - brothers, sisters, mothers, fathers, sons, daughters, grandparents, grandchildren, cousins, aunts, uncles, nieces, and nephews. Some are our best friends, and some our worst enemies. Even the unrepentant doom of this last category grieves the soul of the mature Christ follower. In dwelling upon Psalm 69, Matthew Henry mourns the same:

"Those who reject God's great salvation proffered to them, may justly fear that His indignation will be poured out upon them. If men will sin, the Lord will reckon for it. But those that have multiplied to sin, may yet find mercy, through the righteousness of the Mediator. God shuts not out any from that righteousness; the gospel excludes none who do not, by unbelief, shut themselves out. But those who are proud and self-willed, so that they will not come in to God's righteousness, shall have their doom accordingly; they themselves decide it."

“But Peter and John answered them, 'Whether it is right in the sight of God to listen to you more than to God, you judge.” – Acts 4:19 MEV

Then Peter and John reply. Checkmate. You claim to be the representatives of God, but you command us contrarily to what God commands. Now tell us, which is right? If you've been following along in our study, do you remember what we rehashed yesterday?

"For I will give you a mouth and wisdom, which all your opponents will be able to neither refute nor resist." - Luke 21:15 MEV

Every step of the way, what was spoken unto the Apostles was true. Each step of the way their faith and convictions were affirmed. Each step of the way these followers of the Way (the Truth and the Life) saw and carried the testimony that Jesus Christ, the Son of God, was faithful and true. And as they went, none could refute their truths. The only available responses were to reject the Truth, or to repent and believe and find Life.

" ‘For we cannot help but declare what we have seen and heard.' " – Acts 4:20 MEV

Having received the gift of salvation and the promise of the Holy Spirit, they could not help but declare what they had seen and heard. O, woe is me if I not declare what I've been shown - if I not invite others to share in this joy!

Now let me ask you. Have you felt it? The world wants to silence us. We may lose relationships, opportunities, or careers, but do we follow the lead of the Spirit of God, boldly standing in faith to say, "we cannot help but declare what we've received?" Short of growing to the conformity of Christ in my everything, there is no urge deeper in my soul than this: How could I but declare His Holy Name?

Be ye ready to speak?

Day 26

The Power of the Holy Spirit

" 'And now, Lord, look upon their threats and grant to your servants to continue to speak your word with all boldness, while you stretch out your hand to heal, and signs and wonders are performed through the name of your holy servant Jesus.' And when they had prayed, the place in which they were gathered together was shaken, and they were all filled with the Holy Spirit and continued to speak the word of God with boldness." - Acts 4:29-31 ESV

If you have been reading along, you know Peter and John have just been released by the Sanhedrin with the order to no longer speak to anyone in the name of Jesus. At this point these two "went to their own people and reported what the chief priests and the elders had said to them" (vs 23 MEV). They collectively raised their voices in worship of the Lord God Jesus, the Messiah. That's where we now find ourselves.

Before we consider the verse selection at hand though, take note that they returned "to their own people." Did you notice in the last chapter, as Peter preached the name of Christ, he said, "you acted in ignorance, as did also *your* rulers" (Acts 3:17 MEV). These rulers were the rulers of the people of Israel, but what we see in both these verses is that Peter and John and the other believers were no longer under that old administration. Just as foretold, this new spiritual Israel was no longer the temporal Israel of old, they were now "called by a new name" (Isaiah 62:2 MEV), and thus the Christian Church was born.

Back to our passage though, this new Church stood in the face of extreme threats. The original Greek in which this was written emphasized the Hebraism "let us threaten them with a threat" (Acts 4:17). With Hebrew culture, repetition denoted emphasis. It translates in the NKJV as "severely threaten them." Yet in the face of this kind of danger, look at what they pray.

The prayer begins by glorifying God in their acknowledgement that everything that has happened and is happening is exactly as He foretold.

Then they pray "Now, Lord, look upon their threats," but it's an interesting thing that they don't pray for destruction on those rulers and elders, they don't pray to be free of such threats, and they don't pray for divine protection. What do they pray? Grant us the power of the Spirit to continue boldly preaching the name of Jesus Christ!

How powerful is that? May it be a guide to our prayers and our service, my brothers and sisters. "Take not away from us the trials and tribulations you promised; on the contrary, Lord Jesus, grant us that same power by which you rose from the grave, that we shall fear no evil; grant us the courage, in You, to preach and work faithfully, calling as many as will come to this joy we know so true."

Finally, we see the Holy reply.

"When they had prayed, the place where they were assembled together was shaken. And they were all filled with the Holy Spirit and spoke the word of God with boldness." - Acts 4:31 MEV

Cast thine mind back to Moses at the cleft of the rock and you'll see the Lord descend on the mountain in Fire, with a sound like a wind instrument, the mountain quakes, and "the Lord passed by before him" (Exodus 34:6 MEV).

Lurch forward through the annals of time to Elijah's cave on the same mountain (possibly even the same cleft), and came a wind so strong it broke rocks, but the Lord was not in the wind. Then quaked the earth but the Lord was not in the quake. Next the mountain burst aflame, but the Lord was not in the fire, and then the Still Small Voice. "And behold, the Lord passed by" (1 Kings 19:11 MEV).

Jump forward again and we have the foundation of the Church, upon which the Holy Spirit descended, with a sound like wind, but there was no wind, and with tongues like fire which did not burn (Acts 2:2), and with an earthquake that only affected the room where they gathered, and they were filled with the Spirit of the Lord.

Brothers and sisters, we cannot underestimate the power that we have in the Holy Spirit. It's easy to look back on characters like Moses, David, Elijah, and Daniel, and distance ourselves from the power in which they worked because they were great, anointed prophets of God. But do we fully comprehend the enormity of the fact that the Spirit of God which passed before them - the same Spirit that raised Jesus from the grave - dwells in us?

Now, Lord, grant to your servants to continue to speak your word with all boldness, while You stretch out your hand to heal. In the powerful name of Your Son, Jesus Christ, we pray, embolden us to speak, Amen.

Notes

Notes

Day 27

His Name, Not Ours

"Joseph, whom the apostles called Barnabas (which means, Son of Encouragement), a Levite from the land of Cyprus, sold a field he owned, and brought the money and placed it at the apostles' feet. Now a man named Ananias, with his wife Sapphira, sold a piece of property. He kept back part of the proceeds with his wife's knowledge, and brought a part of it and placed it at the apostles' feet. Then Peter said, 'Ananias, why has Satan filled your heart to deceive the Holy Spirit and keep back part of the proceeds of the land? While it remained unsold, was it not your own? And when it was sold, was it not under your authority? Why have you conceived this deed in your heart? You did not lie to men, but to God.' " - Acts 4:36-5:4 MEV

Remove chapter and verse designations for a moment. For 1500 years, this Bible we study was read without them, and while they're useful to us for referencing locations, they're dangerous when they keep us from seeing the context. So, I ask you today, remove chapter and verse for a moment, and let's just read the book of Acts... If we begin our read at Ananias, it becomes a message about giving, about property, about honesty, and about wealth, but I don't think that's a good starting point. Luke set the story of Ananias and Sapphira in contrast to the story of Barnabas, and when we read it like that, the lesson God speaks is far deeper.

So, who is Barnabas? Here's the man who we'll soon see trusted alongside Saul to carry the gifts of provision to the believers in Judea. The man who, after Peter's vision, the 12 will send out to find Paul and together they first share the Gospel with the Gentile world. Here is the man sent out on a mission, taking and mentoring John Mark, who is quite probably the same Mark that wrote Peter's testimony in the Gospel of Mark. Here is the man who, alongside Paul, tore his clothes and preached only Jesus upon hearing that the Greeks considered them Gods, and it can be noted, they viewed Barnabas as their highest God, Zeus. Clearly, He was a faithful man empowered greatly by the Holy Spirit. He's found over and over again in this book of Acts - seemingly just as used by God as the Apostles themselves - and He is referenced repeatedly in the epistles.

Who is Ananias? Who is Sapphira? They were but a footnote of death.

Such a vast contrast is shown between these three, and it's all laid out here. The son of encouragement lived out his name, giving what he had in sacrificial love. What about "the other two," as I'll so abruptly call them? Take a look at what the Spirit of God speaks to Ananias through Peter. It starts with a group of questions that God would never let Ananias answer.

Much like God's questions to Adam and Eve - "Where are you? Who told you you were naked? Have you eaten from the tree of which I commanded you not to eat?" - He already knew the answers.

Much like God's question to Elijah - "Why are you here, Elijah?" - the questions were intended to direct Ananias and Sapphira's attention to examine their own inner depths.

God asks four questions and the answer to every one of them is the same. Ananias and Sapphira saw the esteem of Barnabas, as he sold his property and laid it at the Apostles' feet. They coveted the same notoriety, but not the same service. They thought they could buy in to the same reputation at a discount. Still, this is not about cost, or wealth, it is about heart.

The difference between Barnabas and "the other two" was in the heart. Barnabas sold his property and laid the earnings at the Apostles' feet in a loving desire to relieve the needy. That's agape love, my friends. The other two just wanted reputation. That's hypocritical self-worship, and it is not of the Spirit, but of the flesh.

Yet here we are, called to live in Spirit while still trapped in flesh. How easily we are tempted to this sort of desire. It's natural for us to hope that people would have a high estimation of our characters. It's natural for us to desire that sort of honor, influence, and name. Translate "it's natural" as "it's flesh."

The Christian is not called to earn a good name for themselves, but by their living sacrifice, to reveal the Glory and Good Name of Jesus Christ, our God. We are not called to look the part before men, but to live the part before God.

"On hearing these words, Ananias fell down and died. And great fear came on all those who heard these things. The young men rose and wrapped him up and carried him out and buried him." - Acts 5:5-6 MEV

Take special note, my friends, that the last words Ananias heard were, "You did not lie to men, but to God." The mask of false piety, that so many of us hide behind, is a stain on the bride's dress. Brothers and sisters, we must drop the mask and truly live out what we profess. There is no reputation to be coveted, but that God's reputation alone be exalted.

Notes

Notes

Day 28

Two are Better than One

"Peter said to her, 'How is it that you have agreed together to test the Spirit of the Lord? Look! The feet of those who have buried your husband are at the door, and they will carry you out.' At once she fell down at his feet and died. Upon entering, the young men found her dead and carried her out and buried her beside her husband. Great fear came on the entire church and on all those who heard these things." - Acts 5:9-11 MEV

I perceive it to be an interesting parallel that at the beginning of all time, in Genesis chapter 3, a husband and wife sin together. One at a time, they are questioned by God, and neither confesses guilt. Henceforth death is introduced to the world. Now at the beginning of the Church, a husband and wife sin together. One at a time, they are questioned by God, as the Holy Spirit speaks through Peter, and neither confesses guilt. Their deaths, each in turn, are instant.

The marriage covenant is a bond with no match among humans, or at least, it was made to be, though we've corrupted it grievously. The two are made one flesh. The husband is made to be the spiritual leader of the family, pointing his wife and children to Christ. The wife is made to be the helper, every bit as important, yet with a similar but somewhat different role. This team, if submitted to Christ, are a force to be reckoned with. If submitted to flesh, they may just trip over one another all the way to the grave.

Just as Adam and Eve were both complicit in their act of mistrust, so were Ananias and Sapphira. When Eve was deceived, it was her husband Adam's responsibility to pick her back up and brush the dust off, but instead, he joined her in the fall. When Ananias conceived the scheme of hypocrisy, it was his wife Sapphira's responsibility to pick him back up and brush the dust off, but instead, she joined him in death.

"Two are better than one, because there is a good reward for their labor together. For if they fall, then one will help up his companion. But woe to him who is alone when he falls and has no one to help him up. Also if two lie down together, then they will keep warm; but how can one keep warm by himself? And if someone might overpower another by himself, two together can withstand him. A threefold cord is not quickly broken." - Ecclesiastes 4:9-12 MEV

Brothers and sisters, for those of us joined in matrimony, we have not only this great blessing from God, but also a great responsibility. When it is said that a cord of three strands is not easily broken, we can know for a certainty that one of those three strands (God), will not be broken. If one of the others is damaged, the two will uphold the one, but if the braid is unraveled, the cord fails. I don't seek to take that imagery too far, though, because we will all stumble, and God is the God who repairs what is broken.

For my married brothers and sisters, we have a great duty to our spouses. This marriage bond is a covenant with responsibility. We must seek to build one another up, and to lift one another up when one falls. Sure, Ananias died on the spot, but can you imagine the torment when his judged soul realized he had led his wife to judgement? Sure, Sapphira died on the spot, but can you imagine the torment when she heard what had happened to her husband by their plot?

Hey man, you married her because you adored her, right? If in that moment of love, you'd have looked forward and seen a man paving her way to destruction, what would you have done to that future you?

Hey woman, you married him because you respected and loved him, right? In that moment of love, would you have been enraged to see your future self smoothing his path to destruction?

Don't underestimate the importance of our duties to support, encourage, and exhort one another.

Notes

Day 29

The Thorn or the Vine

"None of the rest dared join them, but the people held them in high esteem. And more than ever believers were added to the Lord, multitudes of both men and women," - Acts 5:13-14 ESV

The meaning of "none of the rest dared join them," has been the topic of discussion among scholars and theologians for many moons. Some suggest it infers none of the rest of the believers dared associate too closely with the Apostles after the fate of Ananias and Sapphira. This is possibly the case, yet I cannot bring to mind anywhere else in the scriptures where believers distanced themselves, exalting the Apostles in fear. In the previous chapter we saw that the believers, "were all filled with the Holy Spirit and continued to speak the word of God with boldness" (Acts 4:31 ESV).

Others have put forth the idea that Ananias and Sapphira were wealthy, and so no other wealthy Jews joined the Church, only the poor. I don't even know where to begin analyzing that theory, except to cast it out among the fancies of men, based not on scripture, but solely human conjecture.

But I think when we view the contrast here, we do indeed see it related to the two dead hypocrites. Reading chapter five it seems to me that "the rest," is the divergence from "believers [who] were added to the Lord." The rest being those hypocrites who would not truly give themselves to repentance and belief in Christ, yet might otherwise have pretended, and joined themselves to the Church to gain the esteem of men such as we see the Apostles and disciples were occasioned with.

We might ponder why our God, who elsewhere shows Himself so long-suffering, merciful, and patient, cast such immediate destruction upon Ananias and his wife. We might ponder, and we may come across the notion as the Holy Spirit led believers to sell property and give according to need, that these two, in pretending the same faith, blasphemed the Holy Spirit, for which there is no redemption. We might ponder, and our understanding may be that our Heavenly Father, who has set forth to purify the bride for His Son, knew the necessity to nip that blemish in the bud before it bloomed. We can know without doubt that God was both just and wise in that decision. We can look without pondering and see that thorn without blossom in the early church, as "none of the rest dared join them."

But can we look and see that same thorn to be scant of blossom today? I believe that for far longer than I've been alive, we've seen men and women religiously attend worship services, not to worship the Lord they believed in, but because it was where others expected them to be. The show has been perfected to a point where, at first glance, one would not recognize Barnabas from Ananias, but the Lord does not see as man sees. As I've also been studying the life and ministry of Elijah, I recently came across a quote from Charles H. Spurgeon, recorded well over a century ago.

"Many today say, ‘I am worldly but I am religious too!' it can't be done; they are distinct and separate. If God is God, serve Him and do it thoroughly. But if this world is god, serve it and make no profession of religion. 'No one can serve two masters' (Mt 6:24). How many respectable church goers think they can be covetous and grasping in business and grind the faces of the poor and yet be saints? How many women received into church fellowship are found to be full of wrath and bitterness - slaves of mischief and of sin - slanderers and busybodies. If we make a profession to be Christian, we must not pretend to be. If we love the world, then let's love it, but let's cast off the mask and not be hypocrites. The double-minded person, who wears two faces, is the most despicable because he is not honest enough to go through with what he professes."

Can we look at the same thorn and see it without blossom today? I don't believe we have that luxury. Thereby we must look in the mirror. Do we find ourselves attached to the Vine, or to the thorn? No amount of being seen in a Sunday pew, nor serving at the door of the sanctuary, no fish bumper sticker on your car, nor cross logo on your hat, no amount of charitable giving, nor pious lifestyle will assure your place in the good graces of God. We cannot falsely play the part of a believer and expect anything less than to eventually find our portion is the fate of Ananias and Sapphira.

Thanks be to God that this list is not necessary to earn our way through the gate, because even the best actors could not truly perfect that performance. Thanks be to God it's not that complicated. The simple message is repent and believe that Jesus Christ is Lord, and more believers are added unto the Lord.

Whether you've spent your life avoiding the steeple, or you find you've been a lifelong performer in the film of the Church, the call is the same: Submit yourselves, every one of you, to Jesus Christ. Repent (change your mind) and be baptized (declare you have died to self and live for Christ) for the forgiveness of sins. Call on the only Name by which we must be saved.

Notes

Notes

Day 30

The Light of the Son

"And more than ever believers were added to the Lord, multitudes of both men and women, so that they even carried out the sick into the streets and laid them on cots and mats, that as Peter came by at least his shadow might fall on some of them. The people also gathered from the towns around Jerusalem, bringing the sick and those afflicted with unclean spirits, and they were all healed." - Acts 5:14-16 ESV

There are many very extravagant miracles recorded in scripture. Spit-made mud on the eyes of a blind man, healings by word alone, physical contact with lepers, and more. But here is a bundle of miracles worked by nothing more than passing shadows. We can be sure this wasn't just a handful of sick people either. Estimates of the number of people inhabiting Jerusalem alone during the first century range from 400,000 to 1 million or more. The Jewish historian Josephus, who was born in Jerusalem around this time, recorded that there were 6,000 Pharisees alone. In a city of that size, the sick and afflicted would be a relatively large demographic, but Luke goes further to tell us ill people were even brought in from the towns around Jerusalem.

Surely these miracles were a testimony of great significance. The tense implied that this was an ongoing occurrence. Could it have been days, weeks, or months? We don't know, but what we do know is that Luke gave us the context of these miracles.

The language used infers that the carrying out of the lame was related back to the multitudes of believers added daily unto the Lord. What Luke is saying is that these healings were received in faith. The sick were brought out by people who had heard what the Apostles were doing and teaching, and they believed.

Joe heard Peter preach and came to faith. Then he told his buddy, sick Billy. Billy said, "Do you think they could help me?" and Joe responded, "I do have faith that even your affliction is not too great for God, come and see for yourself." Before you know it, Billy is healed and telling his buddy, crippled Johnny. It all harkens back to the many times Jesus said, "Your faith has healed you."

The context can then be brought back around to the completion of these miracles. In mentioning the people brought out and laid in the streets, Luke doesn't immediately record whether they were actually healed or not because it would have been redundant. He immediately after speaks of the ones brought in from surrounding towns and says, "and they were all healed."

Now, it would be easy to lift Peter onto too high a pedestal when we see a sentence so directly attributed to him as, "that as Peter came by at least his shadow might fall on some of them." Yet Peter wasn't the only one. As the leader of the group, and the most outspoken, he was just the most well-known name in the vicinity. If Jesus and all his disciples were all preaching and healing together, it would be said that the sick were brought out that Jesus' shadow might fall on them. Later in Acts we see confirmation that this wasn't some extraordinary grace upon Peter alone. It is recorded that even the handkerchiefs that touched Paul's skin were distributed to heal.

So, in all this, what can we take away? Stand in the sun and look at your shadow. It's a bit of a riddle, isn't it? It is nothing more than the absence of light, but without the light, it wouldn't exist, and thereby the essence of a shadow is light.

Peter and the other Apostles stood in the Son, the Light of the World, reflecting the glory of God into those around them. Even the images they cast upon the ground, as Jesus shined upon them, worked the furtherance of the gospel. That's a testimony of how great His glory truly is. Even a mere shadow of that glory, cast across His disciples can heal the corruption of the flesh.

Brothers and sisters, our God is good in all things, and powerful beyond our wildest dreams. We can look at this shadow, cast upon the infirm, and be reminded that when we stand in the light of the Son to do the works that were prepared for us before the beginning of time, nothing is impossible with God.

So, as you see that image of yourself cast upon the ground today, I petition you to ask yourself, "Am I standing in the sun, or in the Son? Am I living so fully for Christ that even the shadow I cast can make the world a better place? Do people see Christ in me?"

Notes

Notes

Day 31

Speak Life

"they arrested the apostles and put them in the public prison. But during the night an angel of the Lord opened the prison doors and brought them out, and said, 'Go and stand in the temple and speak to the people all the words of this Life.' And when they heard this, they entered the temple at daybreak and began to teach." - Acts 5:18-21a ESV

You may remember that Peter would later be martyred for preaching in faith, and John would suffer much torture, abuse, and even banishment to the prison island of Patmos, but here, an angel of the Lord opened the prison doors and brought them out. When we believe the word of God is true, there's no room for conjecture that this is anything but a supernatural sign; One among the signs and wonders that would accompany the church. There's no room to believe anything less than "God sent an angel to walk them out."

Look at Paul imprisoned in Philippi, later in Acts, and you'll see a guard ready to commit suicide because he knows what would befall him for allowing the escape of his charge, even though he was powerless to resist. Here though, when the officers came to the empty prison, the doors were shut, and the guards were oblivious. Truly an angel of the Lord walked them out of that prison, not some zealous disciple. It wasn't to save them from their suffering though. Much suffering lay ahead for all the Apostles.

"There is no prison so dark, so strong, but God can visit his people in it, and, if he pleases, fetch them out. Recoveries from sickness, releases out of trouble, are granted, not that we may enjoy the comforts of life, but that God may be honoured with the services of our life." - Matthew Henry

The Angel walked them out of their trouble and said, "Go to the most public place, and preach!" What a beautiful expression it is: "Speak to the people all the words of this life." What a wondrous definition of the Gospel, and one we can hold on to. The Gospel is the word of life.

When Jesus finally made a public declaration to being the Messiah, as recorded in John 6, many had trouble with some of the things he spoke.

We were told that many disciples turned away, but the Apostles and several others stayed. Take a look at what Peter says:

"From that time many of His disciples went back and walked no more with Him. So Jesus said to the twelve, 'Do you also want to go away?' Simon Peter answered Him, 'Lord, to whom shall we go? You have the words of eternal life. We have believed and have come to know that You are the Christ, the Son of the living God.' " - John 6:66-69 MEV

"You have the words of eternal life." There is no greater truth than this: we were dead in our sins, each and every one of us, but the Bread of Life came down from heaven, spoke life into 12 men, was betrayed by one unto death, descended to the depths, was raised to life, and lifted up into glory. In His death, we are redeemed, in His resurrection, we are raised from death unto life, and in His ascension to the throne we are equipped to not be overcome by the darkness of the world.

"In Him was life, and the life was the light of mankind. The light shines in darkness, but the darkness has not overcome it." - John 1:4-5 MEV

If you have life in Christ - if you know and are known by Him - you have the light of mankind. The call now, as God's messengers open prison gates of all forms, is not to chase your dreams, or to live your best life now. Those gates are opened for the light to shine and not be overcome. Now go, and speak all the words of this life! However the Holy Spirit may equip and call you to that, go. It will look different for each of us, but if we are in Christ, the call is there, laid on our hearts. However your work was prepared, go. Speak life.

Notes

Day 32

Brambles and Boulders, Muck and Mire

"Peter and the other apostles answered, 'We must obey God rather than men. The God of our fathers raised Jesus, whom you killed by hanging on a tree. God exalted this Man to His right hand to be a Ruler and a Savior, to give repentance to Israel and forgiveness of sins. We are His witnesses to these words, as is the Holy Spirit whom God has given to those who obey Him.' " - Acts 5:29-32 MEV

If you've been following along in our study, you know these early chapters of Acts find Peter repeating this same truth over and over again, in varying company, and with good cause. It could become rather monotonous if in this study we keep hitting the same topic from the same angle though. I recently had occasion to teach from the Psalms, and as Peter proclaims the suffering of the Savior, the guilt of the people, and the witness of His repentant, redeemed disciples, I think we'll take a detour through Psalm 69. Will you follow this Jeeper through the brambles and boulders, the muck and the mire of an alternate two track for a few days? This may be a good time for you to go read it.

Psalm 69 has been labeled by many themes. "A plea for rescue" (CSB), "an urgent plea for help in trouble" (NKJV), "Save me, O God" (ESV), or "a cry of distress, and imprecation on Adversaries" (AMP). Digging in to the text, though, I'd suggest this is the Psalm of the suffering Messiah. This Psalm is quoted as concerning Jesus by the Apostle John in his Gospel account, by Peter in his first sermon which we so recently studied, by Paul in his epistle to the church in Rome, and by Christ Himself.

This Psalm, though written as a personal plea by David in a time of distress, was also prophetically inspired by the Lord, declaring the life and persecution of the Christ. We must consider that it is so much more than that, though, and to confirm this I ask you to look at verse 5: "O God, You know my folly, and my sins are not hidden from You." Dare we never attribute such a verse to the Sinless One. Thereby this Psalm becomes the quintessential Hebrew poetry, always formed as point and counterpoint. We can see it as:

- A testimony of Christ's sufferings, but also
  - A testimony of our joyous redemption in Him.
- A testimony of the perfect righteousness of Christ, but also
  - A testimony of the shortcomings of all mankind.
- A testimony of God's great, merciful grace, but also
  - A testimony of the wrath that awaits those who reject Him.

So, let's start at the beginning.

"Save me, O God! For the waters have come up to my throat. I sink in deep mire; there is no standing place; I have come into the watery depths, and a stream overflows me. I am weary of my crying; my throat is parched; my eyes fail while I wait for my God." - Psalms 69:1-3 MEV

Put this plea in the context of verse 5, and what we see of David's words is that they are essentially a God-inspired demonstration of the sinner's prayer. Save me Lord Jesus, for I drown in my iniquity. There is nowhere I can stand, to overcome on my own. I am weary of mourning with no hope. I thirst for you, O my God.

"Those who hate me without cause are more than the hairs of my head; they are mighty who would destroy me, being my wrongful enemies, so that I must pay back what I did not steal." - Psalms 69:4 MEV

In the midst of this we have verse 4, that counterpoint mentioned above. It seems to be in the same thread, but scripture clarifies to us that it is far beyond such a minuscule view. Jesus quoted it in John 15:25 when He assured us, we need not be surprised if the world hates us, for it hated Him first. He told us that it spoke of his rejection, but that we should not be surprised to find that it also spoke of those who would take up their cross and follow Him. It takes my mind to Peter's encouragement, "if you suffer for the sake of righteousness you are blessed" (1 Peter 3).

Our Lord told His disciples His rejection was a fulfillment of the prophecy, "they hated me without cause." It was fulfilled that the mighty - those high priests, Pharisees, Sadducees, and Roman occupiers - would destroy Him. Today we'll end with the conclusion of this destruction, "so that..."

David prophetically spoke for Jesus, "so that I must pay back what I did not steal." This is the truth of the Gospel. The One who owed no debt took our debt upon Himself. The Sinless Savior took the weight of our sin upon His shoulders, so that we could be redeemed. Jesus Christ hung upon that tree to pay back what He did not owe so that we could be set free and counted by His righteousness.

Brothers and sisters, David penned this Psalm a full millennium before the Sadducees persecuted our Lord. 1000 years in advance, he prophetically foretold exactly what the plan was, formed before the Earth, for our salvation. Tomorrow, we dig into verses 6-12, and we'll see even more, but even in these first 5 verses we can see the truth that God has always fulfilled what He foretold. If all across thousands of years, God has always been faithful to fulfill His words, what cause could we possibly have to doubt He will continue that faithfulness in our meager lifetimes? Take heart, brothers and sisters. Nothing stops our Lord from His will.

Notes

Notes

Day 33

Man of Sorrows

"May those who wait on You, O Lord God of Hosts, not be ashamed because of me; may those who seek You not be humiliated because of me, O God of Israel." - Psalms 69:6 MEV

In studying Acts we took a side trail along the route yesterday, and wound up in Psalm 69. You'll remember that we found this Psalm, which is quoted repeatedly in the New Testament, is a testimony of the Suffering Savior and His redeemed disciples. Now we come to verses 6-12, and they read as if the Messiah Himself spoke the words directly through David's prophetic quill.

First in verse 6 we have Jesus praying over His disciples, "may they not be ashamed because of me." We see this prayer fulfilled in Paul, writing, "for I am not ashamed of the gospel of Christ" (Romans 1:16a MEV), and we see it in the teenage kid who doesn't choose popularity among his peers, above identity in Jesus. Brothers and sisters, the world today wants to shame us into silence, but may we never find ourselves giving in to the pressure, for this gospel we carry is just as Paul continued in Romans 1, "the power of God for salvation to everyone who believes."

"Because for Your sake I have endured insult; humiliation has covered my face." - Psalms 69:7 MEV

This is indeed our Christ. He who for Your sake (God's glory), and for your sake (our salvation), humbled himself. This Messiah, who shared all glory with the Father before the world was formed, stepped down into our world and willingly suffered rejection, insult, and scorn; He who could command armies of angels remained silent as his face was covered with spit, blood, and writhing agony - He allowed the Sadducees to hang Him on a tree - so that we might be saved and made in His image according to the will of God.

"I have become estranged to my relatives, and a foreigner to my mother's children;" - Psalms 69:8 MEV

Though at the beginning of the book of Acts we saw Christ's mother and brothers joining the Apostles in the upper chamber, and though two of His brothers wrote canonical scripture, leading the Church in holiness, we can look back to his life and see a different story. Mark's gospel tells us they had thought He'd lost His mind (Mark 3:21). John's gospel tells us those brothers did not believe in Him (John 7:5). As we studied Luke's gospel, you may remember His relatives and countrymen rejected Him as He taught in the synagogue of Nazareth. Truly, what God prophesied in this Psalm, 1000 years prior, was fulfilled in Jesus of Nazareth.

"for the zeal of Your house has consumed me, and the insults of those who insulted You fell on me." - Psalms 69:9 MEV

Verse 9 confirms for us the truth that this was all prophetic, quoted twice in the New Testament as concerning the Messiah. John testifies that upon seeing Jesus flipping tables, he and his fellow disciples "remember that it was written, 'Zeal for your house will consume me.' " (John 2:17)

Paul quotes the second half of this verse in Romans 15:3, declaring it spoke of Jesus Christ, and exhorting us to humbly serve one another so that in one voice we can declare the praise and glory of God. Brothers and sisters, if our Lord came not to be served in greatness, but to serve in weakness, Paul taught we should follow His example. Now as we read the last few verses of today's selection, cast thine mind to Isaiah's, "Man of Sorrows."

"When I wept with fasting for my soul, it became an insult to me. I also made sackcloth my garment, and I became a byword to them. Those who sit in the gate speak against me, and I am the song of the drunkards." - Psalms 69:10-12 MEV

Read these words and think to the prayer at Gethsemane, to the scorn of religious leaders, to the betrayal plot between those same and the man who was supposed to be His friend, or maybe to the abuse from Roman soldiers.

Brothers and sisters, I remind you today of what we found yesterday. We can look through all of history and see that everything God promised has so far been fulfilled. How can we then have any doubt that He will continue that faithfulness in every promise He has made? How can we doubt that He will work all things to the good for those who love Him? Even when we see the suffering of our lives, we can know that it all works to the plan that leads us into the greatest blessing of all - the presence of the good and holy God.

Notes

Notes

Day 34

Sinner's Plea;
Savior's Service

"Draw near to my soul, and redeem it; deliver me because of my enemies." - Psalms 69:18 MEV

In the midst of our study of the book of Acts, you may remember, we found Peter repeating before the Sadducees, "we must obey God rather than men. The God of our fathers raised Jesus, whom you killed... God exalted Him... as Leader and Savior... We are witnesses to these things" (Excerpts from Acts 5:29-32). It led us to jump back through time, 1,000 years prior, to the prophetic song of the Suffering Savior, found in Psalm 69.

Over the last two days we've found it true to form of the point-counterpoint style of Hebrew poetry; sinner's plea, and Savior's service. As we get to verses 13-18, we again see the sinner's plea, and in 19-21, again the suffering of the Savior is foretold. "But as for me, my prayer is to you, O Lord."

"But as for me, my prayer is to You, O Lord; in an acceptable time, O God, in the abundance of Your mercy, answer me in the truth of Your salvation. Deliver me out of the mire that I may not sink; may I be delivered from those who hate me, and out of the watery depths." - Psalms 69:13-14 MEV

In the most acceptable time, the fullness of time which God so perfectly positioned the human birth of His only begotten Son, He answered every repentant sinner's plea in abundance of mercy. The Truth of salvation was born, taught, healed, and died in our place on that cursed tree at the hands of His enemies.

"Answer me, O Lord, for Your lovingkindness is good; turn Your face to me according to the abundance of Your tender mercies. Do not hide Your face from Your servant, for I am in trouble; answer me quickly." - Psalms 69:16-17 MEV

Those who have yet to find Christ sometimes wonder why a good and loving God would leave people to suffer hell. The answer is, He doesn't. The Lord has not hidden His face from any, unless they themselves turned to not see what was plainly before them. Jesus Christ is the most widely known name across the entire globe, and it has been for nearly 2,000 years. It is the only name by which we must be saved, but it is plenteous enough for any and all who would call upon it. All that remains is that each sinner choose to believe, and upon taking that step, God's face will be revealed unto His servants.

God's lovingkindness is good, and his tender mercies are abundant. So much so, He told His followers to share the good news with all people of all nations. So much so, the very Word of God humbled himself to become like us, yet without all our rebellion, took the stripes of the penalty of our rebellion upon His own back. So much so, He suffered shame and dishonor, insults and rejection by even this Simon Peter who now testifies His name before the Sadducees.

"You have known how I am insulted, and my shame and my dishonor; my adversaries are all before You. Insults have broken my heart, and I am sick; and I looked for some to take pity, but there was none; and for comforters, but I found none. They also gave me poison for my food, and in my thirst they gave me vinegar to drink." - Psalms 69:19-21 MEV

In John's Gospel, as the Lord hung upon that cross, there were two final phrases spoken before Christ gave up His spirit. "I thirst," and "It is finished" (John 19:28-30). Upon his declaration of thirst, "they gave me vinegar to drink" (Psalm 69:21 MEV).

Verses 19-21 swing the pendulum back from the repentant sinner to the serving Savior, and we see again that all of the Old Testament points to Jesus of Nazareth, the Messiah of Israel, and Savior of the world. Matthew Henry makes note:

"The sufferings of Christ we're here particularly foretold, which proves the scripture to be the word of God; and how exactly these predictions were fulfilled in Jesus Christ, which proves Him to be the true Messiah. The vinegar and gall given to him, were a faint emblem of that bitter cup which He drank up, that we might drink the cup of salvation."

What glorious truth we carry, that our Lord drank the cup of God's wrath, so that in the abundance of His mercies we could drink the cup of salvation. What a glorious Truth has saved us, brothers and sisters, and the testimony of a thousand years only scratched the surface of how perfectly God has ordained His plan to redeem us. Brothers and sisters, we are witnesses to these things. We are witnesses of His great love for us. In this light, we must obey God rather than men, not to gain salvation, for only the blood of Christ did that. No, we who have been lifted out of the mire, wash off that muck in thanksgiving to the One who reached down His hand.

Notes

Notes

Day 35

The Time is Now

"But Peter and the apostles answered, 'We must obey God rather than men. The God of our fathers raised Jesus, whom you killed by hanging him on a tree.' " - Acts 5:29-30 ESV

As we've been studying the book of Acts, these early chapters have found Peter's words rather repetitive, and so you may remember 3 days ago we began to take a side trail, through Psalm 69, as it prophesied, quite specifically, of the suffering of the Savior, the redemption of those who turn to Him, the persecution of those same, and now, the judgement upon those who reject him to the end. Oh yes, when we get to verses 22-29 of this Psalm, we find the heat turned up on the enemies of God.

If you've studied along with us for some time, you may remember we've found, over and over again, that all of the Old Testament was a shadow of things to come, and here the shadow is of the return of the Lord Jesus Christ as Judge; That oh so great and terrible day.

For several months now, my pastor, Paul, has been leading us verse-by-verse through the book of the Revelation of Jesus Christ. In that study, we've come across John's vision of the prayers of the saints, wafting up before the Lord as incense from a bowl.

In this Psalm, David prays against those who stood against him. While we're called to pray for our enemies, not against them, this is the natural inner prayer of the spirit of any man, woman, or child who desires a just God; "O Lord visit their injustice." We can safely assume that some of the incense of those prayers is as such.

"May their table become a snare before them, and may security become a trap. May their eyes be darkened so they do not see, and make their sides shake continually." - Psalms 69:22-23 MEV

In his epistle to the Romans, Paul quotes the above verse, revealing the portion of those who reject God to the last, as opposed to those elect whose names are in the book of life. There were many we'll see among the Pharisees who repented of their plot to crucify the Lord, and there was mercy aplenty. But the Sadducees we see in the first century hardened themselves, and so God gave them over to their passions and let their hearts be hardened unto death. There's a vast contrast here, and within it is the gospel call. As long as we have todays, it is not too late to be redeemed, but if you wait for a tomorrow, you may just find your todays run out.

"Pour out Your indignation on them, and may Your wrathful anger overtake them. May their habitation be desolate, and may no one dwell in their tents. For they persecute him whom You have struck down, and they recount the pain of those You have wounded. Add punishment to their iniquity, and do not let them come into Your righteousness. Let them be blotted out of the book of the living, and not be written along with the righteous." - Psalms 69:24-28 MEV

Again, I say to you, though we're called to higher prayers - prayers as merciful as our Lord has been upon our transgressions - the natural prayer within our souls wafts up from these words. Lord, bring justice on an unjust world. Again, when we look at these verses with the knowledge of New Testament revelation, we see a vast contrast. Verse 24, for example, is quoted as prophetic of the perdition of Judas Iscariot in Acts 1:20.

Verse 26, on the other hand - they persecute him whom you have struck down - brings the mind to the persecutors, and I ask you to cast your mind ahead in our study of Acts for a moment, to Saul on the road to Damascus. "Saul, Saul, why do you persecute me?" (Acts 9:4) Saul, the Pharisee of Pharisees who hunted Christ's followers to imprison and kill them, is the epitome of the lesson that none is too far from God to find grace and mercy.

"Those who reject God's great salvation proffered to them, may justly fear that His indignation will be poured out upon them. If men will sin, the Lord will reckon for it. But those that have multiplied to sin, may yet find mercy, through the righteousness of the Mediator. God shuts not out any from that righteousness; the gospel excludes none who do not, by their own unbelief, shut themselves out. But those who are proud and self-willed, so that they will not come in to God's righteousness, shall have their doom accordingly; they themselves decide it." - Matthew Henry

There is no distance too far for us to turn back to God and find he's been right there waiting all along. But there is a time, which none of us knows, that either by our death or His return, we will no longer have the option of turning back. As a witness of God's good grace, I urge you now, don't be found among the latter. Believers, overcome to the end, for we know that trials and temptations will be used to entice us to apostasy. Unbelievers, turn to Christ, before it's too late. Though my soul cries out for justice, the Holy Spirit within me cries out, "May all of creation find His salvation; May even my worst enemies be made new in Christ."

Notes

Notes

Day 36

I Will Praise

"I will praise the name of God with a song, and will magnify Him with thanksgiving. This also will please the Lord more than an ox or bull with horns and hoofs. The humble will see this and be glad; and you who seek God, may your heart live. For the Lord hears the poor, and does not despise His prisoners." - Psalms 69:30-33 MEV

If you've been absent for a few days, you may wonder what we're doing in Psalms, when we were studying Acts. As Peter and John were set free of the prison cell and told to go speak "all the words of this life" (Acts 5:20 MEV), Peter was still establishing the foundation of faith in unbelievers, and so what he speaks in the temple are the same truths we've already delved into a couple times. But not to be repetitive, I mentioned that I recently had occasion to teach from the Psalms, and the Psalm of the week just so happens to "speak all the words of this life."

We've studied the point-counterpoint within, which declared the depravity of man, as opposed to the perfect spotlessness of the Lamb, the suffering of the Messiah as opposed to our joyous hope in Him, and the judgement upon those hardened to the last as opposed to the endless mercy upon the faithful followers of Christ. Now we come to David's response to it all: praise and worship. That occasion to teach, I mentioned earlier, was at practice for the church's worship team, but I'd suggest to you today, that every single redeemed sinner, all the way from Peter to you, is a member of the Church's praise and worship team.

"I will praise the name of God with a song, and will magnify Him with thanksgiving. This also will please the Lord more than an ox or bull with horns and hoofs." - Psalms 69:30-31 MEV

In the last 7 verses of this Psalm, we have an exposition of the joys in which we can worship. First, in verses 30-31, we have the joyous truth that a heart of praise is more acceptable in the sight of the Lord than the most costly sacrifices. I mention often that the calling on the heart of the believer is to become a living sacrifice, sanctified more and more each day into the likeness of Christ and His service. It is true, and yet it can so easily become a trap of works for the believer who wants to please God. The joy we can worship with in these verses is the truth that the greatest path to pleasing God lies in a heart and tongue of praise.

"The humble will see this and be glad; and you who seek God, may your heart live. For the Lord hears the poor, and does not despise His prisoners." - Psalms 69:32-33 MEV

We then see the truth that those who are humbled and ready to seek Him, will indeed find Him, but not only that, they shall, "see this and be glad." Our worship - in songs and in acts - will be a tool for God to share His Gospel. Even when we don't know how to speak the words of life, God promises that our lives given in worship of Him will testify to those who are humbly ready to seek Him. If you know the joy of the Lord, odds are, you know the joy in knowing that He has called more to that joy through your submissive worship. So sing out and live out worship of God, for in this, His glory is testified before all the world.

"Let heaven and earth praise Him, the seas and everything that moves in them. For God will save Zion, and will build the cities of Judah; that they may dwell there, and take possession of it." - Psalms 69:34-35 MEV

Now comes one of my favorite parts. Whether we sing His praises on Sunday morning, July 31st in a congregation of 20 or 2,000, or we sing them in our car Monday morning on our way to work, all of creation sings along with us - the sun, the moon, and the stars. The birds of the air chirp out His praise, and the lion's roar fills the song with bass; the trees whisper His name in the wind, and oceans echo the same. The Old Testament saints and the New Testament saints sing in unison, across the reaches of time, one song, "Holy, Holy, Holy, is the Lord God Almighty. Worthy is the Lamb who was slain." So, whether your praise today is in song or act, smile in the joy that Peter and John, speaking all the words of this life, sing harmony beside you.

"The descendants of His servants will inherit it; and those who love His name will dwell in it." - Psalms 69:36 MEV

Finally, let us sing His praises in the joy that we have inherited the promise that dates back all the way to Eve at the fall. We have been redeemed of all our sin, and in the greatest act of love, we have been called to be the sons and daughters of God. We, who live in Christ, have inherited co-heirship with Christ Jesus; We who love His name dwell in the eternal life which was promised.

Brothers and sisters, whether you find yourself vocally singing His praises today, or silently singing His praises in your heart, sing with greatest joy. Worship the Lord all you peoples. He is worthy, and we are His beneficiaries. Whether you sing in song or in act, sing at the top of your lungs. Magnify Him with Thanksgiving!

Tomorrow we'll return to the book of Acts.

Notes

Notes

Day 37

If it is of God

"Then he said to them, 'Men of Israel, take heed to yourselves what you intend to do concerning these men... Now I tell you, keep away from these men and leave them alone, because if this intention or this activity is of men, it will come to nothing. But if it is of God, you will not be able to overthrow them, lest perhaps you be found even fighting against God.' " - Acts 5:35, 38-39 MEV

Thanks for indulging me to venture on a side trail for a few days. Now we return to Acts, where we find Gamaliel, a Pharisee. You may remember Peter and John were commanded not to preach the doctrine of Christ, yet they continued. They were thrown in jail until the council could convene the next morning, yet they were supernaturally freed. They were commissioned by the Angel to go to the temple and "speak all the words of this life," and so they did. They were then summoned before the Sanhedrin and accused by the high priest and his Sadducean followers, but they retorted, "We must obey God rather than men." The Sadducees were furious and demanded the heads of Peter and John, but now up stands Gamaliel, and he sends the Apostles outside while he speaks.

While we have no definitive evidence, nor scriptural declaration of such, tradition identifies a bit more about this Gamaliel. It was believed of old that this man was of the line of David. That belief continues that he was the grandson of the Rabbi Hillel, one of the premier teachers of the sect of pharisaism. It goes on that he was the son of Simeon, to whom it was revealed he would not die until he saw the glory of the Lord, and declared the fulfillment of that was in the baby Jesus (Luke 2). Furthermore, the Apostle Paul himself states that this "teacher of the law, honored by all the people" (Acts 5:34 MEV), was the principle teacher of a young and zealous Saul of Tarsus.

Surely, he would have been familiar with men such as Joseph of Arimathea and Nicodemus, whose hearts had slowly turned to Jesus Christ. If the tradition is true, he'd have known the testimony of his father that the Messiah had been born in Bethlehem. Even by his words here it seems we may be witnessing one of those "rulers [who] also believed in Him. But because of the Pharisees they did not confess Him, lest they be put out of the synagogue" (John 12:42 MEV).

It sure seems this may be the case. Notice how he commands the Apostles out of the room before speaking. Possibly he feared being outed among his peers. We may have here an Obadiah, respecting of God, but still fearful of men, and used by God in the midst of it all for His good. Maybe we even have here a man who later exposed his faith, even suffering martyrdom, as the Lord changed his heart from fear. Or it could be that he was still just trying to put the pieces together. We just don't know.

Really, it's true that aside from tradition we don't know anything about the man except his words here, but they speak volumes. Surreptitiously Gamaliel defends the Gospel, just as Obadiah had hidden 100 prophets from Ahab (1 Kings 18). He cleverly plants seeds in the minds of his followers. It may be those seeds that save Saul's life, opening his mind to receive Jesus on that road to Damascus, instead of doubling down in his hardening like these Sadducees. What we truly know of this Gamaliel is that God planted some form of wisdom in his head that day, be it by secret belief, or by God's sovereign will. What we truly know is that through him, the high priest and his crew were again given warning and chance to repent when he said, "you may even be found fighting against God" (CSB).

But enough about Gamaliel. This study is about God, and we see a great truth in these words. The Theudas of whom the rabbi spoke is a mystery. He raised an insurrection with about 400 followers, then he was killed and they dispersed, but nothing more is known of his exploits. This is not the same Theudas of whom Josephus wrote, but whose rebellion also came to nothing. Judas the Galilean, upon the defeat of death, also came to nothing. His followers dispersed, and while we have a little more historical acknowledgement of his accomplishments (rather failures), his rebellion also became nothing more than a mark in the historical accounts.

But this study is about God, who stepped down into our world, humbling Himself to become a man like us - like Gamaliel, David, Simeon, Saul,

Theudas, Judas the Galilean, Peter, and John. This study is about the Lord Jesus Christ, who upon His death descended to the depths and was raised three days later. This study is about He who commissioned 11 men (plus countless millions through the centuries) to declare His Kingdom. This study is about the King of Kings, the only King whose kingdom has never come to desolation.

History has shown countless revolutions, rebellions, and governments, and not a single one of them has stood the test of time like the Kingdom of Heaven. That same Kingdom reigns for eternity, brothers and sisters, and you've been invited to co-heirship with the Lord Jesus Christ. Can you fathom what great news that truly is?

There are still false religions abounding in the world and setting their barbs deep in the rebellious hearts of men, but all these rebellions have an expiration date my friends. When Jesus Christ returns and we're raised incorruptible, the corruptible cast aside, Gamaliel will have no more reason to fear men. For we who serve God - He who is outside of time, and saw the end from the beginning - we have no reason to fear anything but the mighty hand of the Lord. What great news it then is that He loves us!

Notes

Notes

Day 38

The True Christ

"They agreed with him. When they had called in the apostles, they beat them, and commanded them not to speak in the name of Jesus, and released them. Then they departed from the presence of the Sanhedrin, rejoicing that they were counted worthy to suffer shame for His name. Daily, in the temple and from house to house, they did not cease to teach and preach Jesus Christ." - Acts 5:40-42 MEV

Here were Peter and John, taken captive and placed before the court repeatedly, threatened, beaten, and threatened again, and yet they rejoice that they were counted worthy to suffer shame for The Name! Where does this fit in the prosperity gospel? Where does the early example of Church which forsook wealth and home for the sake of Christ fit into, "God wants to bless you with wealth on earth"? Where do "they beat them," and, "rejoicing that they were counted worthy to suffer," fit into a prosperity theology of, "physical well-being is always the will of God for Christians on Earth, only restrained by our unfaithfulness"? Where do the compounded pain and disgrace of public whippings fit in this lie that has permeated the last four decades?

Or how about this: Where does the public shame and physical pain of forty lashes minus one fit into the agnostic or atheists doubt suggesting that the Gospel was just a hoax put on by a few men seeking power and fame? I've long watched men and women chasing their endeavors, and I'll tell you, people don't let their backs be torn asunder for that which isn't the deepest conviction in their hearts. They certainly don't rejoice at scars that would cause them both pain for the rest of their lives, and shame that would taint their names to the grave, if they're merely seeking notoriety or wealth. When Christ called him, Saul was already a Pharisee of Pharisees, but he turned away from that life of fortune and fame to later say, "Five times I received from the Jews forty lashes minus one" (2 Corinthians 11:24 MEV).

If, on the other hand, we are "fixing our eyes on Jesus" (Hebrews 12:2 NIV), and "seek[ing] the things that are above" (Colossians 3:2 ESV), then the soul of the Christian, "press[es] on toward the goal for the prize of the upward call of God in Christ Jesus" (Philippians 3:14 ESV).

"Do not be frightened by your adversaries. This is a sign to them of their destruction, but of your salvation, and this from God. For to you it was granted on behalf of Christ not only to believe in Him, but also to suffer for His sake, having the same conflict which you saw in me and now hear is in me." - Philippians 1:28-30 MEV

So again I ask you, where does "it was granted on behalf of Christ not only to believe in Him, but also to suffer for His sake," fit in the prosperity gospel? The "name it, claim it" teachers are lost. Brothers and sisters, do not follow those that espouse lies in the name of God. The father of lies has twisted the word of God since the very beginning, and I tell you now, if that sort of manipulative deception is what started all this, we cannot risk following in those footsteps. If any of those would want to sit next to me and learn the Name of Christ from faithful preachers, it is my calling to welcome him in grace, as a brother, but when they dare stand up to teach, the wolf must be weeded out of the flock.

Millions "brought to Christ" are to no avail if it's not the true Christ. Take note that as Jesus walked the Earth, he did not reject those who were lost in sin, but absolutely opposed those who gained power, wealth, and authority by claiming the Name but not the truth of God.

When, on the other hand, the Name and finished work of Christ is the endeavor of our lives, we can rejoice even when counted worthy to suffer pain or shame. When The Name be glorified, the lost are found. When the Name is taught, the broken are healed. When daily in the temple, and from house to house, they continued to teach and preach the Truth of Jesus Christ, the Church was formed.

Brothers and sisters, Satan's greatest deception involves convincing people of a false version of God. If we already know him, we may never truly seek Him. Whether it's me, your pastor, your neighbor, or the televangelist on channel 35, test every word against the word of God. It is crucial to personally know your Bible. Remember that Satan even tried to use misrepresented scripture against Jesus Himself to overthrow the salvation plan. Do you think he won't try it on you, to keep you from that salvation?

All this to say, spend more time in your Bible than in the teachings of men.

Notes

Notes

Day 39

The First Deacons

"Now in those days, as the disciples were multiplied, there was murmuring among the Hellenists against the Hebrews, because their widows were overlooked in the daily distribution." - Acts 6:1 MEV

As we enter chapter 6, we start to see the first unraveling of the words, "all the believers were of one heart and mind" (Acts 4:32 NIV). It is uncertain how much time has passed before this comes about, but the most commonly given time for Stephen's martyrdom is 38AD, so we know it has been within the first few years. As Joseph Benson wrote, "Ah, Lord! how short a time did pure, genuine, undefiled Christianity remain in the world!"

What we're given to understand by the Apostles' response, is that up until this point, the daily ministrations to the needy were dispersed by their own hands. Remember that some time before, the number had been 5,000 men, plus women and children. Now we're told that all along, the disciples were multiplied. This distribution of charity to the needy had become a great burden on those whose primary calling was to "feed My flock" in spiritual matters. But was there any sign of favoritism?

Clearly the converted Jews of the dispersion thought that the dispersement of charity had become lopsided toward their Israeli counterparts by these 12 Galileans. Whether there was intentional inequity, unintentional exclusion, or merely covetous indignation is not determined by our text. By later teachings in the epistles, we can find it is highly unlikely that the Apostles designed any preference. But whether these Hellenists were actually neglected or not is uncertain.

Having seen so much of this in current culture, and the current American Church, I'd suggest that it is quite possible there was no discrimination. It is quite possible, that in seeing the beginning of that early and primitive church charity run across the worldly limitations of wealth, these Hellenists (Jews who had been dispersed to Greek speaking countries and picked up their language and culture) imagined injustice that was not really there. I do suppose that the covetous human tendency toward victimhood began to chip away at the fellowship even then.

"So the twelve called the multitude of disciples together and said, 'It is not reasonable for us to leave the word of God and serve tables. Brothers, look among yourselves for seven men who are known to be full of the Holy Spirit and of wisdom, whom we will appoint over this duty. But we will give ourselves continually to prayer and to the ministry of the word.' "
- Acts 6:2-4 MEV

Look and see how the Spirit of God led the Apostles to respond. In this first breakdown of the primitive and pure Church, we see the beginning of the variance of Holy Spirit gifts and callings.

I've heard lots of people denigrate local churches and pastors in this same manor. "They don't do _____ for..." "The pastor wasn't there for..." "Pastor _____ never..." When I hear that, it's not the church or the pastor whose image I'm shown...

This is, though, a two-edged sword. As seen by this early disruption, the growth of a church can indeed lead to unintentional discrepancies. While those anointed to preach and to teach have their hands full with giving themselves to "prayer and to the ministry of the word," the Church does still need to handle the other needs of Christian fellowship. Whether or not this disparity was real or imagined, the Apostles responded by forming the first organization of individual duties among the disciples of Jesus Christ.

"And what was said pleased the whole multitude, and they chose Stephen, who was a man full of faith and of the Holy Spirit, and Philip, and Procorus, and Nicanor, and Timon, and Parmenas, and Nicolas, a proselyte from Antioch, whom they presented before the apostles. And when they had prayed, they placed their hands on them." - Acts 6:5-6 MEV

Wisdom shone through, and the office of the deacon was formed. We can note that alongside the name of the first Christian martyr, there are several Hellenistic names such as Procorus, Nicanor, and Parmenas, and even one clarified as being a Hellenist (from Antioch). There was no more room for accusation, and the Church continued to grow. Notice in the beginning of verse 7 we're told in relation to all this, "so the word of God spread."

Brothers and sisters, the Church has lots of needs. When we see a discrepancy and it fills our minds - possibly stings our hearts - it is quite possible that we are the Hellenists here called to fill the need. Rather than, "pastor so and so doesn't take care of," it could very well be that the Holy Spirit is telling us, "I want you to step up and fill this role." If that's the case, take a look at how the Apostles qualified this role. "Men who are full of the Holy Spirit and of wisdom."

Children of God, if our eyes are drawn to a need that's not being filled in our churches, we must ask ourselves, "am I living in the Spirit and growing to maturity? Am I ready and able to fulfill my calling, and is this it? Am I neglecting the spiritual growth and service to which I'm called?" Or maybe we already find ourselves appointed to a role, as these Galilean Apostles were, and the need now is to encourage men and women to step into the gaps they have been shaped by God to fill. Wherever we find ourselves on this scale, the truth is the body needs all the parts, fingers, toes, eyes, ears, tongues, even buttocks; Imagine sitting in a wooden pew without those!

Notes

Notes

Day 40

Priests in "The Faith"

"So the word of God spread, and the number of the disciples grew rapidly in Jerusalem, and a great number of the priests were obedient to the faith." - Acts 6:7 MEV

The ministrations to the poor have been dealt with, the Church begins to grow, and now we see something we have not yet seen in all the New Testament. In a move of God that's been called "a remarkable instance of the power of the gospel... and a striking proof of the power of truth," the priests begin to come to Christ!

This succinct statement was supremely significant. These priests were most closely tied to the Sadducees who persecuted the church. They were the ones who the captain of the temple was said to beat if found asleep on their watch. They were the servants whose daily occupation had them in the presence of those who sought to crush the Gospel preachers. They were the men whose entire lives had been formed around the Old Testament sacrifices. They were men whose former lives were comfortably provisioned, even in a time of poverty.

Yet this great company of priests, who needed a most humbling change from their high places, and who would be the most hated by their former brethren for submitting to the faith, came to Christ.

This great company of priests recognized that the Lamb had been slain, their endless sacrifices were no longer necessary; Indeed, they were fruitless. This simple sentence declares that those who best knew the law of sacrifices could now see that the law was fulfilled in Christ. The old ministry was passed away, and the new had come.

But as previously mentioned, these men would now become to their fellow religious elite, as the tax-collector was to the Hebrews, a most vile traitor. This is not a sacrifice that was made lightly. They would lose house and home, family and friend. Even so, they were obedient to the faith.

I may be wrong, but I do believe this is the first time in scripture that submission to Christ was labeled "the faith." It's a phrase we so often use today, and it's a perfect description of this religion we espouse. Above doctrines, sacrifices, traditions, and works, and at the foot of the cross of our Lord Jesus Christ lies one simple word: faith.

The author of Hebrews would later tackle the difficult subject of the end of Mosaic sacrifices under the Once For All Sacrifice, and in this same epistle he wrote a sentence that may just reflect the Holy Spirit's implanted call within the hearts of this great company of priests:

"And without faith it is impossible to please God, for he who comes to God must believe that He exists and that He is a rewarder of those who diligently seek Him." - Hebrews 11:6 MEV

Whether it requires us to abandon all worldly ties, or merely lay our pains at His feet, faith in the name of Jesus Christ is the substance of what we preach.

Notes

Day 41

The Power of a Seed Planted

"Now Stephen, full of faith and power, did great wonders and miracles among the people. Then some men rose up from what is called the Synagogue of the Freedmen (Cyrenians, Alexandrians, and those from Cilicia and of Asia), disputing with Stephen. But they were not able to withstand the wisdom and the Spirit by which he spoke." - Acts 6:8-10 MEV

Never underestimate the power of a seed planted. Stephen's time in the ministry of Christ was awfully short lived. In scripture, it wasn't even a full two chapters, but in life it was some time less than 4-5 years. Yet in that time this first martyr earned a title that the eldest Christian can desire to attain, namely, "full of faith and (Holy Spirit) power" (vs 8). In that time, the word of God testifies, three times over, that he was "a man full of faith and of the Holy Spirit" (vs 5).

"But being full of the Holy Spirit, he gazed into heaven and saw the glory of God, and Jesus standing at the right hand of God," - Acts 7:55 MEV

While it is the target for which we can always aim, it is not an unreachable goal. Remember that Stephen didn't have a whole lot of time to "grow in the grace and knowledge of the Lord Jesus Christ." Even so, an entire synagogue of those well versed in the scriptures "were not able to withstand the wisdom and the Spirit by which he spoke." This wasn't just laymen either.

“I am a Jew, born in Tarsus of Cilicia, but brought up in this city. At the feet of Gamaliel I was trained in the strict tradition of the law of the fathers, being zealous toward God as you all are today." - Acts 22:3 MEV

When these Libertines brought false witnesses against Stephen, and took him out to stone him, it was Saul of Tarsus (a city in Cilicia), who presided over the execution. Here was the Pharisee of Pharisees, trained up in the law from birth, yet unable to withstand the wisdom the Holy Spirit spoke through Stephen.

While Saul wasn't yet converted, a seed was planted in this young man who would later pen a great majority of the New Testament, but I'd suggest Stephen reached branches far beyond that. His seed may have been small. Maybe it was a few months, or maybe a few years, but it grew. Never underestimate the power of a seed planted.

"He told them another parable, saying, 'The kingdom of heaven is like a grain of mustard seed which a man took and sowed in his field. This indeed is the least of all seeds, but when it has grown, it is the greatest among herbs and is a tree, so that the birds of the air come and lodge in its branches.' " - Matthew 13:31-32 MEV

Later in the book of Acts (chapter 18) we'll be introduced to an Alexandrian name Apollos. The scripture says he was "instructed in the way of the Lord, knowing only the baptism of John" (18:25a MEV). Clearly, he wasn't among these men who persecuted Stephen, or it wouldn't be true that he knew only the baptism of John. And yet, he comes out of nowhere. There's no story of his conversion, either by direct revelation as Saul experienced, or by human preaching as the thousands who heard the Apostles.

Through the years, some scholars have surmised there's a great chance that some of the wisdom spoken through Stephen was carried back by some quietly curious minds; That this influence, this seed, started to sprout back in Alexandria, and maybe took root in Apollos. With that foothold, the Spirit of God began to work, and "being fervent in spirit, he accurately spoke and taught the things concerning the Lord" (vs 25b).

Could it be that Lucius the Cyrene, whom the Bible counts among the prophets and teachers at the church in Antioch, was also a branch of this seed Stephen planted?

When it comes to Kingdom work, never underestimate the power of a seed planted. If Stephen had leaned on his own understanding, he'd have gone to the grave in pain and regret. Instead, being full of the Spirit, he saw the glory of God, and he prayed the Lord's mercy over a young man who would later carry the Gospel to all the nations.

Brothers and sisters, you may never in your lifetime see a seed sprout, but fret not, for it is the will of God that will prevail. You may see what looks like a seed burned in the hottest flame, but do not be dismayed, for even three young men walked out of Nebuchadnezzar's furnace unscathed. It is not your job to harvest the fruit. Your job is to plant the garden. If it is indeed a seed planted in the great power of the Holy Spirit, have faith.

Notes

Notes

Day 42

Through the Ages

"This is the Moses who said to the sons of Israel, 'The Lord your God will raise up for you a prophet like me from your brothers. Him you shall hear.' " - Acts 7:37 MEV

Remember yesterday we looked toward the end of chapter 6, and the arrest of Stephen. The synagogue of the freedmen (aka Libertines, that is, Jews of the dispersion set free from the slavery their families were born into) found offense in what Stephen preached in the Holy Spirit. They could not debate what he spoke, so in the hardness of their hearts, they raised up false witnesses to testify that he blasphemed God and Moses. They testified that Stephen said that Jesus would destroy the temple.

But Stephen, full of the Holy Spirit, is given a chance to retort before the court, and the monologue that ensues is devastating. The deacon lays out history.

Again and again, as he flips through the pages of time, Stephen gives honor and respect to the patriarchs. Likewise, again and again, he points to the hardness of their hearts. Over and over, Stephen reveals how God's work was an evolving, sovereign plan that superseded the failures of men. In the same speech, over and over, he points out how their continual looking back to old ways kept them from embracing the ongoing work of God.

Stephen gives honor to Abraham and God, explaining the covenant of the promised land and Abraham's faithful journey, then he credits the crime 11 brothers committed against Joseph as the tool by which Israel was deposed from that land. Stephen gives honor to Joseph and God, who used this evil for good, and he walks that monologue straight into the death of Jacob and his sons.

Next, this young man gives honor to Moses and Jesus, and he begins this portion of the speech by referencing Pharaoh's command to murder infants, just as Herod had now done in their time. Stephen gives honor to Moses and God, describing how Moses forsook his worldly inheritance as the heir of all Egypt to defend his brethren. He continues by describing how the enslaved Hebrews rejected Moses, causing the rescuer of Israel to flee to the holy ground where he first saw God in a burning bush.

Stephen goes on giving honor to Moses and to God, referencing the Exodus by which they led Israel to freedom, and here's where it gets really interesting. The defendant now starts to reveal where this is going, quoting the prophecy given Moses (Deut 18:15), as well as the hardness of the hearts of those who, in the words of Jesus, put their hand to the plow and looked back.

After all this history comes the beginning of the conclusion.

"Our fathers had the tabernacle of witness in the wilderness, telling Moses to make it as He had commanded, according to the pattern that he had seen, which our fathers, having received it, brought with Joshua into the land possessed by the Gentiles, whom God drove out in front of our fathers until the days of David, who found favor in the presence of God and asked to find a tabernacle for the God of Jacob. But Solomon built Him a house. However, the Most High does not dwell in houses made with hands. " - Acts 7:44-48a MEV

Stephen stood before the court, accused of blaspheming God and Moses. He stood there accused of teaching that Jesus would destroy the temple, in all likelihood, because he was teaching the truth that God now dwelt not in the temple, but within the hearts of his believers, who could now worship him all throughout creation.

"As the prophet says: Heaven is My throne, and the earth is My footstool. What house will you build for Me? says the Lord, or what is the place of My rest? Has not My hand made all these things?" - Acts 7:48b-50 MEV

This first Christian martyr stood at his trial, and what the Spirit revealed through his words was that those who accused him of blaspheming Moses and God in his declaration of the New Covenant, themselves ignored Moses, and blasphemed - even murdered - God. What the Spirit revealed through him is that regardless of tabernacle, or temple, the people who were called by His name were a stubborn people who consistently refused to see the ongoing work of God. At this point, God turns the tables, takes the spiritual gavel from the high priest's hand and puts it in the hands of the defendant.

"Which of the prophets have your fathers not persecuted? They have even killed those who foretold the coming of the Righteous One, of whom you have now become the betrayers and murderers, who have received the law by the disposition of angels, but have not kept it." - Acts 7:52-53 MEV

The high priest and the Sanhedrin hear once again, "this Jesus whom you killed is the Savior we've been waiting for." But now, through Stephen, the Holy Spirit of God also reveals his work through the ages.

I promised you a Holy land. I gave you the pattern for the tabernacle, where I would lower Myself to dwell among you. That wasn't enough for you to be faithful. I allowed Solomon to build me a house, though that was even below me. Even that wouldn't make you faithful. I have now come to dwell inside those of you who will have faith. Yet you stand here accusing them of being what you actually are, stiff-necked just as your forefathers were.

The Sanhedrin had no place to hear this next bit, but through the scriptures which we Christians can today peruse we see a continuance of this truth. Even this indwelling of the Spirit of God within us is not the end of His great work. We have such a wondrous gift in that God has again lowered Himself to live with us, but this is not the end goal of Him who works all things to the good for those who love him.

"It was no dishonour, but an honour to God, that the tabernacle gave way to the temple; so it is now, that the earthly temple gives way to the spiritual one; and so it will be when, at last, the spiritual shall give way to the eternal one." - Matthew Henry

Brothers and sisters, throughout the ages, God has lowered Himself to live with us, but we have a great and glorious future to look ahead to. Rather than lower Himself to our level, through the propitiation of Jesus Christ and sanctification of the Spirit, God promises that when the Lord returns in glory, we'll be raised up to live with him. Hallelujah.

Notes

Day 43

The Heavens Opened

"When they heard these things, they were cut to the heart, and they gnashed their teeth at him. But being full of the Holy Spirit, he gazed into heaven and saw the glory of God, and Jesus standing at the right hand of God, and said, 'Look! I see the heavens opened and the Son of Man standing at the right hand of God.' " - Acts 7:54-56 MEV

Absolute rage pours out of the members and attendees of the court, but a peace that transcends all human understanding reigns in the heart of Stephen. I think most of us have at least some experience with, or maybe live constantly in, fear and anxiety, but has a single one of us been placed alone in a room full of dozens of powerful men with the desire and authority to have us beaten to death? That's what Stephen faced, but notice throughout his entire trial and martyrdom there wasn't a hint of anything short of confident peace.

"When people threaten our persons, reputation, or lives, it becomes us to fix our eyes on the heavenly world; and we shall not look in vain." - Albert Barnes

For an extremely brief ministry, we saw in Stephen a full embodiment of Christ's words, "Do not fear those who kill the body but are not able to kill the soul" (Matthew 10:28 MEV). There was indeed a supernatural peace that filled Stephen's soul, and scripture defines for us from whence it came. Luke explains the extraordinary rage of his accusers, and contrasts it with Stephen's peace: "But being full of the Holy Spirit..."

There is no peace greater than knowing and focusing on the truth that Jesus is Lord and God, First and Last, King and Redeemer. When we can truly know that, with all our being, whom shall we fear?

Now I ask you to consider, as Stephen fully embraces this truth, how greatly he is honored. It must be defined that Stephen was a man like us, fallen short of the glory of God, and in need of the redemption of Jesus Christ, but it is testified of him that such redemption was found. You may remember the Holy Spirit is the down payment of the promise. In this short account of his life and ministry, the word of God three times declares this man, "full of the Holy Spirit." What an honor it is for God to tell all the nations of all the ages such a statement.

"Look!" The honor goes beyond even that testimony, though, and Stephen is shown a glimpse of the throne room as were the greatest prophets of old, but even that wasn't the full extent of the honor. "I see the heavens opened and the Son of Man standing at the right hand of God." To the best of my memory, everywhere else in all of scripture references Jesus as seated at the right hand of the Father. But here, as Stephen overcomes to the last, his Lord stands up!

There is no greater honor given men and women in heaven than to those who were martyred for their faith, and I'd suggest that Stephen stands front dead center of the martyred saints in heaven, asking "how long, oh Lord?" Even so, all the honors that are shown Stephen here are a testimony of where the honor truly lies.

He's credited with being full of the Holy Spirit. Even though that's an honor to him, the true glory belongs to the Spirit that guided this young man. He is granted the honor to be shown a vision of heaven, but it is God's glory which the youthful deacon sees. Finally, he's shown Jesus standing in honor of his sacrifice, but it is the Sacrificial Lamb of God who is seen at the right hand of God.

There is indeed heavenly honor to be had for those who overcome, but the full truth is that even for those of us who receive those honors, we didn't earn an ounce of glory that we didn't already owe in debt. All glory and honor and power belong to the Lord Jesus Christ, and on that wondrous day when we stand before Him, our crowns will be cast at His feet. Amen.

Notes

Day 44

Imitate Him

"They stoned Stephen as he was calling on God, praying, 'Lord Jesus, receive my spirit.' Then he knelt down and cried with a loud voice, 'Lord, do not hold this sin against them.' Having said this, he fell asleep." - Acts 7:59-60 MEV

There are few people that scripture lift higher than Stephen. Even his last few words echo the Savior. These three quick sentences house much of Christian doctrine. I believe, when we look closely into them, we see Stephen living out the greatest and second greatest commands. Allow me to explain.

"And Jesus cried out with a loud voice, 'Father, into Your hands I commit My spirit.' Having said this, He gave up the spirit." - Luke 23:46 MEV

As closely as the young man imitates his Lord's response to persecution, I can't help but wonder if he had been present to witness the crucifixion. Within his reproduction of those words though, there is a crucial difference. The Sinless One, Jesus, was in direct fellowship and communication with the Father, but for the rest of us, that audience isn't available without the atoning blood of Christ. Remember He said, "None can come to the Father except by me."

This is why we pray to the Father in the name of the Son, Jesus Christ. Yet even within Luke's account of Stephen's words, we see a vital truth. Regardless of modern heresies and contradictions, the early disciples indeed knew Jesus Christ as God. Look closely: "he was calling on God, praying, 'Lord Jesus, receive my spirit.' " Whatever arguments may come against us, the Bible teaches the Trinity again, and again, and again.

As mentioned though, I do believe this is also a demonstration of the greatest commandment. Here is Stephen, his body being pummeled to death with stones, and where do we see his mind? On God. Here is Stephen, on the verge of his last heartbeat, and where do we see His soul? Desiring to be with God. Even to his last earthly breath, Stephen loved the Lord his God with all his heart, and all his soul, and all his mind.

"Jesus said, 'Father, forgive them, for they know not what they do.' " - Luke 23:34 MEV

Next, we see the second commandment, that is like it; love your neighbor as yourself. The account of Stephen's passing is quick. " 'Lord, do not hold this sin against them.' Having said this, he fell asleep." Here is a man, like you or me, bleeding and concussed, and his last breath is given to love his enemies; to pray a blessing over those who persecuted him.

Do you know anyone who more fully understands the gospel than that? Not a one of us deserves the mercy we have in Christ, and so those of us who have found it ought to desire that any and all, regardless of their sin, should find the same mercy.

How easy would it have been for him to pray, "Lord, visit their transgression"? But that wouldn't have been the prayer that led to Saul being redeemed and ordained to share the Gospel through all the world.

"And Saul was consenting to his death." - Acts 8:1a MEV

I believe that same Paul often thought back upon Stephen, the first of many stonings over which he would preside. I suppose that visions of the young man's lifeless body probably plagued his dreams. But I also tend to believe that through all the persecutions Paul later himself endured, he thought back to Stephen's example, and imitated the young martyr as he imitated Christ, until, at last, Paul too fell asleep and next awoke in the presence of God.

"Brothers, become fellow imitators with me and observe those who walk according to our example." - Philippians 3:17 MEV

In the words we have between these two covers, we have the example of our Lord. Imitate Him. We have the examples of our predecessors, as they imitated him. Imitate them. And we have, scanning the pages alongside us, the eyes of our peers seeking to imitate him more and more each day. Imitate them.

Brothers and sisters, as we traverse this temporal world to which we no longer belong, let us collectively grow more and more like Jesus. Let us love the Lord our God with all our hearts, and all our souls, and all our minds, and let us love our neighbors as ourselves.

Notes

Notes

Day 45

Speak Christ

"And Saul was consenting to his death. On that day a great persecution broke out against the church in Jerusalem. And they were all scattered throughout the regions of Judea and Samaria, except the apostles. Devout men carried Stephen to his burial and made great lamentation over him. But Saul ravaged the church, entering house by house and dragging out both men and women and committing them to prison. Therefore those who were scattered went everywhere preaching the word." - Acts 8:1-4 MEV

The date is 38AD, and the tides change. No longer are the persecutors found only in the halls of the high priest and the Sanhedrin. The young pharisee gets a taste of blood and he and his peers embark on a savage and unrestricted hunt. No longer are Peter and John the primary targets of this zealous maltreatment. Saul searches high and low for any who would claim the name of Christ, and he does it all in the name of religion...

It's an interesting turn of events when God uses His worst enemies to fulfill His will; when he allows the plans of their evil, deceptive hearts to come to fruition so that His salvation plan would continue forward. It's a peculiar thing when God allows the suffering of the saints so that the Kingdom of Christ would expand in the world and in their hearts. It is certainly a curious manifestation of His eternal omniscience when God uses the sin of those whose names are in the book of life, yet before they've actually found that redemption, to not only advance His work, but also to lead them to the circumstances which bring them to Christ. It is all a great work of God, and I'd suggest that is exactly why Luke includes this blurb.

We can notice that the beloved physician doesn't go into great detail about the persecution. In short order, he tells us there was a persecution, but seemingly only so that God's work of spreading the Gospel has some context. Do you maybe not believe that this is all a work of God? Take a look at some of the final words which our risen Savior spoke to the disciples and Apostles:

"you shall be My witnesses in Jerusalem, and in all Judea and Samaria, and to the ends of the earth." - Acts 1:8b MEV

Check the order there, because I daresay Christ was not careless with His words. First Jerusalem, then Judea and Samaria, and lastly to the ends of the earth. Now return to our current text for a moment:

"And Saul was consenting to his death. On that day a great persecution broke out against the church in Jerusalem. And they were all scattered throughout the regions of Judea and Samaria, except the apostles."

In Jerusalem, we see the man who would later be ordained to carry the Gospel to the ends of the earth, but for now, the disciples of Christ are all scattered throughout Judea and Samaria. Even the stoning of Stephen and the persecution of the men and women of faith, though atrocities committed by the hands of evil men, were permitted by the God who has seen and known all, from beginning to end, and has the entire board perfectly laid out to attain the checkmate that is our resurrection into glory.

While the word "all" is used, it is immediately clarified that not every single Christian fled. The Apostles stayed, the devout men who would honor Stephen remained (though some have surmised these were dissenters from among the accusatory Libertines) and we know others stayed as well, otherwise who would it be said that Saul found and imprisoned searching house to house? Jerusalem would still hear the witness of Christ for years to come.

Even so, the Christian Church was dispersed. Having heard the teachings of the Apostles, received the Holy Spirit, and devoted themselves to spiritual growth, the followers of Christ are broadcast like wheat seeds throughout the Israeli mission field, and those seeds took root. "Those who were scattered went everywhere preaching the word." Reading this, Alexander McLaren sees you - yes you - in that farmer's hand:

"A Christian will be impelled to speak of Christ if his personal hold of Him is vital. He should need no ecclesiastical authorisation for that. It is not every believer's duty to get into a pulpit, but it is his duty to 'preach Christ.' The scattering of the disciples was meant by men to put out the fire, but, by Christ, to spread it. A volcanic explosion flings burning matter over a wide area."

Where have you been scattered?

Do you remain in your hometown, where people remember the old, pre-Christ days in which you terrorized your neighborhood? Do you use that opportunity to preach the redeeming rebirth of Christ?

Have you been displaced to a town where not a soul knows you from Adam? Do you present the witness of Christ at every proper opportunity?

Do you spend your days exploring the restaurants and establishments of your local area? Do the people there know who you belong to?

Do you travel and see the world, visiting landmarks, seeing historical sites, and marveling at God's wondrous creation? Do you carry the Gospel with you, "preaching the word" as you go?

Or do you leave it at home? Do you leave it in the hands of your pastor? Do you only speak his name among the safety of your church friends? Do you silently believe, but leave the witness in the hands of the evangelist?

Tomorrow we will begin to discuss Philip, and this is not the Philip counted among the Apostles. Rather it is Philip, the second of seven deacons, listed immediately after Stephen. But while the primary calling on the lives of the deacons was ministration to the needs of the Church, they clearly did not consider that an excuse to not preach the word. Stephen and Phillip preached the name of Christ.

"Whoever will confess Me before men, him will I confess also before My Father who is in heaven. But whoever will deny Me before men, him will I also deny before My Father who is in heaven." - Matthew 10:32-33 MEV

Brothers and sisters, if you personally know Christ, whether or not you're called to the pulpit, you are called to declare His name. I can personally tell you that yes indeed there will be sacrifices, but need I remind you of what was sacrificed on your behalf?

Notes

Day 46

The Only Begotten Son of God

"Now a man named Simon was previously in the city practicing sorcery and astonishing the nation of Samaria, saying he was someone great," - Acts 8:9 MEV

This Simon is a character study in and of himself. It would appear that the early Church considered the same, as there is much written about him by the early Church fathers. Justin Martyr tells us he was a Samaritan born in a village called Gitton, and his name indicates that either this or Jewish heritage is most probable. Either way, here's a man, raised in the knowledge of the Most High, and yet he sets himself as an enemy of God in the most extreme way. Scripture tells us that Simon claimed to be someone great, and the response of the Samaritans reveals a bit of the nature of that claim.

"to whom they all listened, from the least to the greatest, saying, 'This man is the great power of God.' " - Acts 8:10 MEV

After Jesus had passed through and the believing woman at the well told all the locals about Him, but before Phillip passed through telling all the locals who Jesus really was and what it all meant, we find Simon, using magic and deceiving people to believe he himself was God incarnate.

Most places in the New Testament where we see the word sorceries, the Greek is pharmakeia. It denotes the use of potions - chemicals, medicines, and poisons. Here, on the other hand, we see the one and only use of the word mageuō, literally magic. As our author was a physician, that is quite notable. Whatever sorts of trickery Simon used to bedazzle the people, we know he did it all to make them follow him.

A quick extra biblical study will find numerous accounts of this man being the founder of the first post-Christ cult, the Simonians. It survived into the next century, being a form of Gnosticism, one of the predominant heresies of the first couple of centuries.

"But when they believed Philip preaching about the kingdom of God and the name of Jesus Christ, both men and women were baptized." - Acts 8:12 MEV

Even so, when Phillip arrives in this city, producing actual Holy Spirit miracles, and preaching the true Kingdom of Heaven, the work of God reaches into many a heart, and people are turned from this wickedness. The competition gaining ground did not escape the notice of this son of Satan. Scripture is clear that Simon took note, and he tried to weasel his way in.

"Even Simon himself believed. And when he was baptized, he continued with Philip and was amazed as he watched the miracles and signs which were done." - Acts 8:13 MEV

Simon Magus follows along, claims belief, and gets baptized among the others. I'll discuss that a bit more tomorrow, but today we'll remain with his trickeries. Today it's enough to know that Simon Peter soon declared this man's belief was phony, saying "your heart is not right before God" (Acts 8:21b MEV). Of all the histories of this man, it can be surely noted that he never acknowledged Jesus Christ as the only begotten Son of God.

He works his way in, but this Simon Magus is still looking for an angle. It was not anything we weren't warned about. Jesus told us there would be many deceivers. Simon is proof that not everyone who claims belief in God is a true believer. Here was the first cult leader of many. By adding to, subtracting from, and twisting around the word of God, many through the years have elevated themselves to sit among the gods.

Through the millennia, millions upon millions have been led astray by those who, in the very spirit of the devil himself, raise themselves in rivalry to God. Even today, tens of millions follow long dead men and women who have claimed to receive some special revelation from God; Those who, claiming heavenly insight, have sought to return people to the law, or those who have endeavored to add their own rules, ideas, or imaginations.

Brothers and sisters, you may or may not realize it, but odds are you know someone today whose religion is that of one of these charlatans. The name of Christ, Yahweh, or Jehovah may be used, but like Simon, the

Way, the Truth, and the Life is not their God; the Holy Spirit does not indwell. Hold firm here: Jesus Christ is the only begotten Son of God. Neither Satan nor man is of an equal origin.

Notes

Notes

Day 47

Repent and be Saved

"Even Simon himself believed, and after being baptized he continued with Philip. And seeing signs and great miracles performed, he was amazed." - Acts 8:13 ESV

I must be honest and tell you that I fear to address what is found here. I believe there is great danger in discussing so weighty a topic as this within the confines of space allowed by a devotional format. In the overall context of these devotionals, the truth can be found, but in a single day, words can be twisted. Even so, as we go verse by verse through Acts, our text dictates it a necessity, so let's dive in. Simon believed, and yet...

"But Peter said to him, 'May your silver perish with you, because you thought you could obtain the gift of God with money! You have neither part nor lot in this matter, for your heart is not right before God.' " - Acts 8:20-21 ESV

Peter not only says this man's heart is not made new in Christ; He also tells him he is perishing. The Greek word used here is the same word Jesus used (Matthew 7:13) when he speaks of the wide gate which leads to destruction (perishing). It's the same word He used (John 17:12) when He prayed the assurance that none of His Apostles would be lost except Judas Iscariot, the son of destruction (perishing). It's the same word that Luke's traveling companion, Paul, used (Philemon 1:28) when expressing the contrast between those who have salvation and those who are destined to destruction (perishing). Even more telling, is the fact that it's from the same root as the word used in the most well-known scripture of all, John 3:16. There, in describing the truth that whosoever believes in the only Son of God shall not "perish," we come to the question, what about Simon? It says he believed, yes? The question then lies, did he truly believe that Jesus was the Messiah?

"The Lord is not slow to fulfill his promise as some count slowness, but is patient toward you, not wishing that any should perish, but that all should reach repentance." - 2 Peter 3:9 ESV

After years of leading the Church, no doubt seeing myriads of both true and false believers, Peter (like Paul) contrasts the saved from the perishing, except in one simple sentence, Peter defines a key difference. The saved are they whose belief leads to repentance. This is a topic addressed repeatedly throughout the gospels, the epistles, and even the book of Revelation.

"For godly grief produces a repentance that leads to salvation without regret, whereas worldly grief produces death." - 2 Corinthians 7:10 ESV

So why is it such a dangerous topic? We tend to rally so hard against works based gospels that we go to the far other extreme, holding only one thing: salvation is to all who believe. And that one is indeed true. But many Simons are out there who, while attending a revival tent or teen summer camp with their friends, claim belief merely because it's the thing to do. Simon would lose influence and popularity if he didn't join in the belief. Do we convince them that they no longer need to seek Christ? They've professed belief, right?

We snatch our hands back from works based gospels, and rightfully so, but sometimes we do so with such tenacity that we lose our balance and fall off the other side. Remember not long ago in our study we saw the men of Judea come to faith and ask Peter, "what shall we do," to which he responded, "Repent and be baptized every one of you in the name of Jesus Christ for the forgiveness of your sins, and you will receive the gift of the Holy Spirit" (Acts 2:38 ESV).

"The true penitent repents of sin against God, and he would do so even if there were no punishment. When he is forgiven, he repents of sin more than ever; for he sees more clearly than ever the wickedness of offending so gracious a God." - Charles Spurgeon

We see of Simon that he not only never received the Holy Spirit, but never wanted it. Look at what he offers to buy. He petitions the Apostles for the power to give the Holy Spirit, but he never asks to receive the Holy Spirit. We're shown his heart has never repented of his former ways. He is merely hanging around hoping to buy another scroll of secrets (see Acts 19:19) to wow people into following him.

"Repent, therefore, of this wickedness of yours, and pray to the Lord that, if possible, the intent of your heart may be forgiven you. For I see that you are in the gall of bitterness and in the bond of iniquity." - Acts 8:22-23 ESV

Simon Peter does not beat around the bush in declaring that Simon Magus' profession of belief was empty. He counsels "pray for forgiveness," and defines that this enchanter was still bound in the chains of sin. To consider that any profession of belief in Jesus is equal to saving faith is to declare the Bible fallible, for how else could it say "even Simon himself believed." Many there are who, if asked what religion they claim, would say with a passing shrug, "I'm a Christian," yet who would never tell Christ Himself, "I am entirely yours."

"Or do you presume on the riches of his kindness and forbearance and patience, not knowing that God's kindness is meant to lead you to repentance? But because of your hard and impenitent heart you are storing up wrath for yourself on the day of wrath when God's righteous judgment will be revealed." - Romans 2:4-5 ESV

In declaring the Gospel, we do indeed have a duty to declare that there is no pre-requisite of works. Not a single one of us can earn our way into salvation any more than Simon could buy his way in. On the other hand, we must keep the balance. We cannot "presume on the riches of His kindness," and think that a one time, surface level declaration of belief would grant us freedom from the wrath that is to come.

"and [Jesus] said to them, 'Thus it is written, that the Christ should suffer and on the third day rise from the dead, and that repentance for the forgiveness of sins should be proclaimed in his name to all nations, beginning from Jerusalem.' " - Luke 24:46-47 ESV

We can't even claim that this is the old tradition of law still hanging on in the Apostles, for Christ Himself declared that repentance is a vital part of the Gospel truth.

"And the Lord's servant must not be quarrelsome but kind to everyone, able to teach, patiently enduring evil, correcting his opponents with gentleness. God may perhaps grant them repentance leading to a knowledge of the truth, and they may come to their senses and escape from the snare of the devil, after being captured by him to do his will." - 2 Timothy 2:24-26 ESV

Only God knows, but from what we have in scripture and the histories it would appear Simon Magus never repented; it seems he never escaped the snare of the devil. He went on setting himself in the place of God, creating a cult that lasted generations. Even in his response to Simon Peter we see he never holds Christ to be the Intercessor of God; he never changes his mind. He looks to man and asks the Apostles, "pray for me to the Lord."

If you consider yourself a Christian, I beseech you, without judgement, to look inside. Have you given yourself to Christ, or merely made an empty profession? "Even the demons believe and shudder" (James 2:19 ESV). Has your faith led you to mourn your sin? Has that sorrow led you to hate your sin? Salvation begins at belief, but true belief leads us deeper and deeper into repentance. As we continue in true faith, the Spirit will lead us, more and more, to hate lesser and lesser sins within ourselves.

"True repentance is no light matter. It is a thorough change of heart about sin, a change showing itself in godly sorrow and humiliation – in heartfelt confession before the throne of grace – in a complete breaking off from sinful habits, and an abiding hatred of all sin. Such repentance is the inseparable companion of saving faith in Christ." - J. C. Ryle

Salvation is by faith. True faith inevitably leads to Repentance.

Notes

Day 48

Gospel Change

"Now when they had testified and spoken the word of the Lord, they returned to Jerusalem, preaching the gospel to many villages of the Samaritans." - Acts 8:25 ESV

Peter and John stay for a while, laying out the truth and doctrines of Christ. They lay a solid foundation for this new branch of the Church, and then they pack their bags and head back toward Jerusalem. You may remember though, the last time they began this journey, John was one of two who took a very different approach!

"And when his disciples James and John saw it, they said, 'Lord, do you want us to tell fire to come down from heaven and consume them?' " - Luke 9:54 ESV

The Gospel changes a man, and we see an extreme change in John, both here and beyond. No longer does that fiery zeal seek a pouring out of wrath, but rather pleads that these Samaritans would know the blood which was poured out to redeem them from the coming wrath.

This time though, John doesn't seek destruction, but rather life. He doesn't allow ethnic biases to taint his work, but rather works to preach that which makes all tribes, nations, languages, and races one family.

There is a clear and definite change in the young Apostle, and it came by the Holy Spirit revealing to Him the grace of God. When our eyes are opened in such a way, brothers and sisters - the more fully we understand what was done for us - the change of mind called repentance is inevitable. No longer is there room for hatred, biases, or racism. Love prevails. John is now known as the Apostle of love, but once he was a son of thunder.

The gospel changes the heart of a penitent child of God. Today we cross a short and simple passage, leading to a short and simple devotional, but I ask as you go your way, look within, and question, "has the Gospel of Jesus Christ changed me?"

Notes

Day 49

One Ready Soul

"Then Philip ran to him, and heard him read the book of Isaiah the prophet, and said, 'Do you understand what you are reading?' He said, 'How can I, unless someone guides me?' So he invited Philip to come up and sit with him." - Acts 8:30-31 MEV

An angel is sent to tell Philip to walk into the desert, and with no idea why, he goes. Then the Holy Spirit tells Philip to go to this chariot and he runs to catch up. Having been faithful with the work he was given in Samaria, Philip the deacon is now given more and sent to a prominent foreigner with a heart seeking God. We're not told if this eunuch is a full proselyte (gentile convert to Judaism), or if his heart was merely being drawn to seek God, but we can note that Philip is never said to ask. He's been sent by the Spirit of God, and that's all he needed to know.

In this interaction, the Holy Spirit offers a very different revelation of God's work than we saw in Philip's previous ministry. Having gone and preached the Gospel to all who would hear in a certain city of Samaria, now God draws him toward a single, seeking soul.

He may be a eunuch, but the passenger in this chariot is a man of great importance, yet of humble heart. With command over all the wealth of Ethiopia, he has come to worship the God of Israel among a people with disdain for his foreign origin. With authority over a nation, he humbles himself to admit, "How can I understand, unless someone guides me."

"The eunuch said to Philip, 'I ask you, of whom does the prophet speak, of himself or of someone else?' Then Philip spoke, beginning with the same Scripture, and preached Jesus to him." - Acts 8:34-35 MEV

The sudden fellowship of these two is indeed a work of God. We have both Jew and Gentile, local and foreign, lowly and exalted, but in two worshippers of Jehovah we see two friends sit together. Seemingly hours roll by as the word of God is unfolded in that chariot. The road passes under wooden wheels and as the miles click away, the glory of God comes into sight for one ready soul.

"36: As they went on their way, they came to some water. And the eunuch said, 'Look, here is water. What hinders me from being baptized?' 37: Philip said, 'If you believe with all your heart, you may.' He answered, 'I believe that Jesus Christ is the Son of God.' 38: And he commanded the chariot to halt. Then both Philip and the eunuch went down into the water, and he baptized him." - Acts 8:36-38 MEV

On a side note: Depending upon your translation you may not have verse 37. Many compilers of our modern translations have excluded it because, out of our extant (surviving) manuscripts, it does not show up until the 6th century. Having seen some of the earlier Church fathers (Irenaeus, Cyprian, and Augustine among others) quote these words, I personally believe the omissions in the Egyptian manuscripts were the error, and not the other way around. In other words, I'm given to believe Luke's original documents included these words.

Returning though to our text, we see a heart glad to receive Christ. Look, here is water! Do you hear excitement in those words as I do? All of this was the work of a God who from before the eunuch was born had already seen this moment of heartfelt dedication.

"When they came up out of the water, the Spirit of the Lord took Philip away. And the eunuch saw him no more, and he went his way rejoicing." - Acts 8:39 MEV

Philip was sent as the hands and feet of Christ, then he was whisked away, but the change had already come. A new Christian was reborn and he went his way rejoicing. Do you remember your baptism? Do you remember the excitement that led up to it? Do you remember the rejoicing as you came up out of that water? Do you still rejoice that much? With the love you had at first?

Some early historians (Irenaeus included) suggest that the eunuch took the Gospel back to Ethiopia with him, founding the Church there. Others argue there is no evidence the Gospel made any headway in that land until over 2 centuries later. To my knowledge there's no actual evidence one way or another, and so I suggest to you today that this encounter was a very different revelation of the Kingdom come than the broadcast seed of the Church which we've seen up to this point. This Philip was sent to one single lost sheep, bleating for the Good Shepherd.

Great and fabulous things were happening in the growth of the Church - thousands brought to Christ - but don't think for a second that any of that was any greater than each individual soul, redeemed in Christ. We cannot consider a work of thousands of saved souls as any more or less important than the rejoicing over one single soul turned to Jesus.

Through His good and faithful servant, the Good Shepherd left the 99 in Samaria to find His one lost sheep. It is shown here exactly as He said He works. Glory be to God, and to His Son, Jesus Christ!

Notes

Notes

Day 50

Eternal Perspective

"Saul, still breathing out threats and murder against the disciples of the Lord, went to the high priest, and requested letters from him to the synagogues of Damascus, so that if he found any there of the Way, either men or women, he might bring them bound to Jerusalem." - Acts 9:1-2 MEV

Saul the persecutor still earns his title, and the order of events give the impression this has been going on for some time. It would seem he has satisfied the Sadducean High Priest in having significantly cleansed Jerusalem of this new teaching they hated, but Saul's fiery zeal was not satisfied. The Sanhedrin doesn't approach Saul with a suggestion to widen the scope of his hunt. Rather Saul goes to the High Priest - one of the opposition party with which he has allied in this murderous quest - and requests permission letters which he could take to the Damascus synagogues.

"I was circumcised the eighth day, of the stock of Israel, of the tribe of Benjamin, and a Hebrew of Hebrews; as concerning the law, a Pharisee; concerning zeal, persecuting the church; and concerning the righteousness which is in the law, blameless." - Philippians 3:5-6 MEV

Remembering that Paul was of the tribe of Benjamin, we can look back and see the spirit of prophecy in Jacob's words as he blesses his sons.

"The blessings of your father have surpassed the blessings of my fathers, up to the utmost bound of the everlasting hills. They will be on the head of Joseph, and on the crown of the head of him who was set apart from his brothers. Benjamin is a ravenous wolf; in the morning he devours the prey, and at night he divides the spoil." - Genesis 49:26-27 MEV

While Jesus wasn't of the tribe of Joseph, the life of that young rescuer of Israel - rejected by his brothers, but raised up to glorious power - was a shadow of the coming Messiah. Having blessed Joseph with prophetic words about, "the hands of the Mighty One of Jacob, because of the Shepherd, the Rock of Israel... him who was set apart," Jacob then closes out the blessings of his sons by addressing Benjamin, and the prophecy is told that Saul of Tarsus would persecute the Way. Benjamin (read Saul) is a ravenous wolf; in the morning he devours the prey.

Among the staggering number of cross-references from Old Testament prophecy to New Testament Revelation, we now see one more. The persecutions of Christ's followers through this Saul of Tarsus were foreordained and foretold over 16 centuries before. One cannot earnestly study the scriptures and be left with anything short of awe at the extent of the evidence that this is all the very word of God; to study the scriptures and come to any other conclusion can only come about by a spitefully hardened heart and a stubborn, willing ignorance.

But brothers and sisters, I ask you today to consider the implications in this prophetic revelation of Saul's ferocious pursuit. Over 1600 years before Christ walked the Earth, God declared through his servant Jacob, exactly what would come. In the morning of his life Saul would devour the prey as persecutor, but in the evening, he would divide the spoils as the preacher.

Do you suppose any of his victims noticed this connection while they yet lived? Do you think when they finally entered the throne room, this part of the plan was revealed?

Now I ask, what are you dealing with? What trials and tribulations bring you distress? What's going on at work? In your family? In your church? In your neighborhood? Into what situation are you praying endlessly for God to interject Himself?

We've seen the truth that Saul's persecution scattered the Church so that they could call more to Christ, and so that they would be given opportunities to be faithful with what they'd been given. Don't you think, as their friends and neighbors, mothers and fathers, sons and daughters, brothers and sisters were being imprisoned and bludgeoned to death, that they were praying fervently for God's sovereign hand to step in?

But God's hand was intentionally permitting the zeal of this young man to be so misguided, and it was all to the good.

Wait a minute, hold on, people were unjustly murdered! Indeed, but when they woke up, the greatest honor of all - that of the faithful martyr - was theirs! But people watched their loved ones suffer! Yes, this is true, but their faith was tested, proven, and multiplied throughout Judea and Samaria, and they went on to earn the honor of hearing "well done, good and faithful servant!"

Again I ask, what are you dealing with? Redefine your perspective in the knowledge that God has ordained all things to work to the good for those who love Him. If indeed you know Christ, even what you see as the worst day of your life will eventually be revealed to have been used to the good.

Do you feel the stones? Could you consider the possibility for a moment that God's will, even in our most difficult times, is greater than our most wonderful hopes?

Notes

Notes

Day 51

Saul Sees

"Now as he went on his way, he approached Damascus, and suddenly a light from heaven shone around him. And falling to the ground, he heard a voice saying to him, 'Saul, Saul, why are you persecuting me?' And he said, 'Who are you, Lord?' And he said, 'I am Jesus, whom you are persecuting.' " - Acts 9:3-5 ESV

"Inasmuch as ye have done it unto one of the least of these my brethren, ye have done it unto me" (Matthew 25:40 KJV), had the Lord Jesus Christ spoken, and on this road to Damascus, he revealed this truth to the persecutor. "I am Jesus, whom you are persecuting."

A great imagination cannot fathom the grief of such realization. Unlike the High Priest and his goon squad, Saul's persecutions were driven by a most genuine and all-consuming zeal for God. Everything in this young man cried out for the glorification of the God of Israel. We therefore see that the moment of witnessing said glory and being told that he was "found fighting against God" (as the teacher of his youth had so recently warned), must have been absolutely crushing. We'll come back to that, but first let's digest the truth that he saw the glory of the Lord.

"Since I was blinded by the glory of that light, those who were with me led me by the hand into Damascus." - Acts 22:11 MEV

This was no ordinary light. Paul rehashes this moment repeatedly throughout his ministry, and in that we see the truth that yes, our testimonies, though not themselves the Gospel, do shine the light of Christ when shared in the proper heart of ministry. In one of those opportunities to testify, when addressing King Agrippa, Saul of Tarsus mentions that this light was, "brighter than the sun, shining around me and those who journeyed with me." (Acts 26:13 MEV)

In writing to the Corinthians (1 Cor 15:8), Paul tells of how the crucified and risen Savior was seen alive by the Apostles, then 500 witnesses, and finally, by himself. We need not take Paul's word for it though, for as we soon see, a disciple named Ananias receives a vision from God, then speaks to Saul of "the Lord Jesus, who appeared to you." Not long thereafter, Barnabas, the son of encouragement whom we recently studied, tells the Apostles that Saul had seen the Lord. We're not expressly told here, but I believe the scriptures point to Saul having bodily seen Jesus in that light.

Even the faithful prophet Isaiah, having seen a vision of the glory of the Lord, cried out "Woe is me! For I am undone because I am a man of unclean lips" (Isaiah 6:5 MEV). Try to imagine, then, the utter despair as young Saul sees and hears the God he supposes to serve, only to find out he himself has been the blasphemous enemy he so fervently sought to oppose.

"Saul rose up from the ground. And when his eyes were opened, he saw nothing. So they led him by the hand and brought him into Damascus. For three days he was without sight, and neither ate nor drank." - Acts 9:8-9 MEV

Devastation is a word that cannot reach the depths of the pit he found himself in. For three days, God left Saul in darkness with his thoughts; three days in spiritual death. Three days in which he saw nothing but the faces of his victims. Three days in which the mercy prayers of the dying saints echoed back and forth across his skull, only pausing to emphasize those final breaths. Three days in which his whole world was turned upside down. These three days likely came to mind every time Saul spoke about having died with Christ.

It's been said that we have Stephen's dying prayer to thank for the Apostle Paul's ministry. While there's some truth there, I'd suggest that the Lord saw far deeper, into a heart that truly sought God's glory, yet was grossly misled. Finding this conversion on the road to Damascus, immediately after the record of the lost sheep to which Jesus sent Philip in that carriage on the road to Gaza, is by divine design, a reminder that God will find each of His lost sheep, regardless of how far or which direction they've traveled from Him.

For three days Saul unwittingly gave the world a vision of the beginning of repentance. We witness a mind that experienced a 180° turn; A mind that, within three days, changed completely from demanding the blaspheming of Jesus at threat of death, to personally and publicly preaching that Only name.

I pray, if you're reading this today, you're not found among those who will be hardened to the last. The same mercy that pulled back the veil for Saul on this dusty road is extended in love to you. There is no reason a single one of us should miss this bus. The fare is free, and though the journey is bumpy, the destination is everything.

"Look! He is coming with clouds, and every eye will see Him, even those who pierced Him. And all the tribes of the earth will mourn because of Him. Even so, Amen." - Revelation 1:7 MEV

I pray, if you're reading this today, you're not found among those who will see that glory when it's too late to repent. Saul's sorrow is unimaginable, but it is utterly insignificant compared to the anguish that will be the portion of those who have rejected Him, on that day when there will be weeping and gnashing of teeth; that day when God's mercy is full and Jesus returns on the clouds in judgement.

It's not too late to repent and believe. If you sit in darkness, having seen God's light, and wait for an Ananias to come and introduce you to the Savior, reach out. There is no longer any shame for those who find Christ.

Notes

Notes

Day 52

True Prayer

"A disciple named Ananias was in Damascus. The Lord said to him in a vision, 'Ananias.' He said, 'Here I am, Lord.' The Lord said to him, 'Rise and go to Straight Street, and inquire at Judas' house for someone named Saul of Tarsus, for he is praying, and has seen in a vision a man named Ananias coming in and putting his hand on him, so that he may see again.' " - Acts 9:10-12 MEV

How many times have you heard the wondrous stories of the works of God? Times when you met someone new, and as they told you their salvation story, the coincidental similarities to your own story were too perfect to have been mere chance. Times when you've seen the strangest of circumstances play out so that Bob would be in exactly the right place, at the right time, and in the right state of mind to hear the word which God spoke through Jack, consequently coming to the faith. Times when God told you to go (metaphorically) to the road from Jerusalem to Gaza, and when you got there, the work He had prepared for you from the beginning awaited in a chariot, plain as day.

How many times have you been able to say, this is no mere chance. Too many times to be coincidence? Many of us could answer that question with confident affirmation. That is, too many of us to be dumb luck. How about yourself? Can I get a witness?

As Saul sat blinded in Damascus, praying, and receiving a vision of a man named Ananias coming to lay hands on him, do you think he saw the irony that this was the same name that signed his marching orders to the synagogue? Do you wonder if, as he knelt there pouring out confessions and remorse, he saw the meaning in the name? Ananias was a common name, and the Greek rendition of Hananiah, meaning "Yah has been gracious." I don't suppose this was overlooked, and I don't believe it was a fraction of the mysteriously interweaved workings of God which Paul witnessed over his years in Christ.

We don't know much about this Ananias, except what we read here, and in Acts 22. He was a devout man who had been a strict adherent to the law before finding Christ, and that piety grew after finding Christ so that even the unbelieving Jews held high regard for this Ananias. He was also a follower of the Way (a disciple, a Christian) who when called after by the Lord, did not hesitate to respond, and who when confounded by orders that would have been terrifying, did not fail to follow through. As we see such a man it behooves us to ask, "If placed in this situation, would the word of God record the same faithfulness of me? If/when I'm told 'rise and go,' will my feet carry me as shod by the sandals of the readiness of the Gospel?"

What about Saul though? This is a major turning point in the life of the Persecutor turned Apostle, who was made to carry the Gospel to the gentiles. For three days Saul fasted, and he prayed. As a Hebrew of Hebrews, and pharisee of pharisees, Saul had spent his lifetime praying, but now, for maybe the first time ever, he prayed. Is that confusing? Allow Matthew Henry to explain:

"Now he began to pray after another manner than he had done; before, he said his prayers, now, he prayed them. Regenerating grace sets people on praying; you may as well find a living man without breath, as a living Christian without prayer."

Our generation has seen broken families and divorces in record numbers. The breaking down of marriage after marriage happens often because of a lack of communication. Oh, these men and women don't fail to talk to (or frequently at) each other, but largely they don't communicate with one another. You may have noticed, though, that this was a rather strange interjection, and maybe you even recognized what I'm getting at. There's a difference between saying prayers and praying; a difference between talking at God, and communicating with God.

For maybe the first time in Paul's life, he truly prayed. It was heartfelt, and it was real. He didn't just blurt out his desires, confessions, and regrets, but he left room for God's response, and received a vision from God. Saul didn't just repeat the "blessed are you Lord our God" type prayers so commonly announced in the synagogues to be heard by men. For once, Saul's conversation with the God he loved was genuine.

It may be a rare thing in history to receive visions from God, or to hear His voice give commands, but that doesn't mean He's not present in our prayers. Whether or not you experience as direct of a manifestation as Ananias and Saul did, prayer - sincere, and genuine communication - is a vital part of our relationship with God. As we grow in Christ, we ought to learn that prayer is more than just repetition, and it's more than just a wishlist. We should learn that there must be as much quiet time to hear the Holy Spirit, as there is to pour out our hearts before Him.

"Ananias answered, 'Lord, I have heard from many about this man, how many evil things he has done to Your saints at Jerusalem. And here he has authority from the chief priests to bind all who call on Your name.' But the Lord said to him, 'Go your way. For this man is a chosen vessel of Mine, to bear My name before the Gentiles and their kings, and before the sons of Israel. For I will show him how much he must suffer for My name's sake.' " Acts 9:13-16 MEV

That leads me to yesterday, when I had to drive past the hospital. As I passed, an ambulance stood out front of the Emergency Room. The EMT was wheeling in a woman on a stretcher, and trailing behind was a small girl, hardly taller than the stretcher itself. My mind was instantly brought to the thought of what kind of insecurities, questions, and fears could likely be terrorizing that little girl. Would her momma be ok?

Breaking into tearful prayer, I poured out earthly desires that God would not only be with them in this time, but that He would work through those doctors, and/or through miracles, and assure that this young lady's mother would be ok and would be retained to raise such a helpless child. Then came the response...

"Would your prayer remain the same if I told you that bringing that about would guarantee this young girl never found Christ? You know nothing of this situation. Which is worse? No mother, or no Savior?"

The microphone dropped and I only had one response. "Nevertheless, not my will but yours be done, O Lord."

I don't know what happened to the two who I saw wheeled into the ER yesterday, or what lay ahead for either of them, but that's not what I needed to know. Through that interaction, God reminded me of a truth

He's been trying repeatedly to drive into this thick skull of mine. Our worldly perspectives often give us ideas of what is good, but sometimes God's eternal wisdom deems what we may consider suffering to be the best path for us. It's an interesting "coincidence" that not three hours later, I received news regarding something I have long been praying most fervently and consistently for, and the news illustrated a definitive and painful "no" reply.

Not only must we submit to His will in all things - even when He sends us to Saul of Tarsus, known for his murderous quest - but we can also rejoice in the knowledge that His will is always good, even when it makes no sense to us, or even when it absolutely breaks our hearts. Omniscience, omnipresence, and omnipotence are the hat trick of all hat tricks, and our Lord runs the full gamut of these.

More than just saying our prayers, these prayers of ours should be part of our growth in Christ, just as in a newly converted Saul, God grew a new heart through three prayerful days; these prayers of ours should be genuine submission to, nay eager desire for, God's good will regardless of what it entails, just as God determined to "show him how much he must suffer for My Name's sake."

Notes

Day 53

No Better Proof

"For several days Saul was with the disciples in Damascus. Immediately he preached in the synagogues that the Christ is the Son of God." - Acts 9:19b-20 MEV

Luke fails to mention Paul's retirement into Arabia and so we're left with naught but clues as to when it may have occurred. Unbelievers often reckon this a contradiction of scripture, claiming that Luke's omission and Paul's declaration in Galatians 1 cannot be reconciled. They imagine that Paul's declaration was three years wandering the desert (and how does one entirely neglect three years, saying instead, "immediately"), and I can't blame them. I've heard it taught that way in churches and Christian books as well. It would seem such a belief comes from our own ranks. Look closely at the Apostle's precise words though:

"I did not immediately confer with flesh and blood, nor did I go up to Jerusalem to those who were apostles before me. But I went into Arabia, and returned again to Damascus. After three years I went up to Jerusalem to see Peter and stayed with him for fifteen days." - Galatians 1:16b-18 MEV

Notice, as Paul explains it, the three years did not apply only to Arabia, but included his time in Damascus. We have then the full time frame from Acts 9:18 until vs 26, and it stands as three years, including all within. We don't actually know how long Paul "went into Arabia," and we don't know at exactly which point within these verses he did so. Such has been the discussion of biblical scholars throughout the ages.

It seems, from my feeble perspective, best placed in the midst of what we have as verse 19, between having eaten, and his days with the disciples in Damascus. I believe he broke bread with, at least Ananias if not more, then, with agreement, disappeared toward Mt Horeb to confer with The Lord before returning to join the Damascan Church he had previously come to destroy.

Having laid this fictitious discrepancy to rest, may we take notice in the truth laid out in the comparison of Acts 9 and Galatians 1. Paul says, "I did not immediately confer with flesh and blood," indicating it wasn't the teaching of the disciples that led him to the conclusions he taught.

"But I reveal to you, brothers, that the gospel which was preached by me is not according to man. For I neither received it from man, neither was I taught it, except by a revelation of Jesus Christ." - Galatians 1:11-12 MEV

Another common argument (among those who wage war against the God they claim doesn't exist), is that all this Christianese is merely manipulation's end result in the feeble minded. The Apostle Paul, among so many others, is the ultimate contrast to such a claim. In this brother of ours, we have a highly learned man whose teachers had led him to utterly hate all things Christian, but whose Lord in due time revealed the truth (much like believers who have survived so many modern higher education institutions).

Again, I'm led to believe his excursion came before the fellowship in Damascus, for Paul says his declarations (that the Christ is the Son of God, and that Jesus is the Christ) all came not from the teachings of men, but by God peeling back the veil to reveal the truth he had missed in the scriptures. Finally, after a lifetime among those who would claim, "God has no Son," the young pharisee saw the truth in Psalm 2 and so many other passages of the Old Testament word of God.

You must remember that Saul was a pharisee of pharisees, and to bear false witness in the name of God would have been absolutely out of the question. There cannot even be any question as to whether he was trying to sneak in as a spy, for he affirms of all this, "In what I am writing to you, before God, I do not lie!" (Galatians 1:20 MEV)

"All who heard him were amazed and said, 'Is not this he who killed those who called on this name in Jerusalem, and came here with that intent, to bring them bound to the chief priests?' Yet Saul increased all the more with power and confounded the Jews living in Damascus, proving that this One is the Christ." - Acts 9:21-22 MEV

What is revealed to us in scripture is that Saul was not merely repeating that which Ananias and other disciples taught him. Having the scales peeled back from his eyes, and the Holy Spirit conferred upon him, Saul now properly saw and taught what had always been hidden in the scriptures he knew so well. How could one go about confounding the Jews in the synagogue and prove that Jesus was the Messiah? Only one method could do such a thing, and that is just as Jesus had done for the disciples on the walk to Emmaus, "beginning with Moses and all the prophets, he explained to them the things concerning," Jesus Christ, "in all the scriptures." (Luke 24:27 MEV)

The Jews had long taught and learned the scriptures from flawed human understanding, and thus they killed their Savior. Hearing the true exposition of those same scriptures, they're confounded and the identity of their Messiah is proven. In our time, and among our contemporaries we have the same example; those who have heard weak and flawed teachings find it easy to "deconstruct their faith."

The extreme contrast between those who cannot deny the Lord in these truths, and those who claim contradictions because of false understandings taught within our ranks, is itself evidence of the importance of faithful exegesis of the scriptures. When properly considered, the conversion of Saul becomes one of the most prevalent pieces of evidence of the truth of the Good News of Jesus Christ.

"The example of Saul does not stand alone. Hundreds and thousands of enemies; persecutors, and slanderers have been changed, and every such one becomes a living witness of the power and truth of the Christian religion. The scoffer becomes reverent; the profane man learns to speak the praise of God; the sullen, bitter foe of Christ becomes his friend, and lives and dies under the influence of his religion. Could better proof be asked that this religion is from God?" - Albert Barnes

Could better proof be asked? No. This conversion from persecutor to preacher is ranked among the greatest evidences we have that the long-awaited Messiah was indeed the Son of God, and that Jesus of Nazareth was absolutely that same Messiah, our Christ!

Notes

Day 54

To Speak Another Day

"After many days had passed, the Jews arranged to kill him. But their scheme was known by Saul. They watched the gates day and night to kill him. But the disciples took him by night, and lowered him in a basket through the wall." - Acts 9:23-25 MEV

As we discovered yesterday, the time including his Arabian retreat and his Damascan ministry was three years, and now we see that time end. There can be little doubt that in that time which Paul confounded the Jews in the synagogues of Damascus, many came to the saving faith in the Lord Jesus Christ. Those who remained did so only by venomous adherence to their enmity with the Truth. These enemies of God see their numbers dwindling and conspire to have the converted persecutor put to death. We find out later (2 Cor 11:32-33) that the governor of Damascus, king Aretas, assisted these Jews, placing a garrison on each gate.

"Therefore whoever resists the authority resists what God has appointed, and those who resist will incur judgment." - Romans 13:2 MEV

It is extraordinarily easy to read an individual passage and found our doctrine upon it. Had Paul done this with his own epistle which he later wrote to the Romans, his duty would have been to stay there and die, subject to the governing authorities. This escape of Saul's is therefore a demonstration of the concept of overall biblical context interpreting individual biblical passages.

It was not God's purpose for Saul to yet be martyred, and we see this in triplicate. The Lord ordained this escape to succeed, after which He commanded Saul to flee Jerusalem in a vision (see Acts 22:17-21), and previously Jesus had instructed the Apostles, "when they persecute you in this city, escape into another." (Matthew 10:23a MEV)

"Saul was certain of death if he remained; and as he could secure his life by flight without abandoning any principle of religion, or denying his Lord, it was his duty to do so. Christianity requires us to sacrifice our lives only when we cannot avoid it without denying the Saviour, or abandoning the principles of our religion." - Albert Barnes

The overarching truth which reigns above Romans 13 is that these principles are to be held only up to the point that those authorities demand that which is in opposition to God.

A pattern emerges which has been present on and off through history. The Sanhedrin had used the Roman governing authorities to kill the Lord Jesus. The Jews at Damascus used the local ethnarch in their plot to kill Saul. The adherents to the Roman religions would later use the empirical powers to hunt and murder Christians.

I'm not alone in believing that we soon come to a time when this will again be the widespread experience of the faithful followers of Christ, even in lands originally founded on Christian principles, such as the United States. If Jerusalem wasn't safe from these schemes, neither can we assume the Americas will be. Before such comes upon us, I'd suggest we had better have considered the examples to which we can follow.

The disciples in Damascus followed previous examples. Lowering Saul through a window extruding from the city wall was a direct copy of Rahab lowering the spies through the wall of Jericho as the king there sought to kill them (Joshua 2:15). It likewise mimics Michal lowering David through a window in the wall to escape the murderous intent of Saul (1 Samuel 19:12).

"We are not forbidden to avoid and eschew the dangers and conspiracies that the enemies of God lay for us, but only if we do not swerve from our vocation." - Geneva Study Bible

It can be noted that although Saul fled the persecution which would stay his voice of testimony, he did not allow these threats to silence him. He escaped the city and entered another speaking boldly in the name of the Lord Jesus.

"And he spoke boldly in the name of the Lord Jesus and disputed against the Hellenists. But they tried to kill him. When the brothers learned this, they brought him down to Caesarea, and sent him off to Tarsus." - Acts 9:29-30 MEV

God's will sent him "far away to the Gentiles" (Acts 22:21 MEV), just as Paul later tells us Jesus had revealed to him in a vision. Those who wage war against God may gain authority to demand our silence, to imprison us, or to slay us, but the truth is this war has already been won. The enemy may work hard through those who make themselves his spawn, but God's plan prevails.

Whether in the coming days we find ourselves needing to be lowered from a window (or maybe pray mercy on our executioners), or whether my suspicions are wrong and we live in a time of relative peace, we can take comfort in the knowledge that God has ordered all from beginning to end, and His victory is already final. In this knowledge, let us then "not swerve from our vocation" and continue to speak boldly, as the Spirit so leads us.

Brothers and sisters, when viewing the declarations of glorious honor bestowed upon those who were martyred for their testimony, whilst living in a time of persecution, it could be extraordinarily easy to lay down our necks in anxious wait. That martyrdom complex is not the way of God though. We ought to endeavor to continue to speak His name, as long as He wills for us to work on this Earth. What an interesting balance we then have. On one side, our excitement to be home with Christ, and on the other, our duty to stay and call more to that path.

Notes

Notes

Day 55

Forgiveness

"When Saul had come to Jerusalem, he tried to join the disciples. But they all feared him, not believing he was a disciple. But Barnabas took him, and led him to the apostles, and declared to them how on the road he had seen the Lord, and that He had spoken to him, and how he had boldly preached in Damascus in the name of Jesus. So he stayed with them while coming in and going out of Jerusalem." - Acts 9:26-28 MEV

The first thing we see upon Saul's return to Jerusalem is that he tries to join the disciples. Keep in mind these are the disciples who had watched (for what may have been years) as the zealous young pharisee hunted their brethren with extreme prejudice. What a humbling of heart it must have then taken for Saul to come to them. Yet the Spirit of God deems it ultimately necessary.

Not a one of us who have been reborn in Christ have reason to choose to avoid fellowship. Maybe we are medically unable (and that may be beyond our control), but if by choice, or (as in the case of Saul) enmity, we are not excused from communion with the saints. This new brother did what he must to join the Church, and it was not for his own notoriety. Can you imagine how hard it must have been to walk among those whom you had previously so fervently persecuted?

"For am I now seeking the approval of men or of God? Or am I trying to please men? For if I were still trying to please men, I would not be the servant of Christ." - Galatians 1:10 MEV

As mentioned in recent days' studies, Paul rehashes these early days several times. In one of those, he references this time in Jerusalem (15 days) and he relates it all to giving his heart to God, not seeking reputation among men. This young, born again believer does not join himself to the disciples as Simon Magus had (angling for personal gain). Rather he goes to the place where the most antipathy would lie, and he submits himself to the will of God.

Can we blame the disciples for being hesitant though? These were the few who hadn't been dispersed by Saul's persecutions, and of those, the only ones he had not managed to discover. I don't believe, if placed in their situation, I'd have had any different response.

Although there has been three years since the hunter had left Jerusalem, they knew not what had transpired. The Roman-Jewish historian Josephus informs us that at this time king Aretas of Damascus was very hostile to the house of Herod which was over Jerusalem. Add that skirmish to the facts that it was a six day journey from Damascus to Jerusalem, and that those believers in Damascus were there solely because of the persecution they had experienced in the Holy City, it is no wonder news of the happenings there had not found its way back.

This leads us to the questions of the other characters in today's passage. You may remember Barnabas from our study of the earlier chapters of Acts, and we'll see him again, often with Paul. The scriptures show a natural friendship among these two in the coming chapters. We don't have a definitive answer whether Barnabas had been to Damascus to see those things, or if Saul now approaches him in Jerusalem as an old friend. Many have surmised, as Saul's hometown, Tarsus, was the landing point of the island of Cyprus from where Barnabas originated, that the pharisee and the Levite had grown up together, possibly even studying under Gamaliel together. We'll come back to that.

The next two we see are Peter and James. We're told later in the scriptures that this was James, the brother of Jesus, and that Saul at this time saw no other Apostles. Were they off on missionary trips to the dispersed churches, or was Saul only allowed into the presence of some, on the chance it was still a ploy? We're not expressly told. I'd suggest to you though, that this 15 days with Peter is something we should keep in contextual memory as we enter the coming chapters.

Returning to Saul and Barnabas, I cannot neglect to consider the implications if it is true that these two had grown up together. The scandal of showing his face among the disciples of Jerusalem is one thing, but to come and plead with one such as this is an entirely new level of humility.

Think about it. If a major offense comes from one you have never met before, can you deny that you have an easier time forgiving and forgetting this than even a minor offense from one you had considered a friend? The closer we are to someone, the more it hurts when they inevitably fail us; The easier it then is for us to improperly excuse ourselves from that fellowship where the offense originated.

Such a personal tension may have been the case when Saul and Barnabas came together, no longer as friends, nor enemies, but now as brothers adopted into the family of Christ.

In this moment (or maybe it was back at Damascus) Saul must humble himself saying, "I have done that which is wrong, I have been a great enemy both to God and to you, and I deserve nothing short of the utmost wrath. Glory be to God that in the atonement of Jesus Christ, the Son of God, He offered the forgiveness I could never earn. Can you, now, find room to forgive likewise?"

In this moment (or maybe it was back at Damascus) Barnabas must humble himself saying, "That which was done cannot be undone, for it was a transgression beyond the capability of human pardon. Yet as it were deemed to be thrown into the sea of forgetfulness by Our Lord Jesus Christ, may the Spirit of God within me offer the power needed for me to truly forgive and count you not only my friend, but my brother and fellow Kingdom laborer for eternity. To Him be the glory and power and honor, forever and ever amen."

Brothers and sisters, take note here. Saul's conversion did not lead to self-fulfillment, nor pride of reputation, and neither should it for us. That didn't stop him from sharing either the Gospel or his testimony. Both, when properly spoken, are a witness of God's goodness in spite of our shortcomings, not the other way around. Even in the testimonies of how God has changed us, it can never be about who we are, but always about who He is.

Let it be known that just like Paul, our response to our brethren should be forgiveness, and to the Holy, Holy, Holy God who redeemed us should always be,

"all glory and honor unto thee, not unto me."

Notes

Day 56

Allies in His Name

"And he spoke boldly in the name of the Lord Jesus and disputed against the Hellenists. But they tried to kill him. When the brothers learned this, they brought him down to Caesarea, and sent him off to Tarsus." - Acts 9:29-30 MEV

I ask you to seriously consider the alliances here, because these next few verses match the most epic medieval dramas, and they depict great truths about this life. He spoke boldly in the name of the Lord Jesus, as one who could now truly say, "if God is for us, who can be against us" (Romans 8:31 MEV). How boldly, we might ask, but we need not wait long for our answer. He "disputed against the Hellenists."

These Hellenists, against whom Saul now debated the Messiah, were the same men over whom he'd presided at the stoning of Stephen. They were the same men that for months, maybe years, the young pharisee had led in a ruthless pursuit to render the name of Jesus Christ asunder. These were the same men he had encouraged to hate that Only Name, doubtless with many convincing words and arguments. In case we should miss the importance of this, Luke left a beacon in his text. The word "disputed" is used only one other time in this book, and that of the last time these parties came together, previously against Stephen (Acts 6:9).

While written in another context, one of the two whom Saul now sojourned with (James), later defines the alliances. "Friendship with the world is enmity with God" (James 4:4 MEV). At one time Saul had been found fighting against God, but now he had been joined to the Lord, and that made him, naturally, an enemy of the world (not of men mind you). The newly remade soldier of Christ charges right into the fracas upon which lines he had previously led the opposition, and he earnestly seeks to undo the damage he once caused.

"When I returned to Jerusalem and was praying in the temple, I fell into a trance and saw Him saying to me, 'Hurry! Get out of Jerusalem immediately, for they will not receive your testimony concerning Me.' " - Acts 22:17-18 MEV

Paul recants this episode later in his life, and tells of how Jesus had prophetically called him to retreat to another battle line. Jesus tells him, "They will not receive your testimony." There is a somber truth within this statement. Regardless of God's free gift of grace and the most earnest evangelism of His servants, there are still men and women who will strive to contend as enemies of God until their dying breath. It is not for lack of God's mercy that anyone goes to the grave condemned, but by their own rejection.

On the other hand, we have the testimony of God's goodness through those who are allied under His name. Those disciples of Christ who had narrowly escaped Saul's former crusade, now risk life and limb to support his latter campaign. Within these words we have a testimony of the greatest forgiveness shown in the merciful disciples now presented with their former persecutor. Rather than let him suffer the fate he formerly inflicted, they help him flee.

Take special note of where they took him to though, for that is an even greater testimony of forgiveness. Before sending him off (likely by sea) to Tarsus, they take him to Caesarea. Do you know what else is in Caesarea? The deacon Philip's house was there, and as that was the last place we saw him, probably Philip himself.

Our beloved physician has had an ongoing theme throughout his writings in that he groups names of the disciples by the nearness of their camaraderie. Stephen and Phillip were not only named together, but Philip's testimony picks up the moment Stephen's is laid down.

What a great story we have here; Stephen's friend and Stephen's murderer are reconciled. While Luke does not express certainty, I'd suggest that there is a subtle implication that Saul was taken to rest under Philip's roof before boarding the boat which would carry him to his own homeland. In the face of that sort of ultimate mercy, can we still justify our grudges? Oh, I admit I have them, but try as I might, I cannot find any unworldly justification to continue grasping them. Help me, Lord Jesus.

The next place we see Saul go is back home to Tarsus. the beginning of Saul's ministry is a retracing of his footsteps. He goes from place to place where he had once built alliances with those in enmity of the Truth, and he uses those old connections in an attempt by any and all means to bring some to Christ.

"Then the churches throughout all Judea and Galilee and Samaria had peace and were built up. And walking in the fear of the Lord and in the comfort of the Holy Spirit, they were multiplied." - Acts 9:31 MEV

War. Peace. Fear. Comfort. Martyred. Multiplied. These are all the portion of those allied with Christ.

War with those ideologies which hated Jesus first. Peace with our brethren, peace in the face of persecutors, peace with God.

Fear, not of those who can murder the body but not the soul; Before those, the Spirit of God in us is fearlessness, such as the boldly speaking Saul. Fear of the Lord - that Spirit inspired awe of who God is and all this means. Comfort in the face of such glory, and in the midst of the battle. Comfort in the knowledge that no matter what we've done, or what assault is brought against us, we are His, kept for Him for eternity.

Brothers and sisters, as soldiers in the army of Christ we are in the world but not of it. Our old alliances now wage war against us. Again, we must remember that is not warfare with men and women, but rather with those disputes we once held. Empires rise and fall, thrones are built and burnt, but the Kingdom of God is eternal; the First and the Last reigns forever on the throne under which flag we are allied. Never forget that the word of God calls us more than conquerors. Hey Paul, take it from here and close us out:

"What then shall we say to these things? If God is for us, who can be against us? He who did not spare His own Son, but delivered Him up for us all, how shall He not with Him also freely give us all things? Who shall bring a charge against God's elect? It is God who justifies. Who is he who condemns? It is Christ who died, yes, who is risen, who is also at the right hand of God, who also intercedes for us. Who shall separate us from the love of Christ? Shall tribulation, or distress, or persecution, or famine, or nakedness, or peril, or sword? As it is written: 'For Your sake we are killed all day long; we are counted as sheep for the slaughter.' No, in all these things we are more than conquerors through Him who loved us. For I am persuaded that neither death nor life, neither angels nor principalities nor powers, neither things present nor things to come, neither height nor depth, nor any other created thing, shall be able to separate us from the love of God, which is in Christ Jesus our Lord." - Romans 8:31-39 MEV

Notes

Day 57

Rise and Make Your Bed

"Now as Peter went here and there among them all, he came down also to the saints who lived at Lydda. There he found a man named Aeneas, bedridden for eight years, who was paralyzed." - Acts 9:32-33 ESV

The narrative returns from the origin of Paul, back to the Apostolic works of Peter, but let us not forget that this book is entirely the Acts of the Glorified Christ. As Paul had for 15 days sojourned in Jerusalem with Peter and James (Jesus' brother), the question arose as to why he saw none of the other Apostles. No answer is certain, but it may appear from the immediately following passage, to which we now arrive, that the Apostles were traveling from church to church as Peter now did.

Depending upon your translation you may see Peter went "throughout all quarters," "through every region," "from place to place," "throughout the land," or a myriad of different phrases with similar meanings. The original Greek was more abbreviated though, speaking essentially, "passed through all." If we then consider what the all points toward, I believe we have our answer as to what was being said. Passed through all, "and he came down also to the saints who lived at Lydda." Peter (and likely the rest of the Apostles before him) was making his rounds to all the newly founded churches. The dispersed disciples had carried the gospel with them, bringing many to saving faith, and now the Apostles go among the believers to "make disciples."

In the next chapter we see God inform Peter that the time for the Gospel to be taken to the gentiles had come, but first Luke records the Apostles themselves going throughout all Judea and Samaria. First, here in Lydda we're shown two groups of people: the saints who were there, and those who had yet to turn to the Lord. It's not clarified to which of these Æneas belonged. No statement of faith is made, and he is found in our text between the two groups.

While we don't know the state of his soul upon Peter's arrival, and we don't have any declaration of faith, or baptism recorded afterward, a healing that spanned beyond mere flesh might be implied in Peter's words, and the paralytic took a step of faith. It remains unclarified by our physician, but what we can be sure of is that by the witness of this miracle, worked by Jesus Christ through his servant Peter, many are brought to receive the free gift of salvation. Yet in the midst of anything more certain than this, I'd suggest that what is truly recorded here is, like Jesus' many parables, a metaphor for all the Gospel.

"And Peter said to him, 'Aeneas, Jesus Christ heals you; rise and make your bed.' And immediately he rose. And all the residents of Lydda and Sharon saw him, and they turned to the Lord." - Acts 9:34-35 ESV

Recorded is a man, once able bodied, but now long sick with no hope. Æneas had no strength by which he could lift himself up. He lived in a place known for wealth, for doctors, and for religious schools, but none of the above could pull him out of the palsy and poverty of the bedroll on which he lay. There he laid for eight years, with no escape from the effects of the illness that plagued him. Then, by no merit of his own, Æneas is visited by Jesus Christ who heals him. There is no doubt in our text of who does the healing, as Peter says, "Jesus Christ heals you," but that having been accomplished, Æneas must take the stand, and Peter says, "rise and make your bed." Christ could offer all the healing in the world, but if this man refused to stand, he would remain effectively paralyzed.

Allow me to rephrase that:

Mankind was made pure, but since the original sin we have long been corrupted and sick; we've all fallen short of the glory of God, and we all deserve judgement. There is no amount of good works we could ever do to lift ourselves out of the consequences of our sin. No sages, religions, or politics can cure our world of the effects of this sin, and there isn't enough money in all the world to do so either. Here in our walking death, we stayed for thousands of years, but as we endlessly tried philosophies and charities, ideologies and policies, the prosecution has shown without a shadow of a doubt, that we only make it worse. Then by no merit of our own, glory to God, for He laid down the glory He had from the beginning, and we were visited by the Son of God Himself, who offered the healing solution - His blood. Now His servants declare "Jesus Christ heals you; repent and believe." But though He gave everything, His body and His blood, in the most true and selfless show of love this world has ever seen, Jesus Christ's healing must be taken up to be received. He offers salvation, and He does all the work, but we must take up the faith, for if we refuse this free gift, no other salvation will be found. It is by faith in Christ alone that we can be saved, and without that, we remain effectively under the curse. Every consequence of every sin is still laid upon our charge if we deny the One who paid it all. There's no need for any of us to remain lying on that bedroll.

Notes

Notes

Day 58

Tabitha Arise

"So Peter rose and went with them. And when he arrived, they took him to the upper room. All the widows stood beside him weeping and showing tunics and other garments that Dorcas made while she was with them. But Peter put them all outside, and knelt down and prayed; and turning to the body he said, "Tabitha, arise." And she opened her eyes, and when she saw Peter she sat up. And he gave her his hand and raised her up. Then, calling the saints and widows, he presented her alive." - Acts 9:39-41 ESV

The Apostles have done many miracles up to this point, following in the footsteps of their Master, but not yet has a single one been recorded to raise the dead. Even so, the disciples at Joppa had faith enough to call Peter from the nearby town of Lydda.

Again, we notice Luke records these miracles with definite locations in such a record that could not be denied among the streets, towns, and cities so close to the seat of power which sought to disprove that Jesus was the Deific Messiah. Like Lydda (aka Lud, or Lod), Joppa (aka Jopha or Jaffa as it's known today) is a town that has survived millennia and every rise and fall of various empires. Being the nearest suitable location to Jerusalem for a port, the city has existed in some form throughout history. It was the port through which the wood for both Solomon's and Zerubbabel's temples arrived. It was the port through which Jonah's fantastic tale began. It was now the scene of a miraculous act of God.

It was not only famous among the Hebrews though. Greek legends were also founded around this town. Now Peter was called to this town, which was famous among Jew and Greek alike, and through which many travelers would daily pass. Through this Apostle an undeniable work of God would be performed. Potential questions are never answered whether the disciples at Joppa expected a resurrection from Peter, or whether even he knew what he was to do upon arrival.

Those questions are not defined, but I believe if we read between the lines, we can safely assume these saints had hope that the faithful God would call Tabitha back to earthly service. They laid her in the upper chamber just as Elisha's Shunammite woman had done with her son. They called Peter, having heard he was nearby in Lydda, the news of which no doubt came with the story of the miracle worked in Æneas'. Then they showed him all the ministrations she'd worked for them.

As the widows wept and displayed some of what she had done for them, I cannot reconcile the record to the rest of scripture except to believe that they stood hopeful in the faith that God could resurrect her. What a great faith that must have been in them, but how about for Peter? He's lived the evidence of God's mighty hand working through him and his fellow Apostles, but now to be the voice asked to say "Tabitha arise," must have been humbling, and testing of his faith.

" 'O Lord my God, let this child's life come into him again.' And the Lord listened to the voice of Elijah. And the life of the child came into him again, and he revived." - 1 Kings 17:21b-22 ESV

In the same manner as Elijah (1 Kings 17:17-24), and Elisha (2 Kings 4:32-37), Peter now seeks solitude in prayer. Those were stories of history with which Peter was well acquainted, but he had personally witnessed Jesus raise more than one corpse to life as well.

Tabitha is recognized by two names, Tabitha being of an Aramaic origin, and Dorcas being the Greek equivalent. Although Luke wrote in Greek, Peter chose to not to use Dorcas, and so I believe it's quite probable "Tabitha arise" was spoken in his native Galilean-Aramaic equivalent, "Tabitha Koum" (pronounced koo-me). With that perspective, I have little doubt that Peter's prayers took his mind back to the Lord's words "Talitha Koum" as Jesus resurrected the lifeless body of the synagogue ruler's daughter.

Talitha: ταλιθα
Tabitha: Ταβιθά

Remember that when Jesus raised Lazarus he prayed, "Father, I thank you that you have heard me. I knew that you always hear me, but I said this on account of the people standing around, that they may believe that you sent me" (John 11:41-42 ESV).

When Elijah raised the widow woman's son, it affirmed her faith that Elijah's God was truly God. When Elisha raised the Shunammite woman's son, the same effect came. When Jesus raised the "little girl" (translated from Talitha) those who saw were overcome with amazement. When He raised Lazarus, it was done so that the witnesses would believe he was sent from God.

Now Peter is brought to a certain town named Joppa, through which countless souls would travel, and he's the tool for an Act of Christ which would prove to many that Peter and his brothers told God's truth when they testified that Jesus of Nazareth was the Messiah, the Son of God. May it continue to affirm our faith.

Notes

Notes

Day 59

Except Through Jesus

"In Caesarea there was a man named Cornelius, the centurion of a band of soldiers called the Italian Detachment, a devout man and one who feared God with all his household, who gave many alms to the people and continually prayed to God. About the ninth hour of the day he saw clearly in a vision an angel of God coming in and saying to him, 'Cornelius.' " - Acts 10:1-3 MEV

Throughout Luke's second treatise (and the first for that matter) we've seen specific names and locations used which could have easily been disproved if not true. Now we have an entire band of soldiers. This was the term for a 60th of a legion. The Cornelius of whom Luke here writes, and who possibly even personally gave some of this testimony, was a leader over 100 soldiers.

Somewhere around 25 years passed between this new turn for the Church, and Luke's publishing of the story. Many of those soldiers, friends, and family of Cornelius still lived when this was spread throughout the land. For those who wanted to choke out the Church, Luke's records would have been an extremely easy tool to use; Simply find these men and women, and convince someone to talk. That is, unless these were historical facts. It's almost to the point now though, where these facts and specifics have been so frequent that the continued acknowledgement of such evidence is becoming redundant. So... let's move on.

Our beloved physician leaves an interesting account of this centurion. It sounds very reminiscent of the account of Job; a man who was blameless and feared the Lord to the extent that he had led his whole household to do so as well, with many offerings and prayers.

He's recorded as an extraordinarily upright man. We're told he was a gentile (not a proselyte) who was so benevolent and charitable toward the Jews that even their hatred of the oppressive, occupying forces could not overcome their amity toward him. Yet not only in his works is he shown to have abandoned his national idolatry in a sincere desire for the monotheistic God of Israel. He's also said to have "continually prayed to God."

"And he stared at him in terror and said, 'What is it, Lord?' And he said to him, 'Your prayers and your alms have ascended as a memorial before God. And now send men to Joppa and bring one Simon who is called Peter. He is lodging with one Simon, a tanner, whose house is by the sea.' " - Acts 10:4-6 ESV

In the introduction of Cornelius, we're told of his alms and prayers, but when the angel declares God's recognition, the order has switched, to "your prayers and alms" which ascended before God. Compare this with the greatest (love God: prayers) and second greatest (love your neighbor: almsgiving) commandments, and I believe there's a reason for this alteration. From the perspective of men, the outward alms stood foremost, but God's perspective is not that of men.

We're shown a man that I'd suggest is on par with "my servant Job... a blameless and upright man, who fears God and turns away from evil" (Job 1:8 ESV), and yet, that was not enough.

"The all-important truth in the words is that the prayers and alms {coming from a devout heart} of a man who had never heard of Jesus Christ were acceptable to God. None the less Cornelius needed Jesus, and the recompense made to him was the knowledge of the Saviour." - McLaren

Cornelius was a man who had gained some authority and wealth among the native Roman soldiers. He was born an Italian Roman, not joined to them from conquered lands. We thence know that he was raised in pious adherence to the plenteous polytheistic gods of Rome. Yet he found no God within. When those rituals and beliefs had not brought him to God, he found truth in the Jewish account of the monotheistic Jehovah, yet even though his seeking heart was recognized by God, it wasn't enough. He still lacked salvation.

" 'He commanded us to preach to the people and to testify that it is He who was ordained by God to be the Judge of the living and the dead. To Him all the prophets bear witness that whoever believes in Him will receive remission of sins through His name.' While Peter was still speaking these words, the Holy Spirit fell on all those who heard the word." - Acts 10:42-44 MEV

Cornelius's alms and prayers were heard by God, but the Lord must send an angel and a preacher to reveal to him the truth that "no one comes to the Father except through" Jesus (John 14:6 MEV). Regardless of all his religious devotions and his human attempts at piety and charity, it wasn't until Cornelius and his house heard and believed on the Name and finished works of Jesus Christ that the Holy Spirit came to indwell these gentiles. The same had been true of the Jews.

The enemy is making great gains in the world, and even in self-proclaimed believers right now. He's convincing more and more that there are many ways to God. Throughout the history of the Church, people have erroneously stepped above the Gospel, adding works as a requirement of salvation. But now, as in times past, what we see growing at an alarming rate is not even addition of works, but rather a replacement of Christ by works.

Many now would have you believe that you can earn your way to those streets of gold regardless of faith in Christ. To acknowledge the scriptures' promise of streets of gold, yet simultaneously teach that Christ be not the only way, is a cognitive dissonance beyond any explanation, short of deception by the father of lies who knows his time is short. Be ye not deceived brothers and sisters. Faith in Christ alone is your ticket to heaven. Stick to that ticket like glue.

Notes

Notes

Day 60

Kingdom Hunger

"The next day as they went on their journey and drew near the city, Peter went up on the housetop to pray about the sixth hour. He became very hungry and desired to eat. But while they prepared a meal, he fell into a trance." - Acts 10:9-10 MEV

Have you been reading along with us? If not, here's a brief recap. Saul was visited by the Glorified Christ, who then sent Ananias to this man who was "to bear my name before the gentiles and their kings." After a few years of preaching Christ, Saul was chased out of Damascus at threat of death, at which point he came to sojourn for 15 days with Simon Peter and James, the brother of Jesus. There Jesus comes to Saul again, this time in a vision, saying "Depart, for I will send you far away to the Gentiles."(Acts 22:21 MEV).

Now we find Peter, on a tour of the planted churches which has brought him to Joppa, a port city, where he is staying at a tanner's house by the sea shore. A gentile named Cornelius has been visited by an angel with a message, and subsequently sent servants to go plead for a visit from Peter. It is now mid-day, around noon, and Peter comes up to the rooftop to pray, as was the common secluded retreat of the Eastern religions. He's met with a spectacular view of maritime expanse, then visited with a hunger that was not normal. Allow me to explain.

Most of us are pretty used to threen meals a day, right? Hunger at noon doesn't sound out of the ordinary to us. Well, the Jews and Christians of the first century typically ate two meals. The feasts in the evening, preceded by a small meal in the morning which we might consider a snack - largely milk, cheeses, fruits, and the like. This morning meal was commonly eaten around the 4th or 5th hour (10 or 11am). Either Peter has just finished eating but is now met with an unusual hunger, or he's been fasting, and is unexpectedly unable to continue any longer. Either way, we see the disciples who are with him start making him food, and God drops him into some sort of trance.

Two prayers a day (third and ninth hour) were common at the time, but the highly pious often added a prayer at the 6th. We see Daniel praying 3 times a day in Babylon, and David praying, "evening, morning, and noon" (Psalm 55:17). While Peter doesn't divulge what he was praying, I believe we can be relatively confident that he was praying over what it meant for Saul to preach Christ's Name to the gentiles; what it meant when Christ said "Go therefore and make disciples of all nations" (Matthew 28:19 MEV), or then again, "you will be my witnesses... To the ends of the Earth" (Acts 1:8 MEV).

At the beginning of this chapter, two men's prayers are visited by a response of God. A messenger angel is sent to Cornelius who later tells Peter that the angel had said, "Your prayer has been heard." Could it be that for Peter as well, this trance was an answer to a specific prayer? One tied to his glances across the open sea? We don't have to speculate as to what God was saying in this message. Peter has already done that for us, and God answered.

"Now while Peter wondered what this vision which he had seen might mean, the men who were sent by Cornelius had inquired for Simon's house and stood at the gate, and called and asked whether Simon, who was surnamed Peter, was lodging there." - Acts 10:17-18 MEV

The sheet, tied at the four corners, was God's answer. That which God called clean spanned to the four corners of the Earth and God called Peter to a new ministry. I'd like to get into that some more tomorrow, but for today, I find myself stuck dwelling on the hunger.

I do believe that this hunger was sent upon Peter by He whose "food is to do the will of Him who sent Me, and to finish His work" (John 4:34 MEV). A lot was revealed in this vision, but the hunger was a deeper sign than just an empty stomach. For several years now, his ministry had been fruitful throughout Judea and Samaria, but God put a hunger in him all the more for Kingdom growth.

Take note young single ladies, the old adage "the way to a man's heart is through his stomach," was here exercised, even by God. I know my wife has made good use of that time and again over the years.

This is honestly scratching strange parts of my brain. For the last few weeks, I've had a physical hunger that no amount of food could satisfy, sometimes even that sort of hunger to the point of pain within an hour after eating. I've wondered long hours at what's been going on, but now at such a time I come across this peculiar craving in Peter, and I have more cause to wonder at my own. I may not have a flat roof, but I'll take the Apostle's example and pray about it.

"Then a voice came to him, 'Rise, Peter; kill and eat.' Peter said, 'Not at all, Lord. For I have never eaten anything that is common or unclean.' The voice spoke to him a second time: 'What God has cleansed, do not call common.' This happened three times. And again the vessel was taken up into heaven." - Acts 10:13-16 MEV

I suspect, as we approach the Day of the Lord, all the more, many of us are feeling a deeper and more urgent call to serve. I suspect that among the various gifts and callings, God has prepared far more good works for many of us than what we've actually given ourselves to do.

Like Peter, do we say, "Not at all, Lord," maybe more than once?

Do you have a hunger? Will you rise, kill and eat?

Lord God Almighty, we are your servants, given in humble adoration of You who loved us first. O God, we can't often see what you have working behind the scenes, nor what you have prepared for us to do. Father, we ask your guidance day in and day out. Lord, whether you send an angel, a vision, or merely a knock of a servant at our front doors, we need you to show us what more it is that you would have us do. As the Advocate knocks on the door of our hearts, maybe through our stomachs, help us to know which way we should go. Lord, I believe your Day approaches, and how many more days we have to declare your Name and make disciples is uncertain. Help us that we may not delay. May all the world hear your Good News, oh Son of God. All glory and honor and power is yours, and it's in that precious name of Jesus Christ we pray. Amen.

Notes

Day 61

One Race in Christ

“Then a voice came to him, ‘Rise, Peter; kill and eat.’ Peter said, ‘Not at all, Lord. For I have never eaten anything that is common or unclean.’ The voice spoke to him a second time: ‘What God has cleansed, do not call common.’ This happened three times. And again the vessel was taken up into heaven.” - Acts 10:13-16 MEV

This vision given to Peter must have been quite the conundrum in his mind. As long as we've seen him, Simon has been a headstrong young man, and as we see in his first epistle twenty some years later, his mind is ever on the call to "Be Holy, because I am holy" (1 Peter 1:16, Leviticus 11:44 among others). In that future memo, he is quoting the same chapter of Leviticus in which was laid out the "law for the animals." In the present text though, Peter is clearly hard to convince of a freedom from the ceremonial law.

“To tell a Jew that God had directed those animals to be reckoned clean which were hitherto deemed unclean, was in effect saying, that the law of Moses was done away." - Matthew Henry

Three times Peter declines to eat that which was forbidden, and three times he is exhorted to stop calling these things unclean. This divinely inspired annulment of the law of Moses was not easily accepted, and so we have no reason to wonder at why it was necessary for a trance-like vision to prepare Peter for the approaching gentiles.

The Mosaic Law included numerous regulations, of which some held ties to morality and righteousness seemingly no nearer than trusting and obeying God. The food law which Peter is here told he's been set free from was in large part, a method of separation of Jews from Gentiles. God's plan had meant a certain degree of estrangement between these groups must be held, in order that their idolatries and superstitions would not entirely taint the seed of the woman (Genesis 3:15). They were not to eat what was commonly eaten among the world.

But Jesus has come. He's been crucified, resurrected, and ascended to glory. The Holy Spirit has come to dwell in those who repent and believe, and the Lord now says this law has been fulfilled, that which was deemed unclean is no longer so. As Peter wonders at the application of the vision, he comes to realize that the segregation between Jew and Gentile is no more.

"There is therefore now no condemnation for those who are in Christ Jesus, who walk not according to the flesh, but according to the Spirit. For the law of the Spirit of life in Christ Jesus has set me free from the law of sin and death. For what the law could not do, in that it was weak through the flesh, God did by sending His own Son in the likeness of sinful flesh, and concerning sin, He condemned sin in the flesh, in order that the righteous requirement of the law might be fulfilled in us, who walk not according to the flesh but according to the Spirit." - Romans 8:1-4 MEV

Thousands of years of history proved that the law was unable to make man holy, but the One who is Holy, Holy, Holy was able, in a single act of love, to impute his holiness and righteousness upon us who believe in Him. Peter was shown a vision that declared the separation of Jew and Gentile was needful no longer. When a knock came at the door he followed the command and "came without question" regardless of "how unlawful it [was]." (Acts 10:28-29)

Paul, as a pharisee turned Apostle to the Gentiles, had to make a complete change of mind to accept this as well, but we see he likewise embraced it fully, teaching "everything created by God is good, and nothing is to be rejected if it is received with thanksgiving" (1 Timothy 4:4 ESV). But neither Peter nor Paul thought this an excuse to cease being Holy because God is Holy. We are in the world, no longer Jew nor Gentile, but united alike in our faith in Christ. Even so, that does not free us up to be like the world.

"Do not be unequally yoked together with unbelievers. For what fellowship has righteousness with unrighteousness? What communion has light with darkness? What agreement has Christ with Belial? Or what part has he who believes with an unbeliever? What agreement has the temple of God with idols? For you are the temple of the living God. As God has said: 'I will live in them and walk in them. I will be their God, and they shall be My people.' Therefore, 'Come out from among them and be separate, says the Lord. Do not touch what is unclean, and I will receive you.' 'I will be a Father to you, and you shall be My sons and daughters, says the Lord Almighty.' " 2 Corinthians 6:14-18 MEV

We are called to come out from among them and be separate. If you claim the name of Christ, the separation continues, but it's not the same. No longer are we separated by race, but we are set apart, in Christ, called to be Holy because He is Holy, and exhorted to leave behind all the wickedness of sin. No longer is there Jew and Gentile, but every believer of any race is made one race in the family of Christ; The family that is to the end of days set apart. Come out from among them, all you clean and uncommon; walk in the Spirit not in the flesh. What communion has light with the darkness?

Notes

Notes

Day 62

That None May Boast

"Then Peter began to speak, saying, 'Truthfully, I perceive that God is no respecter of persons. But in every nation he who fears Him and works righteousness is accepted by Him.' " Acts 10:34-35 MEV

We now come to Peter beginning to speak what the Angel had informed Cornelius he would; "He will tell you what you must do" (Acts 10:6b MEV). But first, if you've been reading along in your Bible, we saw Peter enter the house, and Cornelius fall down to worship him. The Apostle tells him, "Stand up, I myself am a man" (Acts 10:26 MEV).

This rebuke of the centurion's misplaced faith is also another affirmation (among so many) of the doctrine of the absolute deity of Jesus Christ. Peter says don't worship me, because I am a man. That's the same Peter who walked on the water with Jesus, afterward falling to worship Jesus alongside all his brethren, saying, "Truly you are the Son of God" (Matthew 14:33 MEV). Even the angels rebuke all who would worship them, saying, "Worship only God." Never doubt that Jesus Christ is the Word who is with God, and who is God.

I must admit though, as I read the beginning of Peter's speech, I find myself in minor disagreement with most theologians and commentators. The widely accepted meaning of Peter's words - "Truthfully I perceive that God is no respecter of persons," - is that he was acknowledging his fault in formerly believing that Jews were any better than Gentiles in God's eyes. He was acknowledging that all of mankind is capable of receiving the Gospel.

I don't dispute that as fact, for it's exactly what this entire chapter describes, and what Peter has already explained. "God has shown me not to call any man common or unclean" (Acts 10:28b MEV). In the same manner, Romans 2:11, Ephesians 6:9, and Colossians 3:25 all teach that God holds no partiality or favoritism. To each is the judgement of their iniquity, excepted only by faith in Christ which is available to all who would believe.

Where I differ is in this specific statement being merely another repetition what Peter's already expressed. The Greek word here translated "respecter of persons," (or "shows no partiality/favoritism" depending upon your preferred Bible version) is prosōpolēmptēs. This is the only use of the word in scripture, and from what I can tell it is used nowhere else at all, except by the fourth century preacher, John Chrysostom. The word is formed from two other, more common words.

prosōpon - appearance, specifically regarding wealth, property, rank, and treatment of others, or lack of the above.

lambanō - to take, to receive, to not reject

When breaking down the word we see that God does not accept any man or woman by their outward appearances. In the second chapter of his epistle, James, the brother of Jesus, teaches that if we exercise partiality based on wealth, or rank, then we are not imitating Christ as we should. I believe this word, prosōpolēmptēs, would fit well in that exhortation also.

Where I'm going with this has to do with how Cornelius is presented to Peter. When his servants arrive, they plead for Peter to come, by describing an authoritative centurion who is devout. They call him, "a man who is righteous and fears God and is of good report throughout the nation of the Jews"(Acts 10:22 MEV). When Peter enters Cornelius' house, and the centurion tells the story for himself, he starts off with, "Four days ago I was fasting until this hour. At the ninth hour I prayed in my house" (Acts 10:30 MEV).

At every turn Peter is appealed to on account of Cornelius' "prosōpon." I truly believe the Apostle was clarifying. He was making sure that right up front they knew that it wasn't to the centurion's credit that he received salvation. "That none may boast."

" 'He will speak words to you by which you and all your household will be saved.' As I began to speak, the Holy Spirit fell on them, as He fell on us at the beginning." - Acts 11:14-15 MEV

God didn't accept you for good works nor your reputation, but he did see your heart that feared and believed in Him, seeking to do what He would want, therefore... Peter then breaks into preaching Jesus Christ, because regardless of alms and prayers, God had sent the Apostle to tell them what they must do. It was just as the Angel had said. So, tell us then Peter, "everything the Lord has commanded you" (Acts 10:33 MEV)

"He commanded us to preach to the people and to testify that it is He who was ordained by God to be the Judge of the living and the dead. To Him all the prophets bear witness that whoever believes in Him will receive remission of sins through His name." - Acts 10:42-43 MEV

Whoever believes in Jesus Christ will receive remission of sins through His Name. Truthfully God is no respecter of persons, for all have fallen short of the glory of God. You cannot earn salvation by any level of pious devotion. Only by the One Righteous (Son of) God, who gave Himself for you, may you be saved. God is not one to respect any of us for good works, because even the best can never outweigh that for which we deserve judgement. It is only by His self-sacrificing love, shown through the Only Begotten Son, which you may be saved.

Notes

Notes

Day 63

Impartial

"Now the apostles and brethren who were in Judea heard that the Gentiles had also received the word of God. And when Peter came up to Jerusalem, those of the circumcision contended with him, saying, 'You went in to uncircumcised men and ate with them!' " - Acts 11:1-3 NKJV

News travels fast. Many, many miles of road were trodden under foot carrying the news that Peter had preached to, and baptized the gentiles. Now, either that news carried with it the witness of the Jewish Christians who had seen the Holy Spirit work in those gentiles, or the messengers were the source of the divisive intent. I tend to believe the former to be the case, as it appears Luke explains, in two simple words, where the division began.

Those of the circumcision contended with him. The men who translated the English Standard Version must have believed there was a link here as well, for they translated it "the circumcision party criticized him, saying..." As we continue in the book of Acts, we'll see this sect of Christianity emerge, seeking to bring the Gentile believers under Mosaic Law. The epistles are likewise filled with exhortations against the circumcision party's teachings.

The entirety of Christendom up to this point (only possibly excluding the eunuch of Ethiopia), were "those who were circumcised" (vs 2 MEV), as some translations would interpret this. Even so, the Greek wording Luke used here, "ek peritomē," is the same exact wording as "those of the circumcision" counted chiefly among the "idle talkers and deceivers" written of in Titus 1:10, and it's the same wording Paul used in Galatians 2:12 describing this party. Look what else he said about them:

"My concern was because of the false brothers [those people masquerading as Christians] who had been secretly smuggled in [to the community of believers]. They had slipped in to spy on the freedom which we have in Christ Jesus, in order to bring us back into bondage [under the Law of Moses]." - Galatians 2:4 AMP

We now find, in Acts 11, the first indication that there were Jewish spies among the Christians, as one would naturally expect considering the opposition they faced. But I don't believe all of these whom we see contending with Peter here were those deceivers. I believe when we see their response to Peter's apologia - "they glorified God, saying 'Then God has granted to the Gentiles also repentance unto life' " (vs 18 MEV) - we begin to understand that some of these were merely the deceived. Those seeking to bring them back under the law had exercised some influence, causing a brief division, but truth spoken in the Spirit of God was able to reconcile those who were true believers.

When you read about these, both true believers and false brothers alike, arguing against the acceptance of those others whom the Holy Spirit had come to commune with, does it cause you to reflect? Does it bring to mind anything you've seen in church? Maybe something you've said or done? Does it bring you to severe caution against partiality, or even subconscious prejudices?

"The imperfect state of human nature strongly appears, when godly persons are displeased even to hear that the word of God has been received, because their own system has not been attended to. And we are too apt to despair of doing good to those who yet, when tried, prove very teachable. It is the bane and damage of the church, to shut out those from it, and from the benefit of the means of grace, who are not in every thing as we are." - Matthew Henry

Until Christ returns, there will always be false believers among our ranks who will seek to hinder God. Sometimes they will merely look like hypocrisy among us, being viewed as in our ranks. Other times they may win influence in our hearts, leading us to unwittingly contend against the salvific work of God. We ought to be extremely careful at all times, that our sincere and eager desire is that all mankind, regardless of our similarities or differences, receives the word of God.

" 'If then God gave them the same gift as He gave us when we believed in the Lord Jesus Christ, who was I to be able to hinder God?' When they heard these things, they were silent. And they glorified God, saying, 'Then God has granted to the Gentiles also repentance unto life.' " - Acts 11:17-18 MEV

Let us never be found contending against God, for He will call men and women to repentance from among every nation and tribe, and from every sort of sinner. Who are we to be able to hinder God? God has granted, to whom He will, repentance unto life. Can anyone walk into your fellowship repentant, or would you turn away someone as different?

Notes

Notes

Day 64

Jesus has Overcome All Our Mistakes

"Now those who had been scattered as a result of the persecution that started because of Stephen made their way as far as Phoenicia, Cyprus, and Antioch, speaking the word to no one except Jews. But there were some of them, men from Cyprus and Cyrene, who came to Antioch and began speaking to the Greeks also, proclaiming the good news about the Lord Jesus." - Acts 11:19-20 CSB

The divided narrative is now united. First, we had the dispersion of the Church by the "persecution that started because of Stephen," and the preaching of Christ to the Jews all throughout the land. Next, Luke took us on an exhibition of the Revelation to Saul, followed by Peter, and finally the many that "God has granted to the Gentiles also repentance unto life" (vs 18 MEV). Now the two stories unite.

My oft preferred version, MEV, along with other translations, has verse 20 as the "Hellenists also." Other translations though, such as the CSB quoted above, NIV, and KJV, interpret this as the Greeks or Grecians. The difference is in whether these were Greek speaking Jews (Hellenists), or gentiles, and the confusion comes because out of our extant manuscripts, some have hellēnistēs and others hellēnēs. Yet if this is not Grecian gentiles then there's no contrast to the preceding sentence as is suggested by the language. I'm of the belief that the mere context of the book infers this is indeed the beginning of Gentilic ministry beyond the house of Cornelius.

Those scattered by the persecution as far as Antioch had been gone from Jerusalem for years. They had no knowledge of what has happened in Caesarea and Jerusalem, so they continued in what they knew, preaching Christ only to the Jews. That is, until some travelers come from Cyprus and Cyrene.

A little geographical context here might help. Antioch is a walk of 300 miles from Caesarea. There's little chance news has traveled that far from Jerusalem. But as we saw after Peter's ministry to Cornelius, the news did spread. For the ships to carry that information from Caesarea to Cyprus and Cyrene is only to be expected. It seems evident that these men from Cyprus and Cyrene, who could have only come to Antioch by boat (Cyprus being an island), are here declared as the first to bring the news of Gentile inclusion to this distant city.

That brings up a specific point in relation to yesterday's devotional. When the word got around about Peter preaching to the Gentiles, some believers indeed made their way to Jerusalem in misguided zeal. What we see here though, is that the Holy Spirit led at least some believers to quickly welcome this new evangelism, and they carried the news abroad.

Those who were deceived and went debating against Peter might have had cause to regret the time they had wasted, and the strife they caused in their broken mistakes. But there's a double truth in Peter's words, "who was I to be able to hinder God" (vs 17 MEV). Peter would not be wise to try to hinder God, but also, he couldn't hinder God if he tried.

As Christians, still in corruptible flesh, not only will we find ourselves in utter futility if we endeavor to fight against the will of God, but we can also take great comfort in the knowledge that even in our greatest mistakes, we are entirely insignificant in the overall scheme of God's will. Even though many went errantly to debate against the Apostle, God still did His work, and others carried the good news to those who were now deemed clean.

Whether intentionally or unintentionally, who are we that we can stand in God's way? When you or I look back mournfully on our continued mistakes and transgressions, with eyes now opened through and to the grace of God, it is natural to feel the bitter disappointment that we possibly got in the way of God's plan; that we missed sharing the Gospel with this person or that. Maybe that we dragged God's name through the mud?

The repentant heart is drawn to such bereavement of soul when we return to our vomit, or are found fighting against God. But there are two truths that we can strangely take comfort in. First, that we are vastly insignificant in the grand scheme of His plan, and second, that God's plan for our individual duties and services already factored in all our shortcomings, long before we were ever born. Take heart, for Jesus has overcome the world; even that worldliness still in us.

Notes

Notes

Day 65

Remain with the Lord

"News of these things came to the ears of the church which was in Jerusalem, and they sent Barnabas to Antioch. When he arrived and saw the grace of God, he rejoiced and exhorted them all to remain with the Lord with a loyal heart." - Acts 11:22-23 MEV

The trek from Antioch to Jerusalem was said to be a 16-day hike. Someone among them thought it necessary to carry news of this conversion of Grecian gentiles back to the Apostles. Whether the news came in a manner of complaint, such as those who had come in regard to Peter's ministry in Caesarea, or it had come as a testimony of the glorious work of God, we're not told. What we do see is the Jerusalem church sending a certain Hellenistic Levite from Cyprus.

There was clear intent here. They sent a man who was most likely to be familiar with the men of Cyprus who had evangelized the gentiles. Along those lines they sent a friend of Saul, the Pharisee appointed by Christ to take the Gospel to the gentiles, and who now resided in nearby Tarsus. Yes, Barnabas was the man for the job, but not because of all this. Barnabas was the man because, "He was a good man, full of the Holy Spirit and of faith" (Acts 11:24 MEV). Barnabas was the man because Christ was in Barnabas.

Upon arrival, the "Son of encouragement" sees something fantastic. No wonder "when he arrived and saw the grace of God, he rejoiced."

Is there anything on Earth more astounding than that all-encompassing grace which brings salvation, overflows with faith and love, teaches penitent sinners to deny ungodliness and worldly desires, is perfected in weakness, and calls men to steward those gifts which he freely gives, working all things to purify the Bride of Christ (Titus 2:11, 1 Tim 1:14, 2 Cor 12:9, 1 Peter 4:10)? Is there any wonder more miraculous than the countless examples of the worst of mankind being made new, regenerate exemplars of morality, set apart as a holy priesthood for God?

“Grace is not simply leniency when we have sinned. Grace is the enabling gift of God not to sin. Grace is power, not just pardon.” – John Piper

Rejoice and be glad when you see these things, for it is all the glory of God. Barnabas did. Then, "he exhorted them to remain with the Lord with a loyal heart." Simplistic? Maybe, but it's the core of the matter.

We add endless theologies, doctrines, and isms, but if it doesn't all boil down to remaining true and faithful to the Lord Jesus Christ with steadfast purpose of heart, then might we have cause for concern? Our exhortations and doctrines, when founded entirely on Christ and his word, are a summation of Him, vital to the Christian walk. On the other hand, if the doctrines of Christ be allowed to overbear the person of Christ, could we be blind to our true state?

"There is a whole world between the man to whom God’s revelation consists in certain doctrines given to us by Jesus Christ, and the man to whom it consists in that Christ Himself. Grasping a living person is not the same as accepting a proposition. True, the propositions are about Him, and we do not know Him without them. But equally true, we need to be reminded that He is our Saviour and not they, and that God has revealed Himself to us not in words and sentences but in a life." - Alexander McLaren

What a balance we must hold. To fully know Christ, we must grow in the knowledge of what we can learn from his Holy Word, but to comprehend that Word in truth, we must fully know and hold to the personal relationship with Christ, first and foremost, and to the last. In the intellectual search of God's word, men have often lost that simplicity, creating endless divisions and schisms by which some of us discount the salvation of others claiming the name of Christ, but look at Barnabas. When he saw the grace of God, he rejoiced and exhorted them to remain with Christ. One can't remain if they aren't already with...

"A pregnant lesson for modern theorists who, on one ground or another of doctrine or of orders, narrow the great conception of Christ’s Church! Can you see ‘the grace of God’ in the people? Then they are in the Church, whatever becomes of your theories, and the sooner you let them out so as to fit the facts, the better for you and for them." - Alexander McLaren

How often I see the discord of schisms taken to the extreme. One denomination argues members of another aren't truly in Christ. One claims that without outward displays of a certain gift, the Holy Ghost is not present. One system of uncertain theology claims the opposing system is entirely apostate and heretical. All of this over things which are not salvation issues; So much dissension over things which the numerous and greatest theologians and scholars of history have been unable to agree upon as common truth. That tells me that all of this is over those things of which God has not yet fully revealed the entirety of truth to mankind.

It is nothing short of pride, in the spirit of the accuser, when we discount the grace of God in the elect, in favor of the doctrines of men. Brothers and sisters, let us never disparage the evidence of grace over that which is not, "in steadfast loyalty of heart remain faithful to the Lord Jesus Christ, the uncreated Son of God, by whom alone we can be saved."

Notes

Notes

Day 66

What's in a Name?

"Then Barnabas went to Tarsus to look for Saul. When he had found him, he brought him to Antioch. For a whole year they met with the church and taught a considerable crowd. And the disciples were first called Christians in Antioch." - Acts 11:25-26 MEV

What's in a name? In the first days, the Church counted themselves by several names, one of which we just saw - the Church. Alongside that, they call one another disciples, brethren, saints, and beloved, all five of which denote a relationship to Christ. We are the Church, the bride of Christ. We are His disciples, posted at His feet to learn from our Master. We are His brethren, united and welcomed into the family as adopted sons and daughters alongside the Only Begotten Son. We are His saints, upon whom the Righteousness of the Sinless One is imputed. We are His workmanship, born once, then born again with the sanctifying work of the Holy Spirit inside us bringing us into the likeness of the Lord.

But where did we come from?

We were estranged enemies of God (Col 1:21). We were darkness, and unwise fools (Eph 5:8, 15, 17). We were dead in our trespasses and sins - hopeless gentiles, apart from Christ (Eph 2:1, 11-12). "We also were once foolish, disobedient, deceived, serving various desires and pleasures, living in evil and envy, filled with hatred and hating each other" (Titus 3:3 MEV). We were lots of things, but none of which would I like to be called.

The city of Antioch held an interesting position in the Roman world. Called the "Queen of the East," "Gateway to the East," or the "First City of the East," it had been built by the former Seleucids, but embraced even more by the new Roman occupiers. Yet even as an occupied land, Antioch was given an unusual level of autonomy and religious freedom. As such, several groups lived out their religion side by side in the city. Licentious rituals with the harlot priestesses of Daphne abounded alongside the Pharisaic legalism of Judaism. Here, shameless sensuality and pious devotion bumped elbows.

It is here, in this land where various religions had been given liberty to continue undisturbed that we find one of the most important cities to the founding of Christianity. The Church remained here for centuries to come, but the Church didn't merely remain here. This was the kickoff point of Paul's three missionary journeys, as well as countless other missionary endeavors. It was through this town which the Name of Christ spread to all the world, and it was here that the disciples of Jesus Christ are first called Christians.

Some believe it was said with a sneer, while others say it arose merely out of necessity, as the heathen world began to recognize that these were not just a sect of the Jews. Already the saints were derided by jeers of "Nazarenes," or "Galileans," by the unbelieving Jews. Now they're called Christians. We know later in the history of the Church, the "Christians" were despised, but it's uncertain whether it began as an insult.

So, what's in a name? If the world is our friend, calling us by terms of endearment, we have reason to be concerned. If, on the other hand, the unbelieving world hates us, calling us names of contempt, we might just have reason to embrace such names. We'll soon see king Agrippa tell Paul, “In so brief an address you almost convince me to become a Christian," to which Paul responds, essentially, "I pray you and everyone here would become truly like me in this way." Clearly, he embraced such a title.

What does the world call you? Maybe our contemporary equivalent is "Jesus freak," or maybe that's even outdated, as now we're labeled "extremists." Do we embrace the insults as part of our fellowship with Christ? Call me what you will, but I am a Christian, a Jesus freak, an extremist because I hold to the age-old testimony in a world that's lost its collective mind. Call me what you will, but God calls me redeemed, and today, if this doesn’t describe you, He's calling out to you. Will you repent and believe? We too were once just like you, but Christ called us out of the darkness and into the light.

Day 67

Prophets in These Days

"In these days prophets came down from Jerusalem to Antioch. One of them, named Agabus, stood up and prophesied by the Spirit that there would be a great famine throughout all the world, which came to pass in the days of Claudius Caesar. Then every disciple, according to his ability, determined to send relief to the brothers who lived in Judea. Indeed, they did, and sent it to the elders by the hands of Barnabas and Saul." - Acts 11:27-30 MEV

"In these days" is rather vague, though we know it to be sometime shortly after Saul's conversion. If we glance ahead to the beginning of the next chapter though, we see "about that time" James, the brother of John, becomes the first Apostle martyred. That happened in 44AD, giving us the idea that this prophecy happened, most likely somewhere within 42-44AD. Claudius Caesar took power in 41AD and reigned for 13 years. There were several smaller famines throughout his administration, but one in particular fit the bill.

The Holy Spirit didn't give a timeline, but these Christians didn't have to wait long for the fulfillment of the prophecy. Beginning in 45AD, and lasting a few years, the annals of history show a famine which extended through the surrounding lands and hit Judea especially hard, causing many deaths by starvation. We're often approached with accusations there's no evidence that any of this biblical mumbo jumbo happened, but this is just one of thousands of examples of historical and archaeological discovery proving that the Word of God is true.

What of this prophet though? We see him again further into Luke's second treatise and again he foretells a troublesome omen. Otherwise though, he's left to obscurity, as I'd suggest could be the greatest hope of any servant of Christ; I must decrease that He may increase. Even so, I tend to believe there is a very direct clarification of doctrine here. Many would argue that since the first coming of Christ, the prophets of old are no more. They even have scriptural basis for this belief:

"God, who at various times and in diverse ways spoke long ago to the fathers through the prophets, has in these last days spoken to us by His Son, whom He has appointed heir of all things, and through whom He made the world." - Hebrews 1:1-2 MEV

Once, God spoke through prophets, but now He has spoken through His Son. "See? There are no more prophets!" Hmmm... Might we then ask, "What of Agabus?" The scriptures continue to talk about prophets even after Christ, placing them right up alongside the Apostles, but that's not necessarily the deciding factor in this debate. The office of prophet had always included two roles - teaching and inspiring in the word of God, and foretelling things to come. One might suggest that these New Testament prophets were just teachers, gifted in comprehension of the scriptures. That doesn't address Agabus though, among others. He stood up and prophesied by the Spirit of things to come.

Those who would make the prophets no more, endeavor to limit the power of God by their own interpretations. I'd rather not be counted as one to do such things. Their doctrinal cousins, on the other hand, suggest that the prophetic gift ended at the end of the Apostolic age. While I'd argue that there continued to be examples of the prophetic in the early Church, even after the last Apostle had gone, that's not scriptural evidence, upon which we must most highly rely. Yet in the same way, those who would make such an argument must discount their usage of the above passage in Hebrews, because the writer pens, "in *these* last days," as if what he told was already so.

I believe that we can easily reconcile Agabus and the prophets to the passage in Hebrews 1 when we consider that Agabus "prophesied by the Spirit." The Holy Spirit was sent by the Son, and came to indwell us because of the redeeming work of the Son. This prophet, just as any servant of God, was only able to work because it was Christ's work. He was nothing more than a willing vessel through which the Son of God continued His work of calling men to repentance, and building His Church.

Brothers and sisters, may we never find ourselves trying to squeeze God into a box of our own understanding. If He is outside our box, we must change the parameters of our understanding, not the parameters of our God. Even so, as discussed in more detail in my first book – Seeking the

Source: Choosing the Path of Wisdom - countless false prophets give us reason to not follow too closely on the heels of those who claim prophetic revelation. In the same manner, when one claims to speak a prophecy of God that definitively doesn't happen, that voice should not be heeded again. We know two witnesses come soon - God's prophets are not done - but don't be led astray by the false prophets.

Notes

Notes

Day 68

It Is All Christ

"About that time King Herod extended his hands to harm certain ones from the church. He killed James the brother of John with the sword. Seeing that it pleased the Jews, he proceeded further to arrest Peter also. This happened during the Days of Unleavened Bread." - Acts 12:1-3 MEV

What a curiously brief record of the martyrdom of an Apostle, wouldn't you say? I mean, consider how extensive the record of Stephen's martyrdom was, and he was a mere deacon. So why would Luke record nothing more than Herod Agrippa killed him by the sword, in the week of Passover, and it pleased the Jews?

You may remember when we parted ways with Luke's first treatise, we entered into the second on the precipice that this latter was truly "the Acts of Jesus Christ," not the Apostles. In chapter 12 we have one short sentence of this Apostolic martyrdom, and nowhere else in all of scripture are their deaths recorded.

That's not for lack of content though. Remember James the greater was an Apostle, labeled one of the two sons of thunder, and consistently one of the three in the most intimate inner circle of Christ Himself. We can be sure this man held a vital position in the early counsel of the Church. Even in the Church histories we have tradition of the importance of this death. The Church historian Eusebius records that the lost writings of Clement of Alexandria had told of how James' accuser had seen him firmly holding to the faith he professed, even before certain death, and was inspired to repent and believe. That tradition continues that this accuser then walked with James to his execution, asking forgiveness, to which James replied, "peace be upon you," and the two died side by side as brothers in Christ.

Yet Luke records simply, "He killed James the brother of John with the sword," because it wasn't about James. The extensive deposition of Stephen's stoning was necessary to show how Christ spread His Church to the four winds. Now in chapter 12, it is necessary to record this martyrdom of James, especially at this time, because it is the evidence that Jesus spoke the truth.

"He said to them, 'You will indeed drink from My cup and be baptized with the baptism that I am baptized with. But to sit at My right hand and at My left is not Mine to grant, but it is for those for whom it is prepared by My Father.' " - Matthew 20:23 MEV

In this brief record of James' death, we have a simple yet vital truth to our reading of the Bible. Brothers and sisters, whenever we open these pages, whether Old Testament or New, the lens by which we should read every one of these pages is that the entire Word of God is, in one way or another, about the Lord Jesus Christ. None of the characters within are recorded as a testimony about them, but rather as a testimony of the work of God.

Whether the Herods over whom God prevailed, raising James to eternal life with the honor bestowed on the martyrs, or the Elijahs through whom God prevailed, calling a nation to repentance, and condemning the hard-hearted kings; Whether the Peters and Pauls, whose blunders and ministrations are recorded in abundant detail, or the Bartholomews and Thaddeuses of whom we're told quite little; all of these characters are a testimony of the One who came down from glory, lived sinless, died as our sin, was resurrected on the third day, and went back up to glory, all so that we could be redeemed and called sons and daughters of God. All of this book testifies of Christ.

Notes

Day 69

Dress Yourself
Follow Me

"Then the angel said to him, 'Dress yourself and put your sandals on.' And he did so. Then he said to him, 'Wrap your cloak around you and follow me.' " - Acts 12:8 MEV

We're told in verse 9 that Peter thought he was seeing a vision, such as the one so recently recorded on the rooftop of Joppa. The misunderstanding is entirely reasonable, or at least, far more than the reality of the thing.

Herod has placed Peter under heavy guard. The night watch was four quaternions of soldiers, that is, four groups of four, taking three-hour shifts. Behind the main, iron gate, a second gate was found with a guard. Beyond that gate, another gate and another guard. Inside the cell lay a sleeping prisoner with each hand chained respectively to each of two guards. Then "the chains fell off his hands" (Acts 12:7 MEV).

For days on end Peter has remained so heavily guarded by a community that no doubt remembered the previous liberation of the Apostles from these walls. For days on end, "fervent and persistent prayer for him was being made to God by the church" (Acts 12:5 AMP). For days on end everything appeared certain that Herod's ruling was already decided; Peter's execution was imminent; So imminent that this is even apparently the last shift of the night, for they didn't discover him gone until daybreak. Yet it is a vivid picture of the peace we have in Christ that we find the Apostle sleeping on what was expected to be his last night on Earth.

Chapter 12 is wrought with imagery but at the present we see, "dress yourself... Follow me." A more direct translation here is gird yourself, as in wrap your loose garment tight about your loins to prepare for action. Yet I think dress yourself is as good an interpretation as any, considering the command continues "put your sandals on. Wrap your cloak around you." There's another passage we commonly know as dress yourself, which in the Greek was also gird, and I believe that there is no coincidence in the comparison of the two.

"Truly, truly I say to you, when you were young, you dressed yourself and walked where you desired. But when you are old, you will stretch out your hands, and another will dress you and carry you where you do not want to go.' He said this, signifying by what kind of death he would glorify God. When He had said this, He said to him, 'Follow Me.' " - John 21:18-19 MEV

There's not a doubt in my mind that God ordained for Peter to be asleep with his garments laid aside so that these words would inform him, with no room in his mind for a shadow of a doubt, that it was not yet his time to die. Many years later, either Peter, or John Mark relating what he'd heard from Peter, told Luke these words with great specificity. Apparently it didn't slip the Apostle's notice either. Dress yourself and follow me, it is not yet time for another to dress you and carry you against your will. I daresay those aren't the only words of the Lord that Peter dwelt on as he pondered the Angel's command.

"Will he not rather say to him, 'Prepare my supper, and dress yourself and serve me until I eat and drink. And afterward you will eat and drink'?" - Luke 17:8 MEV

If you followed our study of Luke's Gospel, you may remember that Jesus taught the disciples that we have full access to the power of God, even by the minutest faith, though we are to grow in faith. He continues, teaching that as long as we live, we are to serve the Master, and He balanced that with the truth that there's no amount of service that can make us worthy of His grace.

In that prison cell, Peter was reminded of his humble human frailty, and he was reminded of the calling on His life to "feed my sheep." The Apostle wasn't yet ordained to die a martyr's sacrifice, but he was still to breathe and walk as a living sacrifice.

Do we need Him enough to pray without cease?
Do we trust Him enough to sleep in peace?
Do we serve Him enough our loins to gird?
Do we love Him enough to follow our Lord?

Sometimes we'll wait in unanswered prayer until the last minute, but it's in those last minutes we so often see the Lord save. Trust, in faith, for the Peace of God surpasses all understanding. Serve in worthlessness, the

Lord who alone is worthy. "Love the Lord your God with all your heart and with all your soul, and with all your mind" (Mt 22:37 MEV) and follow Him.

Notes

Notes

Day 70

Gathered Together

"Realizing this, he came to the house of Mary, the mother of John, whose other name was Mark, where many were gathered together praying." - Acts 12:12 MEV

In the immediate threat of Herod Agrippa's new persecution, we don't find the Church gathered to the temple in prayer, though it may be they yet visited there in the daylight hours. We don't find the Church gathered in all their number in the streets in front of the prison, neither praying nor mourning for Peter's forthcoming final breath. On the other hand, we don't find them all scattered to their homes in secret solitude. Where do we see the church but gathered together in homes, praying through the night. The danger necessitated their hiding, but it couldn't stop them from fellowship and prayer.

"When dangers increase around us and our friends, we should become more fervent in prayer. While life remains we may pray; and even when there is no human hope, and we have no power to heal or deliver, still God may interpose, as he did here, in answer to prayer." - Albert Barnes

This final night, before which Herod would bring charge against Peter, many were gathered together praying. When they finally answered the door and the Apostle was given the chance to narrate what happened, he instructed them to tell the others. Possibly there were several homes in which believers spent this crucial night in supplication. Otherwise, maybe this was believers taking shifts to assure that constant prayers were made in such tumultuous days. Yet what we know is that many were here, hiding behind a locked door, though not all were in attendance.

Granted, it's quite likely that at this time there were still too many disciples in Jerusalem to gather in one home, but even so, there's a lesson in this gathering, and I'd suggest it's one which we quite recently witnessed in the modern Church.

Do you, like me, remember 2020 as if it just happened? The lockdowns, the government orders to close our fellowships, the restrictions on gatherings, and the pastors and churches faced with criminal charges and fines for refusing to bar their doors? In that time, we learned a lot of things about church, one of which was the importance of home church gatherings. The Church was widely reduced to video sermons and digital worship sets. We lost the gathering of the saints; the fellowship of our brethren. Many never returned.

Yet in that time, those who had life groups, home groups, or whatever name you may call them - brothers and sisters in Christ, gathering to converse on the things of God and worship Him together - at least those who continued to meet, found the enormity of necessity of such fellowship. Ask men or women who continued to gather in homes, and I believe you'll get a consistent answer that it was a vital blessing in their faith walk.

Lockdowns or not, we were made for fellowship, not just on Sunday mornings. We were made to gather, and to break bread together. We were reborn into a family, and that family is better in unity. I believe that we'll soon see more of the extreme necessity of home groups, such as we recently experienced, though maybe through different means. Will you be prepared next time? Whose house will you gather at to pray? Or how about this: in the meantime, with whom are you gathering between Sundays to continue in the worship and walk with Christ?

Notes

Day 71

Struck by the Lord

"On an appointed day, Herod, dressed in royal apparel, sat on his throne and gave a public speech to them. The mob shouted, 'It is the voice of a god, and not of a man!' Immediately an angel of the Lord struck him, because he did not give God the glory. And he was eaten by worms and died." - Acts 12:21-23 MEV

In a single chapter of Luke's history, we see two men struck by an angel of the Lord, with two extremely different outcomes. In his typical form, our beloved physician gives medical specifics as to the latter. It appears he believed the king suffered from an acute parasitic infestation. The doctor is not the only source of information from which we have knowledge of Herod Agrippa's curse though.

The Roman-Jewish historian Josephus, who was a young boy under Herodian rule at the time, wrote of this as well. From those records we know that Herod was struck immediately; This wasn't some imagined and far-fetched causation. Josephus records that shortly after he didn't rebuke the crowd, Herod saw an owl perch on a rope behind him, and he instantly recognized it as an omen against his transgression. He didn't even get a chance to go home, but was immediately struck with agonizing pain in his abdomen. So terrible it was, that he was carried out of the place. Five miserable days later he took his last breath.

"But the word of God spread and increased." - Acts 12:24 MEV

Two men were struck by an angel of the Lord. The one, who lived by faith, was granted an impossible rescue. The other, in knowledge of the scriptures of God, accepted blasphemous glory to himself as the pagan kings often did, and was repaid an agonizing death. Two men were struck by an angel of the Lord. The same strike that saved one's life, poured wrath out upon the other.

Peter lay asleep in prison awaiting his sentence in the peace of God, and was set free from his impending doom. Herod had heard the Christian report yet he hardened himself. Oh yes, Herod had heard, but he denied

Christ, persecuted His people, and suffered the weight of the wrath of God. The truth of the matter is, we all deserve that fate. We all belong under the wrath of the Good and Righteous Judge.

"When His disciples heard this, they were greatly amazed, saying, 'Who then can be saved?' But Jesus looked at them and said, 'With men this is impossible, but with God all things are possible.' " - Matthew 19:25-26 MEV

Today two men will hear the Gospel. One will repent and believe and find himself the beneficiary of an impossible rescue. The other will refuse and the weight of justice for which he's already condemned himself will fall heavily upon him. Today two men will be struck by the message of God, with very different outcomes. Will that strike be life undeserved, or agonizing death fully earned? Your choice.

"For to those who are perishing, the preaching of the cross is foolishness, but to us who are being saved it is the power of God." - 1 Corinthians 1:18 MEV

Notes

Day 72

Power

"So, being sent out by the Holy Spirit, they went down to Seleucia, and from there they sailed to Cyprus. When they arrived at Salamis, they preached the word of God in the synagogues of the Jews. And they had John as an assistant. When they had gone through the whole island to Paphos..." - Acts 13:4-6a MEV

With the prophets and teachers of Antioch having laid hands on two men, we now see the outset of the first evangelical mission to the gentiles. Paul, and Barnabas, the Levite of Cyprus, are sent out to preach the Gospel, and the latter's nephew, John Mark, goes with them. This missionary journey makes a direct path to the nearest port, from whence a couple hours' sail lands them on the mining island after which the metal copper takes its name.

This island, like Antioch, had lust filled pagan rituals abounding alongside legalistic Jewish Pharisaism. We see these two men (and their assistant) go through the whole island, from synagogue to synagogue, preaching Christ first among the Jewish population, as Paul made the modus operandi throughout his successive missions. Barnabas, being from here, would have special influence among the locals, making this a good starting point for this journey, but he couldn't have known them all.

History records just a handful of decades later, during the reign of emperor Trajan, that a band of Jews here rose up against Rome and killed what some supposed to be 240,000 Greek civilian inhabitants of the island. Something of that magnitude implies a decent number of Jewish militants, though some of them may have immigrated from the destruction of Jerusalem. That said, this is after many were converted to Christ, so we're given the impression that many Jews were here. Saul and Barnabas had quite the task recorded in a short sentence: "they preached the word of God in the synagogues of the Jews."

Considering the connection to copper, I present you with an analogy which is quite personal to me. I don't write for a living; I am a power lineman, carefully wrangling thousands, and tens of thousands of volts of electric power daily. Wires made of aluminum or copper carry vast quantities of power throughout the land. As the following description is laid out, I implore you to consider the parallels within to God, His Holy Spirit, His evangelist servants, the trials and tribulations they face, and the souls of men and women exposed to the power of God.

It all starts at what we call the source. This is some form of generator (a power creator) that may be a coal fired plant, a nuclear reactor, a solar array, a wind farm, hydroelectric dam, a gas turbine, or more. From there the power is stepped up in voltage to be efficiently carried hundreds of miles. Long spans of aluminum wire (wound with steel strands for strength) carry power from the source to substations around the world. There the voltages are again lowered to either sub-transmission (for shorter distances of transport) or distribution voltages (for local delivery to your home, or business).

These distribution circuits run throughout your neighborhoods, but still being at voltages far above what your home can handle, must be again stepped down by the transformer on a pad in your backyard, or maybe on the pole out front. It's at this point you can finally see the power. Your bulbs illuminate, your stove heats up, your laundry spins, your clocks tell the time. We call that the load.

Behind the scenes are the linemen. We don't flip the switch on your living room wall to keep you out of the dark, but without us, the power would have never arrived to superheat that filament or to excite those fluorescent molecules. On the other hand, without us, other linemen would be trained and equipped to complete the job. Individually we mean little. Occasionally a storm passes through, knocking down the lines, but the linemen respond in the face of danger, and the means of distribution are restored; the power inevitably flows again. In the meantime, some homes have their own connections to power. Gas generators, backup power supplies, batteries, solar panels and the like keep your lights on.

The power lines are dangerous, but in a good way. To the man in the hospital, they deliver the power to operate the machine by which he's healed. To the man who handles them foolishly, death is an agonizing guarantee. To one they are life, to another death. They can illuminate the most gorgeous displays, or ignite the most ferocious fires. The power lines are properly to be feared, but for the lineman, if that respective fear is replaced by paralyzing fear, then being out of a job is far better than the gruesome alternative.

God is our one source, His power sufficient to light the universe. For 2,000 years, His Holy Spirit has been equipping, training, and sending "linemen" to build the lines by which His Gospel travels throughout the land. The line Barnabas and Paul currently built was copper, through Cyprus - a local distribution circuit. But they would soon follow through to build transmission lines across the region, assuring the power of God lit up men and women everywhere. For generations, servants of the Most High, God, have delivered His redeeming power near and far.

Sometimes persecutions have arisen which temporarily hindered the regular missionary flow of that power, but that has never kept individual homes from their connection to God, and those persecutions have always given way to find that Jesus Christ is still here.

The missionaries, preachers, and teachers are the workers through which God has ordained to spread His message, but while their work is crucial, they are not. If Paul had refused or failed, God would have known that and a different worker would have been chosen; God's plan is not hindered.

The power of God is dangerous. Dangerous yet life saving to our old selves, as we die with Christ and are born again new. Dangerous to the unrepentant sinner who upon hearing he is offered free mercy, chooses to refuse; He will only solidify his own agonizing destruction. Most dangerous indeed to the careless preacher, not exercising extreme caution with the Word.

To one, this Word of God is life, abundant, full, and eternal. To another, it is fearful and deadly power. We ought all to tremble before God, whose power, righteousness, and glory should leave us all to burn; Even so, glory be His, for that same God is merciful and abounding in grace. We need not seize where we stand, but step forward, flip the switch, and let his illuminating power make us lights in a dark world.

Paul and Barnabas had a heavy load, but the Source had sufficient capacity for it all.

Notes

Day 73

The War Has Been Won

"When they had gone through the whole island to Paphos, they found a certain sorcerer, a Jewish false prophet, whose name was Bar-Jesus, who was with the proconsul, Sergius Paulus, an intelligent man. This man called for Barnabas and Saul and sought to hear the word of God. But Elymas the sorcerer (which is his name by interpretation) opposed them, trying to divert the proconsul from the faith." - Acts 13:6-8 MEV

Through the Old Testament we saw many prophecies and laws against taking up the sorceries of the heathens, but not so many direct examples of men doing so. Now, in the time of Jesus and His founding of the Church, on the other hand, sorcerers and self-proclaimed magi are seen time and time again. It is not hard to draw the connection as to why this sudden uptick of examples can be found in the scriptures when we read chapter 13 of Acts. What we find in these pages is a false-prophet by the name of Son of Jesus.

Although sorcerers, false prophets, and magi were nothing new, it has been reckoned throughout the ages that this escalation was a strategic move of Satan. The stories of the miracles which Jesus had done spread far and wide. How could they not? Blind men saw, lame men walked, lepers became clean, and thousands ate to satisfaction from small lunch sized portions of food. The dead rose to life for Christ's sake! Not too often you get to use that phrase without taking His name in vain, eh? The reputation of Jesus Christ preceded the missionary preachers in their travels.

In this time, the enemy devised a scheme by which he sought to discredit these stories, and so he sent out his servants to perform tricks which would make those stories seem distant in comparison, common in their experience, or phony, mythical trickery. Look at this sorcerer, and his names. He took upon himself the name Elymas (the Arabian equivalent of magus or wise man), but his name was son of Jesus. People on Cyprus, having heard stories of Jesus, got to witness the false prophecies and sorceries of this bar-jesus. What does God, through Paul, by His Holy Spirit call him though?

"Then Saul, who also is called Paul, filled with the Holy Spirit, stared at him and said, 'You son of the devil, enemy of all righteousness, full of deceit and of all fraud, will you not cease perverting the right ways of the Lord?' " - Acts 13:9-10 MEV

The enemy positioned these sorts of men as an attack, but God has already won this war, and this supposed Son of Jesus is revealed to be a son of the devil. The people called him a wise prophet, but God revealed him to be "full of all kinds of deceit and trickery" (CSB). The sorcerer opposed them, afraid of losing his influence if the proconsul came to faith in Christ, and God calls him "enemy of everything that is right and good" (AMP). Oh yes, these sorcerers and false prophets, whom Jesus warned would come, were indeed positioned strategically across the battle field, but this war has already been won.

" 'Now, look! The hand of the Lord is against you, and you shall be blind, not seeing the sun for a time.' Immediately mist and darkness fell on him, and he went about seeking someone to lead him by the hand. When the proconsul saw what had happened, he believed and was astonished at the doctrine of the Lord." - Acts 13:11-12 MEV

What of this proconsul, on the other end of the spectrum? He is a testimony that God's word is true. Luke was God's chosen vessel to record the founding of the Bride of Christ, and with due cause. He was a physician given to record history with precise detail. The mere fact of Sergius Paulus being labeled the proconsul becomes one of millions of testimonies of the truth of these pages.

Roman provinces were divided into two classes. Those lands which needed Roman soldiers to keep the peace remained under the emperor's authority, and the garrisons would be governed by Prætors. The other, more submissive and peaceful lands, Augustus handed over to the Senate, who governed the land by a Proconsul. Augustus originally claimed Cyprus to himself, but eventually handed the land back over to the Senate, hence the Proconsul. During the later rule of Claudius, Cyprus was governed by a Proconsul.

As for Sergius Paulus, secular authors of the time confirm what Luke records is true, and archaeological discoveries throughout the centuries confirm it. I'll leave a link below, which I'd encourage you to take a few moments to read, because the evidence of history and archaeology in this passage, as in so many others, affirms this faith to which we hold. We must walk by faith, not by sight, but God did not leave us without the proofs of our faith.

https://biblearchaeologyreport.com/2019/11/15/sergius-paulus-an-archaeological-biography/?fbclid=IwAR3auerzDwGAoBUC0csnC93WfpRxAJ7wR_se6CMO46jimRA-4V4QWcr31KI

Notes

Notes

Day 74

Continue On

"Now Paul and his companions set sail from Paphos and came to Perga in Pamphylia. And John left them and returned to Jerusalem, but they went on from Perga and came to Antioch in Pisidia. And on the Sabbath day they went into the synagogue and sat down." - Acts 13:13-14 ESV

We're never told exactly why John Mark left the service to which he had committed. We know he didn't leave the faith, as he later returns eagerly to mission work, joins himself to Peter, writing the Apostle's testimony, and even becomes Paul's fellow worker and "a great comfort to me" in Paul's imprisonment. They do find reconciliation, but first Paul is clearly not impressed by whatever excuse John Mark gives for his abandonment, and it becomes a source of contention between Paul and Barnabas the next time we see them all together.

Could it be that after leaving Cyprus, from where Barnabas hailed, and where surely his cousin had connections, the young man was not as eager to go to a foreign people? Possibly the famine in Judea gave him cause to return and serve his widowed mother in Jerusalem. Or maybe it had to do with the terrain? When Paul spoke of his travels, and "perils of rivers and perils of robbers," this was one of those lands to which he referred.

"On frequent journeys, in danger from rivers, danger from robbers, danger from my own people, danger from Gentiles, danger in the city, danger in the wilderness, danger at sea, danger from false brothers;" - 2 Corinthians 11:26 ESV

The journey from Perga to Antioch in Pisidia (one of 16 cities that the founder of the Seleucid empire, Seleucus, built and named after his father) was a treacherous land. These mountains were littered with perilous rivers, and have throughout history been a haunt of bandits and robbers. Maybe John Mark turned back for fear, or for discomfort, or maybe for a sense of familial duty, but he turned back all the same. Alexander McLaren offers up an extended monologue on this desertion, but for the sake of space I'll resort to sharing just one of his conclusions which currently speaks directly into my life. Maybe it will into yours as well.

"And so in regard to every career which has in it anything of honour and of effort, let John Mark teach us the lesson not swiftly to begin and inconsiderately to venture upon a course, but once begun to let nothing discourage, 'nor bate one jot of heart or hope, but still bear up and steer right onward.' " - McLaren

John, called Mark, may not have continued, but Christ's Gospel cannot be stopped. Barnabas and Paul went into the synagogue and sat down, as teachers - an honor that was affirmed when the rulers of the synagogue invited them to speak to the people. Their preaching will be our topic of study for probably a few days, but today let's leave off with a "word of encouragement for the people" (vs 15).

Brothers and sisters, we are called to be a holy people, an offering unto the Lord. We were not taken out of the world but while still in it were given the Comforter, the Helper, the good and eternal Spirit of counsel. Whether in our ministries and volunteer services, in our hobbies and explorations, or in our careers and studies, can we take warning from one, and encouragement from two, that we would not turn back, but continue steadfast and faithful once a decision has been made. Nothing can stop that which God ordains, and even if we come across a roadblock, or a peril, we can simply readjust our sights to seek the direction His path takes us.

At the same time, must we never leap swiftly to a journey which has not been thoroughly considered. If we are in Christ, and He in us, we have the Holy Spirit to guide us, and our brothers and sisters in the family of Christ to consult. Make use of what we've been given, and don't go it alone. The Christian without God, isn't. The Christian without the Church is an easy target.

Notes

Day 75

The Same God

"So Paul stood up, and motioning with his hand said: 'Men of Israel and you who fear God, listen. The God of this people Israel chose our fathers and made the people great during their stay in the land of Egypt, and with uplifted arm he led them out of it. And for about forty years he put up with them in the wilderness.' " - Acts 13:16-18 ESV

Up until this point we've heard that Paul spoke boldly in the name of Jesus Christ, but we haven't yet seen how he orates the Good News such as we witnessed from Peter and Stephen. We can take special note as we read through his sermon that it is very comparable to Stephen's defense. As the young deacon had spoken boldly in the face of death, you may remember, Paul oversaw those who stoned him. For the Apostle to the Gentiles to now so closely mimic that apologia not only assures us the seed which Stephen planted was not crushed under those stones, but it also confirms Luke's claims that Paul "spoke boldly." Think about it. Saul had personally approved of Hellenists murdering someone he had heard speak these words, and now in a synagogue full of Hellenists, he duplicates them. That is audacious faith.

But the pattern of Peter and Stephen's addresses - beginning with the scriptures of old in a manner that affirms this is the same God and doctrine under which they have so long lived - is ever so minutely altered here in a way that connects his sermon to their response. Keep in mind that although in each town and city Paul always preached to the Jews first and then to the gentiles, he was, specifically, God's chosen vessel to take the Gospel to the latter. In one town after another, he went and preached to the "men of Israel and you who fear God" (Jews and proselytes), and in each of those places some believed, while others hardened themselves in the manner of a different god.

'But when the Jews saw the crowds, they were filled with jealousy and began to contradict what was spoken by Paul, reviling him. And Paul and Barnabas spoke out boldly, saying, 'It was necessary that the word of God be spoken first to you. Since you thrust it aside and judge yourselves unworthy of eternal life, behold, we are turning to the Gentiles.' " - Acts 13:45-46 ESV

We've before seen one who in jealousy contradicted the word spoken, trying to separate mankind from God. The "god of this world," our enemy the devil, took this same tact right from the start, though it began in mere deception and only later grew to violence, stirring up persecution.

This week, Paul presented salvation to all the men of Israel, and some of those found their names in the book of life, but the next week, others were filled with jealousy, and Paul says something I'd like to discuss more thoroughly in coming days; "you thrust it aside and judge yourselves unworthy of eternal life." A stark contrast is found therein.

"For I am not ashamed of the gospel, for it is the power of God for salvation to everyone who believes, to the Jew first and also to the Greek." - Romans 1:16 ESV

The Apostle to the Gentiles came into town, but first he preached the Good News of God to "this people Israel." He began by declaring the truth, much like Stephen had, that this was not a new God he preached, but the newest revelation of the God who had always been their God. Throughout the histories Paul recited, they had a God who long-sufferingly "endured their conduct" (vs 18 MEV), blessing and multiplying them toward a future plan. Now that this plan had been unveiled though, many outright refused the God they claimed to serve. Even that was long foretold.

The everlasting God is the same God from beginning to end. He is the Alpha and Omega, the First and the Last, who has never changed. So, what did change then? The plan progressed, nothing more. From the very start, God ordained the salvation of all the world through this people, Israel, and from the very start, he knew each one of us who would gain eternal life. A knowledge that I am certain brought Him much sorrow was that some would judge themselves unworthy of eternal life and reject Him - even some who were so near as to teach from his scriptures every Sabbath.

When we read Paul's exhortation, remember that it was all framed in the truth that this Christ he preached was the same God who rescued them from Egypt, and the same God who endured their transgressions in the wilderness. Whether we read Old Testament or New, we're reading the same story of salvation that never changes; We are reading of the same God with the same heart and the same purpose. There is no distinct "God of the Old Testament and God of the New Testament." All of this was spoken, endured, and fulfilled so that we whom satan deceived could be reconciled to the God who so loved us.

Notes

Notes

Day 76

God's King

"Then they requested a king. And God gave them Saul the son of Kish, a man of the tribe of Benjamin, for forty years. When He had removed him, He raised up David to be their king, of whom He testified, saying, 'I have found David the son of Jesse, a man after My own heart, who will fulfill My entire will.' From this man's descendants God has raised a Savior for Israel, Jesus, according to His promise." - Acts 13:21-23 MEV

"Then they requested a king." Look back over the previous few verses at what Paul is describing

- God chose their fathers
- God made them prosper in Egypt
- God led them out of Egyptian captivity
- God restrained His wrath against their conduct in the desert
- God cleansed their promised land of wicked men
- God anointed theocratic rulers for them

Then they requested a king. My friends can't you see? A most unexplainably benevolent Monarch you already had! Yet in the manner of the patriarch Adam, you rejected Him, and in the manner of your idolatrous ancestors preferred one of your own making. Oh brothers, can't you see? You authored your own sorrows. Yet One greater than you would not be hindered to author your salvation.

God gave them Saul, who would never be able to fulfill the blessing of Israel, for he was not of the tribe of Judah. As was warned, the kings, starting with Saul, were not an answered prayer, but rather, a curse which would bring centuries of suffering. Even David, though a man after God's own heart, brought some havoc in the land as a result of his sins.

In the typical manner of teachers of his day, Paul quotes various scriptures in one blended sentence. A Psalm, a prophecy and more. The source of the last portion, "who will fulfill my entire will," is a bit of a mystery unless it is an extrapolation from the greater text. But did David fulfill God's entire will? Consider Elijah.

After fleeing from Jezebel, we find Elijah sulking in the wilderness. God speaks to the prophet and tells him to get up and get back to work; he shall anoint three men (1 Kings 19:15-18). Of those three, Elijah himself anointed but one, yet that one became his spiritual son, Elisha. Elisha received the inheritance of the firstborn, the double portion. It is then Elisha who anoints the second man, and subsequently one of Elisha's spiritual sons (Elijah's spiritual grandson) who anoints the third. Elijah fulfilled God's will for his life through his legacy.

Consider then what Paul is saying here. David is a man who will fulfill God's entire will, and so from David's descendants Jesus was raised. Oh "sons of the family of Abraham and those of you who fear God" (Acts 13:26 MEV) can't you see? To their demise they requested a king, but for our salvation God raised up the King.

" 'We preach to you good news: The promise which was made to the fathers, God has fulfilled to us, their children, raising Jesus. As it is written in the second Psalm: "You are My Son; today I have become Your Father." ' " - Acts 13:32-33 MEV

All throughout the Gospels, and this book of Acts, we're told that through Jesus the scriptures are fulfilled, and especially so in Matthew's gospel. At the time of publishing, my pastor, Paul Mowery, is in the midst of expounding on that Gospel, in his verse-by-verse study of the bible. For any who would like to study along with us, you can find our services on the Harvest Fellowship app, on YouTube, or come join us at Harvest Fellowship on Wallen Rd in Ft Wayne, Indiana.

"After John was put in prison, Jesus came to Galilee preaching the gospel of the kingdom of God, saying, 'The time is fulfilled, and the kingdom of God is at hand. Repent and believe the gospel.' " - Mark 1:14-15 MEV

Brothers and sisters, can't you see? The King is on His throne. Nothing else matters. The entire will of God prevails. If, then, God is for us, who can be against us? There is no chance that you will be lost, for in Christ God's good will for you has already been fulfilled. In Christ we have a King that was not made by the hands of men. We may have authored our judgement, but the Son of God authored our salvation. Take heart. Christ has overcome the world.

Day 77

To Know Him

"From this man's descendants God has raised a Savior for Israel, Jesus, according to His promise. Before His coming John had preached a baptism of repentance to all the people of Israel. As John was fulfilling his course, he said, 'Who do you think I am? I am not He. But look! He is coming after me, the sandals of whose feet I am not worthy to untie.' " - Acts 13:23-25 MEV

Throughout his exhortation in Antioch of Pisidia, Paul refers repeatedly to the promises, and "the prophets which are read every Sabbath" (vs 27 MEV). To the Gentiles, the Apostle will have to explain the full Gospel, beginning with the need for atonement and reconciliation to Jehovah, but to these Hellenist Jews, who had always lived under Mosaic Law, what was necessary was merely to help them "know Him" (vs 27).

So, of what does he speak saying, "according to the promise"? We can't really nail it down to one scripture, and yet, the promise is the same promise that has been spoken from the beginning. Remember it is the seed of the woman, Eve, who is promised to trod on the head of the serpent (Gen 3). It is the seed of Abraham through which "all families of the earth will be blessed" (Gen 12 MEV). It is the seed of Isaac of which the promise is repeated (Gen 26). It is Jacob's seed that again holds that promise (Gen 28).

It is the seed of Judah from which the scepter is promised never to depart; that same seed which shall wash His garments in wine (Gen 49). From Judah rose David, son of Jesse. The seed of David is promised a throne established forever (2 Sam 7). That promise is held and repeated over and over again. There was not a Jew in all the earth who didn't know the Messiah comes from the seed of David, the seed of Jesse, the seed of Judah, the seed of Israel, the seed of Isaac, the seed of Abraham, the seed of the woman.

"The Lord swore an oath to David, a promise he will not abandon: 'I will set one of your offspring on your throne.' " - Psalms 132:11 CSB

But when we look at the promise to David's son, Solomon, there's a sudden change. Solomon is promised the throne, only so long as he and his seed remain faithful to the Lord, and it came to pass that in 587BC the family of David, lost the throne. Jesus was the adopted seed of Solomon, from His step-dad Joseph, but He was the direct seed of David, by His mother Mary.

"When your time comes and you rest with your ancestors, I will raise up after you your descendant, who will come from your body, and I will establish his kingdom. He is the one who will build a house for my name, and I will establish the throne of his kingdom forever. I will be his father, and he will be my son." - 2 Samuel 7:12-14a CSB

This promise spoke directly of Solomon filling David's seat and building the first temple, but it couldn't be fulfilled in any mere man. So many of these prophecies spoke in the immediate hereafter, such as Solomon, the son of David, while at the same time speaking in the eternal, of Jesus Christ, the Son of God. The tree of Davidic kings was cutoff at the Babylonian exile, but from the stump a shoot emerged.

"And there shall come forth a shoot from the stump of Jesse, and a Branch shall grow out of his roots." - Isaiah 11:1 MEV

The stump was cut down, but Paul assures the Jews in Antioch of Pisidia that this Jesus (Greek form of the name Joshua), is the promised seed, as testified by John the Baptist. This Jeshua is the promised branch. Again, we can look to "the prophets which are read every Sabbath," and see that while some of those prophecies spoke directly into the lives of men living in their day or shortly thereafter, they couldn't be completely fulfilled by men.

"Hear this, O Joshua the high priest, you and your friends sitting before you, for these men are a sign. I am bringing My servant, the Branch. The stone that I have set before Joshua, on that single stone is seven eyes. And I will engrave an inscription, says the Lord of Hosts, and I will remove the iniquity of this land in one day. "On that day, says the Lord of Hosts, each of you will invite your companion to come and sit under the vine and under the fig tree." - Zechariah 3:8-10 MEV

It is only by our eternal High Priest, Jesus Christ, and what was done the one day in which He died for us, that iniquity could be removed. It is only through that Branch, the seed of David, by which we can be saved. His friends sitting before Him became His witnesses and a sign. The son of Jehozadak became, like so many others, a type - a symbol - of the Messiah. Yet it is Jesus Christ who raises up the eternal temple of the Lord.

"Take the silver and gold and make a crown, and set it on the head of Joshua, the son of Jehozadak, the high priest. And say to him: Thus says the Lord of Hosts: Here is a man whose name is Branch; for he shall branch out from his place, and he shall build the temple of the Lord. It is he who shall build the temple of the Lord; he shall bear the glory, and shall sit and rule on his throne. He shall be a priest on his throne, and the counsel of peace shall be between them both." - Zechariah 6:11-13 MEV

What Paul now spoke to these Hellenists was that the name they'd heard, of Jesus of Nazareth, was the name of their eternal King. No mere man could sit forever on the throne, but no mere god could be the seed of David. In this perfect Son of God, fully man, and fully God, we have the fulfillment of the promise. It came through as hundreds of promises throughout scripture, but it all boiled down to one promise:

"Therefore, brothers, let it be known to you that through this Man forgiveness of sins is proclaimed to you, and by Him everyone who believes is justified from everything from which you could not be justified by the Law of Moses." - Acts 13:38-39 MEV

Brothers and sisters, I encourage you this morning to take a moment to dwell on the glory of the Lord, and the infinitely perfect web which he has woven for us. The promise is true.

Notes

Notes

Day 78

Jesus Christ Lived, Died, and Rose Again

"Because those who live in Jerusalem, and their rulers, did not know Him, in condemning Him they have fulfilled the voices of the Prophets which are read every Sabbath. Though they found in Him no cause worthy of death, yet they asked Pilate to have Him killed. When they had fulfilled all that was written of Him, they took Him down from the tree and placed Him in a tomb. But God raised Him from the dead, and for many days He appeared to those who came up with Him from Galilee to Jerusalem, who are now His witnesses to the people." - Acts 13:27-31 MEV

Sure, I'd like to keep moving forward with our study, but a fruitless study it is if we take not every opportunity to dwell on this truth; that Jesus Christ lived, died, and rose again is the core tenet of this entire book, and it is the only reason we should ever find need to open these pages.

"Now the Apostle has reached the heart of his sermon. He has come to the great cornerstone of the Christian faith. There are no embellishments here - not even an anecdote or an illustration - but just a plain declaration of the great facts of the life and death and resurrection of Jesus Christ. These are the backbone of the gospel, and the more we dwell on these facts, the better." - Charles Spurgeon

Were it not for the life, death, and resurrection of Jesus Christ, there is nothing but ancient history in these pages. If Israel's Messiah had not come to reign, been rejected by His own, been sent down to death, yet lived forever more, then the prophets of old, found in this book, are nothing but liars. Had it not been that the only begotten Son of God condescended to become man like us, lived sinless, died judicially as sin in our stead, and lived again, to reign forevermore, then the Holy Spirit would not live inside us to instruct us from what's beyond the covers of our Bibles.

Without that Savior - without that Spirit He sent - what is written here would avail us nothing. There may be moral lessons within, but we could never attain their fulfillment. There may be guiding truths within, but the path would lead to the same end. There may be great revelations of the foundations of the earth and heavens within, but our grasp of science would yet lead us to false understandings. Without that, it would not be worth the paper it is printed on, but glory to God, for Jesus Christ lived, died, and rose again!

"For I delivered to you first of all that which I also received: how Christ died for our sins according to the Scriptures, was buried, rose again the third day according to the Scriptures, and was seen by Cephas, and then by the twelve. Then He was seen by over five hundred brothers at once, of whom the greater part remain to this present time, though some have passed away. Then He was seen by James and then by all the apostles. Last of all, He was seen by me also, as by one born at the wrong time." - 1 Corinthians 15:3-8 MEV

Sufficient evidence exists of Jesus of Nazareth's life and death on the cross that even atheist scholars - we can reject the baseless bloggers and screaming journalists here - admit that there is nothing but absolute truth in Jesus' existence as a real character of history. The first century Roman historian Tacitus, for example, wrote, "Christus, the founder of the name, was put to death by Pontius Pilate, procurator of Judea in the reigning of Tiberius."

Even the histories of those who cursed Him and demanded his death record his existence. In the Babylonian Talmud (the rabbinic records of post exilic Judaism) a section related to the Sanhedrin records this Jesus was brought before the court, having led many Jews astray, and was crucified on the eve of the Passover.

Any legitimate study of history shows the truth of our claim that Christ lived and died. Yet a person might still claim that there are no secular reports that Jesus Christ was resurrected to live again. Well of course there aren't! If there were, they wouldn't be called secular at all! Those are Christian texts, of which there are plenty.

Look at what Paul writes to the Corinthians, as quoted above: "Then He was seen by over five hundred brothers at once, *of whom the greater part remain to this present time*." The very fact that Christianity wasn't squashed from the get go is evidence that hundreds of men and women claimed to have seen the risen Savior. If it had not been so, then none would have ever given these few swindlers the time of day. Even so, Josephus, an unbelieving first century Jew, was at least a historian enough to record their claim.

"At this time, there was a wise man who was called Jesus. And his conduct was good, and he was known to be virtuous. And many people from among the Jews and other nations became his disciples. Pilate condemned him to be crucified and to die. And those who had become his disciples did not abandon his discipleship. They reported that he had appeared to them after his crucifixion and that he was alive; accordingly, he was perhaps the Messiah concerning whom the prophets have recounted wonders."

Had it not been that these things were true, our Bibles are worthless scrap, but brothers and sisters rejoice! The Lord, He is God. The Promised One is born. The Savior paid our debt on that cross. The Son of God rose again. The King, sits on His throne. The Holy Spirit, He lives inside you, and inside me, if indeed we know Christ. Brothers and sisters rejoice and know what we believe is not in vain. Through this gospel we are saved. Jesus Christ lived perfectly righteous, died as our sin, and rose again, to sit eternal on the throne. Hallelujah, He reigns.

"Now, brothers, I declare to you the gospel which I preached to you, which you have received, and in which you stand. Through it you are saved, if you keep in memory what I preached to you, unless you have believed in vain." - 1 Corinthians 15:1-2 MEV

Notes

Notes

Day 79

Remain Steadfast

"When Paul and Barnabas went out of the synagogue, the Gentiles asked that these words might be preached to them the next Sabbath. When the congregation was dismissed, many of the Jews and devout proselytes followed Paul and Barnabas, who spoke to them and urged them to continue in the grace of God. On the next Sabbath almost the whole city assembled to hear the word of God." - Acts 13:42-44 MEV

While Paul has been speaking the name of Christ for several years now, many consider this monologue we've just studied to be his first missionary sermon. Regardless, it has been completed, Paul and Barnabas walk out, and the gentiles are begging for the Gospel. It's not often that people who don't know the Gospel go seeking for it of their own accord. The question of what drew these gentiles to the courtyard of the synagogue that day can be answered thus: Only by the grace of God.

The Lord led the charge in spreading the good news, and so when these men walk out, they find that He has already imprinted on gentile hearts the desire to know that which they've never heard. The congregation hasn't been dismissed yet, though some may have walked out in hard-nosed disgust. Maybe that disdain by the ultra-religious was the tool by which God sparked their curiosity, but whether it was or not, the Apostle and his fellow preacher walk out to see the grace of God calling the hearts of men.

"When he came and saw the grace of God, he was glad, and he exhorted them all to remain faithful to the Lord with steadfast purpose," - Acts 11:23 ESV

Then they turn back and see those who have just, not only heard the Gospel, but breathed it deep into their souls, coming out behind them. I imagine it gave them a similar emotion as when Barnabas had first arrived in Antioch of Palestine. Both situations led them to the same exhortation. Remain faithful! Continue in the grace of God.

"But he [Jesus] said, 'Blessed rather are those who hear the word of God and keep it!' " - Luke 11:28 ESV

Herein is a lesson that those who are in Christ will be told again, and again, and again. Hold firm to the faith. Having heard a blessing proclaimed on His mother, Jesus turned the tables and proclaimed a blessing on those who hear the word of God and keep it. I'm sure the more self-righteous among the scoffers at Antioch of Pisidia believed themselves to be the ones who "keep it;" the ultra-devout considered themselves the closest to following Mosaic Law. That wasn't of what Christ spoke though. Remember we all fall short. But maybe Paul has some other insight as to what Jesus meant.

"For freedom Christ has set us free; stand firm therefore, and do not submit again to a yoke of slavery." - Galatians 5:1 ESV

To hear the word of God and keep it is exactly what it means to continue in the grace of God. Do not return to your old worldly ways, nor your old self-righteousness. Salvation only comes by grace through faith.

"For by grace you have been saved through faith. And this is not your own doing; it is the gift of God," - Ephesians 2:8 ESV

Holding fast to what we proclaim - that eternal life comes only through repentant belief in Jesus Christ - is a lesson that spans the entire New Testament, including Christ's letters to the churches in Revelation, where Christ repeatedly warns, "be faithful unto death." Even what some consider to be the most legalistic book of the New Testament, written by Jesus' half-brother Judas, hits on this point:

"But you, dear friends, as you build yourselves up in your most holy faith, praying in the Holy Spirit, keep yourselves in the love of God, waiting expectantly for the mercy of our Lord Jesus Christ for eternal life." - Jude 1:20-21 CSB

Keep yourselves in this place of grace. Paul later tells us that he believes nothing in all the world can separate us from the love of God, and yet, he and others repetitively warn of the need to remain in that love. The difference is that the agents of Satan can never divide us from the grace which we ourselves don't walk away from. It's at this point, we should consider the stark contrast.

"Then Paul and Barnabas boldly said, 'It was necessary that the word of God should be spoken to you first. But seeing you reject it, and judge yourselves unworthy of eternal life, we are turning to the Gentiles.' " - Acts 13:46 MEV

There it is again, that word of God which Christ blessed those who keep. Paul and Barnabas mention the necessity which is shown throughout their travels, that it was necessary for the word of God to be spoken to the Jews first, for it had been theirs to receive since the beginning. They then go on, and the next words resound as if spit out of their mouths in disgust. Since you reject it, and judge yourselves unworthy...

What does it mean judge yourselves unworthy? Well, I can tell you one thing for sure, it doesn't carry a meaning as simple as "count yourselves unworthy." No, if anything, what we see is that these infuriated Jews counted only themselves worthy of eternal life. If it were you "believe yourselves unworthy," then I dare say Christ would have scooped them up in His loving grace. Remember, rather, what He said, "when you have done all that you were commanded, you should say, 'We are unworthy servants; we've only done our duty' " (Luke 17:10 CSB).

No, "judge yourselves unworthy" has a different meaning altogether. It means that by rejecting the word of God spoken to you, you have brought down all judgement upon yourselves. The world is saved by Christ, but any and all who reject that salvation seal the sentence upon their own heads. The jury has convened. Judgement is sealed.

Christ said that blasphemy of the Holy Spirit is the only unforgivable sin, and when that Holy Spirit is crying out the gospel of grace in your heart - that same gospel which drew the men both in front and behind Paul and Barnabas (Jew and Gentile) at this point - and you stand in firm opposition, contradicting that word, you've judged yourself already.

If you find yourself today, not yet saved in Christ, but feeling the Holy Spirit tug on your heart, do not delay. Repent and believe, and all of eternity shall be freely given. This great gift of God is not a goal to work toward. It is a gift of grace, the work of God, not of men.

"If you confess with your mouth, 'Jesus is Lord,' and believe in your heart that God raised him from the dead, you will be saved." - Romans 10:9 CSB

Brothers and sisters, if indeed you know the grace of God, remain steadfast in that unto death. The enemy can never take it away from us, but that doesn't mean we can't walk away of our own accord and to our own detriment.

Notes

Day 80

Acting Like Mere Humans

"And when the Gentiles heard this, they began rejoicing and glorifying the word of the Lord, and as many as were appointed to eternal life believed. And the word of the Lord was spreading throughout the whole region." – Acts 13:48-49 ESV

Oh, what a passage, and one which I admit I'm tempted to pass over without comment. Yet while I'd like to entirely avoid the age-old debate in which this passage finds itself a battleground, doing so would not fit the disposition with which we approach this study, namely an eager desire to understand that which I as a reader might otherwise casually overlook. The Calvinism-Arminianism debate rages fiercely over this passage, which can seemingly support the former's claim.

"For it has been reported to me by Chloe's people that there is quarreling among you, my brothers. What I mean is that each one of you says, 'I follow Paul,' or 'I follow Apollos,' or 'I follow Cephas,' or 'I follow Christ.' Is Christ divided? Was Paul crucified for you? Or were you baptized in the name of Paul?" – 1 Corinthians 1:11-13 ESV

Before continuing any further, it should be clarified that I endeavor to be found on neither side of that aisle, but rather sitting on a bench outside the debate hall with my nose in the Good Book. Even so, the debate often spills out into that quiet courtyard, and some of the things I hear, specifically on one side, claim a nature of God which is contrary and disgusting.

Whether those of John Calvin, Jacobus Arminius, John Wesley, Charles Spurgeon, or little ol' me (the far outlier of obscurity and ineptitude in this group), we cannot base our faith on the words of men. They are merely human teachers who are just that: human, flawed, and of little understanding.

"For while one says, 'I am of Paul,' and another, 'I am of Apollos,' are you not worldly? Who then is Paul, and who is Apollos, but ministers by whom you believed, even as the Lord gave to each one?" – 1 Corinthians 3:4-5 MEV

That said, if we look at this passage from the sole perspective of Holy Spirit, I believe the conclusion of Spurgeon stands firm; We have some revelation of the truths of God, yet our feeble human minds cannot attain full understanding of the perfect truth within. Though he considered himself a full-blown Calvinist, he had the presence of mind to recognize the impotence of our intellects.

"It may seem to us as if one truth of God stands in opposition to another, but we are fully convinced that it cannot be so, that it is a mistake in our judgement. That the two things do agree, we are clear, though where they meet we do not know as yet but hope to know hereafter. That God has a people whom he has chosen for himself and who will show forth His praise, we do believe to be a doctrine legible in the Word of God to everyone who cares to read that book with an honest and candid judgement. That, at the same time, Christ is freely presented to every creature under heaven, and that the invitations and exhortations of the gospel are honest and true invitations we do also unabashedly believe."

Where I become disgusted with the division is when I see the arguments of the self-proclaimed reformers, holding so firmly to the doctrines of Calvinism that they fail to acknowledge the implications of their stances.

"For if the reason why these persons believed was only, or chiefly this, that they were ordained to believe, and obtain eternal life, then the reason why the rest believed not must be only, or chiefly this, that they were not so ordained by God. And, if so, what necessity could there be, that the word of God should first be preached to them, Was it only that their damnation might be greater?" – Joseph Benson

But what of our text? "And as many as were appointed [ordained depending on translation] to eternal life believed." As Benson, among others, points out, if this word is properly translated ordained, meaning only that God had made it so that in this city there would be x amount who would believe, and y amount who would perish, then we ascribe to God a greater role in urging men toward their final punishment than

Satan himself. But the Greek word is much more than just appointed or determined.

In Matthew 28:16 the Eleven went to the mountain which Jesus had "appointed" for them, carrying this exact meaning. God ordained it, and thus it must be. On the other end of the spectrum, look ahead to Acts 15:2, when Paul and Barnabas disagree over John Mark's return to their company. In that passage, the same Greek word is used by Luke to describe that the two "determined" to part ways. This same word was used both in some places to show that God had commissioned a thing, and in others that men had chosen a certain path. "Where they meet we do not know as yet."

The very fact that so many faithful men, with lifetimes sincerely dedicated to searching the word of God, have never been able to come to a singular conclusion here, gives me the mindset that our corrupt brains are as yet incapable of the full understanding within. The very fact that the chiefest scriptures of argument on either side of the aisle have such ambiguity of original language as to leave room for this debate, assures me that God has not yet revealed the full truth within, and we ought to be careful not to set our beliefs too firmly to one side or another.

If we endeavor to follow doctrines of men rather than Christ alone, we may find ourselves on the receiving end of Paul's warning, "For whenever someone says, 'I belong to Paul,' and another, 'I belong to Apollos,' are you not acting like mere humans?" (1 Corinthians 3:4 CSB)

I approach this entire study with an inclination to learn all within, yet here I find my learning is simply that we can barely scratch the surface of the unsearchable depths of the love of God. Brothers and sisters, revel in those depths. The love of God stretches far beyond where the greatest human mind can ever fathom. That same love, loves you.

Notes

Notes

Day 81

A Charge Laid on the Faithful Servant

"But the Jews incited the prominent God-fearing women and the leading men of the city. They stirred up persecution against Paul and Barnabas and expelled them from their district. But Paul and Barnabas shook the dust off their feet against them and went to Iconium. And the disciples were filled with joy and the Holy Spirit." - Acts 13:50-52 CSB

You may remember the command of the Lord Jesus, that if they not accept the word, shake the dust off your feet and move on. Do you know the significance? There was a Hebrew proverb that went something like, "The dust of an ethnic city or country pollutes a man." Essentially, for the Jew, the unclean heathens even made the dust of their city unclean, and the devout Jew should be quick to rid himself of all such pollution; it was a show of condemnation on the unclean. Turn it around then, in light of Christ, and what we have here are two evangelists declaring a curse on those devout and prominent Jews of the city who contradicted the word of God. We'll come back to that curse.

The disciples in Antioch of Pisidia are filled with joy and the Holy Spirit. How long Paul and Barnabas stayed with them in this first visit, we're not told, but as they move on to Iconium, we are shown a little more detail; "they stayed there a long time."

"In Iconium they entered the Jewish synagogue, as usual, and spoke in such a way that a great number of both Jews and Greeks believed. But the unbelieving Jews stirred up the Gentiles and poisoned their minds against the brothers. So they stayed there a long time and spoke boldly for the Lord, who testified to the message of his grace by enabling them to do signs and wonders." - Acts 14:1-3 CSB

Iconium was a prominent city - the capital of Lycaonia. The name of the town had several meanings in different tongues. To the Syrians it meant "breast of sheep." The land was known for its sheep feeding, and now, Paul and Barnabas take on Peter's charge - "feed my sheep" (John 21:17). In one city, they shook the dust off, and in another, they stayed and taught. The difference, I suppose, may be found in the specific language Luke uses.

Remember from yesterday that in Antioch, as many as were appointed to eternal life believed. The "devout women of high standing and the leading men of the city," who persecuted Paul and Barnabas were those who rejected the gospel. But here in Iconium they stay because the Jews poisoned the minds of the gentiles against them. For a man to reject the gospel is a curse brought upon himself, but for a man to be deceived from the gospel brings a charge of work upon the faithful servant.

In their travels, we soon see Paul and Barnabas circle back, "strengthening the minds of the disciples and exhorting them to continue in the faith" (Acts 14:22 MEV). Again, we see these towns receive a visit after the Jerusalem council, and it seems to be the region from whence Paul's spiritual son, Timothy originates (see Acts 16:1-2).

This brings us to an interesting point. In 16:6 we'll see Paul, Timothy, and Luke travel through Galatia, and then again pass through in 18:23. Yet both instances give the impression that Paul was instructed by the Spirit to not spend considerable time there. Iconium on the other hand, well, "they stayed there a long time and spoke boldly for the Lord."

The Galatia (in the North) of chapter 16 and 18 was not the only Galatia. The region which included Iconium and Lystra was under Roman rule, and the Roman provincial name was Galatia (in the South). In the late nineteenth century, a man named Sir W.M. Ramsay theorized that this southern Galatia was actually the recipient of Paul's letter to the Galatians. Curiously enough, Ramsay had been educated by those who believed the New Testament was flawed, and yet the Holy Spirit working in him through his studies led the scholar to the exact opposite belief. This Bible we hold dear was, in his opinion (and mine) the incorruptible, inspired word of God.

The southern Galatia theory is extensive and holds much evidence which I won't delve into here. But if this theory is true, then as we read of Paul's travels through this region, first with Barnabas, then with Silas and Timothy, it may be worth reading Galatians in unison. From what I see, I tend to believe this theory. Take a look at some excerpts of that epistle for a moment: Galatians 1:6, 9, 2:9, 3:1-2, 4:13-14, 5:7-9 MEV

"I marvel that you are turning away so soon from Him who called you in the grace of Christ to a different gospel..."

So quickly your minds are poisoned. Not a lot of time had passed when Paul penned this letter.

"As we said before, so I say now again: If anyone preaches any other gospel to you than the one you have received, let him be accursed..." -

Let him be accursed, I shake the dust off my feet.

"When James, Cephas, and John, who seemed to be pillars, understood the grace that was given to me, they gave to Barnabas and me the right hand of fellowship, that we should go to the Gentiles and they to the circumcised..."

Barnabas and Paul did not travel together to ethnic Galatia, but they did to political Galatia. This reference may support the claim that the letter's recipients knew these two evangelists together.

"O foolish Galatians! Who has bewitched you that you should not obey the truth? Before your eyes Jesus Christ was clearly portrayed among you as crucified. I want to learn only this from you: Did you receive the Spirit through the works of the law, or by hearing with faith?"

You received the Spirit. Let me again strengthen your minds that those who would poison your minds against the gospel may not have any influence at all. Continue in the faith.

"You know that it was because of an infirmity of the flesh that I first preached the gospel to you. Though my infirmity was a trial to you, you neither despised nor rejected me, but received me as an angel of God, even as Christ Jesus..."

An infirmity of flesh? Paul is known for poor eyesight, possibly beginning with the blinding glory of Christ on the road to Damascus, but how this may have caused him to preach to Galatians is uncertain. On the other hand, the trip from Antioch of Pisidia to Iconium is a 90 mile, mountainous journey, such as would test the body's limits. Likewise, this southern Galatia is where we're told they tried to worship the brothers, which they rebuked.

"You were running well. Who hindered you from obeying the truth? This persuasion does not come from Him who calls you. A little yeast leavens the whole batch."

Brothers and sisters, in his last charge to Timothy, Paul recants his persecutions in Antioch, Iconium, and Lystra, and he warns that in the last days the evil men, seducers, and deceivers will grow worse and worse. We're seeing that play out, and so we must strengthen our minds to the word of God. A charge is laid on the faithful servant. One such way is to see the evidence, that this letter to the Galatians has sufficient proof of authorship as early as 48 or 49 AD, less than 2 full decades after Christ's crucifixion. The New Testament was not, as some would have you believe, written several centuries later.

Much like the Jews who poisoned the minds of the gentiles, the Judaizers who tried to poison the faith of the Greek believers, and the Tübingen school of thought which tried to poison many like Ramsay, we live in a time where poor and manipulative theology is leading people to deconstruct their faith. We live in a time where a lack of sincere study of the word of God is making us prime targets to be picked off by the enemy, that we might succumb to apostasy.

Brothers and sisters, just as Paul had to exhort the Galatians not to abandon grace for the law, we cannot become like those who are, "always learning, but never able to come to the knowledge of the truth" (2 Timothy 3:7 MEV). On the other end of the spectrum though, we ought to set our minds to the word of God, day and night. No angel of darkness can separate us from the love of God, but the enemy won't stop trying to poison our minds; he won't stop deceiving us in hopes that we may be found, of our own accord, "turning away so soon."

The witness of the Holy Bible is true; It is faithful; It is all the inspired word of God. Trust God.

Day 82

The Snakes and the Dogs

"But the unbelieving Jews stirred up the Gentiles and embittered their minds against the brothers. So they continued there a long time, speaking boldly for the Lord, who bore witness to His gracious word, granting signs and wonders to be done by their hands. But the people of the city were divided. Some sided with the Jews, and others with the apostles. When an assault was planned by both Gentiles and Jews, with their leaders, to attack them and to stone them," - Acts 14:2-5 MEV

It is all too common in the modern Church to deny the witness of the Bible, in relation to Satan, demons, and other things of the spiritual realm. After lifetimes of fairy tales, santa clauses, easter bunnies, tooth fairies, sandmans, and the like, children have grown into adults that file away demons, the devil, and even hell as fables to scare people into submission. If you consider yourself a Christian, but find yourself with this perspective, consider that such a belief is contrary to the Holy Bible, and is thereby claiming fallibility on the part of the word of God, and moreover, on the Word of God, Jesus Christ, who spoke often on these matters.

That said, sometimes the enemy is revealed even through men. What was the devil's plan from the start? Deceive mankind into taking a course of action which would distance them from God. With that in mind, we look again at the Jews of Pisidian Antioch and Iconium. Remember from the last few days of our study, the prominent Jews of Antioch didn't spend a week dwelling on the words Paul and Barnabas spoke, and come to the conclusion it was blaspheme. On the contrary, they came together again the next week, and so did the whole city, but "when the Jews saw the crowds, they were filled with jealousy, blaspheming and contradicting what Paul was saying" (Acts 13:45 MEV).

These Jews in Antioch and Iconium were not upset about the grace of God. They were upset that it was freely offered to so many dogs outside their circle. It should have been just for them! We then see the spirit of the father of lies, the ancient serpent, in how they respond.

"But the unbelieving Jews stirred up the Gentiles and embittered their minds against the brothers." - Acts 14:2 MEV

They tried expelling the evangelists from their city, but it wasn't enough. These prominent men and women of the synagogues take on the form of the enemy, slither into town, and whisper lies in the Gentiles' ears. If they can't separate them from the love of God, they will convince them to separate themselves. "The unbelieving Jews stirred up the Gentiles and embittered their minds against the brothers."

"Then some Jews from Antioch and Iconium came there and persuaded the crowds. They stoned Paul and dragged him out of the city, supposing he was dead." - Acts 14:19 MEV

The same pattern emerges in Lystra, and now we're even told of how these snakes are following the trail of the mission. Being persuaded by these sons of the devil, the crowds stoned Paul. Again, we have the pattern of our enemy. First the snake embittered the minds of Adam and Eve against God, convincing them God was not looking out for their best interest, and then he "wrought upon the heart of [Abel's] brother called Cain, and caused him to kill his brother Abel" (Theophilus of Antioch, to Autolycus book II).

First the Jews embittered the minds of the gentiles against the brothers, then they convinced them to kill the brothers. It even follows the example of Cain, committing this murder with the very stones God had formed.

Sometimes, we must trust the word of God that Satan and his fallen angels are a real enemy, and other times we can clearly see the work of their hands in our lives. Yet on occasion, their existence is testified by those whose master is that dragon of old.

"Then some Jews from Antioch and Iconium came there and persuaded the crowds. They stoned Paul and dragged him out of the city, supposing he was dead. But as the disciples gathered around him, he rose up and went into the city. The next day he departed with Barnabas for Derbe." - Acts 14:19-20 MEV

Brothers and sisters, if we consider ourselves Christians, we should be wary not to deny the truths spoken in this Bible, plenteous as they are. One of those truths is that we have a very real enemy in the spiritual realm, and he enters into those who give themselves to his ways, to work against the grace of God. That should not cause us despair though. Look again, because though they supposed Paul was dead, "he rose up and went into the city." This battle is already won, and no number of deceptive schemes, nor violent plots can stop the snowballing grace of God. Jesus Christ has already triumphed. Now we get to witness that victory play out.

Notes

Notes

Day 83

Of Like Nature With You

"When the crowds saw what Paul had done, they lifted up their voices, saying in Lycaonian, "The gods have come down to us in the likeness of men!" Barnabas they called Zeus, and Paul they called Hermes, because he was the main speaker. The priest of Zeus, who was in front of the city, brought bulls and garlands to the gates to offer sacrifices with the crowds." - Acts 14:11-13 MEV

Yesterday we jumped ahead a bit to the stoning of Paul, but might we today find time to rewind to what happened before. Paul and Barnabas did not tear their clothes at the prospect of being bludgeoned to death with stones, but they did do so at the prospect of being worshipped as gods. Clearly this is not a passage to overlook.

"But when the apostles Barnabas and Paul heard this, they tore their clothes and rushed out into the crowd, crying out, "Men, why are you doing this? We also are men, of like nature with you, preaching to you to turn from these vain things to the living God, who made the heaven and the earth and the sea, and everything that is in them, who in times past allowed all nations to walk in their own ways." - Acts 14:14-16 MEV

The crowds at Lystra held to their beliefs. Though Rome had conquered their lands, the vast quantity of Roman gods did not fully taint their convictions; they still held to the Greek gods of their ancestors. Yet here was a new God being preached, and seeing the miracles done in his name, they could not find any association but that the gods had come down as men.

This is a theme which is seen through so many heathen religions. Their gods were not omnipresent, but would rather manifest in men for a time, as their method of keeping involvement with human affairs. Some would say that the Christian doctrine of the Manifest Word of God, Jesus Christ, is a mere spinoff of such heathen faiths, but the vast differences are too numerous to count.

"That which was a superstition in Lycaonia, and for which the whole 'creation' groaned, became a reality at Bethlehem." - Webster and Wilkinson

For one, all of these gods supposedly came and went, temporarily in the form of men, but Christ came, died on the cross, and rose again, in the form of that man forevermore. This Savior did not need to be on the Earth to deal with our affairs, but rather, by His death He dealt with the all-important matter. He was not gone from us when he died, but now His Spirit lives on inside those who believe on His name. This incarnate Word of God is omnipresent, always everywhere, always sovereign over the affairs of men. The differences span far beyond what I could cover here.

No, the Christian God is not a duplicate of so many other religions. Rather these other beliefs, clinging to a hope that the gods would walk among us, are the natural revelation deep within the blueprint of mankind - that is the testimony in all flesh of God's glory - that we were made by the God who came down in every way like us. Though they would not know it, when God "in times past allowed all nations to walk in their own ways," He was allowing all of creation to testify of His glory. The Lord, He is God.

Notes

Day 84

The Lord Rescued Me

"Then some Jews from Antioch and Iconium came there and persuaded the crowds. They stoned Paul and dragged him out of the city, supposing he was dead." - Acts 14:19 MEV

See the great lengths those opposed to the gospel will go to silence it. The Jews who now came to Lystra traveled somewhere around 130 grueling, mountainous miles for no purpose other than to oppose the teachings of God's grace. See the great lengths those opposed to the gospel will go, but we need not only see it on this page. Just look around our world today, open a newspaper or a magazine, or turn on the TV, and you will see a glimpse of how far the scoffers will go to silence the good news of grace.

"So strong is the bent of the corrupt and carnal heart, that as it is with great difficulty that men are kept back from evil on one side, so it is with great ease they are persuaded to evil on the other side. If Paul would have been Mercury, he might have been worshipped; but if he will be a faithful minister of Christ, he shall be stoned, and thrown out of the city. Thus men who easily submit to strong delusions, hate to receive the truth in the love of it." - Matthew Henry

The corrupt and carnal heart was easily seen in these idolatrous Greeks of Lystra, but theirs weren't the only deceptive hearts of carnality in this history. Look at these Jews from Antioch and Iconium, who dropped everything to pursue homicide, strictly due to their jealousy that the message included eternal life for the gentiles. "So strong is the bent of the corrupt and carnal heart," that it yearns and fights for all others to accompany its descent to the grave.

"the malice of Satan is every way great; if he cannot destroy the souls of these blessed apostles, by making of them to accept of Divine worship, he will do his utmost to kill their bodies." - Matthew Poole

What a sudden change we see in Lystra. One moment Paul and Barnabas are pleading desperately with a crowd to stop worshipping them, only to barely convince them to halt the sacrifice. The very next day forked tongues from the mouths of foreign strangers easily convinced the locals to stone the man to death. That is, the same man they were only barely convinced wasn't a God. If you try to tell me the heart of man is not deceptive above all things, drawn to evil, and inherently sinful from birth, I will struggle to withhold a roaring, deep belly laugh.

"they stoned Paul and dragged him out of the city, thinking he was dead. After the disciples gathered around him, he got up and went into the town." - Acts 14:19b-20a CSB

So, Paul suffers the same persecution which he oversaw when we first met him. Like Stephen, he collapses under the muscle pulverizing, bone breaking blows of stone after stone, yet being dragged out of town, and left for dead, he miraculously stands up and walks back in.

In attempting to picture this scene, I struggle to decide which faces showed more shock. Was it the disciples, preparing to take him off to a proper burial, only to see him stand up, or the persecutors thinking their victim dead, only to see him walk right back into their midst?

"My persecutions and sufferings that happened to me at Antioch, at Iconium, and at Lystra—which persecutions I endured; yet from them all the Lord rescued me." - 2 Timothy 3:11 ESV

In Paul's epistles he often refers back to the many hardships he faced, and specifically to this failed execution, among all the persecutions in Roman Galatia. But he says something of interest to Timothy, who was from this region of Lystra. "Yet from them all the Lord rescued me." Brothers and sisters, if this doesn't make you feel weak, I'm not sure you've really taken it to heart. How often do we look at very inconsequential trials, minor hardships, or first world problems, and wonder why God didn't keep us from suffering them?

"Such sufferings and trials it cost to establish that religion in the world which has shed so many blessings on man; which now crowns us with comfort; which saves us from the abominations and degradations of idolatry here, and from the pains of hell hereafter." - Albert Barnes

Too easy it is for our deceptive hearts to cause us doubt toward the goodness of God when we suffer minor inconveniences, or when we're not prepared for one of our loved ones to be taken into His loving arms. Yet here is a man who has just been unjustly pummeled with stones to within an inch of his life, possibly even being dead for a time (see 2 Corinthians 12:2-4), and he immediately begins teaching that hardships are a necessary part of the road to heaven?

"After the disciples gathered around him, he got up and went into the town. The next day he left with Barnabas for Derbe. After they had preached the gospel in that town and made many disciples, they returned to Lystra, to Iconium, and to Antioch, strengthening the disciples by encouraging them to continue in the faith and by telling them, 'It is necessary to go through many hardships to enter the kingdom of God.' " - Acts 14:20-22 CSB

Despite what we could expect was every muscle aching, the Apostle doesn't lay there and groan, "give me a few days, I'm sure I'll be fine." He immediately stands up, marches back into the lions' den, spends the night there like Daniel, and the next day makes what we now know through archaeological discovery to be a 60 mile trek to another town, where he continues to preach the good news. Yet "the Lord rescued me from trials?"

Brothers and sisters, look at what Paul says when he makes the return journey through these towns. "It is necessary to go through many hardships to enter the kingdom of God." The Lord rescued him indeed, but he didn't restrain the bitter cup of suffering. The Lord rescued him, because he gave him time to continue being a faithful minister of Christ. The Lord rescued him because through it all, Paul never lost the salvation found in Jesus. The Lord rescued him because by the power of the Holy Spirit he never lost sight of the Kingdom of God. The Lord rescued him, because when eventually he was poured out, and his head rolled across the flagstones, Paul gained eternal life in the presence of the Lord. Hallelujah, our God lives, and so shall we!

Notes

Notes

Day 85

What God Has Done

"When they had appointed elders for them in every church, with prayer and fasting, they commended them to the Lord in whom they believed. Then they passed throughout Pisidia and came to Pamphylia, and when they had preached the word in Perga, they went down into Attalia." - Acts 14:23-25 MEV

This first missionary journey is widely believed to have lasted less than three years, from the Spring of 44AD to the Fall of 46. Some of these churches had seen a little time of growth and struggle, but considering the journey, others had maybe a few months of salvation at best before the apostles must appoint elders. The necessity of a Church leadership structure is not lost on the candid reader of these sorts of passages, but how must it have been to appoint new believers as elders over an entire church?

Sure, in Acts 2, some of those who heard the disciples speaking the gospel in all languages were men from this region. Yet we know many stayed among the church of Jerusalem, selling off properties to sustain, and we know that as Paul and Barnabas traveled, they brought the gospel to lands which the Revelation of Christ had not yet been shared. While it's possible these two found some believers of old among the disciples in these cities and villages, it is more likely that they had little choice, short of those spiritual infants whom God would equip.

How great a testimony of the manifold grace of God we now see. Among new converts even, God had elders set aside. That word "appointed" is here clear as day that Paul and Barnabas selected the elders, and yet notice it's done "with prayer and fasting," because it wasn't men who selected leaders. The same Greek word appears in compound form in Acts 10:41, and it means "chosen of God." These baby elders were not elders because Paul decided, "yep, you're it." They weren't elders because of the display of their faith and spiritual wisdom. They weren't elders by any means except that God made them so.

"The praise of all the little good we do at any time, must be ascribed to God; for it is He who not only worketh in us both to will and to do, but also worketh with us to make what we do successful." - Matthew Henry

"From there they sailed to Antioch, where they had been commended to the grace of God for the work which they had completed." - Acts 14:26 MEV

The two brothers commend them to the Lord in whom they believed, and then we're shown the parallel, that Paul and Barnabas were only there because they'd been commended to the grace of God. No matter the mountain nor molehill which God calls us to turn, not a single servant of Christ should ever give consideration to any accomplishment, except that "God has done this. All glory and honor and power are His." Look toward the two evangelists for example:

"When they arrived and had assembled the church, they reported what God had done through them and how He had opened the door of faith to the Gentiles. And there they stayed a long time with the disciples." - Acts 14:27-28 MEV

They reported what God had done, and how He had opened the door of faith. Brothers and sisters, there's no room for personal pride in the Kingdom of God, but there is every reason to boast in Christ. He is faithful, He is good, and He is everything we need for any task He would lay before us. May it never be about what we accomplish, but what God accomplishes through us.

Notes

Day 86

The Judaizers

"After Paul and Barnabas had engaged them in serious argument and debate, Paul and Barnabas and some others were appointed to go up to the apostles and elders in Jerusalem about this issue. When they had been sent on their way by the church, they passed through both Phoenicia and Samaria, describing in detail the conversion of the Gentiles, and they brought great joy to all the brothers and sisters." - Acts 15:2-3 CSB

"Some others" or "certain others" is about as clear as mud, yet the context makes for a sure assessment that, aside from Titus (see Galatians 2:1), some of these others are the Judaizers who had just been at "no small dissension and dispute" (Acts 15:2 MEV) with Paul and Barnabas. Nobody sincere sends only one side of an argument to an arbitrator, and we see Paul's opposition present their case in verse 5. It's there where we're even given the clarification that at least some of the Judaizers, if not all, were of the sect of the pharisees.

I might have suspected. This sect of self-fulfillment of righteousness had been a thorn in Christ's side all along, and now they still have trouble letting go. That doesn't mean they weren't saved in Christ. Notice they're among those who are describing the dispensation of grace to the Gentiles and bringing joy to the disciples. These others may be presently misinterpreting the fullness of His propitiation, but that didn't exclude them from it any more than it did the uncircumcised gentiles. Not the ones who weren't "false brothers" that is (Galatians 2); Not yet at least. If, after the decision of the counsel, they still held to salvation by legalism, the Spirit inspired Paul to some very strict words for them:

"I testify again to every man who is circumcised that he is obligated to keep the whole law. You have been cut off from Christ, whoever of you are justified by law; you have fallen from grace." - Galatians 5:3-4 MEV

We must keep in mind that this doesn't mean any circumcised man loses salvation. Paul himself was a Pharisee and therefore circumcised, and shortly after this dispute is ended, he encourages Timothy to get circumcised (Acts 16:3). That's an interesting case study in itself. Here he is, so firmly standing against the necessity of circumcision and yet, desiring to take Timothy as his student, circumcises him, to appease the local Jews. Note the difference though.

The Judaizers told the gentiles they couldn't be saved unless they were first circumcised. Paul on the other hand, encourages Timothy to "become all things to all men, that [he] might by all means save some" (1 Cor 9:22 MEV).

Had Paul, on the other hand, have been so strict as to imply that anyone who had been circumcised had been cut off from Christ, then he would have been opposing the liberty of Christ in the same manner as the judaizers he disputed with. On the contrary, Paul was teaching that requirements added to the gospel - those by which we would seek to justify ourselves by our own actions - are the path on which we walk away from Christ's justification.

How easily words can be taken out of context though. James and Paul taught the same justification by grace through faith in Christ alone, and yet, James' letter, being written before this dispute, has language that could easily have been misinterpreted and may have even been used in the argument of these Judaizers. Yet James is the one with the final say in the matter, and he rules in Paul's favor. Even to this day many erroneously suppose that Paul and James were at odds over faith vs works.

Paul, on the other end of the spectrum, faced at every turn with legalists and judaizers, frequently wrote furiously about the liberty of Christ, and the enslaving chains of works-based gospels. One could easily take his words out of context and make the gospel a free pass to live as the heathens. The discerning reader will notice though, if read in the context of his entire epistles, and his entire ministry, he also argued the necessity to abandon works of the flesh in exchange for works of the Spirit.

Oh, how easily words can be taken out of context. Often, as I pen what the Spirit reveals in my daily studies, my flesh fears how my words could be misconstrued. Often, I stress over how exhortations to holiness could be taken outside of the context of my entire compendium and interpreted as a call to justification by works. While I believe strongly that we are called to be holy because Christ is holy, those works are only ever encouraged as a response to His salvation. I recognize that like James I sometimes write in absolutes, but I pray I would not lay on anyone a burden which neither we nor our fathers could bear.

"There is a strange proneness in us to think that all do wrong who do not just as we do. Their doctrine was very discouraging. Wise and good men desire to avoid contests and disputes as far as they can; yet when false teachers oppose the main truths of the gospel, or bring in hurtful doctrines, we must not decline to oppose them." - Matthew Henry

I recognize I often write in open contest to that which stands in opposition to the good news, but I pray I would not be seen by God nor men to overstep the bounds of salvation by grace alone through faith alone.

Brothers and sisters, we can easily take any of these passages out of context and misinterpret the word of God. We have good cause to dwell on the word of God, day and night, for we should always be ready to interpret every word or doctrine by the Holy Scriptures. Reading a single devotional, or even a few, out of the context of my entire portfolio could easily give the wrong impression, and likewise, reading a single passage, or even a few, outside of the full context of the Bible can do the same.

So, you've read the bible. Don't think that means you're done! Read it again and again and again, because we'll never find the full understanding of it until we're raised up to live with Christ.

Notes

Notes

Day 87

We All Need Jesus

"After much disputing, Peter rose up and said to them, "Brothers, you know that some time ago God decided among us, that by my mouth the Gentiles should hear the word of the gospel and believe. God, who knows the heart, approved of them, giving them the Holy Spirit just as He did to us, and made no distinction between them and us, and purified their hearts by faith." - Acts 15:7-9 MEV

Peter shows up in Luke's second treatise one final time, and he waits until both sides have had plenty of opportunity to state their cases, then he stands up. This Cephas did not count his apostleship as affording him preeminence, as can be noted by James giving the final judgement. Neither does John, who isn't even named specifically in these arguments, but who Paul affirms in his letter to the Galatians, was instrumental in hearing the case. Peter does, on the other hand, stand up and testify of what God had done.

We can learn a lot from his argument, and specifically what it says.

- God decided that the gentiles should hear the Gospel and believe
- God knows their hearts
- God approved of them
- God gave them the Holy Spirit
- God made no distinction between them and us
- God purified their hearts by faith

"Now then, why are you testing God by putting a yoke on the disciples' necks that neither our ancestors nor we have been able to bear?" - Acts 15:10 CSB

There's been a lot of disputing on the matter, but no human analyses could stand in tempting God. Words have been thrown back and forth across the room, but the word and work of God is now laid down and the matter is settled. In the face of these Pharisees, Peter brings to remembrance the Lord's own words about the group.

"They fasten heavy loads that are hard to carry and lay them on men's shoulders, but they themselves will not move them with their finger." - Matthew 23:4 MEV

In times of old, any foreigner who wanted to join the privileges of Jewish citizenship must be circumcised, just as every Jew must be circumcised on the eighth day. It was a symbol of the covenant with Israel, and carried with it the full requirement of the burden of Mosaic Law, but in the fullness of time, and the revelation of the new dispensation it was shown to have been a mere symbol of the covenant of grace. That symbol now became, as testified by the "God did" statements that Peter has just declared, an inward circumcision of the heart, proven by the indwelling of the Holy Spirit, and His purification.

That old circumcision and the law to which it attested had, throughout history, been proven unattainable. "As it is written, 'none is righteous, no, not one' " (Romans 3:10 MEV). Peter calls them out two-fold. First, it's "why tempt ye God," and then "neither you nor I are any more capable of carrying this load than anyone else."

"But we believe that through the grace of the Lord Jesus Christ we shall be saved, even as they." - Acts 15:11 MEV

Having reminded these judaizers that they were just as guilty, he petitions by the grace of God. You need the grace of the Lord Jesus Christ. I need the grace of the Lord Jesus Christ. They need the grace of the Lord Jesus Christ. Look people, we all need Jesus, not the law.

"For what the law could not do, in that it was weak through the flesh, God did by sending His own Son in the likeness of sinful flesh, and concerning sin, He condemned sin in the flesh, in order that the righteous requirement of the law might be fulfilled in us, who walk not according to the flesh but according to the Spirit." - Romans 8:3-4 MEV

In his epistle to the Romans Paul expounds on Peter's summary, but here at the Jerusalem council, he and Barnabas follow Peter's lead, declaring what God had done:

"The entire assembly remained silent and listened to Barnabas and Paul declaring what signs and wonders God had done through them among the Gentiles." - Acts 15:12 MEV

Brothers and sisters, we can try all we want to debate with our own arguments, or to be justified by the law, but it all comes down to tempting God. Neither our ancestors nor we have been able to bear such a burden. But God has heaved the weight upon His shoulders. The gist of it all? I need Jesus. You need Jesus. They need Jesus. We all need Jesus.

Notes

Notes

Day 88

Joyous Worship

"Simon has declared how God first visited the Gentiles to take from among them a people for His name. With this the words of the prophets agree. As it is written: ‘ “After this I will return, and I will rebuild the tabernacle of David, which has fallen; I will rebuild its ruins, and I will set it up; that the rest of men may seek the Lord, and all the Gentiles who are called by My name, says the Lord who does all these things.” Known to God are all His works since the beginning of the world.' " - Acts 15:14-18 MEV

Peter, Paul, and Barnabas have silenced the opposition by telling what God has done, and now James speaks out. His interjection is recorded almost as if the half-brother of Jesus had sat quietly listening up to this point, waiting to decide the debate’s victors. Maybe he was set aside to be an impartial judge of the dispute. Maybe he was, and maybe he wasn't, but we know he had been raised up as the bishop of the Jerusalem church, and now he speaks the conclusion of the matter.

What does he say? Essentially, "Simon declared what God did, and the word of God is in affirmation of these things." Then he quotes the prophet Amos, just as Stephen had done over a decade before, though most closely from the Greek translation (Septuagint).

" 'On that day I will raise up the tabernacle of David, which has fallen down, and repair its damages; I will raise up its ruins, and rebuild it as in the days of old; That they may possess the remnant of Edom, and all the gentiles who are called by My name,' says the LORD who does this thing." - Amos 9:11-12 NKJV

James' quotation doesn't match our translation well; Ours matches the Hebrew most closely. It does appear rather accurate to the Septuagint, on the other hand, yet with some bits summarized for simplicity. Notice though that in both versions it's not the temple of Solomon which is foretold as rebuilt. This is the Tabernacle of David.

The tabernacle which David built was, like the tabernacle of Moses, a place of worship of the Lord God. The difference was in the type of sacrifices offered there. The tabernacle of Moses, which was succeeded by the temple of Solomon, was a solemn place of blood sacrifice. The tabernacle of David, is where the Lord received joyful and exuberant worship, in song and dance. It's of note then, that the broken temple that was poured out then raised again in 3 days is the same Lord that sits on the eternal throne of David in this tabernacle.

"In mercy the throne shall be established; and one who judges and seeks justice and is diligent in righteousness shall sit on it in truth in the tabernacle of David, judging." - Isaiah 16:5 MEV

The King is on His throne; the Kingdom of Heaven is established forevermore, and the joyful worship of changed hearts is all the evidence "that the rest of men may seek the Lord, and all the Gentiles who are called by My name," are already under his authority. Circumcision was not necessary, for these were already consecrated to the Lord in circumcision of the heart.

"Therefore my judgment is that we should not trouble those of the Gentiles who are turning to God, but that we write to them to abstain from food offered to idols, from sexual immorality, from strangled animals, and from blood. For Moses has had in every city since early generations those who preach him, being read in the synagogues every Sabbath." - Acts 15:19-21 MEV

"We should write to them that they ought to abandon every stitch of their former idolatries," James declares (paraphrased), "but in light of the evidence of God's grace, we should not trouble them with the ceremonial Jewish law."

Brothers and sisters, the King sits in the tabernacle of David. It has been rebuilt and established forever. Let us offer sacrifices of joyous worship, hearts given to sanctification for and by the Lord, and submission to the King of Kings. Brothers and sisters, let us rejoice always for Christ reigns on the throne; He sits on it in truth. Diligent in righteousness, He judges and seeks justice. That's our King.

Day 89

All in Christ
Sons and Daughters

"They wrote this letter by their hand: The apostles and the elders and the brothers, To the brothers who are of the Gentiles in Antioch and Syria and Cilicia: Greetings." - Acts 15:23 MEV

To the brothers who are of the Gentiles... That was quite a statement for a group of first century Jews. For over a thousand years, in the necessity of keeping a bloodline for Christ, the Jews had been set apart from the rest of humanity. They sure knew it too. Granted, no conquered people are going to be amicable toward their oppressors, and age-old wars would certainly put enmity between people groups, but the separation of the Jews had created a sort of national and ethnic pride as well.

Even the Samaritan descendants of Israel, were a lesser class of people in the eyes of the Jews. Consider then where we are:

• we've witnessed the reconciliation of Judeans and Samaritans,
• this council seemingly included Judeans, Galileans, Samaritans, and Hellenists, and
• it's been over a decade since Peter had revealed that God no longer declared gentiles unclean,

But even so, the impression of racial superiority that had been trained in them for generations was hard to break. Yet at the conclusion of these arguments, and James' decision, this letter begins by declaring brotherhood. The gap had been closed. Once again, all men were sons of Adam and Eve.

Oh yeah, there it is. It may have been difficult for the early Jewish-Christian Church to accept the concept that we are all one blood, but the promise of salvation, given to the descendants of Israel, was first given to Eve, from whom the entire human race descended. Remember in Genesis 3, at the declaration of the curse, we witness the first promise of the Good News of Christ. To the serpent, He said:

"I will put enmity between you and the woman, and between your offspring and her offspring; he will bruise your head, and you will bruise his heel." - Genesis 3:15 MEV

Brothers and sisters, in Adam all died, and all were one blood. That blood was rebellious, and rebellion divided us. The hatred, warfare, and racism of our broken world were not present in the garden. They have always been the result of sin. In Christ, on the other hand, all are united. Those who were born of Adam were all one race, one family, divided over millennia, but those who are reborn in second Adam, are reunited as one family, one race, one blood, eternally.

"It seemed good to us, being assembled in unity, to send chosen men to you with our beloved Barnabas and Paul, men who have risked their lives for the name of our Lord Jesus Christ." - Acts 15:25-26 MEV

There is no room in this family for ethnic, national, racial or cultural animosity. If you are born again in Christ, you are my family. We may not share the same language, culture, pigmentation, eye shape, hair texture, or numerous other mutations and variations that separated us over the years, but we are all one race, one blood, assembled as one in unity. We would have an awfully long and miserable eternity if we couldn't get past the hatred of this world. Thanks be to God that He has already proven His Spirit overcomes racial division. Is that Spirit working in you?

Notes

Day 90

Many Others

"Therefore we have sent Judas and Silas, who will also speak to you, saying the same things." - Acts 15:27 MEV

The Church had spread far and wide, and intercommunication was not as simple as logging on to a web forum. It would have been easy to write a forged letter in the name of an Apostle, or leading man of the Church. Actually, several deceivers in the spirit of the enemy did just that. We still have many of those false letters today. We can take note though, that the authoritative letters were not just delivered by a post carrier and read in belief. Leaving the Jerusalem Counsel, we see an example in that the counsel considered even Paul and Barnabas may not have been believed by the recipients, as they had been so firmly on one side of this debate. "Maybe they forged the letter" some might reason. But it pleased the counsel to send witnesses and prophets to teach the same. This pattern of evidence continues frequently in the epistles.

Look at Paul's letter to the Romans, for example, and he pens his intent to visit soon, sends Phoebe with his letter, and name drops several prominent Christians of Rome, who could testify of the teachings therein. If it hadn't been from his hand, it would have been discovered a phony when he did finally arrive and his friends mentioned the letter to him. In his first letter to the church at Corinth, although he unsuccessfully tried to send Apollos with his letter, he again resorts to referencing Aquila and Priscilla, as well as Timothy, the household of Stephanas, and a few men of Corinth who were with him in his travels. Again, if this had been a forgery, it would have been discovered.

The second letter to Corinth comes with confirmation that Paul has recently sent Titus in his stead, and comes himself in a short while. It is there, in mentioning his approaching arrival, that Paul mentions, "Every matter must be established by the testimony of two or three witnesses" (2 Cor 13:1b CSB). While he specifically referenced the issues the Church was struggling with, "every matter" includes his written testimony.

To the Galatians he need not name confirmation - though the letter may have likely been sent with messengers - because he sent the letter as a direct response to what had been reported about the church there, and he indeed passed through on multiple occasions, giving opportunity to confirm or deny his authorship of the epistle.

To Ephesus and Colossus, on the other hand, he expressly sends Tychicus (with Onesimus to the latter). To Philippi, Paul sends Epaphroditus, with intent to send Timothy as well. He also, in common manner, mentions local brothers and sisters who he's served with, in such a manner that they could testify, "yes, I know this Paul and the Gospel he preaches."

The Thessalonians receive a letter referencing the report Timothy had just brought from them to Paul, and another letter written "with my own hand, which is an authenticating mark in every letter. This is how I write" (2 Thess 3:17 CSB). Timothy's letters don't arrive with express references to messengers, but he'd been present and involved in the writing of several of these epistles, so he would certainly recognize that handwriting. Similarly, they are written with very personal detail, even to the point of, "hey, buddy, can you bring the jacket I left behind?" (See 2 Tim 4:13)

Titus is sent 4 messengers, with instructions to help them on their way. Onesimus is again sent with a letter, this time in his own defense, to his master Philemon, and the letter confirms Paul is traveling close behind.

But enough about Paul. James' letter, which most likely predates this Jerusalem Counsel, does not specifically account for any messengers to affirm the authority of it, but we see here in Acts that he was of the mindset to send some. Peter writes his first Epistle "through Silvanus," who is believed by most to be the same Silas which the Jerusalem Counsel has just sent to Antioch. In his second letter, he even references the letters of Paul as confirmation of what he's written.

John's epistles are written later in the history of the Church, and don't expressly reference accompanying messengers. Maybe a better form of assurance had arisen, but it seems from John's words that the best assurance he could offer was that he would come around to confirm. Notice in 3 John, he even mentions that one of his letters had been rejected by a false brother seeking authority of his own. Jude also doesn't reference any carrying messengers, but it's possible that just wasn't his writing style.

Throughout these epistles there are plentiful methods of confirming their authorship, most of which I have not had time to reference here. This is indeed the authoritative word of God, the Master of these servants and Apostles. That said, we have much work to do to "speak to you, saying the same things," and to continue "teaching and preaching the word of the Lord."

"And Paul and Barnabas remained in Antioch, teaching and preaching the word of the Lord, with many others also." - Acts 15:35 MEV

"Teaching and preaching the word of the Lord; the Gospel of Christ; not the word of men, but the word of the Lord, of which he is both the author and subject: this they preached in season, and out of season, with power, purity, plainness, and faithfulness." - John Gill

Since we have this perfect, inspired word of God, and we have His Spirit indwelling us, we have a necessity for "many others" to teach and preach from it. Since we have this redemptive salvation in Christ, we have a cause to serve, and maybe the way the Spirit equips us to serve is to teach and preach. But maybe we find ourselves in churches with teachers and preachers already present. Maybe we use that as an excuse to become mere consumers.

Paul and Barnabas were there, and they were great evangelists, even Apostles. Judas, Barsabbas, and Silas were there, and they're testified to be "leading men among the brothers." Yet even in their company, the church at Antioch didn't consider it an excuse to escape the calling on their lives. Many others preached and taught alongside these men.

"Many others were at Antioch. Where many labour in the word and doctrine, yet there may be opportunity for us: the zeal and usefulness of others should stir us up, not lay us asleep." - Matthew Henry

Maybe you find yourself appointed to mission work. Preach and teach that Holy Name with all boldness and truth.

Maybe you find yourself in a church that is in desperate need of faithful teaching from the word. Does the Spirit call you to fill that gap? Don't hold back.

Maybe you find yourself in a church that's already blessed with many spiritually mature, and Spirit gifted speakers. If that same Holy Spirit indeed calls you to join in that work, their presence does not negate your duty.

Brothers and sisters, whatever gift or gifts the Spirit gives you, faithfully serve the One who so graciously and faithfully served you.

Notes

Day 91

Sharp Contention

"Then there arose a sharp contention, so that they separated from each other. Barnabas took Mark and sailed to Cyprus, but Paul chose Silas and departed, being commended by the brothers to the grace of God. And he went through Syria and Cilicia, strengthening the churches." - Acts 15:39-41 MEV

Oh look, a fight. Should we choose sides?

What a display of something Paul and Barnabas had a few years prior declared, that "we also are men, of like nature with you" (Acts 14:15 MEV). How sad it is to see such a spat leave a scar on the record of the spread of Christ's Church, and divide these two former friends. The truth herein is that which is revealed throughout the Bible; All characters, short of Christ Himself, are just that, short of Christ. We are all marred by the brokenness of flesh. We all need His grace, even unto our final breath.

Over the centuries the nature of this argument has been discussed. Many have reasoned that Paul was in the right, and Barnabas in the wrong. This view gets an early start as even Luke records that Paul left "commended by the brothers" at Antioch. It would seem at least the church there took sides with Paul, but it could be, rather, that the penman, Luke, was the one to do so.

Paul's defense continues in the evidence that his ministry continues to be recorded while Barnabas is never again seen in the physician's second treatise. Many suppose that the sparse record of Barnabas' career after this parting of ways is testimony that he was in the wrong. Look, he went home to Cyprus. They believe he allowed his familial partiality to cloud his vision, and left the will of God.

I'm not alone though in thinking the disagreement wasn't the sin of either man, but rather, how it was handled was. John called Mark may have previously abandoned them, leaving a strain on their first mission, but are we Christians never allowed grace for our mistakes? If not, would this "sharp contention" disqualify both Paul and Barnabas from further mission work, as Paul here implied John Mark's shortcoming had done?

The young man over whom these two friends disputed is, by the supportive hand of his uncle Barnabas, shown still useful in the service of the Lord. He later returns to his first spiritual father Peter, and becomes the most likely candidate for authorship of the Gospel of Mark.

At some point later in his mission work, Paul recognizes the error of his ways, and John Mark is called "helpful to me in my ministry," in the Apostle's second pastoral epistle to Timothy. To the church at Colossae, he writes of Mark being with him in prison, and references that he has previously sent orders to welcome the young man if he comes. To Philemon, a Christian at Colossae, he writes a letter of recommendation for a runaway servant turned Christian, and again references Mark as one known to the man.

Had Mark and Barnabas preached the Gospel in this Greek city, or had Mark at some point joined Paul here, yet also without record, is left to conjecture. There's no explicit record of any of them ever visiting the village. It is even possible that Mark, Paul, and Barnabas found themselves reunited here, though some would argue the latter's disappearance from the book of Acts signaled the withdrawal of God's Spirit of ministry from him. I would personally counter them with 1 Corinthians 9:6.

"Or is it only Barnabas and I who have no right to refrain from working?" - 1 Corinthians 9:6 MEV

At the point of this sharp contention, the brothers had not yet carried the gospel as far as Corinth, but in his second and third missionary journeys, Paul does pass through. We'll get there soon, but first, look at 1 Corinthians 9:6. Paul makes a statement that appears to show Barnabas was still working the mission field, and it appears maybe on one of these trips they even reunited to some degree.

Sure, Barnabas went home to Cyprus, but do we look solely at that and neglect to notice that Paul's direction led him first through his hometown as well? Yeah, the nature of this dispute has been debated through the centuries, but I wonder if like some declare of Barnabas, "we should suspect ourselves of being partial" (Matthew Henry). How easily do we read this Bible through preconceived lenses, and how hard is it to break through that image once it's built?

Brothers and sisters, let's not allow our pre-conceived notions to cloud our vision of God's word, but when they inevitably do, let us not come to such sharp contention with our brethren as these two did. Not over non-salvation issues, to be sure! If Paul had gained his will, we might be missing one of the synoptic gospels. On the other hand, it is the Lord's will that prevails. Glory be to the Lord Almighty. He cannot be stopped, even by our shortcomings.

Notes

Notes

Day 92

To Build up the Name of God

"Then he came to Derbe and then to Lystra. A disciple was there, named Timothy, the son of a Jewess who believed, but his father was a Greek. He was well spoken of by the brothers who were at Lystra and Iconium. Paul wanted him to travel with him. So he took him and circumcised him because of the Jews who were in those places, for they all knew that his father was a Greek." - Acts 16:1-3 MEV

In the same manner of Elijah and his successor Elisha, any study of the works God did through Paul should devote some measure of attention to what was done in and through Timothy. There are several unknowns about Timothy, and yet, more than many characters, we have a lot of background on him. Born to a father who was a proselyte of the gate (uncircumcised and yet God of Israel believing Gentile), and a mother who was a devout Jewess, this Timothy is raised up in the study and piety of the worship of YHWH. It is evident that Timothy, his mother, Eunice, and grandmother, Lois, were most assuredly converted to the Christian faith on Paul's first missionary journey.

"But continue in the things that you have learned and have been assured of, knowing those from whom you have learned them, and that since childhood you have known the Holy Scriptures, which are able to make you wise unto salvation through the faith that is in Christ Jesus." - 2 Timothy 3:14-15 MEV

How old Timothy was on either of these trips, is undefined, but at least four to five years has now passed since Paul and Barnabas first traveled through. We also know that around 12 years after Paul took him under his wing, Timothy is instructed not to let others disregard him due to his youth. Paul also later writes to Timothy of his sufferings at Lystra in a manner that makes Timothy a most probable witness to the stoning on that first missionary trip.

We have then, a young boy, possibly 12 or 13 or even younger, who had been raised to love God sincerely and with all his heart and mind and soul;

a pre-teen who hears a new revelation of the long-awaited Messiah, and believes on that Holy Name of the Lord Jesus Christ. Immediately thereafter, the messenger of this good news is executed by stoning before his very eyes, yet stands up and walks back into town. We have a young boy in whom there could be no faith based on "what God can do for me." A young man in whom there's no room for delusion of grandeur in his devotion to the Gospel work, yet in the absence of this preacher, gives himself fully to the work of the Church.

It may be of special interest that both Paul's and Timothy's paths to the cross begin, in our sight, at the stoning of a saint. I believe this was one of the many ways Paul saw himself in young Timothy, but I don't doubt that instead, it was seeing Christ in young Timothy, that encouraged Paul to take him with him. We're told the churches of Lystra and Iconium both spoke well of Timothy. Even in his childhood, this young man had given himself to the love of God, in much the same manner as young Saul, extremely zealous for the Lord God Almighty, who was raised up a Pharisee of Pharisees.

Both of these men started out as boys extremely well versed in the ancient scriptures. Both, having known these things, and been introduced to the risen Savior saw in the word of God that Jesus of Nazareth was the Holy Word of God, Lord, King, and Christ. Both saw the importance of this message, and had God-given sympathy for the lost, broken, and hurting. Both devoted their lives to sharing the good news, and strengthening the believers.

As I pray this morning over my 2-year-old son, and my influence in his life for Christ, I recognize that whether spiritual or physical sons or daughters, the godly impact we have on those who live after us is our great legacy. Paul may have had an entire book written about what God did through him, and he may have written the majority of our New Testament, but the fact of the matter is, without a lasting impact on those who remained after him, it would all mean nothing.

Tradition says that after Paul's execution Timothy settled into Ephesus as his home base for gospel service, eventually sharing in the martyr's end. Imagine all the lives turned to Christ by this young boy Paul turned to Christ. Imagine all the missionaries, elders, teachers and others who were built up by this young disciple, and the countless souls each of them reached.

Brothers and sisters, each of our lives is but a blink of the eye in the timeline of God's work. If our grand desire is to build a name for ourselves, and if we ever even accomplish that, it may last a few weeks, years, decades or generations. But when our grand desire is to build up the name of God, all of eternity will know the great things God has done.

Notes

Notes

Day 93

Strengthened

"Paul wanted him to travel with him. So he took him and circumcised him because of the Jews who were in those places, for they all knew that his father was a Greek. As they went through the cities, they delivered to them the decrees to observe, that were set forth by the apostles and elders at Jerusalem. So the churches were strengthened in the faith, and increased in number daily." - Acts 16:3-5 MEV

Again, we come to this conundrum. To circumcise or not to circumcise, that is the question. But the question has been answered. Timothy is a unique case to the overall context, because Paul didn't demand his circumcision as a precursor to baptism. Rather he encouraged the young man to be circumcised, not as a gentile joining himself to the law, but as a true (half) Israelite, showing himself unashamed of his blood, and becoming a Jew to them that were Jews, for the sake of ministry. You see, Paul's method remained, enter the synagogues and preach Christ first to the Jews, then to the Gentiles. But young Timothy would have hindered that ministry if he remained in the uncircumcision of his father.

If you want confirmation of this, look straight to the very next sentence; they delivered the decrees to observe. Notice it's not "they spoke," or "they taught," but "they delivered." Luke is very clear that they were carrying exact copies of the letter from the Jerusalem Counsel to Antioch. Here we have the first biblical record of how our New Testament really came to be, as the individual letters to individual churches - in their specific trials - were recognized as helpful for the building of the faith, and therefore dispersed widely among the Church. This sort of pattern is why there are more surviving ancient copies of the Holy Scriptures than any other ancient text.

It is also our evidence as to the accuracy of Luke's records of the decree. Many copies were made and dispersed, and many were available to read. Moreover, we see quite soon that Luke reveals himself among this mission trip, so he most certainly had read it himself in his careful study.

So here we have these decrees which the gentile believers could hold up in response to any Judaizers. Do not be obligated as a gentile to circumcision, but abstain from all the symbols and acts of your former idolatries. You profess Christ, good, now make certain He's your only God. The obligations which the Jerusalem Counsel did see fit to lay on the gentile believers were nothing more than this: a list of the things which those in Antioch would formerly perform in worship of their false gods, from which they must now distance themselves.

"So the churches were strengthened in the faith, and increased in number daily." The word here translated as strengthened, or established, depending upon your preferred Bible version, is used one other time by our beloved physician. Well, twice actually, in one circumstance.

"He took him by the right hand and raised him up. Immediately his feet and ankles were *strengthened*... And His name, by faith in His name, has *made this man strong*, whom you see and know. And faith which comes through Him has given him perfect health in your presence." - Acts 3:7, 16 MEV

If you've studied along with us, you may remember a certain man, lame from birth, laying at the temple gate. The same Greek word that is used to describe his legs coming to life under himself so that he could walk, and jump, and praise God, is the same word Luke used here of the churches. In this new doctrine, the believers were brought past an unfaithful teaching that was brought by those the Church hadn't commissioned. They were strengthened to stand in Christ, to leap in faith, and to praise God for all that He had done.

Brothers and sisters, may we evermore be strengthened by the truth of the word of God, by His good news, and by the burden which was not laid upon us - that which neither we nor our fathers could bear.

Notes

Day 94

When We Can't See

"They went through the region of Phrygia and Galatia and were forbidden by the Holy Spirit to speak the word in Asia. When they came near Mysia, they tried to go into Bithynia, but the Spirit did not allow them. So they passed by Mysia and went down to Troas." - Acts 16:6-8 MEV

Luke doesn't give detail as to how the Spirit of Jesus (as this reads in many of the original manuscripts) forbade them to speak the word in Asia, or to enter Bithynia. It's quite possible they didn't fully understand it themselves. In your Christian life you may have experienced these moments when God clearly closes doors, when His still small voice gives warnings or suggestions, or when He clearly implants the knowledge of what should be done. Sometimes we only recognize His hand in retrospect. We just don't know How the Holy Spirit restrained the Apostle and his team. For all we know, the God of all creation could have taken their voices in Asia, or organized the air molecules into an invisible and impenetrable wall through which they could not pass.

What is certain here, is that God exercised the authority of His command at this point in the journey. What can also be known is that it was all part of a great plan for growth. The Lord's church will not be stopped. Considering the great compassion for the lost that both Paul and Timothy are shown to have, and the same compassion that would have driven Luke to become a physician, it was likely a hard to swallow pill, to walk through these idolatrous lands and not introduce them to the God of salvation. Yet whether by utter obedience on their part, or forceful determination on God's part, they succumbed to the order.

"We must follow Providence: and whatever we seek to do, if that suffer us not, we ought to submit and believe to be for the best." - Matthew Henry

It may have been hard to understand (and it may be even as we read today), why God would not allow them to preach to these people, but God's benevolent omniscience is not to be underestimated. It could be said that the greatest growth a Christian may ever find in his or her walk is in those days when every ounce of our understanding is tried; When seemingly every door is shut, every earthly hope is crushed, and every plan of men is pulverized in the mortar and pestle of the Lord. When long, hard days are spent in faithful prayer, with no end in sight, the faithfulness of His saints is strengthened.

The Lord left these lands to hear the Gospel from their neighboring regions through which the gospel had been preached. He kept these lands in reserve for other instruments in His hand to preach to. The gospel must, at this point, protrude westward.

"During the night a vision appeared to Paul: A man of Macedonia stood and pleaded with him, saying, 'Come over to Macedonia and help us.' After he had seen the vision, immediately we sought to go into Macedonia, concluding that the Lord had called us to preach the gospel to them." - Acts 16:9-10 MEV

Sometimes years or decades pass by before we can see how God worked all things for the good in our lives, even in those most difficult moments. Sometimes He is right up front and reveals a better plan than we could have conceived. Sometimes, as in this passage, we just need to sleep on it.

Brothers and sisters, whatever it is God ordains for your life, fear not, the Lord of angel armies is always victorious. His redemptive work is already finished, and His evangelic work is already ordained. His plan for your life is far better than you could ever imagine on your own. In this life you will have times when you can't, for the life of you, figure out what God is doing, or if He's even still seeing your ordeal. Hold strong to the faith, and even moreso in those moments, because "faith is the substance of things hoped for, the evidence of things not seen" (Hebrews 11:1 MEV). God won't let you down. Don't walk away just because you can't see what He is doing right now.

Notes

Day 95

No Exultation of Self

"From Troas we set sail on a straight course to Samothrace and the next day to Neapolis, and from there to Philippi, which is the main city of that part of Macedonia, and a colony. We stayed in this city several days." - Acts 16:11-12 MEV

Were you here for yesterday's study? Did you notice the word "us" in Luke's treatise? It's no longer "they traveled," "they entered," or "they departed." Our beloved physician has, at some point along the way, joined with Paul, Silas, and Timothy on this journey. It is quite probable that the only gentile author of the New Testament is first introduced to the gospel here in Troas. Later in this chapter, after Paul's imprisonment and release, Luke is again not traveling with them for a time.

Yet here, they stay in Troas for an undetermined but apparently short duration, and Luke's curiosity is caught. He hops on a boat with these strangers, likely for an opportunity to hear more. It's characteristic of the physician, in his manner of eager search for the truth, which we've seen over the past 8 months, starting in Luke 1 (Volume 1). We've seen over and over again, the excruciating detail he has drawn from his witnesses. Names, places, customs, travel routes, and more have all been accurate in a way that scholars are in agreement affirm a first century authorship.

Here, as before, he is very specific about their travel route, this time with first-hand knowledge. The ship leaves Troas. It would be fighting the strong current, but the wind carries them on a straight course to an island where they dock for the night. The next day they set sail again, and make landfall. Finally on the third day, the gospel comes to the Philippians. If you were to look this city up on a map today, you'd find it on the outskirts of a modern town named Krinides, Greece. There the ruins of this city remain, with a Roman aqueduct, Greek and Latin inscriptions, and Romanesque columns. The ruins even attest to the truth of Luke's details that this was a prominent city, and a colony of Rome.

"On the Sabbath we went out of the city to a riverside, where prayer was customarily offered. And we sat down and spoke to the women who had assembled." - Acts 16:13 MEV

I'll come back to Lydia, in verses 13 through 15, but first, I ask you to notice something we've been seeing over and over again. Luke doesn't give any emphasis to his own involvement. He never introduces himself, or tells of his own conversion. He never makes a big deal of his involvement; it's just simple fact. We went here, and did this. There's no fanfare or pageantry, no exultation of self. Merely the facts that, we served Christ where He sent us. Similarly, Paul would not bear any celebrity brought upon himself.

"On one occasion, as we went to the place of prayer, a servant girl possessed with a spirit of divination met us, who brought her masters much profit by fortune-telling. She followed Paul and us, shouting, 'These men are servants of the Most High God, who proclaim to us the way of salvation.' She did this for many days. But becoming greatly troubled, Paul turned to the spirit and said, 'I command you in the name of Jesus Christ to come out of her.' And it came out at that moment." - Acts 16:16-18 MEV

The Greek word here translated spirit of "divination" is actually "python" - "spirit of python." This is very much not the Spirit of God working to affirm their ministry. No, this is a demonic possession. The serpent slithers to and fro, seeking to be made a god. To these people of Philippi, python was the nickname of one of their Greek gods, Apollo.

Several questions arise which are not answered by our text. Was this demon forced by God to cry out and display what James had written, "even the demons believe - and they shudder" (James 2:19 CSB)? Was the girl inside fighting back against the demon, and crying out in a desperate plea that these men would take pity on her and rescue her? Or maybe these declarations were made in mocking fashion?

Whatever the case may be, for several days this demoniac followed the mission team and cried out to all, "look at what they're doing." It could have been useful. We're told that her masters made lots of money off her possession, so clearly these people listened to her, and here she was pointing celebrity their way. A girl with the spirit of the god these people served was essentially telling all the people that Christ is the Most High, and the only way to salvation. It could have been useful. But instead, it greatly troubled Paul.

No doubt, her possession troubled him, because compassion for the devil's captives is the name of the game for Paul, yet I believe there's more. I'd suggest Paul quickly grew tired of the finger of attention being pointed at them, when all he was trying to do was point every eye to Jesus Christ.

It all reminds me of a few songs. The first, by Francesca Battistelli, is "He knows my name," and I love the line, "it's all His stage."

"I don't need my name in lights
I'm famous in my Father's eyes
Make no mistake
He knows my name
I'm not living for applause
I'm already so adored
It's all His stage
He knows my name"

The second, "Nobody," by Casting Crowns, is another favorite of mine.

"'Cause I'm just a nobody
Trying to tell everybody
All about Somebody
Who saved my soul
Ever since You rescued me
You gave my heart a song to sing
I'm living for the world to see
Nobody but Jesus"

Let your heart sing out, "only Jesus," because no amount of human applause received is worth even a fraction of a percent of revealing the glory of God. All glory and honor and power be to God the Father, and His Son Jesus Christ.

Notes

Day 96

Insignificance and Greatness

"On the Sabbath we went out of the city to a riverside, where prayer was customarily offered. And we sat down and spoke to the women who had assembled." - Acts 16:13 MEV

Yesterday, Luke's humility in not introducing himself drew my eyes to the insignificance of worldly notoriety, and so I drilled down on that with the promise to return to Lydia (vs 14-15). But in my morning study of those two verses, I found it necessary to first study that verse which led us there - verse 13. Normally these morning devotionals are written entirely by my own hand, barring useful and eloquent quotations which I cannot pass on utilizing. But today, looking at commentaries on verse 13, I'm entirely caught up with the words of Alexander McLaren, so I ask you suffer me to step aside and let that 19th century servant of God speak into your life for a moment:

"The apparent insignificance and real greatness of Christian work.

"There did not seem in the whole of that great city that morning a more completely insignificant knot of people than the little weather-beaten Jew, travel-stained, of weak bodily presence, and of contemptible speech, with the handful of his attendants, who slipped out in the early morning and wended their way to the quiet little oratory, beneath the blue sky, by the side of the rushing stream, and there talked informally and familiarly to the handful of women. The great men of Philippi would have stared if any one had said to them, 'You will be forgotten, but two of these women will have their names embalmed in the memory of the world for ever. Everybody will know Euodia and Syntyche. Your city will be forgotten, although a battle that settled the fate of the civilised world was fought outside your gates. But that little Jew and the letter that he will write to that handful of believers that are to be gathered by his preaching will last for ever.' The mightiest thing done in Europe that morning was when the Apostle sat down by the riverside, 'and spake to the women which resorted thither.'

"The very same vulgar mistake as to what is great and as to what is small is being repeated over and over again; and we are all tempted to it by that which is worldly and vulgar in ourselves, to the enormous detriment of the best part of our natures. So it is worth while to stop for a moment and ask what is the criterion of greatness in our deeds? I answer, three things - their motive, their sphere, their consequences. What is done for God is always great. You take a pebble and drop it into a brook, and immediately the dull colouring upon it flashes up into beauty when the sunlight strikes through the ripples, and the magnitude of the little stone is enlarged. If I may make use of such a violent expression, drop your deeds into God, and they will all be great, however small they are. Keep them apart from Him, and they will be small, though all the drums of the world beat in celebration, and all the vulgar people on the earth extol their magnitude. This altar magnifies and sanctifies the giver and the gift. The great things are the things that are done for God.

"A deed is great according to its sphere. What bears on and is confined to material things is smaller than what affects the understanding. The teacher is more than the man who promotes material good. And on the very same principle, above both the one and the other, is the doer of deeds which touch the diviner part of a man's nature, his will, his conscience, his affections, his relations to God. Thus the deeds that impinge upon these are the highest and the greatest; and far above the scientific inventor, and far above the mere teacher, as I believe, and as I hope you believe, stands the humblest work of the poorest Christian who seeks to draw any other soul into the light and liberty which he himself possesses. The greatest thing in the world is charity, and the purest charity in the world is that which helps a man to possess the basis and mother-tincture of all love, the love towards God who has first loved us, in the person and the work of His dear Son.

"That which being done has consequences that roll through souls, 'and grow for ever and for ever,' is a greater work than the deed whose issues are more short-lived. And so the man who speaks a word which may deflect a soul into the paths which have no end until they are swallowed up in the light of the God who 'is a Sun,' is a worker whose work is truly great. Brethren, it concerns the nobleness of the life of us Christian people far more closely than we sometimes suppose, that we should purge our souls from the false estimate of magnitudes which prevails so extensively in the world's judgment of men and their doings. And though it is no worthy motive for a man to seek to live so that he may do great things, it is a part of the discipline of the Christian mind, as well as heart, that we should be able to reduce the swollen bladders to their true flaccidity and insignificance, and that we should understand that things done for God, things done on men's souls, things done with consequences which time will not exhaust, nor eternity put a period to, are, after all, the great things of human life.

"Ah, there will be a wonderful reversal of judgments one day! Names that now fill the trumpet of fame will fall silent. Pages that now are read as if they were leaves of the 'Book of Life' will be obliterated and unknown, and when all the flashing cressets in Vanity Fair have smoked and stunk themselves out, 'They that be wise shall shine as the brightness of the firmament, and they that turn many to righteousness as the stars for ever and ever.' The great things are the Christian things, and there was no greater deed done that day, on this round earth, than when that Jewish wayfarer, travel-stained and insignificant, sat himself down in the place of prayer, and 'spake unto the women which resorted thither.' Do not be over-cowed by the loud talk of the world, but understand that Christian work is the mightiest work that a man can do." - McLaren's Expositions of the Holy Scriptures

Notes

Notes

Day 97 *The Lord Opens the Heart*

"One who heard us was a woman named Lydia, from the city of Thyatira, a seller of purple goods, who was a worshiper of God. The Lord opened her heart to pay attention to what was said by Paul. And after she was baptized, and her household as well, she urged us, saying, 'If you have judged me to be faithful to the Lord, come to my house and stay.' And she prevailed upon us." - Acts 16:14-15 ESV

We return to Lydia, and again see secular evidences of Luke's claims. Thyatira was known for its production of purple dyes. Both secular writings, and discovered archaeological inscriptions confirm that there was a trade guild of such there. This woman was seemingly either unmarried, or widowed, and carried on the business which her kinsmen were famed for. Most believe that Luke's phrase, "who was a worshiper of God," indicates this woman to be a proselyte, not a Jewess, and I must agree. If memory serves, everywhere else I've seen the physician use that phrase, it was a distinction from the physical descendants of Israel.

Look what else he says of her though: "The Lord opened her heart to pay attention to what was said by Paul." The fourth century Bishop of Antioch, John Chrysostom, is said by many to be the greatest preacher to ever step into the pulpit. At minimum, he was one of the most faithfully bold. Having preached to the impoverished and the wealthiest just the same, he pictured Paul, Silas, Luke, and Timothy sitting alongside that river bank, and speaking, and he saw the turn of Lydia's heart.

"The opening of the heart was God's work, the attending was hers: so that it was both God's doing and man's" - Chrysostom

Truly, "No one can come to me unless the Father who sent me draws him" (John 6:44a ESV). At the same time, notice that the Lord opened her heart only so far as she must pay attention to His word spoken through these servants. At some point or another, God calls to each of us.

From a combination of the knowledge of God shown in scripture, as well as my experience, and the testimonies of so many others I've heard, I am absolutely confident that the Lord knows the most perfect time to do so; God knows that moment and situation in each of our lives when we are most likely to turn to him, and listen with all our hearts, and He chooses that time to open our hearts. He chooses that time, because Christ came not, "to condemn the world, but that the world through Him might be saved" (John 3:17b MEV). He chooses that time, because if we're called and don't choose to attend to that word, we condemn ourselves, which is not the will of God for any of us.

At one point in each of our lives, the Father draws our hearts to Christ. Maybe today you feel that draw. Are you attentive? Maybe today, God is reaching in and opening your heart. Let not the flesh nor the world hold you back. If that's you today, freedom is just a simple step away. Repent and believe on the Name and finished work of Christ. Believe in your heart and confess with your mouth that Jesus Christ is Lord, and that by His death on that cross, your debt is paid. By His blood, your sin is washed away. By His resurrection, you are raised up to life and born again. By His glorification you are adopted into the family of Christ, more than a conqueror, but a co-heir to the eternal throne of heaven. Maybe God has opened your heart today. Don't delay. Scratch that... Delay everything else if you must, and listen to the word of the Lord. He loves you and He wants you to be reconciled to Him.

If, on the other hand, you're already reborn in Christ - you've been baptized in His death and raised up to life with Him - take note of Lydia's immediate response. "If you have judged me to be faithful to the Lord, come to my house and stay." The "If you have," is rather a given. They've just baptized her into the family. The implication here is, since you recognize me as follower of the Lord, please accept the service I have to offer.

Purple was expensive. Aside from the purple ribbons of the Jewish tradition, it was mostly reserved for kings and the ultra-wealthy, and it was the color of the official Roman toga. Lydia's career was profitable, and it showed in that she had a household in Philippi complete with servants, though she lived in Thyatira. What did she have to offer? She had financial offerings. Each and every Christ follower has something they can give, some sort of offering unto the Lord, be it finances, skills and trades, laborious services, or whatever. God has given you something you can give back. What is it? Do you give it eagerly and with joyous heart?

Notes

Notes

Day 98

"When her masters saw that the hope of their profits was gone, they seized Paul and Silas, and dragged them into the marketplace to the rulers. And they brought them to the magistrates, saying, 'These men, being Jews, greatly trouble our city and teach customs which are not lawful for us, being Romans, to receive or observe.' " - Acts 16:19-21 MEV

Read that again focusing on what Paul and Silas were charged with. No, it wasn't teaching customs that were unlawful for Romans. These two were charged with ruining the business of those who would sacrifice morality for profit. That's not what was spoken before the magistrates of course, but it is the cause of their arrest. The masters of the possessed girl had no quarrel with the teachings of the Christians until they, "saw that the hope of their profits was gone." The same occurs throughout the ages, even unto today, and we soon see it again in Ephesus with the silversmiths (ch 19).

Yes, this charge rages on still today, and if you look through the history of the early church, business and profit is the underlying cause for many of the persecutions. Today it can be witnessed in nations like China where the Chinese Communist Party persecutes Christians in what boils down to their attempts to keep the financial stranglehold they have over the most populous nation on earth.

Some of you aren't going to like what is said next, though. This charge is just as prevalent, if not more, in the land of the woke and the home of the compromise. Yes, in the United States, this is the root of the charge of most anti-Christian activity. Companies can't legally make this their direct excuse, but many won't hire those who are the most outspoken for the truths of God, for fear they may end up another in the list of businesses which have been publicly castigated by the media. Men and women who openly declare the doctrines of Christ have become a liability on the profits of business in the "woke" era.

"For the love of money is a root of all kinds of evils. It is through this craving that some have wandered away from the faith and pierced themselves with many pangs." - 1 Timothy 6:10 ESV

It has become so direct that if you ask many American Christians why they don't publicly profess the Gospel, and if you were to get an honest answer, many would admit, "it just doesn't work that way in our economy. I can't do that in my career. I wouldn't have a job." You might even hear, "that's against the code of ethics of my career." The truth is though, without a single moral standard, given by a Supreme Authority, there is no such thing as ethics.

For many, this compromise becomes a restraint - a barrier - keeping them from the growth in Christ that the Spirit is seeking to lead them through. For others, it becomes the catalyst for their apostasy. This is nothing new. From the moment Paul, Silas, Luke and Timothy set foot in Europe, money has been a tool through which Satan works. If you look at the financial aspect of the first century Levitical high priesthood, you'll see it was the underlying theme of even the charges of blasphemy which the disciples had previously endured from their Jewish brethren.

Business has always been a tool of the enemy, and the love of money a root of all kinds of evil. Brothers and sisters, we ought not walk ourselves into persecution. Just as Paul and Barnabas had fled persecution in Iconium, we have the right to avoid it when we can, but if self-preservation and financial advancement come into conflict with what the Word and Spirit of God command of us, then we must be very careful which god we choose to make our Lord. It may not be easy, when looking at the woke economy, but that's not where we're supposed to be looking anyway. We are exhorted to fix our eyes on Christ, on the coming of the Kingdom of God, and on our eternal inheritance.

"Whoever finds his life will lose it, and whoever loses his life for my sake will find it." - Matthew 10:39 ESV

Day 99

God is There Still

"Having received this order, he put them into the inner prison and fastened their feet in the stocks. About midnight Paul and Silas were praying and singing hymns to God, and the prisoners were listening to them," - Acts 16:24-25 ESV

Beaten with rods,
and feet in the stocks,
in the most secure cell,
God is there still.

We read on and find this jailer is turned to Christ, but how many of these prisoners do you think came to know the Lord? I am all but certain this joyful faith in the most extreme and hopeless circumstances turned more than one soul to salvation that night, but I guarantee it did more than that.

"The leg feels not the stocks when the mind is in heaven. Though the body is held fast, all things lie open in the spirit" - Tertullian, Ad Martyras (to the martyrs)

Paul may have been one of the greatest heroes of the faith, but there are several inconsequential words there.

Paul - inconsequential
Greatest - inconsequential
Heroes - inconsequential
Faith - now we're talking...

Paul may have been the servant of God to bring thousands of gentiles to faith and build the Church in the gentile world - the one to write one epistle after another, exhorting us to uncompromising faith in all circumstances - but even Paul needed God to work in him through faith.

Think about it. Just over a decade before, this man had been positioned for a life with the silver spoon. Wealth, power, and authority were all but his. Now here we find him, bruised, battered, restrained, and in the deepest hole. Everything would have certainly felt desperately hopeless.

That is, unless he kept his eyes on the promises of God. And so it is, that we find Paul and Silas making a joyful noise unto the Lord so that all could hear. And so it is, that we find Paul and Silas praying and singing hymns to God so that their souls could hear the sound of His goodness.

"I am not saying this because I am in need, for I have learned to be content whatever the circumstances. I know what it is to be in need, and I know what it is to have plenty. I have learned the secret of being content in any and every situation, whether well fed or hungry, whether living in plenty or in want. I can do all this through him who gives me strength." - Philippians 4:11-13 NIV

Brothers and sisters, whatever circumstances the world has surrounded you with, "godliness with contentment is great gain" (1 Timothy 6:6 MEV). I suspect, as Timothy read these words, the sounds of Paul's songs echoing from inside the jail came flooding back to memory. Even Paul knew that contentment in any circumstance came from Christ alone. It is "Him who gives me strength." Whether we're on our mountaintop moments, or beaten and thrown in the inner cell, we must keep our eyes fixed on Christ, because He is all we need.

Notes

Day 100

Do Yourself No Harm

"When the jailer awoke and saw the prison doors open, he drew his sword and would have killed himself, supposing that the prisoners had escaped. But Paul shouted, 'Do not harm yourself, for we are all here.' " - Acts 16:27-28 MEV

The charge upon this jailer was not a mere trifle. Having supposed he had lost his prisoners the man could only expect to suffer their sentences as was the custom. It was enough of a weight, he'd rather die, but our God is the God who brings the dead to life, and His servant leaps to the rescue with four simple words. "Do not harm yourself."

"Paul cried aloud to make the jailer hear, and to make him heed, saying, Do thyself no harm. All the cautions of the word of God against sin, and all appearances of it, and approaches to it, have this tendency. Man, woman, do not ruin thyself; hurt not thyself, and then none else can hurt thee; do not sin, for nothing but that can hurt thee. Even as to the body, we are cautioned against the sins which do harm to that." - Matthew Henry

The jailer was a dead man walking, but Jesus, through his servant Paul, says, "Lazarus come out." After spending a night sleeping to the sounds of hymns and prayers - and no doubt questions and answers about the gospel of Christ from within the cells - the jailer is awake, and he now has a question of his own.

"Then he called for a light, ran in, and fell down trembling before Paul and Silas. And he brought them out and said, 'Sirs, what must I do to be saved?' So they said, 'Believe on the Lord Jesus Christ, and you will be saved, you and your household.' Then they spoke the word of the Lord to him and to all who were in his house." - Acts 16:29-32 NKJV

What must I do to be saved? This was the absolute most important question the jailer would ever utter, and the fact he led them out of the cell indicates he had some sense of that weight. What must I do to be saved? His question harkens back to the cry of the girl with the spirit of python. "These men... proclaim to us the way of salvation" (vs 17).

Such a simple gospel. "Believe on the Lord Jesus Christ, and you will be saved." And they spoke the word of the Lord to him. The simplicity of the gospel is that all we must do is believe on the Lord Jesus Christ, but that's not only believe that Jesus existed. Even the demons do that. It is to believe upon the name and finished work of God's Christ; to place the fullness of our faith, the weight of all our terrors, upon Him, just as we see this jailer did.

"In that hour of the night he took them and washed their wounds. And immediately he and his entire household were baptized. Then he brought them up to his house and set food before them. And he rejoiced with his entire household believing in God." - Acts 16:33-34 MEV

In that same hour... A lot happens within a tick of the little hand. An earthquake signals the man's error in imprisoning the servants of the Most High. Fearing the sentence of the magistrates which would soon lay upon his shoulders, this lost man endeavors to commit suicide. The servants of God cry out in absolute forgiveness, "stop," then lead him to salvation by the Lord Jesus Christ. And now, like Lydia, he offers up the service he has (he cleans their wounds).

"When the fruits of faith begin to appear, terrors will be followed by confidence and joy in God." - Matthew Henry

A lot happens in a single hour, and this jailer goes from a dead man walking, to the joy of the Lord. "He rejoiced with his entire household believing in God." A dead man is reborn, and all of heaven rejoices. Among the sounds of the angels' cheers are the sounds of a household given to the worship the Lord. Do you remember when you first came to truly know Christ?

Maybe you remember an instant relief such as this, as the Crucified Lord took the weight of your burden upon his spread shoulders. Maybe you remember instant and previously unexplainable joy such as this, as the Risen Savior signed your name in His book of life. Or maybe you're still the walking dead. Tomorrow I'd like to dig into the evangelists' response to the jailer a bit more, but today, if you have not yet, will you place your hope and trust on the Lord Jesus Christ? Will you repent and believe?

Until you make that decision, you'll never understand the joy with which this man and his household rejoiced.

Brothers and sisters, if you know that peace, how on earth could you love like Christ without sharing the news of the greatest joy the world has ever known? How on earth could you reflect His love without calling the dead to life? How on earth could you love your neighbor as yourself except to cry out, "wait, do thyself no harm"? Brothers and sisters, if indeed you are in Christ, and He in you, then the word of the Lord says you are now to be an ambassador of Christ. The dead walk all around us. They're dying in wrath with no idea why. Do we speak the truth and call them to life?

Notes

Notes

Day 101

What Must I Do to be Saved

"Then he called for a light, ran in, and fell down trembling before Paul and Silas. And he brought them out and said, 'Sirs, what must I do to be saved?' So they said, 'Believe on the Lord Jesus Christ, and you will be saved, you and your household.' Then they spoke the word of the Lord to him and to all who were in his house. And he took them the same hour of the night and washed their stripes. And immediately he and all his family were baptized. Now when he had brought them into his house, he set food before them; and he rejoiced, having believed in God with all his household." - Acts 16:29-34 NKJV

What must I do to be saved? Maybe give to the church, care for the poor, make amends with those I've wronged, abandon my vices, follow the doctrines of religion, and all the churchy stuff? No, Paul and Silas reply, "believe on the Lord Jesus Christ, and you will be saved." It's the beauty of this great plan of God that salvation can be summarized in so few words. It is simple enough for the basest mind to grasp in a moment, and complex enough for the most curious intellect to explore for decades to come. We should note though, that these words weren't the fullness of the reply, but rather, the beginning of the explanation. "They spoke the word of the Lord to him."

No, it is not enough to just believe in a man named Jesus. The same Sadducees and priests who demanded his crucifixion had no choice but to believe he existed, yet many of them still found no salvation. No, it's not enough to believe that Jesus is a Christ (annointed one of God). Even the demons believe that, and they shudder. It's not even enough to believe this man was a great Lord and religious master. The rich young ruler considered Him the good teacher, but it wasn't enough. On the other hand, yes, it is absolutely enough to "believe on the Lord Jesus Christ." So, what does that mean?

We believe that Jesus Christ is Lord of all heaven and earth, and specifically, that he is Lord of each of us, the One in whom we now follow. No longer do our worldly endeavors hold lordship over us.

We believe that the Lord Jesus is the Christ Messiah, the One who was foretold from the very beginning; the only One who descended from heaven fully God, and became fully man, to die in our stead, so that we may have life and have it to the full.

We believe that God's Messiah is Jesus (salvation from God), the only name by which we may be saved; that there is but one way to be reconciled to God and it is in this person, Jesus of Nazareth.

Believe on the Lord Jesus Christ. There is no other way to salvation which has ever been honestly proclaimed by any true servant of the Most High.

Truly works of man can't earn our way in. The TV show "My Name is Earl" may have had a funny premise, leading to ridiculous comedy, but it was no premise of salvation. We can't undo or outdo our sin. The message of the gospel is repent and believe.

Repent is a simple word that we often don't fully comprehend. In essence, it means nothing more or less than "change your mind."

In depth, it means change your mind about who Jesus is - the Lord Messiah. He lived, He died, He was resurrected, and He was raised up in glory, King of Kings forevermore, the First and the Last.

No more must we listen to the secular lies about the Bible, spoken by biased and hardened hearts that know far less about it than they may ever come to admit. No more must we believe the claims that there's no evidence of the tenets of Christianity, and Jesus Christ, of which we have more historical evidence than any other claim of history, ten times over.

Change your mind about what you prefer - no longer does the pursuit of worldly pleasures guide our steps, but rather, having been reconciled to God, a Christian pursues "just a closer walk with thee."

Change your mind about what God has said, that no longer are the commands of God burdens, but rather the deepest desire of a benevolent God, for our own good. What He commands of us is what's best for us, and all these lifestyles we've previously chased were nothing less than self-destructive tools of the enemy. Satan offered us a trojan horse, and we brought it in, but the God who never sleeps offered the Commander of His army to defend us and help us push that horse back out the gate.

Change your mind about what you've done - at one point the jailer was only afraid of what the magistrates would do to him, having no fear of the consequence of sin, but now realizing that's no longer a threat, he trembles before the servants of the Most High. No more have we any reason to fear what the world can do if we follow God, but we come to the realization that without salvation, we must fear the wrath that is to come.

Then Believe. Believe that the Lord God Almighty came into our world as a helpless baby, lived as a humble, sinless servant, died with the weight of our sin upon his shoulders, was resurrected bodily, and seen alive by over 500 witnesses, and was raised up on the clouds to sit on the heavenly throne - our only Intercessor and High Priest. He will return in judgement, but those who've believed on Him will be spared by the most selfless act of grace and mercy the world will ever know. The Creator of all heaven and earth watched us rebel against Him in self-destructive sin, then He gave of Himself to bring us back into the good garden.

"For with the heart one believes unto righteousness, and with the mouth confession is made unto salvation." - Romans 10:10 NKJV

Believe on the Lord Jesus Christ, the only begotten Son of God, and you will be saved, you and your household... No, your belief can't save your children, your spouse, or your friends, but when the fruit of true belief shines in your life, many will see and be saved. The jailer believed, with all his household. This was clearly known because in rejoicing, he declared the confession of faith. Repent and believe. Jesus Christ is Lord and God, and our only path to salvation.

Notes

Notes

Day 102

Unjust Accusations

"But Paul said to them, 'They have publicly beaten us, who are uncondemned Romans, and have thrown us into prison. And now do they secretly throw us out? Certainly not! Let them come themselves and bring us out.' The sergeants reported these words to the magistrates, and they were afraid when they heard that they were Romans. So they came and entreated them. And they brought them out, asking them to leave the city. They went out of the prison and entered the house of Lydia. When they had seen the brothers, they exhorted them and departed." - Acts 16:37-40 MEV

There are a few things of note here. First, we can note that Paul reveals these magistrates are guilty of the very thing he was imprisoned for. They did what it was not lawful for Romans to do. When the Roman statesman and lawyer Cicero rose into our history books, it was by bringing a case against Verres, the governor of Sicily. Of all the charges he brought, the highest of them was violent, degrading punishment of Roman citizens. This was a severe matter. It was contrary to a law which had stood for over 3 centuries. Paul and Silas were unjustly punished under the false accusation that they taught things which were unlawful for Romans to observe, but the magistrates who commanded their punishment were openly guilty of committing the things which were unlawful for Romans to do.

We might wonder, though, why the sudden change of heart? The previous evening, these magistrates gave a strict charge to guard the prisoners in an act that assured more judgement to come, but then the morning shows their intents change and they order the prisoners quietly released. Could it be that the earthquake made them question what they'd done? Maybe the news from the happenings at the prison reached them and they feared more than just worldly retribution. We're not really told, but it's something that will be a pattern for things to come.

The Lord's return will be preceded by many signs and wonders such as this. These calamities will be nothing short of God's final attempt to call hearts to His freely offered salvation. Sadly, just as these magistrates are never shown to echo the question of the jailer, the book of Revelation tells us in those days there will be men and women who will refuse the gift, even to the end. Yet, we see in these magistrates a type of that day, and those who have falsely accused the followers of Christ will have every reason to fear the judgement they've brought upon themselves. While they've apologized to Paul and Silas, the heavenly judgement still weighs heavily. Salvation stands beyond mere earthly amends.

As for those of us who already find ourselves in the grace of God, take note of Paul's actions here. The man has taken unjust abuse without making this strong case before. This isn't the first time he's been held without trial. Here though, he makes the case, and quite probably it's not for the sake of his own defense. Remember where he went to preach. There was no synagogue here. There were just women gathering to pray at the riverside. The few, new Christians he would leave behind would, in this community, have little support, and virtually no defense. But Paul leaves this charge hanging in the air, almost as if to say, "I'll let it slide, but mess with these little ones, and I'll be back."

Moreover, notice he doesn't take his just retribution on the magistrates. These two men had every right to seek punishment against their abusers, but they didn't. Vengeance is mine, saith the Lord... Instead, they make the case of justice, and leave it at that. They also didn't cower in fear. They were asked to leave the city, but first they went to Lydia's house. Again, I can't help but wonder if this was not only to speak to and encourage the believers, but also to make a point to the magistrates. "These are ours. Leave them be."

Brothers and sisters, we may come across all sorts of unjust accusations. In our attempt to love unconditionally we are often accused of hate, by the most hate filled members of our society. The example of our predecessors shows that, on occasion, it is acceptable and maybe even necessary to make the case for justice, but that doesn't excuse us from the command to forgive, just as Christ has forgiven us. Anything less than this, and we're no different than those who accused us. That's not who we are. We are the children of God, reborn in spirit, and made new, more and more into the likeness of Christ.

Day 103

Opening the Scriptures

"According to his custom, Paul went in, and on three Sabbaths he lectured to them from the Scriptures, explaining and proving that the Christ had to suffer and to rise from the dead, and saying, 'This Jesus, whom I preach to you, is the Christ.' Some of them were persuaded and joined with Paul and Silas, including a great crowd of devout Greeks and many leading women." - Acts 17:2-4 MEV

With their backs flayed open, these servants of the Most High continue to carry the Gospel across grueling distances. 33 miles to Amphipolis, 33 more to Apollonia, and 37 to Thessalonica where they find a synagogue. We see again Paul's formula for his ministry, as he preaches Christ to the Jew first, and then to the gentile, so he goes in and "opens" the scriptures. Most English translations bring this into our tongue as "explaining" the scriptures, but the original Greek word "dianoigō" properly meant "opening," as you would a closed door.

"And Sha'ul [desired], as his manner was, went in unto them, and three Shabbat [rest] days reasoned with them out of the scriptures, Opening and alleging, that Moshiach [Messiah] must needs have suffered, and risen again from the dead; and that this Yeshua [God is Salvation], whom I preach unto you, is Moshiach [Messiah]." - Acts 17:2-3 NMV

I tend to think we're missing out on the context when we don't see this word as "opening" the scriptures. Remember, Paul was preaching to the Jews. They knew these scriptures as well as anyone, but only within the closed minds of those who had been taught, generation after generation, how they were supposed to understand them. So, Paul must open the minds of the Jew, explain the scriptures in a way they hadn't been able to process before, and prove that the Messiah must suffer, die, and rise again, and that Jesus was that Messiah.

Raise your hand if you were brought up in certain understandings of scriptures, only to later have the Holy Spirit (maybe through another servant of God, or maybe even through private study) open your mind to the true meaning and depth of the word of God. Ok, so I can't see you raise your hands, but I believe many could claim such an experience.

There is indeed value in the accumulated knowledge and understanding of our forefathers in faith, but at the same time and within that treasure trove of teaching, each of us is responsible for our own relationship with Christ. Look at these two towns, Thessalonica and Berea, and we'll see a vast difference; the latter "examined the scriptures daily to see if these things were true" (Acts 17:11). We'll dig into that more tomorrow, but for now, it is enough that the Messiah must suffer for us, and that Jesus, son of Mary, is that Messiah.

"He must needs suffer for us, because he could not otherwise purchase our redemption for us; and he must needs have risen again, because he could not otherwise apply the redemption to us. We are to preach concerning Jesus that he is Christ; therefore we may hope to be saved by him, and are bound to be ruled by him." - Matthew Henry

Looking back on the scriptures through the lens of what we know of Jesus, it's easy to see how not only the prophets, but also all the types and anti-types of Christ made it clear he must suffer for our redemption. If there was any other way, Jesus would have been spared the cup of wrath, but instead He drank of it willingly, because it was necessary so that we could be saved. Brothers and sisters, this is our Christ: Jesus, the Son of God, who came, lived, died, and was resurrected for our salvation. This is our King.

Notes

Day 104

It is Me They Have Rejected

"But the Jews who did not believe became jealous and, taking some evil men from the marketplace, gathered a crowd, stirred up the city, and attacked the house of Jason, trying to bring them out to the mob. But when they did not find them, they dragged Jason and some brothers to the city officials, crying out, 'These men who have turned the world upside down have come here also, and Jason has received them. They are all acting contrary to the decrees of Caesar, saying that there is another king, Jesus.' " - Acts 17:5-7 MEV

Jealousy is not a good look on you. We've seen it over and over again in this post-Jesus ministry. Some of the Jews hear of God's gift and, refusing to accept it for themselves, become jealous when it's offered to the Gentiles. In their response to the gospel, they provide us the true evidence of how far the unbelieving soul is from the Kingdom of God.

Not only do they reject their king, but they also endeavor to war against His conquest of the hearts of all men. Not only do they hate that He would be the Good Shepherd over all, Jew and Gentile alike, but they resort to allying with evil men to wage this war. Not only do they place themselves in enmity with God, but the case they make is that Caesar is the only rightful ruler, and Jesus Christ cannot be accepted in the heart as King.

If only they'd looked through the scriptures, they'd see that their ancestors had long suffered trouble for not accepting God as their only King. If only they'd properly studied 1 Samuel and the histories that followed, they'd realize that they were walking a treacherous path. Even a few simple sentences should have caused them to re-think this assault.

"The Lord said to Samuel, 'Obey the voice of the people in relation to all that they say to you. For it is not you they have rejected, but Me they have rejected from reigning over them. Just as all the deeds which they have done to Me, from the day I brought them up from Egypt even to this day, in that they have forsaken Me and have served other gods, so they are doing also to you now. Now then, obey their voice. Only you will testify against them and proclaim to them the judgment concerning the king who will reign over them.' " - 1 Samuel 8:7-9 MEV

If only they had examined the scriptures for themselves, they might have found a different eternal outcome; Maybe one more like the Jews in Berea.

"The brothers immediately sent Paul and Silas away by night to Berea, and when they arrived they went into the Jewish synagogue. Now these Jews were more noble than those in Thessalonica; they received the word with all eagerness, examining the Scriptures daily to see if these things were so. Many of them therefore believed, with not a few Greek women of high standing as well as men." - Acts 17:10-12 ESV

We're shown two cities, and two bodies of Jews. One goes merely off of their traditional understandings of the scriptures and absolutely rejects the very Word of God. The other group examines the scriptures daily to see if these things are true, and they receive the word with all eagerness. There's a world of difference there. One group is of the world, and the other is of the Kingdom of Heaven.

If the Lord and His servants were to walk into our churches today, which group would He find? Looking around us, it wouldn't be too hard to fathom the former group being a vast majority, and some of the studies that have been published as of late seem to confirm such a tragedy. It's one thing for atheists to have pre-conceived notions contrary to scripture though they've never thoroughly studied it, but it is a great affront to God when the people who call themselves by His name, in their failure to engage with scripture, hold beliefs about Him that are so contrary to who He is, that were He to stand before them, they would choose the enemy.

"But when the Jews from Thessalonica learned that the word of God was proclaimed by Paul at Berea also, they came there too, agitating and stirring up the crowds." - Acts 17:13 ESV

Brothers and sisters, if you find yourselves among the millions who would check the box of "Christian" on a survey, but never open your Bibles between Sundays, you are in severe danger of being deceived. If you listen every day to preachers and teachers, and read every Christian author you can find, but never immerse yourself in a personal study of the true word of God, you, likewise, are in danger. Religion can tell you all about who Jesus is, but a personal relationship with Him is how you are to know and be known by God.

So, here's my charge: if time spent reading my devotionals takes up the only time that you could find to study the scriptures for yourselves, please stop reading my meager scribblings. The Holy Bible is living and active, and sharper than any two-edged sword. It will speak far better truth than I could ever hope He could do through me. Don't neglect time in your Bible in favor of doctrines of men. There is only one King, and anything that gets between us and Him is dangerous territory.

Notes

Notes

Day 105

Spirit Provoked Within

"While Paul waited for them in Athens, his spirit was provoked within him as he saw that the city was full of idols. Therefore he disputed in the synagogue with the Jews and the devout persons, and in the marketplace daily with those who happened to be there." - Acts 17:16-17 MEV

Are you a traveler, an art connoisseur, a museum patron? Have you seen the great temples, statues, and busts of history? The craftsmanship of mankind's most skilled hands can truly inspire a sense of awe and wonder in the viewer, but what lies beneath the sculpted surface of these hewn images? When the answer is man's worship of his own creation, there is nothing for the Christian spirit but to be provoked to sympathetic distress.

"The first impression which the masterpieces of man's taste for art left on the mind of St. Paul was a revolting one, since all this majesty and beauty had placed itself between man and his Creator, and bound him the faster to his gods, who were not God." – Baumgarten, as quoted by Jamieson, Fausset, and Brown

Oh, how far from truth these career students made themselves. The first century author Petronius wrote of this city, "it was easier to find a god than a man there." Paul wandered the streets of Athens and everywhere he looked were busts, and statues of false gods; "objects of worship" (vs 23 MEV). Pliny claimed there were 30,000 statues, not counting those of private ownership.

The King James translates Luke's description of the city as "wholly given to idols," but among many other translators and commentators, I don't believe that is accurate. The city was indeed, "full of idols," but unlike some of the other communities the Apostle has, to this point, visited, the people weren't fully given to anything, short of novelty. Look further down the page (vs 19-21) and you'll see what they were fully given to was "hearing something new."

As Paul goes to speak before the Areopagus, he says of them, "I perceive that in all things you are very religious" (vs 22 MEV), but the Greek word he used (deisidaimōn) was telling. It carried two meanings. When used in the positive sense, it indeed meant "religious," but if spoken in a more negative context, the word meant "superstitious." It's not the word the Athenians would have used of themselves (theosebês), which more completely meant "worshipper of God." It is no coincidence that Paul chose not to use this word of them who knew nothing of the one true God.

"Here then we have a full proof of the insufficiency of science and philosophy to guide men in matters of religion. 'The barbarous Scythians, the wild Indians, nay, the stupid Hottentots,' as Mr. Scott observes, 'have never deviated further from truth, or sunk into grosser darkness, in respect to God and religion, than the ingenious and philosophical Athenians did!' " - Joseph Benson

In a city full of idols, whose inhabitants were always on the lookout for the newest wisdom, or just the latest trend in thought, there was nothing left but waning rationale. Even the religion they considered worship was nothing more than crass superstition. Here was a city that would worship anything, and thereby didn't truly worship anything. Without devotion to a standard of truth, these men would accept any new disposition which tickled their fancy. Sound familiar? Our media has advanced but the absurdity is the same.

One can't hardly open his or her eyes in the morning but be assaulted by our society's insatiable appetite for something to change. We've come to a generation in which people are so desperate for something new that truth is considered flexible and relative. The idea so prevalent in this hour of our land is that each person can decide their own version of truth, and that it is then self-validated. Such a concept is absolutely impossible to follow through any depth of assessment. If any conjecture is truth, and any one person's supposition absolutely contradicts another's hypothesis, both can't be truth; in seeking to accommodate both "truths," neither will stand. The very nature of truth is that only one truth can be.

"When they heard of the resurrection of the dead, some scoffed. But others said, 'We will hear you again concerning this matter.' So Paul departed from them. However, some men joined him and believed.

Among them were Dionysius the Areopagite, and a woman named Damaris, and others with them." - Acts 17:32-34 MEV

That's not to say we can't hear anything new. Look at these Athenians - look specifically at Dionysius the Areopagite - and it is evident that had he never heard anything new, he'd have never come to learn of salvation in Christ. On the other hand, Dionysius and Damaris and the others weren't merely following the latest movement of thought. They believed, and joined him. In essence, they repented (changed their minds), and the truth they had longed for was finally found. The days of searching for something new were over.

Do you ever stand here in our nation and find your spirit provoked within you? Provoked to absolute horror that so many today bow and worship to the works of their own hands and imaginations? Provoked to concern, with both agitation and pity, at the enslaved nature of the idolatrous mind? Paul demonstrates the spirit of the Christ follower in such a situation, "ready to plead for [the cause of Christ] in all companies, as occasion offers" (Matthew Henry).

There can be but one absolute truth, and it has been long revealed among us. Let not the passing fancies of chaotic opinions lead you astray, and likewise, bear not that such disoriented souls would pass through our spheres of influence without hearing the absolute truth. These men, and women, boys, and girls, must have an opportunity to decide for themselves, and if all said souls ever hear are the newest delusions, well then, I daresay we've failed in our charge.

"How then shall they call on Him in whom they have not believed? And how shall they believe in Him of whom they have not heard? And how shall they hear without a preacher?" - Romans 10:14 MEV

Notes

Notes

Day 106

As if He Needed Anything

"God who made the world and all things in it, being Lord of heaven and earth, does not live in temples made by hands. Nor is He served by men's hands, as though He needed anything, since He gives all men life and breath and all things." - Acts 17:24-25 MEV

We can define the word "repent" all day long, or we can offer example. Look at Saul now. Less than two full decades before, he had stood on the receiving end of this statement - "the Most High does not dwell in houses made with hands" (Acts 7:48 MEV) - and it spurred him to murderous rage. Now, his mind has changed, and the declaration of Stephen is the very same truth he pronounces.

Back then, it was spoken to the religious Jews in relation to the temple, and now to the polytheistic and superstitious searchers of all things. Their graven images and statues of the dead held nothing more within than the atomic structures which God had stitched together by His Word. He does not dwell in temples made by hands. Yet, God's Spirit does dwell inside our created bodies, those of us redeemed, who are the temples of His Holy Spirit.

Turn on your radio and you may hear a popular Christian song all about the Father's house. Don't get me wrong. I enjoy the song and often catch myself singing along, but just because it's popular does not necessarily mean it's accurate. The Father does not dwell in houses made by human hands. The Father's house is where Jesus went to prepare a place for us, where we cannot yet follow. The church where you attend worship is not the Father's house.

We can then cast our eyes to the Christian temples through history, and along our neighborhood streets. They range from massive works of craftsmanship and art which bewilder the senses, to high school gymnasiums with a handful of folding chairs set up for an hour or so. Some of the former serve the wealthy within their walls, while leaned along the outer wall the poor are forgotten. Some of the latter work great things for the Kingdom of Heaven. Make no mistake, our churches are not built to house the Lord, but rather to provide a place for His children to gather in fellowship, worship, and service. Nothing more.

That leads us to the second pronouncement of the Apostle; the Lord of Heaven and Earth is not served by men's hands as if he needed anything. Mic drop.

Maybe you're just joining us today, but if not - if you've been following along so far - you have likely noticed I often spur the reader into the service of God. These works of God which were prepared for us to do from before the world began are nothing more and nothing less than acts of worship. I say again, nothing more.

Plant this firmly in your head, in your spirit, and in your soul: God does not need you. He does not need anything you can do for Him. Take Billy Graham, for example. He's reportedly the tool through which millions came to know Christ, and yet, were he to have spent his life quietly in a pew, the Lord God, Creator of heaven and earth would not have missed reaching into the hearts of each and every one of those saints.

It is our prerogative to take part in the coming of His Kingdom, and yet, that Kingdom is in absolutely no need of us peasants. How amazing it then is, that the God who had no need of us, chose us, sent His Son to die for our redemption, and raised us up with Him as co-heirs to the throne. The King sits forevermore on His throne, and He has no need for us, yet he sees the works of our hands and smiles at the hearts that lie behind them. He invites us to sit with Him, to dine with Him, and in an act of Deific humility which I may never cease to be amazed by, to be again served by Him.

Oh, brothers and sisters, dwell on that today, as the Spirit dwells within you; God does not need you, and yet, He loved you. How much then are we spurred to love Him?

Notes

Day 107

From One Blood, Every Nation

"He has made from one blood every nation of men to live on the entire face of the earth, having appointed fixed times and the boundaries of their habitation, that they should seek the Lord so perhaps they might reach for Him and find Him, though He is not far from each one of us. 'For in Him we live and move and have our being.' As some of your own poets have said, 'We are His offspring.' " - Acts 17:26-28 MEV

Gasp! "Can you believe what this foreigner just said? We Greeks, and Athenian scholars to boot, are the same blood as those wretched barbarians? How dare he make such a claim? All evidence points to our superiority. Why, my young son is more advanced than their wisest men! He even dared call us ignorant. Us!"

"Hey, uhh, buddy, have you met the Jews? The race from which this man comes holds similar opinions of us. It seems no more an assault on our own biases, than it is on his own. Could it be you take offense because you secretly recognize your guilt in this?"

Here we are again and the Pharisee of Pharisees - this chiefest among the chosen race - tells us there is no room for bigotry, no place for a superior race. At the height of all learning these Athenians hear something new; "God has suffered your ignorance along with all the rest of humanity. You are no different, and no better."

From the beginning blood of two (Adam and Eve), God created all mankind. At Babel and other fixed times, He dispersed us to appointed boundaries, where various climates and conditions would warp us all to a multitude of appearances yet still, we are from one blood. Through this, God led us, so that we may seek His truths, His face, His salvation, and be again made one blood in Second Adam, that is, the Lord Jesus Christ.

These Athenians were the evidence of this plan. At the height of all learning, their poets declare a truth of God, though they've not yet met His Truth. At the height of all learning, they yearn for more, still aware they have not found the Truth. At the height of all learning, it is declared,

"God overlooked the times of ignorance, but now He commands all men everywhere to repent" (Acts 17:30 MEV).

Though they've been idolatrous heathens, miles from the God who created the heavens and the earth, He was "not far from each of" them. The very simplest cells of their being called out for the Master, leading them to this lifelong desire for understanding. Without His truth, they have desperately sought for Him and reached, and now, here, He reveals Himself to them.

Among the hearers of this pronouncement, we see three groups. The first are scoffers, self-assured in the pride of their own, clearly, vastly superior understanding. Resurrection from the dead is a fairy tale. The second still had their doubts, as the enemy dug in his claws, yet they seem to have recognized there may be something here, and asked to hear more. The third group, "joined him and believed." Finally, the ignorance they felt, deep within their souls, was answered.

It could be said that the Jews who accepted Christ only did so because they had come from such closed minds that they'd be easily manipulated. It could, but it couldn't when we also see that some of these Areopagites with the most open minds of all - these who spent every waking moment trying to speak or hear something new – also discovered that absolute truth was found in the Lord Jesus Christ. From all walks of life, all races, all cultures, and all backgrounds, Jesus has touched the souls of those who would accept His salvation. Just as Paul spoke, God made all mankind to reach for Him, and for the appointed time, He overlooked our ignorance, but now He calls all of us, of every nation, to repent.

Notes

Day 108

Good God

"God overlooked the times of ignorance, but now He commands all men everywhere to repent. For He has appointed a day on which He will judge the world in righteousness by a Man whom He has appointed, having given assurance of this to all men by raising Him from the dead." - Acts 17:30-31 MEV

Mercy, patience, and grace are among the most notable attributes of our holy God. He looked upon our race, entirely and ignorantly in rebellion against Him throughout the ages, and said, "I would suffer for them." Can you imagine that? Isn't the very act of such self-sacrifice, in and of itself, a command that cuts deep into our souls to submit to that kind of loving God?

There's a story from Billy Graham's extensive ministry in which he was speaking at a university. An unbeliever stood up and said, "if God is God, I give him 5 minutes to strike me dead." Oh the presumption of human pride. But the Holy Spirit inspired an immediate response out of the preacher, "do you think you can exhaust the mercy of God in only 5 minutes?" If that were the case, each and every one of us would be a lost cause. His long-suffering mercy extends leaps and bounds beyond my comprehension. Why would God not have destroyed me long ago? Because of His righteousness, grace, love, and glory.

"When the Son of Man comes in His glory, and all the holy angels with Him, then He will sit on the throne of His glory. Before Him will be gathered all nations, and He will separate them one from another as a shepherd separates his sheep from the goats." - Matthew 25:31-32 MEV

Even when we do look ahead to the judgement that is to come, we can see how good, righteous, and glorious He is. In all truth, God the Father has every right to judge all of us with the utmost condemnation, but for our sake, He hands that authority over to another. God the Son, is given all authority, including the seat of judgement on that appointed day. Do you realize what that means?

God could judge as He is, but instead, He sends his Son to live as one of us before taking that throne. This man came, lived subject to all the temptations and trials we face, remained wholly righteous, and died willingly for our redemption. Now we have as our Judge, not only the perfect, omniscient, and omnipotent power of God, but also the understanding, sympathetic, and familiar Brother who knows what we've experienced. There's no room to question His judgement on that appointed day.

"I saw heaven opened. And there was a white horse. He who sat on it is called Faithful and True, and in righteousness He judges and wages war." - Revelation 19:11 MEV

Christ came in humble service to mankind, and we crucified Him. But the Holy Spirit of God raised Him bodily from the dead with many witnesses, so that we would have assurance of those things He spoke. Soon we will see Christ return, as the judge of all mankind, believer and unbeliever alike. When all is revealed even Graham's heckler will have no room but to admit that the judgement rendered is right and fair. Oh how simple an offer we have, to be judged not by our works, but by the righteousness of Christ, and all we must do is repent and believe. That's a good God.

Notes

Day 109

You Are There

"After this, Paul left Athens and went to Corinth." - Acts 18:1 MEV

We come to 9 simple words (12 in the original Greek), but they began a ministry that may have been among the most fruitful of this mission. The two epistles to the church at Corinth testify of the importance of this. They alone make up a tenth of our entire New Testament. So, what was Corinth, and why does such a simple sentence matter?

Corinth was a city on the Isthmus (a sort of land bridge to what was otherwise an island). A port on each side made commerce between Asia and Europe a great boon to Corinth, and with luxury came the utmost licentiousness. This city was rife with vulgarity and immorality. Yet it's here where we see one of the greatest successes of the Apostle. After limited success in Athens, it's no wonder Paul can later write, "I thank my God always on your behalf for the grace of God which has been given to you through Jesus Christ" (1 Corinthians 1:4 MEV).

In a city of carnal debauchery, the servant of Christ "lectured in the synagogue every Sabbath and persuaded Jews and Greeks" (Acts 18:4 MEV). Contrast this to where Paul has been coming from. Chased out of Thessalonica and Berea, then met with rather reserved response from the self-assured Athenians, Paul wanders alone. He's got no friends, no fellow workers, and little to hold up saying, "my labor is not in vain. Look at what God is doing." Yet a short journey later, either by land or by sea, he comes to Corinth.

We recently dwelt upon what it meant that in a city full of idols, "his spirit was provoked within Him," and now, in a city full of the depravity of flesh, "He was compelled by the Spirit" (vs 5 NKJV). Paul's been on a bit of a rollercoaster, and now (at least once Silas and Timothy arrive) he reaches a spiritual summit after a long, dark valley, but his ministry remains the same; Preaching Christ, and Him crucified. There's a consistency in the Apostle to which much credit can be given.

Consider this: If the Lord let the Apostle Paul go through a time of trial, testing his faithfulness to the preaching of the gospel, how could we let anyone convince us that turning to Jesus Christ will make the world all sunshine and puppy dogs? On the other side of the same coin, in both, those darkest valleys, and the peaks of our highest mountaintops, God says, "I am with you" (vs 10 MEV). In this world we will have trouble, but take heart for Christ has overcome the world.

"If I ascend to heaven, You are there; if I make my bed in Sheol, You are there." - Psalms 139:8 MEV

Notes

Day 110

Roller Coaster

"He found a Jew named Aquila, a native of Pontus, who had recently come from Italy with his wife Priscilla, because Claudius had commanded all the Jews to leave Rome. And he went to them. And because he was of the same trade, he remained with them and worked, for they were tentmakers by trade." - Acts 18:2-3 MEV

Remember that long valley of trial we discussed yesterday; The one that seems to have now come to an end? It has been my experience, when we remain devoted to Christ and His Gospel through such times, that God often ends them with extraordinary displays of comforting love. Case in point: not only does Paul now move into a town where His ministry is met with great success, and not only does he come to a period where the violent assaults are momentarily relieved, but now he finds companions of the utmost confirmation that "I am with you."

Take a closer look at Aquila and Priscilla. Aquila's name, as recorded by Luke, is the Greek transliteration of the Latin word for "eagle." It was common among the Jewish slaves of the dispersion to receive names of animals in the native tongue of their masters. It is thereby most likely that this man was one of the class of the "freedmen."

Before we move on from here though, let's clarify the facts that we know from the authoritative scriptures. Paul stayed and worked with a Jew named Aquila and his wife, Priscilla. Aquila was, like Paul, a tent maker, and this couple had left Pontus when Claudius Caesar issued a decree banishing Jews from Rome. More than that, we can only find conjecture from Luke's language, from cross-references and context, and from historical accounts. Speaking of historical accounts, the Roman historian Seutonius recorded this decree from Claudius.

"He expelled the Jews from Rome, who were continually making tumults, being moved thereunto by one Chrestus,"

Some accounts record that the Roman letters for e and i were relatively difficult to discern in verbal communication, and when we consider that these dispersed Jews likely carried a bit of an accent compared to the native Roman, many scholars have come to the conclusion that this Chrestus, of which Seutonius wrote, was none other than Christus, that is, the Lord Jesus Christ. Most everywhere we've seen Paul preach that gospel up to this point, the description "continually making tumults" seems a good description of the Jewish reactions which the cities experienced. Yet this leads to an interesting theory.

Notice that Aquila and Priscilla are never said to be converted to Christianity, and Paul is never specifically recorded to have preached Christ directly to them. The question of whether Claudius expelled Jews because of tumults in Rome or because of what he heard of from regions like Galatia, remains uncertain, but it's now been two decades since the Pentecost. For the Jews in Rome to not have learned of the happenings in Jerusalem is rather far-fetched, and even in scripture we have hints that maybe the gospel has come this far prior to Paul's arrival.

Remember that among those who marveled at the Holy Spirit displays on that day of Pentecost were Jewish and proselyte "visitors from Rome" (Acts 2:10). Did these men carry back news of Jesus Christ? Quite probably. Likewise, consider the words of Paul concerning a few other Romans. At the end of his letter to the Roman believers, Paul sends greeting to Aquila and Priscilla, but then among a long list of names he mentions two others:

"Greet Andronicus and Junia, my kinsmen and fellow prisoners, who are noteworthy among the apostles, who also came to Christ before me." - Romans 16:7 MEV

Of these Romans Paul declares they came to Christ before him. Did the gospel reach Rome before Paul brought it, and were Aquila and Priscilla already believers? I'd suggest it may be all but certain.

So, let's get back to where we started. After Paul's faithful dedication through the extended time of trial, not only did God bring him out of the persecutions for a time, and not only did he bring him to a place where he'd see the grace of God working extensively. On top of all that, God at the same time introduces new friends, workers of the same trade, and above all, fellow believers in the Lord Jesus Christ. If Paul did not see that as an affirmation from God, he wasn't paying attention.

Brothers and sisters, do not be surprised when this faith walk to which we are called rides like a roller coaster. Sometimes we'll be plunged at breakneck speeds into deep and fearsome trenches. At other times, the views of God's glory will be all around us as we "click, click, click" our way to the top of the highest peak. As mentioned yesterday, God is right beside us through it all. If you've been on the receiving end of those affirmations, you'll know what I'm talking about when I say, God makes it impossible to not see that He has perfectly orchestrated everything. Remember those moments next time you are plunged into despair. If you haven't had those highs yet, or haven't recognized them when they came, trust me; God is with His children through thick and thin.

Notes

Notes

Day 111

Pressed Upon by the Spirit

"He lectured in the synagogue every Sabbath and persuaded Jews and Greeks. When Silas and Timothy came from Macedonia, Paul was pressed by the Spirit and testified to the Jews that Jesus was the Christ." - Acts 18:4-5 MEV

Over the past couple of days, we likened Paul's arrival at Corinth to the upswing of a rollercoaster, but as of yet, he hasn't reached that mountaintop view. Still the "click, click, click," as the car climbs the hill, leaves Paul in a downcast state of fear and weakness; "look what my European mission has led to thus far, so how treacherous a drop do I now approach?"

"Brothers, when I came to you,... I was with you in weakness and in fear and in much trembling."- 1 Corinthians 2:1a, 3 MEV

Yet even so, as we have already discussed, Paul did not let his fears, his afflictions, nor his distress keep him from his calling. He lectured every Sabbath and persuaded souls to Christ. On the other hand, when we look at the first 4 verses, we can notice there's less emphasis on his mission work than normal, and more on his trade. There's a notable restraint from his typical urgency. His fear and trembling do appear to have had an effect, but we see those chains break when Silas and Timothy arrive. Paul is "pressed by the Spirit." Other translations bring this through to the English as, "Paul devoted himself to preaching the word" (CSB).

What was it about the arrival of his fellows that caused such a stir in his soul? The Apostle hasn't seen Silas since Berea, but a detail Luke failed to record was that Timothy did actually make it to Athens with Paul. How do we know? Well, it is at this point - when Silas and Timothy join Paul in Corinth - that the three write the First Epistle to the Thessalonians. At the beginning of chapter 3, Paul tells us that he had sent Timothy from him at Athens to go check on the church at Thessalonica.

"But just now Timothy has come from you to us and brought us good news of your faith and love, and that you always have good memories of us, desiring greatly to see us, as we also desire to see you. Therefore, brothers, during all our afflictions and distress, we have been encouraged about you through your faith. For now we live, if you stand strong in the Lord." - 1 Thessalonians 3:6-8 MEV

You may remember that when the three were hustled out of town by the brethren there, the unbelieving Jews joined forces with evil men and, failing to find Paul, took out their anger on the newly converted Christians. Now, if you've got a few minutes, stop for a moment and go read 1 Thessalonians with this context. It is only 5 relatively short chapters. When you come back, you'll understand why Paul is suddenly reinvigorated.

What are you doing here? I'll wait.

Back so soon? Do you see what I mean? Paul receives report that not only did the trials of faith not chase off these new babes in Christ, but instead, the light they now shone illuminated the whole region. He receives report that in his absence, and faced with such hostility, they've not apostatized; His labor was not in vain. These missionaries were being led from city to city, where they received depressing results, but going back they find the kindling ignited in their wake and entire regions were transformed by the flame of the Gospel. That is an encouraging thought for any carrier of the Good News. Upon receiving this report, we see the passionate flame resuscitated in our Apostle.

"Therefore you were examples to all who believe in Macedonia and Achaia. For the word of the Lord sounded out from you not only in Macedonia and Achaia, but also in every place your faith in God has gone forth, so that we do not need to say anything. For they themselves declare how we were received by you, and how you turned to God from idols, to serve the living and true God, and to wait for His Son from heaven, whom He raised from the dead—Jesus, who delivered us from the wrath to come." - 1 Thessalonians 1:7-10 MEV

Brothers and sisters, this morning I reiterate what we've discovered over the past few days. The faithful Christian life will come with ups and downs, joys and fears, but God is with us always, His plan is perfect, and His victory is already set in stone. Fear, anxiety, and depression are natural emotions, and ones which even Paul struggled with, but it is not for us to excessively remain in them. We can send out our Timothys, and receive report of all that God has done. When we objectively look back on the faithfulness of God in our lives, it will be evident to each and every Christ follower, no matter the valley of the shadow of death we may presently walk in, that He will not leave us nor forsake us.

I'd ask that we all draw another lesson from today's passage as well. As Alexander McLaren said, "The impulse to utter the word that we believe and live by seems to me to be, in its very nature, inseparable from earnest Christian faith." Whether Paul in Corinth, or Jason in Thessalonica, the Spirit presses upon the heart, to varying degrees and duties, the urge to declare, "I was blind but now I see." Do you realize, though, that by following this impulse with faith and love, you not only spread the gospel to the heathen world, but you also encourage the Christian world?

Your preachers and teachers are encouraged to find their labor is not in vain. Those who faithfully prayed for your previously unbelieving Spirit are encouraged in the sight of answered prayers. Those who walk surrounded by darkness are encouraged by the glimpses of light that emanate from your new life. Those who approach their final breaths are encouraged that the word of the Lord which went out will not return void. Those who have just come to faith are encouraged that there are great things prepared for the servant of God.

"Let us firmly hold the profession of our faith without wavering, for He who promised is faithful. And let us consider how to spur one another to love and to good works. Let us not forsake the assembling of ourselves together, as is the manner of some, but let us exhort one another, especially as you see the Day approaching." - Hebrews 10:23-25 MEV

Does the Spirit press upon you?

Notes

Notes

Day 112

Blow the Trumpet

"But when they opposed him and blasphemed, he shook out his garments and said to them, 'Your blood be upon your heads. I am innocent. From now on I will go to the Gentiles.' " - Acts 18:6 MEV

It stands to reason that this opposition and blaspheme may be the inspiration for 1 Corinthians 12:3. "No one speaking by the Spirit of God says, 'Jesus be cursed!' " Having heard the debate every Sabbath for what was likely several months, there were some here who refused to believe, and not only that, but they put themselves on the offensive, as enemies of Christ. For Paul to shake the dust off his garment at them was no small symbol, but it was not a hasty response either.

He's exhausted every human effort and word, but they still would not believe. There's a time in Christian evangelism where pursuit of the same course in the face of obvious defeat becomes nothing more than pride, and Paul has come to that sort of wall of unbelief. Yet take note that he doesn't do so with contempt. The Apostle doesn't leave the city, and he doesn't even cross to the other side. No, he sets up shop right next door, in the house of a proselyte (vs 7) as if to say, I've left you, but you can still come find me and the gospel I preach. Keep reading and the very next verse (8) reveals that distance did indeed make the heart grow fonder, and the ruler of the synagogue himself came to Christ.

To give up efforts on any soul is a solemn affair, and one which the Spirit may lead us to in our ministries (whatever they may be), but while we may be led to walk out the door, may we never close it behind us, nor lock it if it is closed in our wake. We must remember the long-suffering grace of God, how extensively it was proffered unto us, and how the will of God calls all men to repent. All that said, look at Paul's parting words. No doubt these words referenced a passage that he'd argued in this synagogue over the recent months, namely Ezekiel 33.

"then whoever hears the sound of the trumpet and does not take warning, and a sword comes and takes him away, his blood shall be upon his own head. He heard the sound of the trumpet yet did not take warning. His blood shall be upon himself. But he who takes warning delivers his soul." - Ezekiel 33:4-5 MEV

At the Parousia - the second coming of Christ - the judgement we face will be individual, not national. None will be able to say, "it's not my fault." Rather, each who falls unredeemed before the Lord that day will have nothing more than, "His blood is on our hands" (Matthew 27:25 MEV). The sentence each of these blaspheming Jews suffers on that day will not be passed off to another in blame. Their blood and the blood of the Messiah weighs on their own heads; The watchman blew the trumpet, they heard the sound, yet they did not take warning. So it is with many, all throughout history.

"Now as for you, son of man: I have set you a watchman to the house of Israel. Therefore you shall hear a word from My mouth and warn them from Me. When I say to the wicked, 'O wicked man, you shall surely die,' and you do not speak to warn the wicked from his way, that wicked man shall die in his iniquity. But his blood I will require from your hand. Nevertheless, if you on your part warn the wicked to turn from his way and he does not turn from his way, he shall die in his iniquity. But you have delivered your soul."- Ezekiel 33:7-9 MEV

Clearly Paul felt the individual call to service to God. He heard and could not refute the call. "For you will be His witness to all men of what you have seen and heard" (Acts 22:15 MEV). Here was the watchman, hearing the word of the Lord to "Rise, be baptized and wash away your sins, and call on the name of the Lord" (Acts 22:16 MEV), and he sounds the trumpet to all men.

Can we hear that call and leave the trumpet silent? Yes.

Can we choose to not warn the wicked and yet be held blameless for the souls who slumber to the sound of the sword? That's a different story.

"Now as for you, son of man, say to the house of Israel, 'You have said this: "Our transgressions and our sins are heavy on us, and we are wasting away because of them! How then can we survive?"' Tell them, 'As I live — this is the declaration of the Lord God — I take no pleasure in the death of the wicked, but rather that the wicked person should turn from his way and live. Repent, repent of your evil ways! Why will you die, house of Israel?' " - Ezekiel 33:10-11 CSB

The trumpet of warning and the trumpet of grace and glory may just be one and the same. Keep reading further into this chapter of Ezekiel and you'll see a prophecy that preceded Christ's ministry by six centuries, yet it laid out His Gospel. Verses 10 through 16 are among my favorite Old Testament passages, while 17 through 20 tell another story; the devastating and mournful story of people such as these blasphemers.

"Yet the sons of your people say, 'The way of the Lord is not right,' when their way is not right." - Ezekiel 33:17 MEV

Brothers and sisters - those of us who are pressed by the Spirit to shod our feet with the sandals of the readiness of the gospel - we must blow the trumpet. Let it ring out loud. Many may hear it and scoff, but the one soul of Crispus makes worth of the effort.

More than once has the Spirit pushed me to speak yet remained I silent. No more, oh Lord, help me in my weakness. Provide your strength. Fill me with your breath to blow that trumpet loud. Christ be magnified.

Notes

Notes

Day 113

The Leaders of the Synagogue

"Crispus, the ruler of the synagogue, believed in the Lord with his entire household. And many of the Corinthians, who heard, believed and were baptized." - Acts 18:8 MEV

There are several undefined factors in this portion of Luke's writings, to which we could see various details. For example, there are two rulers of the synagogue listed in this chapter - Crispus, and Sosthenes. What we do not know is which of the following three potentials is accurate: There may have been more than one person at a time raised up to this title, as was sometimes the case. There's also a chance, in such a thriving city, that there was more than one synagogue. It could also have been - and this is where my belief stands - that the unbelieving Jews expelled Crispus from the role upon his turning to Christ, replacing him with Sosthenes.

"Then all the Greeks seized Sosthenes, the ruler of the synagogue, and beat him before the judgment seat. But none of these things mattered to Gallio." - Acts 18:17 MEV

We then continue in the chapter and find another unknown with the introduction of Sosthenes. If you compare English translations at this verse, you'll see a split, where some state the Greeks seized Sosthenes, and others simply say "they," "they all," or "the crowd." On the surface, it may seem an argument that our bibles are flawed because "they are just copies of copies of copies," as the common atheist argument stands. If we honestly look at where this disagreement comes from though, it is actually evidence to the contrary.

We have more ancient copies of scripture than any other book of the time which those same atheists will teach as truth in their universities. They were all hand written, and translated individually. Of those copies, some show the word Hellēn (the word for "Greeks" in their native language), while others exclude the word. The very fact that this uncertainty rises is because we have so much evidence of the early language of these writings. If the Lord allowed this uncertainty in His inspired word, we can be sure it is inconsequential.

The context does, though lead me to the belief that Crispus was replaced, then Sosthenes led the Jewish charge against Paul before the Roman governor, causing an uproar much like those which got the Jews expelled from Rome. Then, seeing the Roman governor shake them off, the Greeks chased the leader of this riot out of the tribunal with fists. That being the case, let's consider an implication of this Crispus' faith.

It does appear, from Luke's language, that Crispus did not come to faith until Paul shook the dust off and left the synagogue. Can you blame him? The flesh is a strong contender. Please allow me a moment to explain. To be the "ruler of the synagogue" was a very esteemed title. It was so distinguished that these men would rest in graves labeled with their appellation. Their families would even have a sense of pride in that one of their own had risen to such preeminence. Here in the synagogue, this man who would have found such a title by a lifetime of dedication, saw the opposition his brethren held toward this gospel. He knew that the achievement of a lifetime would likely be forfeited to follow this Jesus as Messiah. Yet once the ultimatum was laid forth, he "believed in the Lord with all his household."

"Then Jesus said to His disciples, 'If anyone will come after Me, let him deny himself, and take up his cross, and follow Me.' " - Matthew 16:24 MEV

The very fact of this Crispus' conversion was noteworthy. He is among a select group of men and women whose names are given, some because of their social standing, others due to their recognition within the church, and some, well there are some I'm sure Luke added for a reason that I'd be curious to figure out some day. But Crispus is noteworthy. Not that one soul is worth more than any other. A soul saved is a soul saved and there is no favoritism with God.

Yet Paul clearly recognized the usefulness of such a convert. His faith served as an affirmation of the truth of what Paul taught. "Here is one whose dedication to God and His word has long been established in your midst, and see, he believes." Paul clearly recognized this value, and he departed from his normal refusal of performing baptisms. In 1 Corinthians 1:14 Paul tells us he personally baptized Crispus. Clearly the man's faith alone was a great service to God.

There's more to the story though. Look at 1 Corinthians 1:1, and you'll see another name. "Sosthenes, our brother." In the manner of Nicodemus, these spiritual leaders examine the scriptures and hear the good news and slowly they come to realize, this is the truth of God, undefiled, and pure. Jesus of Nazareth is the long-awaited Messiah, the Son of God, who from the beginning was with God and who was God; the One who descended from heaven to die as the silent Lamb in our stead - the perfect atonement - then was raised up as the Lion of Judah, King of Kings forevermore, with all authority in heaven and earth.

There's no favoritism with God. Your soul, my soul, the soul of the crackhead down on main street, or the soul of the most religious in all the city, they all are nothing more or less in God's eyes than one soul saved, one child adopted, and one lost sheep found. Yet from the perspective of men, let's take special note that those who knew the Hebrew scriptures better than any of us, while hindered by their pride and pleasures, eventually came to repent and believe.

Notes

Notes

Day 114

Battle Plan

"The Lord spoke to Paul in the night through a vision, 'Do not be afraid, but speak and do not be silent. For I am with you, and no one shall attack you and hurt you, for I have many people in this city.' So for a year and six months he sat among them, teaching the word of God." - Acts 18:9-11 MEV

Fear continues. If that weren't the case, why would the Lord have need to come and say, "Be not afraid"? Can you blame Paul though for a bit of anxiety? He's still got scars across his back, and most certainly vivid memories of Jewish crowds chanting for his abuse and imprisonment. Now he's converted the ruler of the synagogue in what was reportedly one of the most sinful cities in all the land. What can he expect, but that either Jew or gentile will soon come against him with violent intent. Needless to say, they eventually do, but first God has a message.

"Speak and do not be silent." God tells Paul, fear not, and continue the work to which you've been called. He is given two reasons, a sort of battle plan - first the defensive strategy, then the offensive.

Defense: I am with you! Is there any greater defense for any child of God? "If God is for us, who can be against us?" (Romans 8:31 MEV). Not only am I with you, but as I charge you to speak, I promise you that none here shall attack you and hurt you.

"So for a year and six months he sat among them, teaching the word of God. When Gallio was proconsul of Achaia, the Jews in unity attacked Paul and brought him to court, saying, 'This man is persuading men to worship God contrary to the law.' " - Acts 18:11-13 MEV

Ok, wait a minute. Surely enough, Luke equips us to comprehend that Paul was faithful to the command, but then we see that after a year and a half of safety, the unbelieving Jews do indeed attack him. Yet notice God's promise is not "none shall attack you NOR hurt you." What He did say was "none shall attack you and hurt you." Their attack isn't contrary to the promise, as we immediately thereafter see the assault thwarted, and it's the leader of the opposition who is instead hurt.

"Wait a minute," you may say, "if you're going to get specific about words, the promise wasn't 'nobody here will hurt you,' it was 'no one shall' hurt you. Didn't the Apostle continue in imprisonments and finally lose his head on the chopping block?"

"Who shall separate us from the love of Christ? Shall tribulation, or distress, or persecution, or famine, or nakedness, or peril, or sword? As it is written: 'For Your sake we are killed all day long; we are counted as sheep for the slaughter.' No, in all these things we are more than conquerors through Him who loved us." - Romans 8:35-37 MEV

Yes, all of that is true, but the Lord pointed out to us that we are not to fear the one who can destroy the body but not hurt the soul (Matthew 10:28). Remember it is Paul who tells us, "all things work for good to those who love God." To this day, at the moment you read this devotional, Paul remains unhurt. In eternal life, his soul worships in the presence of His Lord. No more scars, no more pain, no more anxiety, and no more fear. At their worst, all men could do to him was set his eternal soul free from its corrupted flesh tent.

So, what about that offense? "I have many people in this city." God wasn't telling Paul about the people who already sat in the gathering of the saints to listen to his teaching. Though it's true they are His people, the Lord had no need to tell Paul that. He was relating it to the command, "speak and do not be silent." What God expressed was that from the beginning of time he had already seen many more hearts turned to Christ by the Apostle in this city.

Think about that. In the midst of their deepest transgressions, God already knew them and counted them. He had already seen their absolution day. He had already felt their worship; that which those men and women hadn't even conceived of yet. The Lord knew, from before the foundation of the earth was laid, each and every one of us who will repent and believe before taking our final breaths.

"I have other sheep who are not of this fold. I must also bring them, and they will hear My voice. There will be one flock and one shepherd." - John 10:16 MEV

Maybe you're reading this today and you haven't yet come to the saving knowledge of the Lord Jesus Christ. Maybe He has already seen the day you will, and if so, He already watches you, one of his lost sheep. Maybe that day is today. Do not delay.

Maybe you're reading this today, faced with fears and anxieties about sharing the Gospel. Do not be afraid, but speak and do not be silent. For God is with you, and he will not let any harm come to your eternal soul, if you remain in Him. He has many sheep still wandering. Will you carry the Shepherd's news?

Notes

Notes

Day 115

The Vow

"Yet Paul remained many days. He had his hair cut in Cenchrea, for he had taken a vow. Then, bidding farewell to the brothers, he sailed to Syria, and Priscilla and Aquila were with him. He arrived at Ephesus and left them there. But he himself went into the synagogue and lectured the Jews. When they asked him to remain for a while longer, he did not consent, but, bidding farewell, said, 'I must by all means attend this upcoming feast in Jerusalem, but I will return to you if God wills.' And he set sail from Ephesus." - Acts 18:18-21 MEV

The vow of which Luke references is not specified, and has caused much debate among the scholars and commentators of history. Some see it as certain to be the vow of the temporary Nazarite.

"And the Nazirite shall shave his consecrated head at the entrance of the tent of meeting and shall take the hair from his consecrated head and put it on the fire that is under the sacrifice of the peace offering." - Numbers 6:18 ESV

If that's the case, he's technically required to have his head shorn at the entrance to the temple. Yet it was arguably not required for those whose vows found them abroad, and it was not uncommon for those Jews who took this vow outside of Jerusalem, to cut their hair elsewhere and bring it back to Jerusalem for the sacrifice. If that's the case, we have the explanation of Paul's sudden urgency to return for the feast.

On the other hand, the Jewish historian Josephus records a common practice of vows which other commentators believe may have been the case.

"for it is usual with those that had been either afflicted with a distemper, or with any other distresses, to make vows; and for thirty days before they are to offer their sacrifices, to abstain from wine, and to shave the hair of their head." - Josephus, Wars of the Jews 2.15

The Jews (and gentiles for that manner) had many forms of vows, often related to a distress, but one that was common in this time also required the hair to be shaved and offered with the sacrifice. Quite honestly, it seems, to me, to be hardly different from the Nazarite vow, and either one explains the rush trip back for the feast. Other vows have been suggested, but maybe Albert Barnes has a point when he suggests, "where nothing is recorded, conjecture is useless."

The same really goes for "this upcoming feast." Which feast it is that Paul rushes off to is not specified. Some seem certain it was Pentecost, while others point out that traditionally, the word "feast" used without an identifier implied Passover. I'd suggest a third option, that it wasn't specified because it no longer mattered. Paul's been gone for years now and missed several feasts, but that was no big deal. As he said himself, we are no longer under the law of sin and death. Take a look at what he teaches the church at Colossae:

"Therefore let no one pass judgment on you in questions of food and drink, or with regard to a festival or a new moon or a Sabbath. These are a shadow of the things to come, but the substance belongs to Christ." - Colossians 2:16-17 ESV

It seems most evident to me that the only real reason he must so suddenly attend this feast, is to fulfill his vow. That brings up a point in which I think we can learn from his example. The Apostle to the Gentiles has been redeemed from his former ignorance and sinful pride for the grand purpose of carrying the news of Christ to the gentile world. He's shown the utmost passion and fervor in that calling. From this history of Luke's, as well as Paul's own words in his epistles, we can deduce a most severe compassion in the man for the lost world. Yet he "must by all means attend this upcoming feast."

Paul lives out an example, that what is right and good must always take priority. Sometimes, such as this, it is hard to decipher. Isn't it right to fulfill his calling to preach the gospel abroad? Yet more immediately, he had a vow to fulfill, and we can't accomplish good ends for the Kingdom of Heaven, by means of sacrificing individual sanctity. That didn't stop him from heading back out, and continuing the ministry, nor from sharing the news in Jerusalem of what God has done. In closing today, I think we can look at his words to the Ephesians.

"I will return to you if God wills."

Paul was not one to preach, "do as I say, not as I do." In his farewell, he lives out something James, the brother of Jesus, would soon teach the church.

"Come now, you who say, 'Today or tomorrow we will go into such and such a town and spend a year there and trade and make a profit'— yet you do not know what tomorrow will bring. What is your life? For you are a mist that appears for a little time and then vanishes. Instead you ought to say, 'If the Lord wills, we will live and do this or that.' As it is, you boast in your arrogance. All such boasting is evil. So whoever knows the right thing to do and fails to do it, for him it is sin." - James 4:13-17 ESV

Instead you ought to say, "if the Lord wills..." Brothers and sisters, we come up with many plans in our hearts. I doubt there's anyone here that would argue if I said that those plans rarely work out how we had anticipated, even when they are plans for good. How easily, when we make human plans for the glory and purpose of God, are we drawn to question Him when those plans fall apart? That's not His error, but rather ours. If we had only taken this example to heart, maybe we'd keep the perspective that His plans are always better than our own. Let us rather plan, "If the Lord wills we will do such and such."

Notes

Notes

Day 116

More Accurately

"Meanwhile a Jew named Apollos, born in Alexandria, who was an eloquent man and powerful in the Scriptures, came to Ephesus. This man was instructed in the way of the Lord, knowing only the baptism of John, but being fervent in spirit, he accurately spoke and taught the things concerning the Lord. He began to speak boldly in the synagogue. When Aquila and Priscilla heard him, they took him and explained the way of God more accurately." - Acts 18:24-26 MEV

Not a lot is known of Apollos, beyond what is told here. We know from Paul's writings to the Corinthians, and to Timothy, that the Apostle respected him as a fellow teacher of Christ. We also know from the same source that, of no fault of Apollos', the people lifted him improperly onto a pedestal in their minds. We know of his birth in Alexandria (the source of the Septuagint translation, and a hotbed for Jewish scriptural engagement), and we know he knew of and shared what he learned of John the Baptizers ministry - that Jesus is the Messiah.

What we don't know, is, well, it's extensive, and considering the almost cult like status he unwittingly started to gain, I'm sure God had a reason for that. Eloquence is a dangerous gift when speaking the gospel. Yet, considering today (when originally posted) is Reformation Day, it may be worth a passing note that Martin Luther held the belief that this Apollos was the mysterious author of the book of Hebrews. Could that be? We really don't know, but it is an interesting conjecture which I find no reason to rule out. On the other hand, the Lord saw fit to keep both that author, and Apollos rather veiled from our historical magnifying glass.

What we can know though, is that even without the Holy Spirit, and without instruction in the full counsel of the Gospel, this man's own spirit was on fire for the Lord of Hosts. We are told he taught accurately concerning the things of the Lord, but we're also told that Aquila and Priscilla explained to him, "the way of God more accurately." That's an interesting conundrum, isn't it? How can one teach accurately, but then be taught more accurately.

Let's be clear that this isn't elementary mathematics. I can't teach that 2x3 is somewhere around 5, and be said to teach accurately, only to be taught more accurately later that the solution is 6.

What it is, is the Gospel of Christ, the Alpha and Omega, whose grace runs deeper than our greatest minds can fathom, and the depths of whose love is unsearchable. It is as simple as "Christ died for our sins, so that those who believe on His name may be redeemed," and it's deeper than the Mariana trench.

Apollos was powerful in the scriptures, yet he could still be taught a deeper explanation of them. Whether an infant in the faith, brought to salvation 5 minutes ago, or a lifelong believer with seminary doctorate, and 5 decades of preaching under your belt, not a one of us will ever outgrow the need of studying the scriptures. God forbid that flame dies out in the active preacher - that all he has is recycled sermons, and a cooling soul.

There's another implication here as well. Apollos taught accurately, though more accurately was possible. Christians are quick to demean other preachers of lesser or even different understanding, and those whose words may sometimes be slightly altered for a better outcome. We belittle the man who, in fervor of spirit, speaks the name of Christ, yet not quite exactly as we understand it. If you recognize yourself in those statements, please allow me to ask one question: how many pieces would you have the body of Christ divided into?

Notice Priscilla and Aquila don't belittle Apollos, but rather edify him to even higher service. Paul likewise doesn't disparage him. Tomorrow we'll see Apollos "destroy arguments and every lofty opinion raised against the knowledge of God," (2 Corinthians 10:5 ESV), but when it comes to disagreements among believers over issues of understanding that are not essential tenets of salvation, we're far too apt to denigrate the bride of Christ. It's nothing less than the same pride that led to Satan's fall.

"Oh look how this beloved child of yours is failing, God..."

Day 117

God Gave the Increase

"When Apollos intended to pass into Achaia, the brothers wrote to encourage the disciples to welcome him. On arriving, he greatly helped those who had believed through grace. For he vehemently refuted the Jews publicly, proving from the Scriptures that Jesus was the Christ." - Acts 18:27-28 MEV

Remembering where we were, Paul preached in Corinth, returned to Ephesus, and then started making his way back to Jerusalem for the feast. Apollos shows up on the scene, preaching Christ from what he knew of John the Baptist, though having never heard the full Gospel. Aquila and Priscilla edify him to higher learning; they explain more fully those things he's missed. Now, Apollos endeavors to go to Achaia.

Achaia, being the region within which we find Corinth, sang out to Apollos' ministerial heart. Could it be that some Corinthian disciples had, like Aquila and Priscilla, followed Paul to Ephesus, and now having heard Apollos speak, urged him to go teach their countrymen? Or maybe, his upbringing in Alexandria making him a great candidate to reason with Jew and Greek alike, he simply desired to go. I'd suggest though that it's quite probable that whether or not the interests of men played a factor, it was God who drew his eye to the region, much as he had directed Paul's second mission to Europe. What does Paul say?

"Who then is Paul, and who is Apollos, but ministers by whom you believed, even as the Lord gave to each one? I have planted, Apollos watered, but God gave the increase. So then neither is he who plants nor he who waters anything, but God who gives the increase." - 1 Corinthians 3:5-7 MEV

It would seem that Paul's words indirectly speak both to this route planning, as well as to the actual saving faith of the disciples. Paul could preach with passionate fire, and Apollos could preach with eloquence and scripture, but the listeners "believed through grace." Likewise, if the Spirit of the Lord had not restricted Paul and his fellows from entering Asia, and had the Lord not drawn this Apollos to go and water that garden in

Achaia, this church would not have preached the Good News to lost souls for years to come.

"The business of ministers is to preach Christ. Not only to preach the truth, but to prove and defend it, with meekness, yet with power." - Matthew Henry

Notice though, Apollos didn't just stand in their fellowship halls and preach a message to people who would come sit there; he doesn't preach a message that was carefully worded so as not to offend the contemporary Jewish or Greek ethos. The words Luke used told a very different story. This minister "vehemently refuted the Jews publicly, proving from the Scriptures that Jesus was the Christ." Now, what does the inspired word of God say of this tactic? "He greatly helped those who had believed through grace."

This Corinthian church continued to have issues, as we see in the clear frustration of Paul's epistles to them, but nonetheless they were believers counted saints by the power and grace of God. Neither is the one who plants, nor he who waters anything, but God who gives the increase, and neither then are those who believed, saints by anything more than God's grace. It is the gift of God.

"For by grace you have been saved through faith, and this is not of yourselves. It is the gift of God, not of works, so that no one should boast." - Ephesians 2:8-9 MEV

Notes

Day 118

Holy Spirit Come

While Apollos was at Corinth, Paul passed through the upper regions and came to Ephesus. He found some disciples and said to them, 'Have you received the Holy Spirit since you believed?' They said to him, 'No, we have not even heard that there is a Holy Spirit.' " - Acts 19:1-2 MEV

Apollos and Paul we've met, but is anyone else here drawn to the curiosity of these "about twelve men in all"? Luke calls them disciples, yet what is revealed is they knew not the gospel. Like Apollos they appear to have been Jewish disciples of John the Baptizer, or maybe just heard of his message. Yet while they awaited the One coming after John, "One mightier than I, the straps of whose shoes I am not worthy to stoop down and untie"(Mark 1:7 MEV), they clearly had not been instructed in the Good News of the resurrection of Christ and the coming of the Holy Spirit. Yet Luke describes them as disciples.

I'd suggest this actually shines a light on a question that's been asked through the ages. What of those who believed, yet died before the coming of Christ? Take John the Baptizer himself, for example. Did he die outside the salvation of Christ? Not a chance in Satan's eternal prison... Even as far back as Abraham, the New Testament defines that faith was credited as righteousness. The saving grace of our crucified God-Man is just as outside of time as God is Himself. Those who believed before He was fully revealed were still followers of the Lord. And so it is that they're counted among the disciples, but what was missing?

Paul comes, and he finds these men. It would appear they haven't been in Ephesus long, or they would have been instructed more accurately, just as Apollos. Yet that's not out of the ordinary. We'll see Paul stay in this city for two years and with good cause. People came and went in droves, from all around, and for many reasons. These men, having seemingly just strolled into town, found themselves drawn to a group who appeared to believe the same as them - the Messiah has come. But what they found was not themselves. Hallelujah.

Paul comes, and he finds these men, then he asks, "have you received the Holy Spirit since you believed." We are not told why. Maybe because he saw they were new and uninformed, or more likely, considering the direct and specific nature of the question, he recognized the lack of the signs of the down-payment of the promise. So he asks a question for the ages.

"The question suggests, though indirectly, that the signs of the Spirit's presence are sadly absent in many professing Christians. Paul asked it in wonder. If he came into modern churches, he would have to ask it once more." - Alexander McLaren

Paul asks, and it is revealed they're missing the indwelling of the Spirit. To call yourself a Christian means nothing without a heart turned to Christ. To believe in a higher power does not put you in the good graces of that power without the redemptive blood He spilled. Even to believe in Yahweh, as the Jews we'll soon see in Ephesus, is not the key to eternal life; At least not after hearing of Him and declining the chance to believe in the Way. Look at these "about 12 men" for example.

He said to them, 'Into what then were you baptized?' They said, 'Into John's baptism.' Paul said, 'John indeed baptized with the baptism of repentance, telling the people that they should believe in the One coming after him, that is, in Christ Jesus.' " - Acts 19:3-4 MEV

These men live repentance, and believe in the coming Messiah. They even believe He's come, but they don't yet believe on the Name of the Lord Jesus Christ, eager as they are to do so. When, on the other hand, they hear who the Messiah is (and most certainly Luke has severely abridged Paul's responsive instruction), they believe and are baptized in the name of the Lord Jesus Christ.

"If you then, being evil, know how to give good gifts to your children, how much more will your heavenly Father give the Holy Spirit to those who ask Him?' " - Luke 11:13 MEV

I assure you, not one soul who has truly placed their full belief on that Only Name has been left in the dark. Yet at the same time, as McLaren once said, "If [Paul] came into modern churches, he would have to ask it once more." Be not fooled brothers and sisters. There walk among us the dead. Attendance upon the Sunday service is not the supreme sign of a soul saved; The Spirit is. We cannot simply assume that even the man or woman who has sat among us in worship for a decade or more is not in need of the Gospel. We should likewise not assume that our own place under the steeple has made us "those who bear His name."

"But many are deceived in this matter, and think they have received the Holy Ghost, when really they have not. As there are pretenders to the gifts of the Spirit, so there are to his graces and comforts. We should therefore strictly examine ourselves on this subject; and inquire whether we have received the Holy Ghost since we believed?" - Joseph Benson

Paul is not walking into your church this weekend to preach Christ and ask you, "Have you received the Holy Spirit since you believed." Take the time in prayer, and introspection in your heart of hearts to inquire, "Have I received the down payment of the promise? Have I truly laid all my belief upon the Lord Jesus Christ?" Fear not if you find a negative answer, but believe, for the heavenly Father knows how to give the good gift to His children.

"When they heard this, they were baptized in the name of the Lord Jesus. When Paul had laid his hands on them, the Holy Spirit came on them, and they spoke in other tongues and prophesied. There were about twelve men in all." - Acts 19:5-7 MEV

The book of Acts makes it clear that the Holy Spirit comes upon believers in different stages. Some received the Holy Spirit at Pentecost, others at baptism. To the house of Cornelius came the Holy Spirit even as they first heard the word spoken through Peter, and others received Him with the laying on of hands. We cannot place the Holy Spirit in a box, suggesting there is a singular method, display, or time of receiving, except to say that universally He comes only subsequent to true faith.

"The tree is known by its fruits. Do we bring forth the fruits of the Spirit, love, joy, peace, etc., all goodness, righteousness, and truth. Are we led by the Spirit? Do we live and walk in the Spirit? Do we experience his renovating power, and are we under his government?" - Benson

Brothers and sisters, if indeed that we are, let each of us inquire within ourselves this question. Have we received this gift? Does the same Spirit that raised Jesus from the grave truly indwell these earth tents of ours? If you can say, without a shadow of a doubt, "Yes, indeed. Thank you, Jesus," then, brother or sister, let us not forget that the world inside our chapel doors needs Jesus just as much as the world outside does.

Notes

Day 119

Separate and Preach

"He went into the synagogue and spoke boldly for three months, lecturing and persuading concerning the kingdom of God. But when some were hardened and did not believe, but spoke evil of the Way before the crowd, he withdrew from them and took the disciples, lecturing daily in the school of Tyrannus." - Acts 19:8-9 MEV

What a mercy it is that this Apostle, the chosen vessel of God's, to bear His name before the gentiles and kings, goes first to the Jews. Consider the state of these people's hearts. The gentiles were no better to them than unclean animals. For a Jew to even dine with them would get him excommunicated. If Paul had walked into any of these cities and neglected the Jews in favor of the gentiles, it would have immediately hardened the hearts of every one of them to the Way. As it is, he reasons with them first, from their own scriptures, and in the face of tiresome opposition.

The work pays off too, for look, "*some* were hardened and did not believe." There is a subtle implication here, as elsewhere, that this method of going to the Jew first did not find God's word returned void. *Some* did not believe, informs us that others did. God's mercy worked great things, even in the midst of such hardening of hearts, but there were some who would rebel to the end, and harden themselves. That's risky business, because God is in the habit of finishing the work of hardening those who harden themselves against Him. That's not His will though. We're told God desires that all men, everywhere should repent, yet He also knows that won't be the case for everyone. Look at Psalm 95, encouraging us to "make a joyful noise to the Rock of our salvation" (vs 1 MEV).

"For He is our God, and we are the people of His pasture and the sheep of His hand. Today if you hear His voice, do not harden your hearts, as at Meribah, and as in the day of Massah in the wilderness," - Psalms 95:7-8 MEV

It was the way of Israel, and all mankind for that matter, to rebel against God, and we had proven it for thousands of years, but the Way of salvation - the Way of the Lord, the Way of God, and the Way of faith - is our Lord Jesus Christ, the Way, the Truth, and the Life, by whose name and finished work we are brought back into fellowship with the Father. Rebellion is abandoned, at least, by many, while some others harden their hearts.

"For we are to God a sweet fragrance of Christ among those who are saved and among those who perish. To the one we are the fragrance of death, which brings death, and to the other the fragrance of life, which brings life. Who is sufficient for these things? For we are not as many are who peddle the word of God. Instead, being sent by God, we sincerely speak in Christ in the sight of God." - 2 Corinthians 2:15-17 MEV

The Gospel is the fragrance of death unto death for some, and the fragrance of life unto life for others. Once the two groups have been distinguished, it behooves us to separate from those who are hardened to death. Anything else and we just pile heaping coals upon their heads. Let me tell you, that's not what I would like to see come of my service. There's a point where all we have left to save those "some" is prayer.

Did you notice that when Paul departs from the synagogue, he "took the disciples"? The word "aphorizō" is more directly translated, "separate," as we see in the KJV and NMV. Paul "departed from them, and separated the disciples." It's the same word used when Jesus teaches of the end, saying, "the angels will come out and separate the evil from the righteous" (Matthew 13:49 MEV), and it's the same word used when our Lord similarly says of His return, "He will separate them one from another as a shepherd separates his sheep from the goats" (Matthew 25:32 MEV).

Paul doesn't just walk out saying "come along brothers." No, this is a very distinct line in the sand. The taking of the disciples implies a far more explicit separation. "We are no longer affiliated with them, and will no longer let our minds be poisoned by their deceptions and blasphemies." The prayer of Jesus reveals that although we weren't taken out of this world, we are protected within it, yet at the same time, we are not to tempt the Lord our God. There's a time for evangelism to the heathen world, and there's a time to, "above all else, guard your heart" (Proverbs

4:23 NIV). Don't expect that you can spend your life among anti-Christian influences and not be influenced.

We shall soon come across the people of Asia separating themselves to the point of burning some of their most valuable possessions, and yet, in our modern faith, we seem to think we can play both sides.

"I know that show has vulgar sexual content, and advocates sinful lifestyles, but it is entertaining and it's just a TV show. I'm still a Christian." Well brothers and sisters, I'm here to break the news that this is not the Way. We are still in the world, yes, but we are called to be holy. That word means nothing less than "set apart." Yeah, plenty of people enjoy the little pleasures of this world, but that's not who we are saved to be. There's a reason Satan is called "the god of this world," and we'd do well to remember that. Whose children are we, really?

So Paul leaves, he separates the disciples, and he teaches Christ daily in a classroom.

"This continued for two years, so that all who lived in Asia heard the word of the Lord Jesus, both Jews and Greeks. God worked powerful miracles by the hands of Paul." - Acts 19:10-11 MEV

He stays for two years and "all who lived in Asia heard the word of the Lord," that is, all who would not refuse to hear. As mentioned yesterday, this city was a central hub where all of Asia would come. Some came to worship at the temple of Diana (Artemis). Others came for international trade. Some came for the skilled craftsmen, and others came to set sail from or land in the port. Endless reasons brought people to and from this city, and the Church here is credited for their service of evangelism to the Asian world by Jesus Himself, in Revelation chapter 2, though, notice again, it is God who worked the miracles, and God who equipped the preachers to speak. When we're told that all in Asia heard the word of the Lord because of the ministry in Ephesus, this is a word which history declares truth.

Brothers and sisters, Paul preached to the Jews until they would not be saved, but then he turned to those who would. God proves, over and over again, that He is a God who works powerful miracles and won't lose a single sheep. The goats choose their damnation, but the sheep hear His voice. If you are among the sheep, separate yourselves and be holy, because He is holy. We ought not let ourselves be again stained by a filthy world because we know it is Christ's blood that has washed us clean.

Notes

Day 120

Uncommon Miracles

"God worked powerful miracles by the hands of Paul. So handkerchiefs or aprons he had touched were brought to the sick, and the diseases left them, and the evil spirits went out of them." - Acts 19:11-12 MEV

At the risk of sounding like a broken record, we again come to a reminder that any great "Acts of the Apostles," were nothing less than "Acts of God." Notice the definite language; "God worked powerful miracles by the hands of Paul." While I am usually a particular fan of the MEV, if we were to read that solely we would miss an emphasis that sets the stage for this entire chapter. I believe the ESV brings it through among the clearest of translations, calling them "Extraordinary miracles." The original Greek language which Luke wrote was, "ou ho tygchanō," literally translated as "those not common." Put that into context of where we are.

This is Ephesus, where magic charms are uttered everywhere, every day. At the conclusion of this display, people burned their books containing magical arts, spells, and incantations, to the tune of 50,000 silver (the specific coinage of this silver is unknown, but it's the equivalent of somewhere between 4 million and 1.6 billion USD). "Common" is a rather relative word, and in this town, nothing they considered common would be anything less than extraordinary in our daily lives. So, consider what degree of "powerful miracles," God really wrought here as He did "miracles, and those not common."

"God was pleased to confirm the teaching of these holy men of old, that if their hearers believed them not, they might believe the works." - Matthew Henry

Remember that Luke was a physician, very specific in his examination of the medical instances throughout these years, and he says these were "diseases... and evil spirits". By the hem of his garment, Christ healed a woman. By the shadow of Peter, Christ healed the sick and cast out evil spirits. Now, by the sweaty and tool-stained cloths of Paul's tentmaking trade, Christ healed the sick and cast out evil spirits. Truly Jesus Christ assured that His Gospel was not easily disbelieved. Luke then records for us, a contrasting example.

"Then some of the itinerant Jewish exorcists invoked the name of the Lord Jesus over those who had evil spirits, saying, 'We command you to come out in the name of Jesus whom Paul preaches.' There were seven sons of a Jewish high priest named Sceva doing this. The evil spirit answered, 'I know Jesus, and I know Paul, but who are you?' Then the man in whom the evil spirit was jumped on them, overpowered them, and prevailed against them, so that they fled from that house naked and wounded." - Acts 19:13-16 MEV

Several ancient historians discussed these sorts of vagabond Jewish exorcists. They wandered the landscape, often in the superstitious and magic practicing Asian cities, using formulas and incantations to expel demons. Josephus, in his "antiquities," describes some of these arts or spells as having come down from Solomon. Yet this instance in Ephesus shows the true nature of their work. It wasn't a work of faith, but rather, a desperate grasping for anything that might work to earn them wealth or fame.

See how they invoke His name. It is not, "Jesus Christ our Lord," or even as Paul had cast out one demon, "I command you in the name of Jesus Christ." Au contraire, these sorcerer Jews command, "in the name of Jesus whom Paul preaches." They saw something work, and thought they'd use it to their gain; just another trick up their sleeves.

Even through their iniquity, God works the furtherance of his gospel and this demon is forced to declare Christ's superiority, then he makes a very public spectacle of those who would use His name in vain. Seven men are overpowered, stripped naked, and beaten bloody, by one demon possessed man, that is, one demon who could be cast out of the man merely by a garment that had touched one of Christ's faithful teachers.

"This became known to all Jews and Greeks living in Ephesus. And fear fell on them all, and the name of the Lord Jesus was magnified." - Acts 19:17 MEV

The purpose of any of these miracles was for one aim alone. That the Name of the Lord Jesus be magnified. The very fact that these exorcists had made a habit of using these charms of Solomon shows that God had, in times past, allowed them to be successful. To what end? That the name of Yahweh, the God of Abraham they invoked, would not be made a spectacle before the nations. Now though, Jesus' words are fulfilled "by whom do your sons cast them out? Therefore they will be your judges" (Matthew 12:27). These sons of a high priest try to use the name of Jesus for personal gain, without any faith at all, and the truth is revealed for all to see.

"Truly, truly I say to you, he who believes in Me will do the works that I do also. And he will do greater works than these, because I am going to My Father." - John 14:12 MEV

The words of Jesus were shown true, and the miracles He worked through His servants magnified His name in all the land. But any who would claim the name of Christ, without personal faith in Jesus should take heed. The enemy won't recognize an unbeliever attached to that Holy Name. As for those brothers and sisters who truly believe on the Lord Jesus Christ, we can also take heed of this demon's confession.

"I know Jesus, and I know Paul."

If indeed we are in Christ, and He in us, we are known in the heavenly realms - children of the one true God. The demons can oppress us, but they cannot possess us, nor harm our eternal souls. To the Father, we are known by Christ's righteousness, and to the enemy we are known by Christ's power. Fear not these demons, but don't pretend they're non-existent either. It is not possible to believe in the infallibility of scripture, while at the same time discounting Satan and his minions as fables. They're real, and to us who are in Christ, they're nothing more than temporary inconveniences; enemies who have already lost to the King.

Notes

Notes

Day 121

Abandon All Ties

"And this became known to all the residents of Ephesus, both Jews and Greeks. And fear fell upon them all, and the name of the Lord Jesus was extolled. Also many of those who were now believers came, confessing and divulging their practices. And a number of those who had practiced magic arts brought their books together and burned them in the sight of all. And they counted the value of them and found it came to fifty thousand pieces of silver. So the word of the Lord continued to increase and prevail mightily." - Acts 19:17-20 ESV

History confirms that Ephesus was known for its magic arts. Charms and incantations, written in books and sold for great amounts were aplenty, but some of these books were sold for a high price as rarities, or even containing exclusive charms. Ephesian letters, organized to be spoken with certain intonations, or written on medallions and parchments to be worn, brought the superstitious and desperate from miles around.

Now in this same city, God has shown, through His apostle Paul, and these sons of Sceva, that the Name of Christ is above any other name, and that it is not to be trifled with, nor is the religion of Christ to be corrupted with these heathen practices. Fittingly, and as we should expect, considering the situation, Luke records "fear fell upon them all." Then we see a living example of what it means to "be holy, for I AM holy" (Lev 11:44, 1 Pet 1:16). These who were now believers put themselves forward to be "a people set apart."

Just as we saw at John's baptismal ministry, we have the disciples coming and confessing their sins, and as the ESV puts it, "divulging their practices." The former magicians declared the secrets of how they had fooled people into following them. Try to get a magician to explain all his craft today, and you'll understand this was no small thing. There's no going back from that. To make such public revelation, they've come to decide that they can never go back to their old ways. They can't trick people who know their tricks. That's a sign of faith. The double-minded are not fit for the Kingdom of Heaven, but these disciples were far from double-minded.

Yet they do more than just divulge their secrets. These men and women burn the very books in which these incantations and charms are written. Not just a few books either. The type of silver coin is not specified, so we can't know for sure what this value is, but estimates range from 4 million to well over a billion modern US dollars. This was no small sacrifice. Ask yourself this: would we make a similar sacrifice today?

I'd be surprised if most of us would. Maybe we'd sell the books to reclaim their value, but then we'd be passively corrupting someone else. Some of us might hold on to them, you know, just in case this Jesus thing doesn't work out. Or possibly we would stuff them in a box in the attic, because we're just not ready to entirely give up the old life.

Brothers and sisters, let it not be so. If indeed we believe, let's follow the example of these and become a holy priesthood, dying to our former selves, and abandoning all ties to our iniquity, except the confession of such. Let's do what we must to rid the world of our former sinful influence, and be faithful servants by whom God works that, "the word of the Lord continue[s] to increase and prevail mightily."

Notes

Day 122

Pressing On

"After these things happened, Paul determined in his spirit to pass through Macedonia and Achaia and go to Jerusalem, saying, 'After I have been there, I must also see Rome.' He sent two who ministered to him, Timothy and Erastus, into Macedonia, but he delayed in Asia for a time." - Acts 19:21-22 MEV

Can we just spend a day taking ministerial inspiration from the Apostle? Would you look at that? Would ya just look at it? Seriously, this man has been through the wringer. He's been brought before numerous courts, imprisoned, beaten with rods until his back flesh was torn, and constantly accused of blasphemy of the God he served by the very people he worked to save. Yet at the same time, he's not necessarily driven by an unmet urge to overcome these obstacles and finally see success. The man, by the will and work of God, has already found extensive success, introducing countless souls to Christ's redeeming salvation. Yet onward he runs the race.

"Now concerning the collection for the saints, as I have given instruction to the churches of Galatia, so even you must do." - 1 Corinthians 16:1 MEV

Luke tells us Paul purposed in his heart to pass through Macedonia and Achaia, then return to Jerusalem, yet he first delayed in Ephesus, due to the importance of the locale in the spreading of the Gospel. But while he's there, Paul writes (among other epistles) the epistle to Corinth, chief city of Achaia. It is from that letter that we can discern Paul's intent in going to Jerusalem.

Paul instructs the church in Corinth to collect alms for the poor at the church in Jerusalem. In verse 3, he says he'll send a selected messenger to deliver the blessing, and in verse 4 says, "If it is fitting that I go also, they will go with me" (MEV). This seems to always be the attitude of the man. If God wills. Once he reaches Macedonia he writes a similar letter, but this time, to a church he has not yet been able to visit.

"making request if, by any means, now at last I might find a way in the will of God to come to you." - Romans 1:10 MEV

In this letter, we see Paul, more than once, declare these desires of his reborn heart to "see Rome." It is in these passages that we see the city's majesty is not what he endeavors to see, but rather Christ's Church there. This is something we see has long been the goal of his missions, though God has not allowed this dream to come true. Yet, in due time, Paul will come to learn that God had placed that dream there for a reason.

"Paul sought not to rest, but pressed on, as if he had yet done nothing. He is already possessed of Ephesus and Asia. He purposes for Macedonia and Achaia. He has his eye upon Jerusalem; then upon Rome; afterward on Spain. No Cesar, no Alexander the Great, no other hero, comes up to the magnanimity of this little Benjamite. Faith, and love to God and man, have enlarged his heart even as the sand of the sea." - Johann A. Bengel

In each of his three recorded missions, the Apostle is restricted by the Spirit from going all the way to Rome, much less Spain, but that doesn't stop him from chasing dreams of greater and greater works for the Kingdom of God.

"For this reason also I was often hindered from coming to you. But now, no longer having a place in these regions, and having a great desire for many years to come to you, whenever I go to Spain, I shall come to you, for I hope to see you when I pass through and to be helped on my way there by you, when I have first enjoyed your company for a little while. But now I am going to Jerusalem to minister to the saints." - Romans 15:22-25 MEV

Oh Paul, little did you know how this trip to Rome would come about, or how you would continue to be "hindered from coming to" the church at Rome. Over the next several chapters, we'll witness in detail (likely because of Luke's admitted presence for the proceedings) Paul's return to Jerusalem, and his nearly immediate imprisonment. The Lord had his will, and through trial after trial, Paul becomes, just as God had said, "a chosen vessel of Mine, to bear My Name before... Kings." The journey through court after court leads him exactly where he desired to go, and exactly where the Lord had told him it would.

"The following night the Lord stood by him and said, 'Take courage, Paul. For as you have testified about Me in Jerusalem, so you must also testify at Rome.' " - Acts 23:11 MEV

After a shipwreck on their way to Rome, Paul eventually realizes his dream of seeing Rome, though certainly not how he had intended. He arrives and spends two years chained in a private house, where we'll see our beloved physician's inspired writings come to an end, but we know from history and other epistles, such as those to Timothy, Paul's ministry did not end there. He was released, and well, we can't be sure, but the early Church fathers were of the belief that Paul did actually make it to Spain. Clement of Rome, for example, wrote a letter to the Corinthian church in which he says Paul, "had gone to the extremity of the west."

Now place yourself in Paul's shoes. For decades the man chased a dream of taking the Gospel to the head city of the empire. His heart for Christ even drew him to desire to go to the western extent of the Mediterranean nations. All along the way he's been slapped down, by God and by man. How many of us would have continued? I'd be surprised if many of us could, in utter honesty, say that we wouldn't have given up and redirected our goals a dozen times along the way.

You know, sometimes that is fitting, because our dreams are not always aligned with the will of God but rather our old hearts of stone. Sometimes, on the other hand, God has placed those dreams in our hearts, and the journey toward them through which he wills us travel, may seem as endless failure. Those are the purposes of our new heart, where we'd do well to remember the Proverb, and continue in what God wills and establishes for us.

"Ponder the path of your feet, and let all your ways be established. Do not turn to the right or to the left; remove your foot from evil." - Proverbs 4:26-27 MEV

Notes

Day 123

Greater Treasure

"For a silversmith named Demetrius, who made silver shrines for Artemis, brought much business to the craftsmen. He gathered them together with the workmen of similar trades and said, 'Men, you know that by this trade we have our wealth. And you see and hear, not only at Ephesus, but almost throughout all Asia, that this Paul has persuaded and turned away many people, saying that these things made by hands are not gods. Now not only is our trade in danger of coming into disrepute, but also the temple of the great goddess Artemis, whom all Asia and the world worship, may be discredited and her magnificence destroyed.' " - Acts 19:24-27 MEV

Luke introduces this by saying, "about that time great trouble arose about the Way." If we were to ask, from where did it arise, we must simply employ the generalization, "follow the money." The crowd ends up chanting, "great is Artemis of the Ephesians," but we're not there yet.

First, we read "A silversmith named Demetrius," and we're given an identity, then we see, "who made silver shrines for Artemis," and we're introduced to his trade niche. "Brought much business to the craftsmen," reveals to us from where his influence stems. He begins to speak, saying "Men, you know that by this trade we have our wealth," and we see both his motive, and the basis of his petition. He continues, "Paul has persuaded and turned away many people... Our trade [is] in danger," and his concern is revealed. Notice that almost the entirety of this introduction is about wealth. Follow the money.

"For where your treasure is, there will your heart be also." - Luke 12:34 MEV

Yes, this Demetrius appeals to religiosity, but only secondary to greed; His priorities, and those of his fellow tradesmen are clear. Look at what those other arguments are. He points to Paul "saying that these things made by hands are not gods." I've built or rebuilt many things in my years, and not a one of them, even before coming to Christ, could ever reasonably cause me to think, "this is a god." Either this man is so entirely blinded by his greed that he's lost all sense of reason, or he is not truly appealing to defend these gods, but rather to defend "these things made by hands, which we sell." I'd suggest the content of the rest of his speech makes clear it is the latter.

"Men are jealous for that by which they get their wealth; and many set themselves against the gospel of Christ, because it calls men from all unlawful crafts, however much wealth is to be gotten by them. There are persons who will stickle for what is most grossly absurd, unreasonable, and false; as this, that those are gods which are made with hands, if it has but worldly interest on its side." - Matthew Henry

Yet he also warns that the temple of Artemis (synonymous with Rome's goddess Diana) will be discredited, "and her magnificence destroyed." Clearly, he needed a hook. If Demetrius and his buddies ran out in the streets shouting, "great is our source of wealth," well, you can imagine how their neighbors might respond. If, on the other hand, they run out and stir up the population with shouts of "great is Artemis of the Ephesians," then the streets would be, "filled with confusion. And in unison they seized Gaius and Aristarchus" (Acts 19:29a MEV).

Once they get into the theater we again see, "the assembly confused" (vs 32a). Here a great trouble arose, and nobody, except those who started the fuss, knew what they were even angry about. But they must defend their little goddess and her temple, or else her magnificence might be destroyed.

Do you notice the placement of this specific concern? In verse 27 we have the silversmith warning that their goddess, "whom all Asia and the world worship," might have her magnificence destroyed. They need to stir up the entire city to rise up against a little, weak, and battered Jew and his small, peaceful band of traveling companions. But just 10 verses earlier, without ever lifting a finger from his daily endeavors, Paul is part of a story in which, "the name of the Lord Jesus was magnified."

Nobody worships Artemis anymore. Even those fanbases of Greek mythology, when describing her, use the past tense, indicative verb, "was." Compare that to our Lord, who does not need us to raise mob mentalities of violence in defense of His magnificence, and yet to this day we know The Lord Jesus Christ as, "Him who is and who was and who is to come" (Rev 1:4 MEV). The magnification of His Name needs not our defense, for Christ is inherently magnificent. He was here before the foundation of the Earth, and He'll reign when its foundations are torn asunder. This is no god made by human hands.

What should we children of His take from this though? Follow the money may be a functional phrase when it comes to investigation of facts and motives, but it is altogether a most dangerous approach when it comes to our hearts. If (or maybe a better word is "when") we find ourselves at a sudden financial development, for better or for worse, we should be extra cautious of where our treasure lies. Whether faced with the fears of financial hardships, or the temptation of financial blessings, let's keep in mind that the greatest treasure we could ever set our eyes on is to know and be known by our Christ. We cannot let the glorification of our God become second to the multiplication of our wealth.

Say, for example, you have come into some extra cash. You could go down to the dealership and buy that new car you've been wanting. It would be a great status symbol, and really would increase your comfort level. Or... You could browse the web to illumiNations.bible and choose a people group which hasn't yet been reached with the word of God in their own language, anonymously donate a selected amount. You would help in translation for a people who hasn't been able to read the word of God for themselves, as if funding Martin Luther and William Tyndale themselves.

Which would be a greater treasure in your eyes?

Notes

Notes

Day 124

Stand Firm

"So the city was filled with the confusion, and they rushed together into the theater, dragging with them Gaius and Aristarchus, Macedonians who were Paul's companions in travel. But when Paul wished to go in among the crowd, the disciples would not let him. And even some of the Asiarchs, who were friends of his, sent to him and were urging him not to venture into the theater." - Acts 19:29-31 ESV

These few verses hold several characters to which we can devote a quick study. First, we come to this confused crowd, with the universally dangerous mob mentality. We (and Paul) can easily see the danger these posed to Gaius and Aristarchus. The Asiarchs could see the danger they posed to Paul. The town clerk could see the danger they posed to themselves (vs 35-40).

We were created in the image of God, but in our iniquity, we're often no brighter than lemmings or cattle. Get us in that herd, and we'll trample anyone or anything, and follow the crowd right over a cliff of our own demise. As we're remade into the likeness of Christ, brothers and sisters, we ought not allow ourselves to be drawn into the world's mobs, and God forbid we build mobs like this in His Name.

Gaius and Aristarchus, on the far opposite end of the spectrum, are little more than ragdolls in this scene, dragged in and dropped in the midst of a crowd of potentially thousands of berserkers - it has been observed that this theater could hold 25,000 people - but while we see no recordable action or reaction from them in these verses, as we continue further into scripture, we'll discover they did something enormous. These two traveling companions of Paul's, are found in his continuing travels. They stood in the face of death, listening to hours of chants that could be paraphrased, "give up, you're surrounded," and they stood firm in the faith.

We may not live in lands or times in which we'll find ourselves singled out for our faith, literally surrounded by thousands chanting for our heads. Nevertheless, it behooves us, as followers of Him who was first hated by the world, to diligently inquire of ourselves this question: If that were me surrounded, with no hope of survival, could I - would I - hold fast to the testimony of my faith?

"There ought to be in all Christians, and especially in the ministers, an invincible steadfastness which may not by any storms or assaults be overcome, which nonetheless must modestly allow itself to be governed by wisdom." - Geneva Study Bible

The quote above stands in the gap between this pair and their traveling companion, Paul, to whom we now arrive. There are several characters in scripture of whose size we are informed, but Paul is not one of them. There are, though, several hints in the Bible which lend plausibility to the observation of one second century church father who described him as a large nosed, balding, and bow-legged man of medium to small stature. With that context, look again at Paul, ready to charge in before thousands.

This man is not fueled by self-confidence, but rather God-confidence. This isn't Samson, ready to charge in and fight a thousand men with nothing more than the jawbone of an ass. This pathetic little preacher sees his friends in deep waters, and cannot in good conscience, stand by without joining them to see what God would do. God did, indeed, do something, but first Paul must be coached back in God's wisdom by his brethren, and shown confirmation in an extraordinary way.

About that extraordinary way, we come to the Asiarchs. Now your preferred translation may present them as "rulers," "chiefs," or "officials" of Asia, but the original Greek was a single word, literally translated as Asiarchs. That's important because these weren't just praetors, governors, judges, and kings. The Asiarchs were an entirely different class. It was an annually elected position; chosen men of influence and wealth, who would preside over, and even pay for the sacred games and festivals to their gods - namely Artemis. Many of them were even priests and high priests of these Greek gods.

Their job in Ephesus was literally to make sure that Artemis was properly worshipped, yet God raised up men to defend Paul from among those who, by all reason, we should expect to see lead this riot. Many commentators have deemed them cowards for not directly standing up in authority to calm the crowd, and maybe that's a fair assessment, but I tend to believe they, in the nature of elected politicians, commissioned the town clerk in their stead to stand up and silence the tumult.

We don't know if these Asiarchs ever came to Christ or not, but from Luke's language - "friends of [Paul's]" - we can safely conclude that these were not, at this time, disciples of Christ. Yet something about this pathetic, little, repentant pharisee earned their esteem. As his friends I have no doubt that they had heard the Gospel extensively, though they had not submitted to the Lord. If that's you today, feeling the tug of God on your heart - if you're reading this today - and you have not yet submitted your heart to the Lordship of Jesus Christ, I plead humbly, do not delay. None of us is ever guaranteed another day to live. Until He returns there is never a today that is too late to turn to Christ, but tomorrow may just be a bridge too far.

Notes

Notes

Day 125

Noise and Clamour

"Some of the crowd prompted Alexander, whom the Jews had put forward. And Alexander, motioning with his hand, wanted to make a defense to the crowd. But when they recognized that he was a Jew, for about two hours they all cried out with one voice, 'Great is Artemis of the Ephesians!' " - Acts 19:33-34 ESV

There's a word toward the beginning of verse 33 here, which has caused a variety of interpretations (instructed, brought, drew, prompted), because of the various meanings of the original word. For an English demonstration of what I mean, take a look at the word "right." The right (correct) interpretation, if we seek to determine between right (morally) and wrong, as it pertains to a basic human right (legal or moral claim to), can be found by studying the parchment to your right (directionally). This word was similarly fluid, but I like ESV's translation, for the word "prompted" seems to have, to the best of my vocabulary, the closest connection to all intents.

That's not been the only subject of debate among scholars though, in studying this passage. Ask yourself, "who is Alexander?" There are a few things we can draw from the passage, among which primarily I note that Luke gives no definition of who Alexander is. It's as if the man is so known that he need not be introduced as the others, "who were disciples," "sons of the high priest ___," "his traveling companions," "of Achaia," and on and on. Luke, writing his history, need not introduce Alexander, and so we can deduce the receipt of this letter would be met with clear understanding of who this man was. Yet the centuries melted away, and so did his notoriety, and we are now left to conjecture.

Various beliefs about this man stand, one being that he was a Christian who the Jews put forth maliciously. I personally don't believe Luke's specific language supports the claim. The 17th century political theorist and theologian, Hugo De Grotius (among many others), believed this to be the same Alexander of whom Paul wrote to young Timothy, and I find myself in the same camp of thought.

"Alexander the coppersmith did me great harm; the Lord will repay him according to his deeds. Beware of him yourself, for he strongly opposed our message." - 2 Timothy 4:14-15 ESV

If this be the case, we find some definition as to why the Jews put this man forward. Chiefly, he was a coppersmith, one of Demetrius' artificers, and would therefore have more sway among this mob than any ol' Jewish priest or trader. There was, though, another instance of Paul discussing this Alexander, and it gives details enlightening us to another strategic angle for the Jews.

"This charge I entrust to you, Timothy, my child, in accordance with the prophecies previously made about you, that by them you may wage the good warfare, holding faith and a good conscience. By rejecting this, some have made shipwreck of their faith, among whom are Hymenaeus and Alexander, whom I have handed over to Satan that they may learn not to blaspheme." - 1 Timothy 1:18-20 ESV

Before stating that "he strongly opposed our message," Paul declared that to attempt a correction of the blaspheme of Alexander, he took the action which he advocates in 1 Corinthians 5:5. Remember that Paul had actually written that Epistle during his over two year stay in building the church in Ephesus. He wrote a difficult matter to Corinth, but not as one who didn't practice what he preached. Paul was likely enforcing this discipline, as he instructed the Corinthians to do the same.

"You are to deliver this man to Satan for the destruction of the flesh, so that his spirit may be saved in the day of the Lord." - 1 Corinthians 5:5 ESV

We then come back to 2 Timothy - written somewhere up to 7 years after 1 Timothy and upwards of 15 years after the Ephesian ministry - and see the man hasn't repented. He truly made a shipwreck of his faith. So, what does all that have to do with the Jews in the tumultuous Ephesian theater? Here was a man with knowledge of Christian doctrines, who had apostatized to Judaism. Add that to his influence earned by shared trade, and he's their perfect weapon to defend the argument, "hey don't look at us, we're not with those (spit) Christians."

It's a sad thing to consider that some who had apparently turned to Christ will be again enslaved by the devil in apostasy, but it cannot be whitewashed from scripture. Some of these, even to this day, we will find to be the most greatly opposed to our message, but while they may be the loudest voice in the room at times, we must keep in mind there is no voice more potent than that which spoke the heavens and the earth into existence. Immediately after warning Timothy about this Alexander, Paul writes a heartfelt bitterness which was sweetened by the truth of God.

"At my first defense no one came to stand by me, but all deserted me. May it not be charged against them! But the Lord stood by me and strengthened me, so that through me the message might be fully proclaimed and all the Gentiles might hear it. So I was rescued from the lion's mouth. The Lord will rescue me from every evil deed and bring me safely into his heavenly kingdom. To him be the glory forever and ever. Amen." - 2 Timothy 4:16-18 ESV

I can't help but wonder, as the Apostle wrote these words, if he saw the parallel to the situation Gaius and Aristarchus had found themselves in. Could Paul have bolstered his faith by remembering how God had rescued his traveling companions from the lion's mouth when he, himself, had not come to stand by them?

Look now again to our selected passage in the riot at Ephesus, as this apostate blasphemer stood up to join in the charge, greatly opposing them. He's never even given a chance to speak, and the mob loses their collective minds.

"Great is Diana of the Ephesians — This was all the cry for two hours together; and it was thought a sufficient confutation of Paul's doctrine, that they are no gods which are made with hands! and thus the most sacred truths are often run down with nothing else but noise and clamour and popular fury!" - Joseph Benson

Truly, walking out of that theater, Gaius and Aristarchus could say, "The Lord will rescue me from every evil deed and bring me safely into his heavenly kingdom." Today we certainly face "noise and clamour and popular fury," as the anti-Christian trends gain exceedingly greater reign across media platforms. The vocal minority is increasingly swaying the minds of the vacillating and indecisive. But fear not, my brethren, "wage the good warfare, holding faith and a good conscience."

The Lord's omnipresent voice echoes across the ages. He stands by us and strengthens us so that the message might be fully proclaimed. He will rescue us from every evil deed, and carry us "safely into His heavenly kingdom. To Him be the glory forever and ever. Amen." Stand firm in the faith. The clamor and popular fury will continue to grow, but we know it will be silenced.

Notes

Day 126

All Night Long

"On the first day of the week, when we were gathered together to break bread, Paul talked with them, intending to depart on the next day, and he prolonged his speech until midnight. There were many lamps in the upper room where we were gathered." -Acts 20:7-8 ESV

The uproar in Ephesus dies down, and Paul endeavors to get back on the move. He travels around to the Macedonian churches, edifying them to higher levels of faith and understanding, then spends 3 months in Greece. Getting ready to head out, he learns of a plot against him, and changes his travel plans, doubling back through Macedonia, to where we now find him, in Troas.

Luke is again traveling with the apostle, and we get the detail that they stayed here for 7 days. Now it is the first day of the week, but also, their last day before again sailing out. The Sabbath has come and gone, and it is now the Lord's Day. As we've recently discovered, the first epistle to Corinth has already been written in which Paul makes note of this first day as a special day for the alms-givings of the followers of Christ.

"On the first day of the week let every one of you lay in store, as God has prospered him, so that no collections be made when I come." - 1 Corinthians 16:2 MEV

After decades pass, the Apostle John, in his Revelation prophecy, also makes special mention of this day saying, "I was in the Spirit on the Lord's Day" (Revelation 1:10a MEV). Whether or not it had, at this point, become the standard day of fellowship, as it would officially in the fourth century, is not really defined, though there's evidence that the Lord's supper was being regularly shared on Sunday evenings even then.

What we've seen throughout Luke's history though is that Paul at times preached every Sabbath, and at times preached every day. His ministry was not constrained to a single day. It would seem evident from the overall context, that for this seven days Paul was teaching every chance he got. He knew this to be the last time he'd see them.

But why all night long? Aside from the factor of heat, many of these children of God were still slaves under heathen masters, or even freedmen, still in the employment of their old service. It is almost certain that at least some, if not most or all of these men and women had worked hard all day, and chose to spend their night sitting in discourse with the Apostle - that is, asking questions and learning all they can before he was gone. That's not just an hour after work. Eutychus fell out of the window around midnight, but they continued the discourse until dawn (vs 11).

"How seldom are hours of repose broken for the purposes of devotion! but how often for mere amusement or sinful revelry! So hard is it for spiritual life to thrive in the heart of man! so naturally do carnal practices flourish there!" - Matthew Henry

Did that hurt a little bit? Have you ever sat wondering when your pastor was going to wrap it up? "He's running long today." You're not going to beat the crowd to the store, or the restaurant. Tap, tap, tap goes the toe. If you showed up to church on Sunday, and the service kept going all day and maybe even into the night, would you make your displeasure heard? Let me back up and ask, would you be frustrated, or excited about what God's doing? If your church held an all-night service, would you be as excited as you are for that concert, game, or maybe even bar, that'll keep you up all night next weekend?

Notes

Day 127

His Life is in Him

"A young man named Eutychus sat in the window, falling into a deep sleep as Paul spoke for a longer time. Being overcome by sleep, he fell down from the third floor and was taken up dead. Paul went down and leaned over him, and embracing him said, 'Do not be troubled, for he is alive.' " Acts 20:9-10 MEV

There have been many things said about poor Eutychus over the years. Some use him to shame those who snooze in the pews. There are those who believe the verbiage "taken up dead," and "his life is in him," imply he wasn't really dead at all; this was no miracle, just the observance of a man laid across a seriously wounded boy, feeling either heartbeat or breath. Still others present the idea that the young man falling out the window was organized by the devil to interrupt Paul's final teaching in this city.

Think of the context though, and it's hard to compare Eutychus to the man sleeping through a 45-minute sermon at 10am on Sunday. Here it is at midnight, in the Middle Eastern springtime, and Paul is teaching and answering questions all night long. With many lamps and many bodies in a small room, the window is open to let heat and fumes out. If you've ever been in a place that's so stuffy you can barely breathe, then found a comfortable place to sit, where there is fresh, cool air, you may have found yourself, as I have, struggling not to doze. I doubt we can fairly blame the boy. Even Luke's words, "being overcome by sleep," indicate a positive struggle to stay attentive.

Or how about the idea that he wasn't really dead after all? Remember that traveling with Paul we again see our beloved physician, whose attention to medical detail has been verging on obsessive. Likewise, Paul gets up from the boy saying, don't worry, he's alive, then goes back upstairs and eats (whether communion, agape meal, or just refreshment to strengthen for the rest of the evening we don't know). They listened to him the rest of the night and were greatly comforted. The boy just fell 3 stories for crying out loud. Would you be greatly comforted if your son, fell out a window, and lying unconscious, was declared alive by a man who then says, come let's eat and chat? You'd probably think the man was a complete jerk.

Add to all that something that doesn't come through in English, and I think we have a clear refutation of the claim. In Mark 9, Jesus expels a demon from a boy who is "as one dead" (hōsei nekros), but Jesus reveals he's actually alive. On the other hand, the Greek words which Luke so specifically chose were "airō nekros." This word "airō" is a verb of movement. He was literally "taken up dead." What Luke is telling us is someone who loved him ran down, grabbed up the corpse in a desperate attempt to find some sign of life. Tears are flowing! It's hard to believe, his mother, brother, wife, or whoever, with his head on their lap, was not wailing out for the doctor they knew to be present. Even Paul's response, "do not be troubled," is more accurately translated "make ye no ado." He literally tells them to quit wailing, with the same word Jesus uses when asking "why make this uproar and weep" (Mark 5:39 MEV). Luke most certainly verified the boy was dead. This was the record of a miraculous healing in the style of Elijah (1 kings 17:21) and Elisha (2 kings 4:34).

So, was this a devilish plot to disrupt Paul's teaching? I'm not sure we could really say one way or another. It surely happened. Was it pure luck? Maybe an attack of the enemy? Whatever the case may be, we may apply the words of Jesus at the news of Lazarus' death. "Lazarus is dead. And I am glad for your sakes that I was not there, so that you may believe" (John 11:14b-15a). Why does God let bad things happen to good people? Well, here we have one instance, much like the death of Lazarus, where it was the necessary step to boost faith in many.

"Jesus' healings are not supernatural miracles in a natural world. They are the only truly 'natural' thing in a world that is unnatural, demonized, and wounded." - Jürgen Moltmann

Yes, God could, in an instant, end all death, and sickness and suffering. What would happen? We would return to the choice of Adam and Eve, and in unbelief, again choose the devil's lies. Death would re-enter, and we'd start all over. It is "natural," in our fallen state, to wonder why God allows such suffering, but the truth of the matter is, He's already working the solution - The Only Solution.

Jesus' ministry of miraculous healings in the Gospels and the Acts, were nothing short of glimpses into his final work of restoring the believers back to the perfect garden. About Moltmann's profound statement above, Dane Ortlund makes an observation I'd suggest applies to this book of the Acts of Jesus' Christ as well.

"We tend to think of the miracles of the gospels as interruptions in the natural order... We are so used to a fallen world that sickness, disease, pain, and death seem natural. In fact, they are the interruption." - Gentle and Lowly

The boy fell, in a fallen world. Any one of us could hear of a boy falling out of a third story window, and if we didn't immediately assume him dead, we at least would be hard pressed to be convinced he was not seriously injured and suffering great pain. That is the result of us being conditioned by a lifetime in a fallen world.

Brothers and sisters, as you see these great miracles in the Holy Bible, or maybe you've seen great miracles in your life, take heart. Let your faith be multiplied and strengthened, for what God has done is to show you what lay ahead for the believer who holds fast to the testimony of this faith.

Good things, beyond our worldly comprehension are in store, brothers and sisters. We can read about no more tears, or pain, no more suffering, or death, streets of gold, rivers of living water, and so much more, but I don't believe that we have the capacity, or even context to truly understand how wonderful the promises we have really are.

"And [they] were greatly comforted" (vs 12b MEV).

Paul was leaving these men and women for the very last time. God allowed some temporary suffering, and by it all, this church was left with a confirmation they could never forget. "So that you may believe." This man preached to them by the power of the one true God. Never again would they have legitimate cause to doubt.

Notes

Day 128

If it Seems Advisable

"Paul had decided to sail by Ephesus, to avoid spending time in Asia. For he was hurrying so he could be in Jerusalem, if possible, on the day of Pentecost." - Acts 20:16 MEV

About a week ago we considered a passage from the previous chapter in which Paul "determined in his spirit to... go to Jerusalem" (19:21 MEV). We acknowledged his normal submission to God's sovereign will, and even referenced his first letter to the Corinthians where he tells them he will send a messenger with their alms to Jerusalem, then writes, "if it is fitting that I go also, they will go with me" (1 Cor 16:4 MEV). Today though, as we again come to Paul's determination in the spirit to go, I'd suggest we revisit those passages from a different angle, and even skim ahead a bit as well.

Depending upon your preferred translation, when you look at 19:21, you'll likely either see "in the Spirit," or "in the spirit," and if you're paying attention, you may notice the variance in capitalization. You see, by the original language we don't really know for absolute certain what was being said. Was Luke saying that the Holy Spirit was leading him to Jerusalem, or was it Paul's own evangelistic spirit for his own people that led him through this journey? I personally believe the MEV got it correct, saying he purposed "in his spirit," and there are some clues that lead me to that belief.

First and foremost, let's look at the cues we have in the language. The interpretation of many Greek words is dependent upon context found in the words surrounding them. Thayer's Greek Lexicon is a great tool for deciphering the meaning of the Greek in a specific passage, based upon the inflection, context, and more. What do they say specifically of this passage? The language indicates a clear meaning, "To propose to oneself."

Next, we can look back again at that letter to Corinth, and take note. He deviates from his standard M.O. Notice it's not "if the Lord wills, I will go with them." The sudden departure in his verbiage seems a bit Freudian, as he says, "if it is fitting" (MEV), or "if it seems advisable" (ESV). But did it seem advisable? We can now look forward in Acts, and I'd say we have our answer.

"And see, now I go bound in the spirit to Jerusalem, not knowing the things that will happen to me there, except that the Holy Spirit testifies in every city, saying that chains and tribulations await me." - Acts 20:22-23 NKJV

The disciples at Tyre, "told Paul through the Spirit not to go up to Jerusalem. But when our days were over we parted and traveled on" (Acts 21:4b-5a MEV).

At every turn, Paul is getting signs from God that it is not advisable, but he's being about as stubborn as a mule. Now at Caesarea the prophet Agabus is given prophecy by the Holy Spirit that, in Jerusalem, Paul would be bound and handed over to the Gentiles. "When we heard these things, both we and the residents implored him not to go up to Jerusalem" (Acts 21:12 MEV).

"So when he would not be persuaded, we ceased, saying, 'The will of the Lord be done.' And after those days we packed and went up to Jerusalem." - Acts 21:14-15 NKJV

What we're looking at here is a man, with a right heart about him - notice in 21:13 he says he is ready to be imprisoned or even die "for the name of the Lord Jesus" - yet even so, his mind is straying from the will of God. With every warning, he continues in what he has decided, and what he has purposed. You must remember that every human character in this book, short of Jesus Christ Himself, paints a picture of broken flesh for us. We cannot idolize this Paul. He was just a flawed human like you or I. But God.

"Christianity is the story of the faithfulness of our God, not the faithfulness of us." - Paul Mowery

But God, having given every warning, carries Paul alive, though battered, through the lion's den. Christ brings Paul out the other side of his folly, and the man finally makes it to Rome and beyond where his ministry for Christ continues. This Apostle pushed forward, hundreds of miles, as all along God was standing before him saying, "hey son, you're headed the wrong direction." Even so, we don't see God say, "ok, good luck, I'll just find someone else then."

"The following night" - that is, after Paul has tried his way only to see God was right - "the Lord stood by him and said, 'Take courage, Paul. For as you have testified about Me in Jerusalem, so you must also testify at Rome.' " - Acts 23:11

Have you ever walked in stubbornness, maybe even with good godly intentions, yet against the will of God? When He finally opens your eyes, it's extremely disappointing, isn't it? Are you maybe walking your own way right now, afraid to look back and see God's expression? Brothers and sisters, take heart. The Lord saw all of that before He chose to die for you. It doesn't matter if you've walked hundreds of miles in the wrong direction, He's still right there with you, waiting to put you back into the good fight. So don't let, "if it seems right," keep leading you to bondage. Turn back and allow, "if the Lord wills," to guide your life into the Way.

Notes

Notes

Day 129

Beneficial Necessity

"I did not keep from declaring what was beneficial to you, and teaching you publicly and from house to house, testifying to both Jews and Greeks of repentance toward God and of faith in our Lord Jesus Christ." - Acts 20:20-21 MEV

Declaring what was beneficial, both repentance toward God and faith in our Lord Jesus Christ. I could sit here all day yet never find a more succinct sentence to summarize the whole gospel. Paul spent years in Ephesus testifying and edifying, introducing men and women to Christ's salvation, and appointing these elders to Christ's employment, but this single sentence is the very essence of all he spoke. The beneficial necessity of repentance toward God, and faith in the Lord Jesus Christ.

"... repentance towards God, and faith towards our Lord Jesus Christ, with their fruits and effects. Without these no sinner can escape, and with these none will come short of eternal life." - Matthew Henry

There is no Jew, nor Greek, American, nor Iranian, Caucasian, nor Asian, Hispanic, nor African, native, nor alien who does not need this gospel. When it comes down to the day that each and every one of us is brought to judgement, there will be no distinction; All need the salvation of Jesus Christ, and all who have that have need of nothing else.

Without that, doubters ask, why would a good God allow such evil in the world. What we fail to account for, when posing such a question, is that He is not allowing it at all. We chose evil. "Truly, these times of ignorance God overlooked, but now commands all men everywhere to repent" (Acts 17:30 NKJV). The fact of the matter is, God is not allowing evil, He is allowing us time to repent - that is change our minds - and abandon evil before he destroys it. The truth is, if He shouldn't allow evil right now, every single one of us should perish with it, but that is not the God who saves. The Lord is long-suffering, that we may turn toward Jesus.

"... we have here a brief summary of all Gospel preaching. And it is easy to see why repentance is here put before faith; for the former must of necessity precede the latter. There is a repentance subsequent to faith, the fruit of felt pardon and restoration. It was this which drew the tears with which the Saviour's feet were once so copiously moistened. (Lu 7:37, 38, 47; and compare Eze 16:63). But that is not the light in which it is here presented." - Jamieson-Fausset-Brown study bible

What these three men wrote is absolutely true. There is no such thing as faith in the Lord Jesus Christ, unless one first believes in the need for His redemption. That, my friends, is the result of repentance toward God. Only by turning from sin toward God, can we begin to realize how far we've fallen, and the just punishment we deserve. Yet Charles Spurgeon notes a very specific warning which many in the pews should reflect upon. "There is a repentance that is faulty because it is not toward God." He goes on:

"In some there is a repentance of sin that is produced by a sense of shame. The evildoers are found out... They are repentant because they have dishonored themselves. If they had not been found out, in all probability, they would have continued comfortably in the sin, and even have gone further in it. Their shame is not evangelical repentance, and a person may go to hell with a blush on his face."

"Some again have a repentance that consists in grief because of the painful consequences of sin. There is no true repentance that only consists of being sorry because one is smarting under the consequences of sin."

"Others exhibit a repentance that consists entirely of horror of the future punishment of sin. If we have no repentance for the sin itself, it is in vain that we should stand and tremble because of a judgement to come." - C.H. Spurgeon

What Charles works up to is a summary that all repentance is fruitless, unless it's the true repentance toward God; That even if we were promised no consequence, shame, or punishment, we'd still choose God over sin. Repentance toward God that leads to faith in the Lord Jesus Christ, is that very acknowledgement of the truth that every path of sin that has ever enticed men and women with promises of pleasure and enrichment, only ever, in their end, led to suffering and impoverishment; God's rule was always right - the only Way to true joy and peace.

Notes

Notes

Day 130

None of These Things Move Me

"not knowing the things that will happen to me there, except that the Holy Spirit testifies in every city, saying that chains and tribulations await me. But none of these things move me; nor do I count my life dear to myself, so that I may finish my race with joy, and the ministry which I received from the Lord Jesus, to testify to the gospel of the grace of God."
- Acts 20:22b-24 NKJV

A couple of days ago, we considered the very real possibility that Paul is now headed toward Jerusalem, with good intent, yet against the will of God. Whether or not that is accurate, I ask this morning to examine the determination in the Apostle's service. If you've been following along with me through this study of Acts, you may have tired of the question, "would I hold firm the declaration of faith in the face of persecution?" It may be one that is beneficial for us to regularly ponder in our mostly peaceful lives, marked by the freedom of religion. We're building muscle memory of the brain, so to speak, in the event we ever face such tribulations. And so, whether we exhaust of this query or not, as we study those who faced it every day, we continue.

"It adds a great force to this, and all the other passages of Scripture, in which the apostles express their contempt of the world, that they were not uttered by persons like Seneca and Antoninus, who talked elegantly of despising the world in the full affluence of all its enjoyments; but by men who daily underwent the greatest calamities, and exposed their lives in proof of the truth of their assertions." - Joseph Benson

We can count ourselves among the likes of Seneca or Antoninus, as we enjoy the luxuries of peaceful lives, in our homes, with our friends and family, worshipping safely in our churches on Sunday morning, yet pondering this question. God gave us a great tool, though, in His authoritative word, and especially in Dr. Luke's history, as we can study those whose lives were truly given to the cross.

We can look at men like Paul, a citizen of Rome, and Pharisee of Pharisees, who gave up all the affluence and notoriety the ancient world had to offer, for the promise of "chains and tribulations." We ought to try to place ourselves in their shoes, and look out from their eyes, as we can with Paul here, staring off across the Mediterranean toward Jerusalem, and saying, "none of these things move me."

"The powerful influences of the Holy Spirit bind the true Christian to his duty. Even when he expects persecution and affliction, the love of Christ constrains him to proceed. None of these things moved Paul from his work; they did not deprive him of his comfort. It is the business of our life to provide for a joyful death." - Matthew Henry

Whether or not Paul's mission was now pitted against the will of God, he earnestly believed himself to be doing the Lord's work. That can be dangerous if we're not in tune with His will, and Paul suffers for it, but this is a matter of a wrong head, not a wrong heart. What lay in his heart, is the ever-present mission of his life, to fight the good fight to the end, run the race to completion, and be counted innocent of the blood of all men. Here's the watchman, seeing the warning, and he's giving his all to pronounce it to the people. The man truly lives what he teaches.

"For I consider that the sufferings of this present time are not worthy to be compared with the glory which shall be revealed to us."- Romans 8:18 MEV

No amount of worldly suffering could move Paul, because he knew it to be but a blink in the eternal life of those who are resurrected in Christ. So "[he] press[ed] on toward the goal for the prize of the upward call of God in Christ Jesus" (Philippians 3:14 ESV). He knew not how bad things would become, or if he would die in Jerusalem, but the man went forth, believing in his heart of hearts that the Lord's service was all that truly mattered in this world.

Do you know anyone who just by being around them you feel inspired to do better, be better, serve better? Can you count Paul as one of those today? We don't currently face the sufferings he so regularly knew (though I suspect we will in our lifetimes), yet as we flip through the pages of his life, can we take inspiration into our own lives? For those of us in

Christ, we all walk toward that same, "glory which shall be revealed to us."

"We have no such obstacles in our course as Paul had in his, but the same spirit must mark us if we are to do our work. Consciousness of a mission, fixed determination to carry it out, and consequent contempt of hindrances, belong to all noble lives, and especially to true Christian ones." - Alexander McLaren

As you read McLaren's words here, I ask you to run them by Henry's commentary, "It is the business of our life to provide for a joyful death." All our lives we've been programmed to "provide for a joyful death," but in oh so wrong a way. Slave hard, save hard, stuff the bank, and bank much stuff, because the goal of life is to end with more than the next guy, right? Wrong, brothers and sisters. We are those who are called to store our treasures not here on earth, but "in heaven, where neither moth nor rust destroys and where thieves do not break in and steal" (Matthew 6:20 ESV).

Children of God, hear this: "Consciousness of a mission, fixed determination to carry it out, and consequent contempt of hindrances, belong to all noble lives, and especially to true Christian ones." By faith alone in Christ alone you are saved. No amount of work can earn you one more ounce of salvation than you already have. Even so, there are treasures and rewards awaiting our service in heaven. Brothers and sisters, serve as if your eternal lives depended upon it.

"But I do not account my life of any value nor as precious to myself, if only I may finish my course and the ministry that I received from the Lord Jesus, to testify to the gospel of the grace of God." - Acts 20:24 ESV

Notes

Notes

Day 131

The Whole Counsel of God

"Therefore I testify to you this day that I am innocent of the blood of all men. For I did not keep from declaring to you the whole counsel of God. Therefore take heed to yourselves and to the entire flock, over which the Holy Spirit has made you overseers, to shepherd the church of God which He purchased with His own blood." - Acts 20:26-28 MEV

It's been said that there is no more important lecture for the minister of Christ to heed than Paul's final address to the Ephesian elders. Indeed, the Apostle considered these words of utmost value. These men were the best of the best, from the church where he had, to this point, spent more time than anywhere else, and from whence the gospel spread as it had from no other place.

We can now look back and see the fruit of these words, as we have the history of the Church at Ephesus gracing historical documents all through the ages up to the ninth century. In Paul's 3 years there we were told all of Asia (that is Asia minor, or mostly what we now know as Turkey) heard the word of Christ. Imagine the count of the flock our Good Shepherd appointed to the care of these undershepherds!

But Paul now leaves, knowing that "none of you... will see my face again." Surely, there is no coincidence that having made such a statement, he proceeds by echoing the parting words of Moses, and says, "I testify to you this day" (See Deuteronomy 8:19). Just as Moses, repeated all the warnings God had given him for Israel, and was thereby innocent of their blood (Ezekiel 33), so Paul now reckons himself the watchman commanded to blow the trumpet, and having faithfully done so, he reiterates the warning. The instruction of the Lord given to the prophet Ezekiel seems to have been ever present in the mind of Paul. How many times has he referenced it now?

But recognizing his own innocence in this matter, Paul is not content to leave it there. He gives grand instruction to these ministers, from which we have much to learn. Yes, that means we, who are given to some form of ministry for Christ, but don't discount yourself from that if you are not a pastor, deacon, elder, or the like. Do you have children at home? The Lord has placed you as an overseer of a portion of His flock. Have you opened your home to a small group? The Lord has placed a portion of his flock in your care. Are you the mature Christian in a workplace with both new believers, and some very worldly influencers? The Lord has strategically positioned you on the front lines, to fend off the wolves. "Therefore take heed to yourselves and to the entire flock."

"Take heed to yourself and to the doctrine. Continue in them, for in doing this you will save both yourself and those who hear you." - 1 Timothy 4:16 MEV

It cannot be overlooked that both here, and in the first pastoral epistle to Timothy, Paul places "take heed to yourself," first. "For if a man does not know how to manage his own house, how will he take care of the church of God?" (1 Timothy 3:5 MEV). Whether the Lord has ordained you pastor of a congregation of 10,000, or the parent of a single child, you are warned to first remove the plank from your own eye.

"He said to him again a second time, 'Simon, son of John, do you love Me?' He said to Him, 'Yes, Lord. You know that I love You.' He said to him, 'Tend My sheep.' " - John 21:16 MEV

The true Christian has the right to say, "we are those who love Him, because He loved us first. You know that I love you, Lord," to which the Lord Jesus Christ replies, "feed My lambs" (John 21:15). That makes Paul's address vital daily instruction to all but the monk, hiding alone in a castle hidden among the mountaintops. What does Paul say but "I am innocent of the blood of all men, For I did not keep from declaring to you the whole counsel of God."

If we are to take heed to ourselves first, and to the whole flock, do we test all teachers we listen to against the word of God? The preacher of the word of God has dangerous influence over our perspectives of the Lord's truths. Look at how lost Israel had grown under the blind leadership they followed. I've honestly lost count of how many times the New Testament (not to mention the Old) warns us to beware of false prophets, wolves in sheep's clothing, or as Paul describes in verse 29, "dreadful wolves [who] will enter among you, not sparing the flock."

"But there were also false prophets among the people, just as there will be false teachers among you, who will secretly bring in destructive heresies, even denying the Lord who bought them, bringing swift destruction upon themselves." - 2 Peter 2:1 MEV

Do you ever read "Christian" books and wonder where the scripture is? Maybe you sit in church and hear a great motivational speech, with maybe a passing reference here or there to a single passage or two? Or maybe, if you've been attending the same church for a long time, you've noticed you only ever hear the same few hundred verses, over and over again, on repeat; the same recycled sermons from 2 years ago?

We wonder why kids these days are growing up absolutely unable to believe that the Christianity they were raised in is anything but hypocritical superstition. But how could we expect them to believe if what they were hearing was not the full truth of God? If passages, taken out of context are used by false teachers, to present a false gospel - or even by well-intentioned teachers presenting a partial gospel - should we expect them to follow that? Would we want them to? Brothers and sisters, we've been charged with a great duty to tend the flock for our Shepherd. We must be vigilant, and we must be tenacious when it comes to holding off those who play loose with the word of God.

"All Scripture is inspired by God and is profitable for teaching, for reproof, for correction, and for instruction in righteousness, that the man of God may be complete, thoroughly equipped for every good work." - 2 Timothy 3:16-17 MEV

The whole counsel of God is not something to be tossed aside. Sure, there are some verses that are more widely applicable than others. Indeed, like Paul and Ezekiel 33, we may find passages that the Holy Spirit implants firmly into the forefront of our minds. But brothers and sisters, when we see a question like, "what verse do you lean on in hard times," do we consider how much we're missing out on by leaning solely upon a verse, when this entire living and active Word of God is our connection to His strength? Take heed to yourselves, that you study the whole counsel of God, and take heed to the flock for the same. Don't let your Christianity balance upon the words of any preacher or teacher, but especially not on one who only cares for certain portions of this Holy Bible.

"For you know that you were not redeemed from your vain way of life inherited from your fathers with perishable things, like silver or gold, but with the precious blood of Christ, as of a lamb without blemish and without spot." - 1 Peter 1:18-19 MEV

The Lord redeemed you with His very own, precious blood. The wolves smell blood, my brethren, and they're hungry. To whatever degree God has made you an undershepherd, tend His flock. Keep your eyes peeled, and your wits about you. They bring destructive heresies, even denying the Lord who bought them. Do you not see how even our children are on the menu these days?

Notes

Day 132

Breaking Stones, Building Walls

"Now, brothers, I commend you to God and to the word of His grace, which is able to build you up and give you an inheritance among all who are sanctified." - Acts 20:32 MEV

When we witness the departure of a faithful minister, leaving with knowledge that deceivers lay in wait for the flock he leaves behind, the real strength of our foundation is revealed. It was never in men, though the walls of this temple include their contributions. It was and will always be the rock of our foundation, the Lord Jesus Christ. Paul, leaving behind this church which for three years he has warned about men speaking perverse things to draw away the disciples, commends them "to God and to the word of His grace."

We cannot lay too great an emphasis on this truth. For the immature believer, the indwelling Spirit of God, and the word of His grace, are vital to build up a maturity that can endure the heresies scattered in our path as caltrops. For the mature believer, just the same, these are the true necessities of the overcomer.

"The most advanced Christians are capable of growing, and will find the word of grace help their growth." - Matthew Henry

As we grow in Christ, we members of His body and His Bride, are merely stones in the wall, each dependent upon the full structure - upon our brethren which sharpen as iron, and upon our ministers which expound on the word of His grace - but noneso more than upon the Cornerstone Himself, without which there is no structure to build.

After 30 years as pastor of a Scottish church, Alexander McLaren prepared himself and His congregation for his extended departure to Australia. Amidst the fears of what they may experience in his absence, McLaren preached his parting sermon on this passage of Acts, saying he could leave no instruction more than, "cleave to the Lord with full purpose of heart," and "cleave to the word of His grace."

"You have your Bibles and you have God's Spirit. And if my silence shall lead any of you to prize and to use these more than you have done, then my silence will have done a great deal more than my speech. Ministers are like doctors, the test of their success is that they are not needed any more. And when we can say, 'They can stand without us, and they do not need us,' that is the crown of our ministry." - Alexander McLaren

So Paul, preparing to be seen no more, says, "I commend you to God, and to the word of His grace, which is able to build you up." You may pour through endless biblical commentaries and find no clear definition as to whether this is the word of His grace, as in scripture, or the Word of His grace, as in Jesus Christ, John's "Logos." Like any of those students of scripture from ages long gone, I cannot be certain, though I've come to believe that is because there is less distinction than our feeble minds would like to impose here.

The word Paul spoke to these elders for "word" is the same word with which John began his Gospel, expounding Jesus' deity as "the Word." The word for "word," if you will, was Logos. Say that ten times fast. When John was given the prophecy of Revelation, it was closed with a curse upon any who would add to or take away from these words (logos). Before that though, the angel tells John, "These words are faithful and true" (Revelation 22:6 MEV). Earlier in the book, the Lord Jesus Christ is called the Faithful and True.

I'd propose that what Paul spoke was interchangeably, the word of His grace found in scripture, and the Word of His grace that is the manifestation of the Word who was with God and who was God, because the former is but a glimpse of the latter.

"Is not My word like fire, says the Lord, and like a hammer that breaks the rock in pieces?" - Jeremiah 23:29 MEV

My grandfathers were both brick layers. When my dad was young, he and his brother broke field rock, so it could be used to build walls, chimneys, and more. Those rocks were not fit to the purpose until they were broken. Brothers and sisters, sometimes the Word has to break us, in order to build us up. When we cleave to the word of His grace, we won't be exempt from the breaking moments. Often those are the moments that make us "those who are sanctified" (Acts 21:32 ESV).

" 'Then the King will say to those at His right hand, “Come, you blessed of My Father, inherit the kingdom prepared for you since the foundation of the world.” ' " - Matthew 25:34 MEV

When we see Paul leave the Ephesians, we see him declare the only way he could trust them not to lose faith. He committed them into the hands of God and the word of His grace. These are the necessities that we must always lean upon, because we are living stones, being built into the sanctified temple, and holding the promise of inheritance. We can only be built up because of the Cornerstone.

"He said to me, 'It is done. I am the Alpha and the Omega, the Beginning and the End. I will give of the spring of the water of life to him who thirsts. He who overcomes shall inherit all things, and I will be his God and he shall be My son.' " Revelation 21:6-7 MEV

Notes

Notes

Day 133 *Truly Family*

"When we found the disciples, we remained there seven days. They told Paul through the Spirit not to go up to Jerusalem. But when our days were over, we parted and traveled on. Everyone, with wives and children, escorted us until we were outside the city. And we knelt on the shore and prayed. After bidding farewell to one another, we boarded the ship, and they returned home." - Acts 21:4-6 MEV

We haven't expressly seen Paul in Tyre up to this point, though it is estimated that the route he took from Syrian Antioch to the Jerusalem Counsel led him through the town, "declaring the conversion of the Gentiles" (Acts 15:3 MEV). Paul was not the man to evangelize this place. These Christians knew little of him, though it's probable they knew Saul well. Many believe that Phillip, the deacon evangelist who settled in Caesarea was the one to bring the gospel here. You may remember him as a friend of the deacon Stephen, over whose martyrdom Saul presided. That may give these believers great cause to reject this weary traveler, but it seems they didn't.

These disciples were also Jews, remember, and we're seeing more and more, the judaizers gaining ground in a hatred of the gentile inclusion of this gospel. Again though, they did not cause trouble for Paul and his companions. That brings us back to our passage.

"When we found the disciples." When you travel, what go ye to see? Personally, I love mountains. Wind swept, snowcapped, and rocky protrusions from the ground. Lakes hidden deep in valleys of Colorado Spruce. Moraine fields with wildflowers springing up from boulders bigger than your house. The creation of our wondrous God is quite the sight to behold, but what greater creation has He than, "all those who are sanctified" (Acts 20:32 ESV)?

When the wheels of the plane touch down at Thanksgiving, do you not leave straightaway to head toward family? Does that journey not find you among your brothers and sisters, mothers, fathers, nieces, nephews, aunts, uncles, and grandparents? Is it different when you travel to a new land? When stepping foot on ground you've never before seen, do you seek out the family - your brothers and sisters in Christ?

Honestly, it's something I've never done. I've traveled an awful lot, and while I'll be sure to catch up on the recorded sermons I've missed from my local fellowship, I have yet to seek out a local fellowship while on the road. What am I missing? What wondrous works of God have I not seen by passing on the fellowship of our global family?

It truly is a family, and regardless of political differences, you still gather for Thanksgiving and Christmas, right? I believe we see the same forgiving and loving family nature here, as Paul walks into Tyre. They don't just say, "OK, hi Saul. Welcome to Tyre." Rather, Paul is welcomed into their fellowship for seven days. That means he's there for their Sabbath, and for the Lord's Supper on the Lord's Day. Moreover, they don't just send him off with a "see ya later." Instead, they stop what they're doing, and take their entire families to go see him off at shore. They pray over his journey, and having rejected their warnings, he receives their best wishes.

Brothers and sisters, do you realize the full implication of the truth that we are, in Christ, brothers and sisters; we are the adopted sons and daughters of the Most High, promised eternal inheritance, side by side for all time. Do you realize how we who are bought by the blood of Christ truly are family? If you were to end up in the fellowship of complete strangers, yet strangers who are fellow disciples, would you act as such? Or might you even consider not just accidentally ending up in their presence, but rather seeking them out? His children are of one blood, regardless of our differences. We are family.

Notes

Day 134

The Lord Has a Plan

"When we had come to Jerusalem, the brothers received us gladly. On the next day Paul went with us to James, and all the elders were present. He greeted them and recounted one by one what God had done among the Gentiles through his ministry." - Acts 21:17-19 MEV

As Paul returns to Jerusalem with the alms for this poverty-stricken branch of the Church, we find none of the 12 Apostles present. Paul went in to James and the elders. Now, I'm not here to argue the Catholic/Protestant division, but this is not James the lesser, as some would suggest. There are those who refuse to accept this as James, the half-brother of Jesus, twisting and ignoring words until it's just a nickname such as John, the one whom Jesus loved. No matter how much I study this though, I cannot find any excuse to deny that this man was the brother James, referenced by Christ's neighbors who rejected him in Matthew 13:55.

"When they had entered, they went up into the upper room, where they were staying: Peter, James, John, and Andrew; Philip and Thomas; Bartholomew and Matthew; James the son of Alphaeus and Simon the Zealot; and Judas the son of James. These all continued with one accord in prayer and supplication, with the women and Mary the mother of Jesus, and with His brothers." - Acts 1:13-14 MEV

Both James the greater and James the lesser are listed among the 11 apostles in the upper room, and then Jesus' mother and brothers are listed distinctly. There are at least 3 times in scripture when we're told that after the Virgin Mary gave birth to Jesus, she and Joseph proceeded to give Him brothers. The bishop of Jerusalem, and author of the Epistle under his name, is none other than the half-blooded brother of Jesus. He was the son of Mary, but not the Son of God. So again, we return to Jerusalem with Paul, and find the Apostles have been scattered to the winds, leaving James to tend this parent church.

Scripture doesn't tell us where most of the Apostles went, though history gave us some details, and tradition suggests some more. James the greater we've already seen martyred in Acts 12, and his brother John we see later in scripture exiled to Patmos, but what of the others? Peter, for example, after what may have been a brief stint as bishop of Antioch, ended up in Rome, where he was martyred. Andrew is said to have preached to Greek communities before being martyred in Patras.

Phillip's journeys are a bit of a mystery, though he was said to have ministered to the Hellenists before his martyrdom. Bartholomew is either a mystery, or quite the man on the move, as various traditions place him all over the place. Matthew, likewise, was on the move around the Mediterranean, before being martyred in Ethiopia. Thomas took the Gospel to India, where his tomb remains. Judas Thaddeus earned the title Apostle to the Armenians, before being martyred in Beirut. Simon the zealot is said to have been with him. James the lesser is said to have gone into Egypt, to a city name Ostrakine, where he was crucified. The replacement Apostle, Matthias, is said to have built a church in Cappadocia, where he was eventually beheaded for his faith.

What's my point? Every one of these men, of whom Jesus said, "...you will be my witnesses... to the end of the earth" (Acts 1:8 ESV), did just that. The Lord Jesus Christ was not flawed in His prediction, nor ignored in His command. These men committed their lives to share this gospel and to keep His command, and eventually they gave their lives in that service.

Brothers and sisters, the Lord has a plan for your life. He has prepared good works for His children from before we were born. We are those who were bought by His very blood. Can we really sit back, comfortable in our daily lives and satisfied with the pleasures of this world, and not feel the pull of the Lord? Can we seriously ignore that purpose for which God weaved each of us in the womb, and not fulfill what He has in store for us? Or, my brothers and sisters, shall we not die to self, and live Christ, wherever, whenever, and to whatever He leads us? This world has nothing to offer us in comparison to what the Lord has in store for those who love Him.

Day 135

Stiff-Necked

"When they heard this, they glorified the Lord. Then they said to him, 'You see, brother, how many thousands of Jews there are who believe, and they are all zealous for the law. They have been informed concerning you that you teach all the Jews who are among the Gentiles to forsake Moses, telling them not to circumcise their children nor to observe the customs. What then shall be done? The assembly will certainly meet, for they will hear that you have come.' " - Acts 21:20-22 MEV

Having read through this, over and over again, I cannot break the feeling there's a bit of a cordial peeing match going on here. Paul comes and tells all that the Lord has been doing among the gentiles through Him, and James responds, "you see, brother, how many thousands of Jews we've got here who believe." Come on, man. Maybe it's just a prejudice inside my perspective, but I cannot read these words, "you see, brother," except in the voice of one who says, "hey there, friend," with a sly grin as he sidles up, knife in hand.

James is, like any of us, human, and it appears we catch him now, in the flesh, as he makes the same mistake that oh so many leaders before him had. What does he explain, but these Jewish believers are zealous for the law of Moses, and they're upset about the lies they're hearing about Paul. But it was more than a brotherly concern addressing something to which they could work out a solution. James had already decided what he thought a solution was, and it was to bear under the weight of their stubbornness.

"Then the Lord said to Moses, 'I have seen this people, and certainly, it is a stiff-necked people.' " - Exodus 32:9 MEV

As mentioned, this was not the first time one of the leaders of Israel fell prey to error as the bishop of Jerusalem now did. When Moses was delayed on the mountaintop, these "stiff-necked people," demanded a forged god from Aaron, and his compliance to their demands - making the golden calf - brought the anger of the Lord upon them. (See Exodus 32)

"The Lord spoke to Moses and Aaron, 'Because you did not believe in Me, to sanctify Me in the eyes of the children of Israel, therefore you will not bring this assembly into the land which I have given them.' " - Numbers 20:12 MEV

It wasn't too much later than that, when again these stubborn people thought they knew better, and Moses bowed to their complaints, smiting the rock, and extending their years of aimless wandering.

This kind of weakness among the people and their leaders was a constantly repeating story, over and over again, throughout their history. But now James' own brother, Jesus, had come to redeem the nations, to unite us all in one blood, and to set us free from the law of sin and death. Even so, these hard-nosed pharisees among the believers sway James to the same mistake. The shadows were sub-standard to the light which had now shined upon their very faces, yet James capitulates to their clutch of the ceremonial laws.

"It was great weakness to be so fond of the shadows, when the substance was come." - Matthew Henry

What James demanded was not the will of God. When we look ahead in the chapter, we see Paul likewise submit to the demands, but he's never allowed to complete the task. James suggested that Paul should go out of his way to appease the Jews among them, but it was through the attempted execution of this act that the Jews outside their fellowship brought charges against Paul; charges which would place him in the chains of imprisonment for many years to come.

We have here, a sign of the importance of a true balance of faithfulness that can only be kept by submitting fully to the leadership of the Spirit of God. On the one end, the ultra-religious Christians held so firmly to that which had already been fulfilled, that they tipped the scales of grace toward a legalism that was willing to impose on a man who wasn't even guilty of their charges. On the other end of the spectrum, the ultra-religious non-Christians held so firmly to their impression of racial superiority, that they tipped the scales of law so far from grace that they falsely charged a man with bringing gentiles into the inner temple, merely because he had earlier been seen with one in the outer court.

Brothers and sisters, there is no end to the importance of letting the Spirit guide our steps, our actions, our words, and our thoughts. There is no room in such submission, to compromise with that from which He leads us away, whatever form that may take.

Notes

Notes

Day 136

Taken in the Act

"When the seven days were nearly concluded, the Jews from Asia saw him in the temple, stirred up all the people, and laid hands on him, crying out, 'Men of Israel, help! This is the man teaching all men everywhere against the people and the law and this place. He even brought Greeks into the temple and has defiled this holy place.' For they had previously seen Trophimus the Ephesian in the city with him, whom they supposed Paul had brought into the temple." - Acts 21:27-29 MEV

While we've considered that Paul may have forced his own will to come to Jerusalem, above the will of God, who warned him every step of the way, and we just considered the likeness of this vow, to Aaron, and Moses, and so many other leaders who kowtowed to the demands of the people, it's hard to fault the man. I mean, we see all along, the heart he has behind every step. If you're having trouble picking up what I'm putting down, read this, and consider what Paul's just agreed to do:

"To the Jews, I became as a Jew, that I might win the Jews; to those who are under the law, as under the law, that I might win those who are under the law; to those who are outside the law, as outside the law (being not without God's law, but under Christ's law) that I might win those who are outside the law. To the weak, I became as weak, that I might win the weak. I have become all things to all men, that I might by all means save some. This I do for the gospel's sake, that I might partake of it with you." - 1 Corinthians 9:20-23 MEV

The Apostle quite literally agrees to pay for the vows of 4 men, who in Christian liberty were no longer bound by ceremonial law, but were likewise not forbidden from it. Essentially, Paul went out of his way to show he wasn't trying to "teach against the law," as the accusation which is now brought against him. Sometimes it doesn't matter how good your intentions are, nor how noble your actions; unjust charges will be brought against your name. Paul now finds himself in that situation as the Jews from Asia, who had caused so much trouble in his missions, now recognize him here at Pentecost.

I don't believe we have any way to know whether this was just Jews who had similarly made the pilgrimage for the feast and happened to spot him, or if they had deliberately come plotting to destroy him, having heard of his determination to make it to Jerusalem for the feast. Either way, these men stir up a great tumult here in Jerusalem, as has been done so many times before, but this time they've got their players strategically positioned on the board and they knock over this pawn saying, "check."

Some time has passed since archaeologists were able to confirm just how serious this charge was. An inscribed slab was found, and translated. "No man of alien race is to enter within the balustrade and fence that goes round the temple. If anyone is taken in the act, let him know that he has himself to blame for the penalty of death that follows." Surely, these Asian Jews would have to defend their charges that he taught against the law and the people, and this had never worked yet, but the racial prejudice concerning the uncircumcised and the temple was a sure-fire assault. Even if there was no Greek found in the temple, the mere suggestion caused the non-Christian Jews' blood to boil.

"Then the whole city was provoked, and the people ran together. They seized Paul and dragged him out of the temple. And immediately the doors were shut. While they were trying to kill him, news came up to the commander of the battalion of soldiers that all Jerusalem was in an uproar." - Acts 21:30-31 MEV

Thus it is that we read here that Paul is physically dragged out of the temple by a mob that numbers in the tens of thousands, and they proceed to make a solid attempt at beating the life right out of him. Here we find God's pawn, laying in a pool of blood, surrounded by bishops and rooks, looking to be the failing last line of defense for the King, but around the corner the King sends an unexpected knight. "When they saw the commander and the soldiers, they stopped beating Paul" (Acts 21:32 MEV).

"He is not a Jew who is one outwardly, nor is circumcision that which is external in the flesh. But he is a Jew who is one inwardly. And circumcision is of the heart, by the Spirit, and not by the letter. His praise is not from men, but from God." - Romans 2:28-29 MEV

The temple at Jerusalem was but a shadow of things to come. Soon every knee shall bow before Christ in the temple where the King now sits on the mercy seat. When that day comes, what will matter is not how religious each one of us was. The only thing that will matter is were we Christ's?

"For we are the circumcision who worship God in the Spirit, and boast in Christ Jesus, and place no trust in the flesh," - Philippians 3:3 MEV

When that day comes, and everyone is "taken in the act, let him know that he has himself to blame for the penalty of death that follows." Checkmate! Here were the unbelieving, trying to use their religion to gain victory, but what they really did was give Paul a stage to testify against them that day. Surely, when they fall before the judgement seat, they will have no room but to know they were warned, and yet they remained stubborn in uncircumcision of the heart. They have no one to blame but themselves for the penalty of death that follows.

"Circumcise therefore the foreskin of your heart, and be no longer stubborn." - Deuteronomy 10:16 ESV

If your name is not yet in the Lamb's book of life, here's your warning, and the promise of redemption which is offered to you. It's not too late to repent and believe. God loves us in spite of our sin, and He is calling all men everywhere to turn to Him. In Christ you can be, not only forgiven, but adopted into the family of God. Oh what love, that we can be called sons and daughters of God. Won't you join us?

Notes

Notes

Day 137

Testimony

"As Paul was about to be brought into the barracks, he said to the commander, 'May I speak to you?' He replied, 'Do you know how to speak Greek?' " - Acts 21:37 MEV

Picture the scene here. Paul has been assaulted by what the Jews called "the rebel's beating." This was extrajudicial "justice," executed on the greatest offenders of their religious laws, and varied greatly from the forty lashes minus one which Paul has already repeatedly endured. It was mob fury. For example, if a priest ministered in his uncleanness, his fellow priests would capture him, and drag him out, at which point the young priests would proceed to physically beat him to death with fists, clubs, and staffs. You can imagine what sort of shape Paul was in by the time the commander arrived with hundreds of soldiers.

Yet what had been a great affront to the temple in days past - the "castle" (KJV) spoken of in verses 34 and 37 - came to be the saving work of God for this temple of the Holy Spirit, or the flesh tent which Paul presently inhabited. To secure control and combat uprisings, Rome had taken what was formerly a priestly structure from the Asmonaean era, and built it up more (under Herod, who dubbed it Antonia) into their barracks. This was a literal stone castle, built against the northwest corner of the temple, situated upon a massive rock 75 feet high, the main structure of which was another 60 feet tall, and some of the turrets of which towered as high as 100 feet above the rock. The place was enormous, and able to house an army, from such close quarters of which, Paul's rescue now comes.

"When he came onto the stairs, he was carried by the soldiers because of the violence of the people. For the mob of people followed, crying out, 'Away with him!' " - Acts 21:35-36 MEV

The stairs up to this Antonia were grand in stature, and now became an unmatched stage for Paul to exercise the greatest mercy he could muster. As he's led up the stairs, the mob that had been temporarily stayed from their attempt on his life, now press in again - the fires of violence rekindled. In the midst of this, what does Paul do, but beg of the commander a chance to speak. Being granted his request, he turns around and makes an attempt to win some to the Gospel; the bruised and bloodied Apostle looks upon them through the blood that drips across his swollen eyes, and from his split, fat lips gives his testimony to these very same people in their own language.

"Paul said, 'I am a Jew, from Tarsus of Cilicia, a citizen of no common city. I beg of you, permit me to speak to the people.' When he had given him permission, Paul stood on the stairs and motioned with his hand to the people. When there was great silence, he addressed them in the Hebrew language, saying," - Acts 21:39-40 MEV

While I'm all for cutting off heresy at the root, there are those who become so zealous in the heresy hunt, they miss the mark entirely. One example is a phrase that was going around a while back: "your testimony is not the Gospel." While that is, by strictest definitions, true, the very concept of what it portrays altogether disregards the chapter that we will soon find ourselves in (Acts 22). One of the greatest evangelists of all history is given the perfect stage to share the gospel with lost and broken people who are exactly like he once was, and he doesn't reason with them from the scriptures. No, he tells the testimony of how far he had been misled in the same zealous rage they now find themselves in, and how the Lord Jesus Christ, once dead but now alive, had come into his life and changed everything!

There is indeed a difference between your testimony, and the gospel, but the two are not mutually exclusive. Rather, your testimony is as much the "Acts of Jesus Christ" as is this book we now study. It is the evidence of the long-suffering love of the Father, the redemptive mercy of the Son, and the sanctifying work of the Holy Spirit. Your testimony is among the greatest tools in your arsenal, and when you stand on the steps of the Castle that is the Rock of our Foundation, the work of God in your life is not something to neglect to share. It is the glory of God. May He be evermore magnified by the stories of His work in our miniscule lives.

Day 138

Inspired and Inerrant

"And he said, 'Do you know Greek? Are you not the Egyptian, then, who recently stirred up a revolt and led the four thousand men of the Assassins out into the wilderness?' " - Acts 21:37b-38 ESV

The commander who arrested (and thereby rescued) Paul, is in a bit of a bind right now. He's charged with keeping the peace in Jerusalem, and this day he was confronted by a massively explosive fit of rage in the temple. Having found what would appear to be the culprit, he demands answers as to why Paul was being beaten, but much like in Ephesus, the crowd was confused, all giving different answers. From the charges the Asian Jews brought against Paul, we can deduce some of the things the commander heard that day.

"He's been wandering all around, claiming to serve a false God, and leading Jews and Gentiles away from our law."

"He spoke against the law"

"He defiled our temple, bringing in those who don't belong."

The commander didn't rise to his rank without some great wits about him. The man is in this position in Jerusalem because he is a very intelligent man, capable of deducing the facts behind great mysteries. Consider him like the chief inspector, and he's now leading Paul up the stairs, trying to figure out what is going on. Then Paul speaks to him in Greek, and he gets a clue. "Ah, maybe this is the troublemaker we've been looking for."

How about we interpose some history here, to explain who the Egyptian was? The Jewish historian Josephus was quite accurate as a historian, though his numbers were reportedly often rather exaggerated. He tells of a Jew that had recently come from Egypt claiming to be a prophet. This Egyptian gathered an army of bandits and zealots - assassins named for the small curved knives (sicarii) they carried. The commander declares it was a band of 4,000, though Josephus claims 30,000.

History tells us the false prophet led the men to the Mount of Olives, and through the wilderness, telling them that God had shown him how Jerusalem would fall, and he would lead them to overtake the city. But the Roman procurator, Antonius Felix (after whom this castle was named, and whom we'll soon see Luke introduce), had gotten word of the Egyptian's plot and, leading a counterstrike, overthrew the rebellion. Josephus tells us that the Egyptian escaped the fray. The commander now suspects, that maybe Paul is this man, to which Paul responds, "no sir, I'm from Tarsus."

But what does all this matter to us? Throughout the centuries, the hard-hearted have made claims that this Bible is the errant word of men, rather than the inerrant word of God. They'll claim that it's all made up rubbish, written hundreds of years later, by a church trying to seize control of the people. One of their greatest allies sought to prove this, but only succeeded in proving his prejudice wrong.

In the late 19th and early 20th century, the Universities of Edinburgh, Oxford, and Aberdeen employed an archaeology professor who in his day earned notoriety as the foremost expert on the history of Asia minor. Sir William Mitchell Ramsay was even knighted for the excellence of his work. This professor, as with so many influencing our young people today, was a staunch biblical skeptic.

Considering his area of expertise, the man took particular aim at our beloved physician's history. Ramsay was so determined to prove that the book of Acts was littered with historical inaccuracies, and thereby disprove Christianity, that He traveled across Asia Minor, Greece, and more with the sole intent of finding evidence to discredit Luke's words.

"I may fairly claim to have entered on this investigation without any prejudice in favor of the conclusion which I shall now attempt to justify to the reader. On the contrary, I began with a mind unfavorable to it, for the ingenuity and apparent completeness of the Tübingen theory had at one time quite convinced me."

Ramsay spent many years investigating the places and events which Luke records, with the preconceived notion that he would prove the physician wrong. By the end of his exhaustive probe, Ramsay, having set out to disprove the Bible, had found every reason to believe it, and became, himself, not only almost (see Acts 26:28), but entirely as Paul was, a Christian.

“Luke is a historian of the first rank; not merely are his statements of fact trustworthy, he is possessed of the true historic sense ... in short, this author should be placed along with the greatest of historians.” Sir W.M. Ramsay

The professor in question rests in Christ today, but his name lives on among the greatest archaeologists to ever live. Look at the findings of his life's work. Having determined to prove the Bible wrong, the man found every single historical detail of Acts to be trustworthy, ranking Luke among the greatest historians to ever live.

The deceptions of the heart which would lead the self-important to believe the word of God flawed are absolutely incapable of being evidenced by any man, woman, or child who would sincerely look at the details and facts and come to the conclusion of their summary. The God of the Bible inspired this inerrant book, and that same God is the one true "God who made the world and everything in it, being Lord of heaven and earth," (Acts 17:24 ESV) just as Paul had told the Athenian scholars.

Notes

Notes

Day 139

Saw the Light,
Heard The Voice of Him

"Those who were with me saw the light and were afraid, but they did not hear the voice of Him who was speaking to me." - Acts 22:9 MEV

"The men traveling with him stood speechless, hearing the voice, but seeing no one." - Acts 9:7 MEV

Uh oh, a contradiction! Ok ladies and gentlemen, it's been fun, but I guess I can't believe anymore. Oh wait, nevermind. Faith won't be overcome so easily. Yet what can we make of the variance between Luke's investigative record in chapter 9, and his record of the words he heard Paul speak in chapter 22? As we saw yesterday, it cannot be denied that he was an absolute giant among historians, so how could he let something like this happen within the confines of a single book he's written?

Look closely at what the two accounts are saying. Paul says they "saw the light," but Luke says they "saw no one." This happened in the Middle East at noon. This might be among the unmatched places on earth for the sharpness of the mid-day sun. Yet Paul soon tells Agrippa, "At midday, O King, I saw along the way a light from heaven, brighter than the sun, shining around me and those who journeyed with me" (Acts 26:13 MEV). They all saw the light, but only Paul was blinded, because on that road, only Paul truly saw the glory of the Lord, as he declares in 1 Corinthians 15:8. His companions merely saw the visual echoes, if you will - the residual glow.

With that in mind, look again at the two accounts, paying attention to the slight variances. Luke says they heard, "the voice," whereas Paul says, "they did not hear the voice of Him who was speaking to me." It's easy enough to explain in English, but let's first look at the Greek as confirmation. The word for voice, used in both these accounts was "phōnē." It was used 141 times in the New Testament, and depending on context and form it meant anything from "sound," to "speech," and from "voice," to "articulation."

All three synoptic gospels record the baptism of Jesus and the "phōnē" (articulate voice) of God speaking "this is my beloved Son," for all to hear. At the other end of Christ's ministry, on the other hand, we're given specific details about all the words He spoke from the cross, but when he gave up the ghost, there were no words. "And Jesus cried out again with a loud voice, and yielded up His spirit" (Matthew 27:50 NKJV). It's the same word.

We can see the same in the English. If I were to sing out the melody of a great hymn of old, yet with no words - just "ahhhhhhahhhahhhh" - you would hear my voice, though there would be no articulation. If, on the other hand, I were to recite the words of the same hymn, you would hear my speech - the articulation of my voice.

"To see and hear the risen Christ was a privilege given to St. Paul alone." - Pulpit commentary

Paul and Luke didn't contradict each other, they merely emphasized different portions of the same truth. In chapter 9, Luke defines that they didn't directly see Christ, and thereby explains why they weren't blinded by His glory. In chapter 22 Paul says that they didn't hear the words He spoke, thereby explaining why they weren't there also to testify of what Christ had declared unto him.

If you find yourself in unbelief because of the supposed contradictions of scripture, please look at the facts, as we found yesterday that Sir W.M. Ramsay did. No legitimate search for the truth will leave you outside of His grace.

If on the other hand, my brothers and sisters, you are my fellow believers, and come face to face with the claims of those who haven't truly studied the depths of his word, let not their unbelief lead you astray. I have yet to find a supposed contradiction that is anything less than flawed human understanding. Overcome to the end in faith, for the promise of inheritance belongs to those who remain in Christ.

Day 140

Off the Face of the Earth

"They listened to him up to this point. Then they raised their voices, shouting, 'Wipe this man off the face of the earth! He should not be allowed to live!' " - Acts 22:22 CSB

As Paul neared the top of the stairs, and the fury of the Jews rekindled, they had shouted out "away with him," but here at the interruption of his defense we see the true meaning of what they were saying. It wasn't, "throw him in a cell." No, they say, "away with such a man from the earth" (MEV), or as NIV puts it, "rid the earth of him." There's no justice here, no request for a trial, only a purely homicidal demand.

Yet look at the overall situation. Paul, reaching the top of the stairs, is suffered a chance to turn and speak to them. "Paul stood on the stairs and motioned with his hand to the people. When there was great silence he addressed them" (Acts 21:40 MEV). Then the Apostle begins his apologia with a respectful address, calling them (national) brothers, and (spiritual) fathers. "When they heard that he addressed them in the Hebrew language, they became even more quiet" (Acts 22:2 MEV).

The man is given a chance to plead his testimony, as so many martyrs in his wake. The Jews are silenced, though we don't know their hearts. Clearly, they're appeased by the respect, by Paul's history as a student of the great Gamaliel, by his zeal for the law, as well as by his being evangelized by "Ananias, a devout man according to the law, who was well spoken of by all the Jews living there" (Acts 22:12 MEV).

"Yeah, that all sounds good. I have no complaint," they may be thinking. Even the story of seeing the crucified Jesus alive - a story they've no doubt heard before considering the decades that Christians have now inhabited Jerusalem - seems not to upset them. Were they inkling toward belief, like Agrippa, almost convinced to become Christians? Or maybe they were content to write it off as the flawed understanding of just another sect of Judaism, as the Sadducees thought of the Pharisees, and vice versa. What we know, is that they silently listened to him, right up until Paul declares this proposed Messiah sent him to the gentiles.

All hell breaks loose, and they're so furious that the commander, not having understood the language Paul had spoken, assumes Paul must be a murderer or something. What could provoke these people to such levels of intensity? Well, Claudius Lysias, Sir, they're enraged that the man claims you have a right to God's mercy.

"Resolute and stubborn pride will neither embrace the truth itself, neither allow others to receive it." - Geneva Study Bible

It's one thing for these "brothers and fathers," to neglect the call to redemption for themselves, but what sort of hardened heart must it take to then demand others should not be given the same offer? They've put themselves in a catch 22. If, what Paul spoke of Jesus was not true, then what harm could it do to let him speak lies to gentiles? They won't be any more or less God's chosen people for it. Even the people's nationalistic pride couldn't complain, if Christianity was a myth. But if, on the other hand, they're upset that Paul preaches the true Messiah to the gentiles, yet they don't themselves hang their hats on that Only Name, then they've decidedly chosen to leave the fellowship of God.

This sort of "resolute and stubborn pride" has scarred every page of time. Look around in our lives. Christians speak publicly, encouraging each other with scripture, in response to which the unbelieving demand our silence, rather than ignoring our "silly myths." Christians put up decorations and the staunch atheists take it to court. The gospel gets spread in the media, and we're "shoving it down their throats," even though ungodliness reigns over 95% of modern media.

But brothers and sisters, that all concerns us no more than that we can pray for their hearts to be made new, and their eyes opened. It concerns us no more than we can respectfully remain available and willing to share in the event of such a turn. What should concern us is that in chapter 22 we see this stubborn pride not from atheists (though that is a religious belief in and of itself), but rather from the ultra-religious who believed in the God of Abraham.

Brothers and sisters, children of God, when it comes to the truth of God, we must remain vigilant, for we are not, by any means, exempt from the temptation of pride. It could be said that the religious are possibly even more prone to pride, though I wonder how we can look at our failures in light of God's grace, and still have any room for pride.

"Condemned sinners are struck blind by the power of darkness, and it is a lasting blindness, like that of the unbelieving Jews. Convinced sinners are struck blind as Paul was, not by darkness, but by light. They are for a time brought to be at a loss within themselves, but it is in order to their being enlightened. A simple relation of the Lord's dealings with us, in bringing us, from opposing, to profess and promote his gospel, when delivered in a right spirit and manner, will sometimes make more impression than laboured speeches, even though it amounts not to the full proof of the truth, such as was shown in the change wrought in the apostle." - Matthew Henry

Notes

Notes

Day 141

Born a Citizen

"The commander answered, 'I bought my citizenship for a large sum.' So Paul said, 'But I was born a citizen.' " - Acts 22:28 MEV

And those who were to beat him backed up and the commander became terrified. This encounter is a straightforward, historical case study in Valerian law, and yet there's a parallel imagery that makes this word of God almost a parable, such as those spoken by the manifest Word of God, Jesus Christ. First, let's rewind a bit.

"The commander ordered him to be brought into the barracks and examined with scourging, so that he might learn what crime they were alleging against him. As they stretched him forward with straps, Paul said to the centurion standing by, 'Is it legal for you to flog an uncondemned Roman citizen?' " - Acts 22:24-25 MEV

To examine with scourging was, just as it sounds, the gross technique used throughout the world and across the pages of time; It was a method of drawing a confession by torture. Whether or not such methods might draw false confessions or not, seems to have mattered not. It was a lawful and common practice on slaves and foreigners, and so we see the soldiers "stretched him forth," to tie his hands to the whipping pillar, some 30ish inches high. From this bent position Paul speaks.

"On hearing this, the centurion reported to the commander, saying, 'What are you doing? This man is a Roman citizen.' " - Acts 22:26 MEV

Suddenly the mood changes. If Paul falsely claimed citizenship, they had the charge they needed to condemn him. Impersonation of a Roman citizen was a grievous crime, but if he spoke the truth, the soldiers, the centurion overseeing them, and the commander who ordered the scourging would be guilty of a far greater crime. Roman citizens were exempt from any uncondemned punishment or examination, and they held special privileges to judicial trial. Even the binding with chains had gone too far. So, the Centurion wisely covers his own butt and reports to the Commander, who jumps to react.

"Are *you* a Roman?" The Greek language carries an inflection of emphasis here. "Really," Lysias asks, "you impoverished, persecuted, Jew, from Tarsus? You are a Roman?" How specifically Paul was born a Roman has become a great question through the ages, with some supposing that the liberty given the city of Tarsus afforded resident citizenship. If that were the case, the commander is an idiot, because he's already been told Paul is from Tarsus and he's now in disbelief of Paul's citizenship. The most likely scenario is that Paul's father or grandfather had been granted citizenship for outstanding military service.

"The commander answered, 'I bought my citizenship for a large sum.' So Paul said, 'But I was born a citizen.' Therefore those who were about to examine Paul immediately backed away from him. And the commander feared, knowing that he was a Roman citizen and because he had bound him." - Acts 22:28-29 MEV

Paul speaks up "wise as a serpent and harmless as a dove," and makes demonstration of a principle of which Matthew Poole writes: "It is very reasonable that a good man should make use of such lawful privileges as the place in which he lives doth afford, and in his condition may be allowed." With the context laid forth, will you humor me to go back and read this encounter as if it was one of Jesus' parables? As I do, please keep in mind this is extra-scriptural, and not the word of God.

The Kingdom of Heaven is like a man who, being stretched forth for the scourging of a slave, is given special privilege by his birthright, for which the accuser must leap back and tremble in fear. The enemy bursts in, most certain he has the right to accuse our condemned souls, saying, "for the great cost of eternal damnation I bought my authority as the god of this world," to which the redeemed of God reply, "but I was reborn a child of God, and citizen of the Kingdom of Heaven!"

This, my brothers and sisters is the birthright of those reborn in Christ. The demons leap back and shudder, trembling at the Name of Jesus. The accuser bursts in enraged, but he has no authority here, for these temples belong to God.

You, my friend, my fellow saint, were reborn a citizen.

Day 142

In All Good Conscience

"Paul looked at the Sanhedrin and said, 'Brothers, I have lived in all good conscience before God until this day.' The high priest Ananias ordered those who stood by him to strike him on the mouth. Then Paul said to him, 'God will strike you, you whitewashed wall! Do you sit judging me according to the law, yet order me to be struck contrary to the law?' " - Acts 23:1-3 MEV

Two men stand in opposition here. One, with his bailiffs doubling as bodyguards, and another, with his religious subordinates acting as his enforcers. When it all pans out though, we see in these two men the battle between good and evil, heaven and hell, God and those who make themselves His enemies. Two men stand in opposition and one declares "I have lived in all good conscience." Let's start there.

Since his conversion it would be hard for us to deny Paul's assertion. The man has demonstrated with every breath what it means to deny oneself, take up his cross, and follow Jesus. The scars of his back would testify of how faithful he had been to the ministry given him since the road to Damascus, but what about before that life changing day?

Surely it could be said that at the time, he lived by his conscience, even though he placed himself in enmity to God. The Pharisee was exceedingly zealous for what he thought was the will of God. There were lots of priests, rabbis, and more who were in their places for personal gain, but it is evident that Paul legitimately sought to serve his God. It might be disappointing that through his blindness so many suffered, but I believe God used that transgression for good to give Paul the drive and testimony that was necessary for the work that lay before him.

Surely Paul doesn't think, though, that just because he had good intentions, he was exempt from the consequences of sin. No, this is not one of those who might argue, "surely my good deeds will outweigh my bad deeds, and God will forgive me." On the contrary, Paul knew more than anyone his need for the salvation of Jesus Christ. This is the man who calls himself the chiefest of sinners, and who in his epistles and speeches used the word grace possibly more than the rest of the Apostles combined. Good conscience did not equal salvation in Paul's mind, and it doesn't for any one of our lives either.

Across the room, Ananias commands, "slap that insolence off his lips!" Do you wonder why though? Paul hasn't really said anything of consequence yet. He hasn't, "taught against the law," or even spoken of the inclusion of the gentiles. Maybe it had to do with who Ananias was. This was no longer Ananias the father-in-law of Caiaphas, who claimed the high priesthood which wasn't officially his, during the days of Jesus. That man had long passed. This Ananias is possibly the son of Caiaphas, and possibly a few other characters of history by the same name, but what we do know of him is rather telling.

This Ananias had indeed held the rank of high priest. The man was so known for injustice, cruelty, and greed that it's been recorded for all the world to see. He would keep the offerings for himself and his own family to such an extent that the lower priests would literally die of starvation. Toward the end of this chapter, we'll meet Felix the governor, but Felix's predecessor, Quadratus, had actually sent this Ananias, bound in chains, to the emperor Claudius for trial, his crimes were so great.

It may just be that the man's fit of rage against Paul was the sting of his conscience, having heard of such honor from his opponent. There's more to the story though. Paul responds by the Spirit of prophecy, "God will smite thee." Within five years after this encounter, the household of this Ananias had come to utter ruin, culminating eventually in his untimely death.

"Those who stood by said, 'Do you criticize God's high priest?' Paul said, 'Brothers, I did not know that he was the high priest. For it is written, "You shall not speak evil of the ruler of your people." ' " - Acts 23:4-5 MEV

This brings up an interesting question though. How could the Holy Spirit lead Paul to transgress the law? God does not tempt men to sin. If this man was the high priest, then God caused Paul to sin, but again, there's more to the story.

Our chapter begins with Paul "looking intently at the council" (vs 1 ESV). The last time he was here, some 25 or so years earlier, he was on the other side of the table. Some of the faces had surely changed, but others I'm sure he recognized, and there's little doubt he had been apprised of some of the more notable details. One such detail would be very relevant, and is surreptitiously alluded to by his response, "Brothers, I did not know he was the high priest" (vs 5 MEV).

Back in the days of the trial in Rome, Quadratus ousted Ananias from the high priesthood, installing a priest of his choosing, by the name of Jonathan. Jonathan was rather vocally opposed to Quadratus' replacement Felix, who eventually had Jonathan assassinated. From that point, until well after this trouble with Paul, the seat of high priest remained vacant. What Paul spoke was the truth. He did not know Ananias to be the high priest, because he knew the man officially was not. Take a look at Romans 13 and you'll see that Paul was well aware that God had used these Roman invaders to depose this evil usurper of the seat of Aaron.

Brothers and sisters, clean conscience or not, Paul's ministry was clear, in the leading of the Spirit, that all mankind need repent and believe for salvation in Christ. No amount of good intent exempts us from the consequence of sin. Once you have that, it is to the glory of God that we live, "in all good conscience." Chapter 23 begins with 2 opponents, and through the interaction we see again the verification that this book is both true to history, and matched to the truths of God throughout His word.

Notes

Notes

Day 143

The Hope of the Resurrection of the Dead

"When Paul realized that one part of them were Sadducees and the other part were Pharisees, he cried out in the Sanhedrin, 'Brothers, I am a Pharisee, a son of Pharisees. I am being judged because of the hope of the resurrection of the dead!' When he said this, a dispute broke out between the Pharisees and the Sadducees, and the assembly was divided. For the Sadducees say there is no resurrection, and neither angel nor spirit, but the Pharisees affirm them all." - Acts 23:6-8 CSB

Talk about divide and conquer! Paul recognizes an old division he knew so well, and he takes advantage of it. Again, we see Paul giving heed to Christ's words, "be wise as serpents and harmless as doves" (Matthew 10:16b MEV). There was no dishonesty or guile here. He merely stated the facts in a way that would make great use of their division.

The Apostle says, "hey Pharisees, I am indeed one of you, raised in strictest adherence to the law, and the full knowledge of scripture, but these Sadducees who don't believe in anything but the Pentateuch, and don't believe there is any separation of spirit from body, are judging me because, like you, I do have hope in the promises of the afterlife found in our scriptures." He defines it a bit more specifically in the next chapter when addressing Felix.

"However, I affirm that in accordance with the Way, which they call a sect, I worship the God of my fathers and believe everything written in the Law and in the Prophets. I have hope in God that there will be a resurrection of the dead, both of the just and the unjust, which they also expect." - Acts 24:14-15 MEV

It didn't take much to throw this room into upheaval. The Sadducees believed so firmly that there was no spiritual realm, no spiritual beings, no afterlife, and no division between spirit and body, that they even thought God was a fully corporeal being. That makes it a little easier to understand how the higher classes of priests, who were almost entirely Sadducees, were so corrupted that they used the commands for sacrifice to such personal gain.

If there is no afterlife, no threat of punishment, nor promise of reward, then what can be gained in this life is all that matters. If God is a physical being, He is no longer omnipresent and omniscient; He is reduced to the same state as the devil, prowling around. He can't see your corruption, and isn't standing there before you to deal with it anyhow. There's no profit or risk in whatever one does in this life, because nothing will happen after death anyway, so the only goal of life is to seek worldly happiness and prosperity. This sect literally made their god the devil, yet called him by the name "Yahweh."

Do you see now what I mean when I say atheism is itself a religion? You can believe that God is watching everything and working everything out toward his will for our eternal salvation, or you can believe that there is no God, no life after death, and no heaven and hell, but you're still believing in something. The latter belief is about as close to the Sadducean Priests as anyone could hope to be, short of the prosperity gospel teachers who should really consider fearing the eternal consequences before them.

Leading up to Christ's first manifestation, this belief spawned and grew, even in the people who were called by His Name; The idea that there is no spiritual realm, no afterlife, no heaven, nor hell, and thereby, no future state of heavenly Kingdom worked its way into the world. To come to such a conclusion, these religious leaders had to disown vast portions of the word of God, and interpret those they kept as merely allegorical.

I hate to say it brothers and sisters, but in our lifetimes, leading up to Christ's return, the same sort of beliefs are again spawning. The word of God is often no longer believed to be literal truth from the very mouth of God. The warnings of eternal fire are not welcome, even in many Christian circles, and thereby the promise of reward becomes inconsequential and unbelievable.

We can be called all sorts of names for holding to the age-old biblical truths, but whether I'm a hardline fundamentalist, a fool for Christ, an extremist, or whatever, I will gladly continue to believe that this Word is true! Though there are metaphors within the book, it is not, overall, allegory nor metaphor.

This is the hope that is within us, that Christ came, lived as one of us, died sinless, but as our sin, was raised again on the third day, then ascended to His heavenly throne, from which He promises to come again soon, bringing an eternal Kingdom in which those whose names are written in His book of Life will be raised to live forevermore. The hope of the resurrection of the dead.

In the end, every single soul will be judged on their belief, whether it is hope in the resurrection of Christ, or the lack thereof. What a simple way to gain salvation. Why would we succumb to the treachery of the enemy's lies?

Notes

Notes

Day 144

The Enemy of my Enemy

"There was a great outcry. The scribes that were from the sect of Pharisees stood up and argued, 'We find no evil in this man. But if a spirit or an angel has spoken to him, let us not fight against God.' When much dissension arose, fearing that Paul would be torn to pieces by them, the commander ordered the soldiers to go down and take him from them by force and bring him into the barracks." - Acts 23:9-10 MEV

The Sanhedrin has been divided for quite some time, but we saw yesterday how Paul poked the bear, inflaming the passions of their disagreement. The Sadducees, on the one hand, had no part in the Kingdom of Heaven. They didn't even believe it was possible, having put God in a small box of their own design. To come to faith in Christ, those men would have had to abandon everything they believed, and start as newborn babes, but pride would never allow that.

The Pharisees, on the other hand, are just inches from faith, having belief in the promise of the Messiah, a strong foundation in the Holy Scriptures, and awaiting the promise of a resurrection state, aka afterlife. The scribes of the party of the Pharisees (that is the most learned among the sect) stand up and defend what Paul has said, but we cannot take this as a statement of faith on their part. Read between the lines.

Paul had told them he saw the Risen Lord Jesus, but they instead say "a spirit or an angel." Depending on your translation, you may or may not see the end of their statement, "let us not fight against God." The problem is, none of the oldest manuscripts contain that portion. It seems to be a later addition, taken from Paul's own Rabbi, Gamaliel, from Acts 5:39. It would appear that this addition was the work of later transcribers to finish the sentence Luke left open, probably just as he heard it.

These scribes of the Pharisees are recorded in an aposiopesis. It is an intentional cutting off mid-sentence, to pose the suggestion as an implied question. Essentially what they say is, "but if he did get a vision of a spirit or an angel... then what of it?" They weren't affirming the faith of Christ, by any means. What these men did was choose the enemy of my enemy, then twist his words to make an argument on behalf of their own beliefs. If he did see an angel or the spirit of a dead man, it proves the Sadducees wrong.

"Men are not always very careful about the exact correctness of their statements when they wish to humble a rival." - Albert Barnes

What we find in these Pharisees, while not as distant from the truths of God as the Sadducees, is a group of men who could have easily heard the words of Elijah, "how long will you waver between two opinions" (1 kings 18:21 CSB). They are willing to make use of Paul's statements, and defend his guiltlessness not because they've been convinced Jesus is Lord, but because his claim benefits their argument.

We see the same quite frequently in modern two-party politics. Partisan politicians, and politically vocal citizens often don't care about truth anymore; Not half as much as they care to win the fight. Honesty and truth have become casualties of division, and that will not end well. Except in the case of faithful Christians caught in the middle.

"There is no true friendship among the wicked, and in a moment, and with the utmost ease, God can turn their union into open enmity." - Matthew Henry

Paul stands in the middle of this room, ready to die for the Gospel of Jesus Christ, and with every indication pointing to that being the case, but once again, God turns the cards in his favor, turns the wicked and unbelieving against each other, and sends in rescue. You can imagine what the room looks like at this point, by Luke's verbiage. The commander thought the men would tear Paul apart, they had pitted him in the middle of such a tremendous dispute. It's gotten so out of hand, Luke says that the soldiers had to "take him from them by force."

That doesn't look good for the child of God, and it's the evidence that just being a child of God will not exempt us from the tribulations to come. At the same time, this is another among a line of evidences that God will rescue us from such circumstances.

"The following night the Lord stood by him and said, 'Take courage, Paul. For as you have testified about Me in Jerusalem, so you must also testify at Rome.' " - Acts 23:11 MEV

It wasn't yet time for Paul to be rescued up to heaven, and so he was rescued from the absolute chaos found in the Sanhedrin that day. Brothers and sisters, it's hard to stand here with eyes open to the things of God yet not see the signs that we are coming closer and closer to the final days. In the midst of all that, take heart. Whether or not we end up in the middle of the most terribly chaotic disputes, God will rescue His own. Whether that means we find ourselves ushered into His presence, or carried safely through the fray, we have nothing to fear.

Notes

Notes

Day 145

Anathematized

"When it was morning, the Jews formed a conspiracy and bound themselves under a curse not to eat or drink until they had killed Paul. There were more than forty who had formed this plot. These men went to the chief priests and elders and said, 'We have bound ourselves under a solemn curse that we won't eat anything until we have killed Paul. So now you, along with the Sanhedrin, make a request to the commander that he bring him down to you as if you were going to investigate his case more thoroughly. But, before he gets near, we are ready to kill him.' " - Acts 23:12-15 CSB

We must take into account the intensity of hatred that can be spawned by zealotry for religion which has strayed from the heart of God. These men plotted to kill Paul, amidst a detachment of Roman soldiers, on a very short walk from the castle Antonia to the Sanhedrin. While the assumption that they were capable of such an assassination lends itself toward the hypothesis that these men were the Sicarii Zealots (as in the disciple Simon the zealot), who normally plotted and trained to assassinate Roman authorities, it can only really be concluded that they were so convinced it must be done, that they were willing to die in the process.

It is interesting, especially if these were indeed Sicarii, that those who would normally kill and die to free the nation of Israel from foreign invaders (assuming it part of God's messianic promise), would now turn the same homicidal conspiracy against one of their own for preaching that very same Messiah. Not only so, but look with what intensity they make such a determination.

Odds are, your preferred translation renders this passage as, "they bound themselves under an oath," but the true weight of this oath is not done justice by the word. The Greek word with which Luke records this "oath," is "anathematized." You may recognize that word from 1 Corinthians 16:22. "If anyone does not love the Lord, let that person be cursed" (NIV), or "let him be anathema" (KJV). The oath meant to bind oneself to the strictest curse, or literally under the wrath of God. In other words, this was as close as a man could get to literally selling his soul to the devil. They endeavored to murder the servant of God, and if they failed, they committed themselves - soul, body, estate, and family - to be fully cursed and rejected by God himself.

That would sure seem to be absolute insanity, but it can be observed that such a curse meant little to these men. In the name of religion, these 40 men (and oh so many more like them) utterly deserted their fellowship with God, but you know, if you asked them, they would see it differently. "You're the heretic, buddy, not me. I'm God's hammer."

The problem is that the Jews had evolved these curses to be of little consequence. If such had not been the case, these men would have eventually starved to death, and then suffered the wrath of God. I'd suggest, though that only the latter most likely happened, but we'll come back to that. It was not uncommon for men to make these sorts of oaths, and then being unable to fulfill the vow, they would go to the rabbis who alleged to have the authority to absolve them of the curse.

An example would be if you anathematized yourself to not eat for 40 days, but then the commanded feast came around. The Rabbi might ask you, "did you not know the feast would interfere," to which you could passingly reply, "nope, I never even looked at the calendar." Poof, your soul is saved because some priest or teacher says so. After all, you can't skip the command of God, right? The strange thing about it is, these were the same men who took such offense to their manifest God saying, "your sins are forgiven."

Again, we see it all stems from religion that has strayed far from God, no matter how much the name is claimed. The authority to exonerate the soul belongs solely to the Lord Jesus Christ, and to downplay that by suggesting any other man can forgive sin is the exact blunder which opened the door for these men to place their souls in the hands of "your father the devil" (John 8:44).

You know what's really amazing though? Even these men hadn't gone too far to truly be redeemed by the Lord Jesus Christ. Aside from Luke's usage of this word "anathematized," it appears in scripture one more time. In the gospel which Simon Peter testified to John Mark, the Apostle rehashed his darkest night. Just before the crow of the rooster, when confronted the third time with the accusation that he was one of Jesus' disciples, Simon tells us something terrible.

"Peter began to (anathematize) invoke a curse on himself, and to swear, 'I do not know this Man of whom you speak.' " - Mark 14:71 MEV

Here was the Petra, the stone, who would feed Christ's sheep, but before he was redeemed by the crucified and risen Savior, he put himself under the same sort of curse. On the one hand denying His Lord, with whom he walked so closely, and on the other, placing himself under the wrath of God if it was a lie. All on the night Christ was condemned by men. I don't know how far you've strayed from God, but I could confidently place a very healthy wager that you haven't gone anywhere near that far.

Do you know, that you're just a turn away from complete and unconditional forgiveness? Do you know that all it would take is to repent and believe on the name and finished work of Christ, and the remembrance of your iniquity will be no more before God? Just that simple step, and all your curse will be washed clean in His blood, your sins will be put away from God as far as the East is from the West.

That, my friends, is religion that hasn't strayed from the heart of God, but we must still be careful, for Ecclesiastical history is littered with accounts of men who, having come to that belief, set their eyes on a point in the distance and let their feet carry them to it, leaving the Way along the way. The history of religion testifies how easily zeal can lead us to the same treachery as these 40 men. Brothers and sisters, don't underestimate the propensity of our hearts to wander in this direction, and don't let pride convince you you're immune to such misdirection. We must stay in the closest fellowship with Christ at all times, filled afresh with the Holy Spirit every day.

Notes

Day 146

The Lord Reigns Sovereign

"Then he summoned two centurions and said, 'Prepare two hundred infantrymen, seventy mounted soldiers, and two hundred light infantrymen with spears to go to Caesarea at the third hour of the night. And provide mounts so Paul may ride and take him safely to Felix the governor.' He wrote a letter that went like this:" - Acts 23:23-26 MEV

There is little known of the commander Claudius Lysias outside of scripture, but the same can't be said of Antonius Felix, the procurator of Judea. Starting with Lysias, we're never told in scripture of his coming to faith. That doesn't necessarily mean it never happened, though I'd incline to believe, considering the pattern of Luke's history, that he didn't convert during his brief time with Paul. At least for the time being we can be relatively confident that this man was an unbelieving gentile, given sufficient reason to defend Paul at all costs.

Look at the detachment he sends. 400 men on foot, 70 cavalrymen, and enough "mounts" (horses, mules, or whatever) for Paul and his companions. They roll out at the start of the sleeping hours, around 9 or 10 PM, while Paul's assassins are resting up to prepare for their suicidal assault the next day. By morning they reach Antipatris, some 40ish miles away, and having moved Paul a safe distance from the conspirators, the footmen are sent home, leaving the cavalry to guard him the final 26 miles to Caesarea.

Clearly Lysias feels the importance of keeping Paul safe, though it's decidedly a self-preservation sort of move. Under Roman law, he was utterly bound to the safety of this uncondemned Roman prisoner, and already teetered on the edge of condemnation himself for having arrested Paul in the first place. Notice what he writes to Felix. "Learning he was a Roman, I came and rescued him." Excuse me, but that's not how I remember it sir.

"Claudius Lysias, To His Excellency Governor Felix: Greetings. This man was seized by the Jews and was about to be killed by them. When I learned that he was a Roman citizen, I came with soldiers and rescued him. Being minded to learn what crime they alleged, I took him to their Sanhedrin. I found him being accused of controversial matters about their law, but charged with nothing worthy of death or imprisonment. When it was revealed to me that there was a plot against the man, at once I sent him to you and ordered the accusers to state before you their charges against him. Farewell." - Acts 23:26-30 MEV

So, what of Felix? I hesitate to say this of anyone, but historical records do a fair enough job of declaring him pure filth. Felix started out as one of two brothers who were slaves in the household of the emperor Claudius' mother, Antonia (from whom this governor assumes his surname). Upon both being freed, Felix's brother became the best friend of the emperor, and petitioned for Felix to receive honors. The freedman is given rank as procurator of Judea, but while it can often be expected of those raised in royalty to be rather overbearing and heartless to the people they govern, this former slave, Felix, was a real piece of work.

Though the man came from humble beginnings, he rose in vulgarity and violence at an unprecedented rate. The Roman historian Tacitus tells us he ruled with "the power of a tyrant in the temper of a slave." At the beginning of chapter 24, as Felix begins to hear the case against Paul, the lawyer that Ananias brings begins by sucking up to Felix, praising all the peace, foresight, and reforms the man brought.

While it is true he did come in and decimate the gangs of bandits and marauders, the man was an utterly cruel and violently oppressive ruler, even making use of the Jewish Sicarii assassins for his own purposes. "He was an unrighteous governor, a base, mercenary, and bad man" (Adam Clarke). It was so bad, that when he left rank in Judea, the Jews of Caesarea went to Rome bringing charges of insufferable cruelty against him. The only reason he escaped the charges was because of the influence of his brother.

"There are many plans in a man's heart, nevertheless the counsel of the Lord will stand." - Proverbs 19:21 MEV

Paul receives a visit from Jesus telling him the oh so familiar comfort of scripture, "don't be afraid." Actually, it was, "Take courage, Paul," but pretty much the same thing when we then see God work through these ungodly men. Both of these authorities show the desires of their own hearts. Lysias, having spent tremendous wealth and diligent work to get to where he is, endeavors to cover his own backside above all, but God uses the man to rescue Paul from the Jews and start the journey to Rome. Felix, endeavoring to squeeze bribes out of Paul, and gain favorability among these Jews who had grown weary of his oppressive tyranny, keeps Paul safe there for two more years, giving the Apostle time to rest from his missions, and practice his apologia before all the who's who of Rome's regional leaders in Judea.

"Many are the afflictions of the righteous, but the Lord delivers him out of them all." - Psalms 34:19 MEV

Brothers and sisters, whatever dark and evil plans lie in the hearts of men, the Lord's will prevails, even there. When it's all said and done, even that man who earns the rank of most severely opposed to Jesus, will be seen to have played right into the overall plan of God. That doesn't mean their plots and schemes don't throw afflictions in our paths, and it doesn't mean God condones their evil, but nevertheless, God prevails.

Moreover, if the Lord exercises sovereignty even over the hearts and plans of them who are most opposed to His authority, how much more in those of us who desire to follow His lead? When we fail and make missteps, it is oh so easy to think we've ruined God's plans for us, but the truth of the matter is, we're not that big.

"All hearts are in God's hand, and those are blessed who put their trust in him, and commit their ways unto him." - Matthew Henry

Notes

Notes

Day 147

Troublers of Israel

"When he was summoned, Tertullus began to accuse him, saying, 'Since through you we enjoy much peace, and your foresight is bringing reforms to this nation, with all thankfulness, most excellent Felix, we always welcome it everywhere. But not to detain you further, I beg you to briefly hear us in your patience.' " - Acts 24:2-4 MEV

Oh the flattery. It would seem from the opening statements of both Tertullus and Paul, survival in the courtroom of Felix required a certain level of adulation. In honesty these words meant nothing, because a mere 2 years later the complaints against Felix will have piled up so deep that Nero will have no choice but to remove him from power, and the Jews of Caesarea will travel hundreds of miles to Rome to file suit against him. Sooner or later the praise of mankind comes to nothing.

" ' We have found this man a troublemaker, instigating riots among all the Jews throughout the world, and a ringleader of the sect of the Nazarenes. He even tried to profane the temple. So we seized him and wanted to judge him according to our law.' " - Acts 24:5-6 MEV

Oh the indictment. These men who have made themselves the enemies of God accuse Paul of the exact things they are guilty of. Think back. Was it Paul who instigated riots, or the Jews who hated what he peacefully and lovingly spoke? Was it Paul who profaned the temple, or Ananias and his cartel who had turned it into their own personal tool to extort every dime from the children of Israel? History tells us even the way these men would say the word "Nazarene," was as an insult, spit out in disgust.

"God's prophets were charged with being troublers of the land, and our Lord Jesus Christ, that he perverted the nation; the very same charges were brought against Paul." - Matthew Henry

They say history repeats itself, and when we look at the history of Israel, that is certainly shown true. Look at Elijah, and he's called "you troubler of Israel," by the idolatrous king Ahab. Look at Amos, and you'll see a prophet of God, told not to prophesy anymore because of the king and the temple. Jeremiah was repeatedly accused, imprisoned, and beaten.

"Then they said, 'Come and let us devise plans against Jeremiah. For the law will not be lost from the priest, nor counsel from the wise, nor the word from the prophet. Come and let us strike him with the tongue, and let us not give heed to any of his words.' " - Jeremiah 18:18 MEV

Hanani was imprisoned, and Micaiah was slapped in the face then imprisoned. Uriah was struck down by the king's sword, and John the baptizer likewise had his head removed by the king. Zechariah, the son of Jehoiada, was stoned to death, and before being similarly stoned to death, the deacon Stephen asked, "which of the prophets have your fathers not persecuted" (Acts 7:52 MEV).

There was a common denominator both in every one of these martyrs and confessors, and in their accusers. Those faithful to the word of God were consistently the ones accused and persecuted as troublers of Israel, while those who provoked God to anger against His people were the accusers and the ones citing the law as being on their side.

"If a man comes and utters empty lies — 'I will preach to you about wine and beer' — he would be just the preacher for this people!" - Micah 2:11 CSB

Though God commanded capital punishment upon the false prophets, they were always the ones accepted by Israel, while His faithful servants suffered for speaking His truth. That's not something that's merely history. While (at least in the USA) we're no longer martyred for standing firm, the accolades of men reveal this is not ancient history. The record still skips on the same old verse. Those who will sugarcoat or pervert the gospel often fill stadiums, while the faithful preachers are the ones even so-called Christians consider too hard-nosed.

"Today if God's servants preach the truth of God, or if they will hold to it and dare to live it, they will soon meet with some contemptuous title or other. Pare down the gospel, cut away its angles, draw out the lion's teeth, and then you will be friends with the world. But hold the doctrines of grace, bring forth the atonement, speak out plainly, have your convictions and state them, and soon the hounds will be after you full cry." - Charles Spurgeon

Brothers and sisters, servants of the One True God, it is easy for us, in looking to see the success of God, to play the numbers game. Butts in seats, social media reactions, affirming conversations and more become easy metrics to see if we're good stewards of the word of God. The record of His Word reveals that they're not accurate measurements though. If anything, faithfulness to God's truth, and the accolades of men are, more often than not, inversely proportional.

Sure, we can play all sorts of games with our techniques, but if the full truth of the Gospel is in any way malleable, suffering for the sake of reach, then it is not God's influence for which we work. Marketing strategies have become all too common in Christ's modern Church, and the evidence in the hearts of our land shows how harmful they've been. I daresay marketing has no place in the Church if we can't absolutely subject it to God's word.

Paul and Felix may have been cast in certain lights by the words of Tertullus, but when it comes down to that day when everyone is judged of God, the tables will be turned. These men will be seen in very different lights. The most flattering worldly comments will come to nothing when Jesus Christ sits to judge the world. Only faithful adherence to Christ will find any one of us hearing positive affirmations that day. Only His righteousness matters, for the rest is all vanity.

Notes

Notes

Day 148

Guilty of Loving Christ

"Neither can they prove the charges they are now making against me. But I admit this to you: I worship the God of my ancestors according to the Way, which they call a sect, believing everything that is in accordance with the law and written in the prophets." - Acts 24:13-14 CSB

Tertullus and "the Jews also" (vs 9) have stated their case, and now Paul is given the chance to make his apologia, and a good defense does he make. He points out how verifiable it is that it's only been 12 days since he came to Jerusalem, most of which have been spent in Roman captivity. Next, he declares the fact that he was not the one found causing a disturbance. No, instead, he was found worshipping the God of their fathers, ritually cleansed in the temple in the manner of their own religious law. He points out that it was the Jews from Asia who had caused the riot, then asks where are they to be found in this courtroom?

Paul appeals to a well-established Roman law, that the people of each land be allowed to worship their own gods in the manner of their religion, to which he says, "look, I was doing exactly that, even as by their own established ways and beliefs." Finally, the Apostle closes out by saying essentially, "if they're not here to present their case, let those who are tell what charges they have against me." In the midst of all that, though, we find Paul make a confession. "I worship the God of my ancestors according to the Way,"

"If blamed for being more earnest in the things of God than our neighbours, what is our reply? Do we shrink from the accusation?" - Matthew Henry

The one accusation Tertullus makes against Paul which holds a shred of truth, is entirely true, and entirely to be embraced by the small Benjamite. I am indeed of this sect they call the Nazarenes. I worship the same God as my countrymen, keeping His same laws, but in the understanding of said laws which is found in the Lord Jesus Christ! Do what you will with that, but the other charges are all false.

"If there is any sight pleasing to the God of our salvation, and a sight at which the angels rejoice, it is, to behold a devoted follower of the Lord, here upon earth, acknowledging that he is guilty, if it be a crime, of loving the Lord who died for him, with all his heart, and soul, and mind, and strength. And that he will not in silence see God's word despised, or hear his name profaned; he will rather risk the ridicule and the hatred of the world, than one frown from that gracious Being whose love is better than life." - Henry

We're here in the flesh, and will still fall to sin, to temptation, and to error, but it is the new heart of those redeemed in Christ which inspires and empowers us to live, more and more, according to the righteousness by which we are already known. That sort of devoted life will find us, less and less condemnable by earthly laws, except for those laws which stand in opposition to God Himself. Whatever charges may be raised against our names, let us endeavor with every breath to be blameless in them all except for one - that we be the devoted followers of the Lord Jesus Christ, with our eyes set on His promise of eternal life.

Yet, it could be said that's often not the case...

"How many in the world would rather be accused of any weakness, nay, even of wickedness, than of an earnest, fervent feeling of love to the Lord Jesus Christ, and of devotedness to his service! Can such think that He will confess them when he comes in his glory, and before the angels of God?" - Henry

How many of us will go about our daily lives, just as the rest of the world? How many go to work, hiding our faith, you know, in case it may be a hindrance to that promotion we've been chasing? How many act as any others of our friends, never declaring the hope that is in us, because they might not be our friends anymore? How many shrink from the declaration of sin, only sharing a partial gospel (and we know it), because the world says the other part is bigotry and hatred? We wouldn't want to offend, after all, would we? How many of us will find the Lord remembers these compromises in the day of judgement?

Ask me this, am I a follower of the Way? Oh yes! Do what you will with it, but I believe in the Lord Jesus Christ, by whom everything was created that was created, and by whom every atom of the universe is held together. I believe that He manifested as one of us, suffered every temptation as we do, lived sinless, died as the propitiation of our sin, was resurrected on the third day, then raised to glory in the presence of many witnesses. I believe He sits on the throne making intercession for us, and has sent the Holy Spirit to continue this work which was begun in us, right up until that day when He, the King, returns to judge the world. I believe on the day of judgement all will be resurrected, some to eternal life by faith in His grace alone, and others to the just payment of their sin.

This I confess: I am a follower of the Way.

How about you?

Notes

Notes

Day 149

Peek-a-boo, God Sees You

"I have a hope in God, which these men themselves also accept, that there will be a resurrection, both of the righteous and the unrighteous." - Acts 24:15 CSB

It seems a safe bet to assume at some point in your life you've played peek-a-boo with an infant. They don't know much, but they know that when they can't see you, you can't see them. At least, they think that's what they know. All through time men have thought they knew so much. Not too long ago, they knew the Earth was the center of the universe, and that it was flat, with the sun and moon orbiting us. Granted, some still think they know that. Many, many others still know "if I can't see you, you can't see me."

The height of human intellectual achievement has always leaned toward the stance that it has reached the pinnacle of all knowledge. That is, at least, the height of prideful intellectuality. Those who really seek to know the truth are consistently amazed to greater understand how little we actually understand. Yet some things can be known for a certainty, and among those are the things which have been unambiguously declared in the word of God - that truth which never changes. One of those things is that yes, God can still see you, regardless of whether you cover your eyes.

“Many of those who sleep in the dust of the earth shall awake, some to everlasting life, but others to shame and everlasting contempt." - Daniel 12:2 MEV

None are righteous, save those who are known by the righteousness of Christ, but they aren't the only ones who should expect resurrection. While those who die in Christ will be resurrected with incorruptible, glorified bodies, those who die having rejected Him to the end will also be resurrected, after the thousand-year reign (see Rev 20:6). It's at that time when Revelation 21:8 tells us the unrighteous "shall have their portion in the lake that burns with fire and brimstone" (MEV), calling it the second death.

"Do not marvel at this. For the hour is coming in which all who are in the graves will hear His voice and come out—those who have done good to the resurrection of life, and those who have done evil to the resurrection of judgment. I can do nothing of Myself. As I hear, I judge. My judgment is just, because I seek not My own will, but the will of the Father who sent Me." - John 5:28-30 MEV

It was prophesied long ago, but it was confirmed by the words of Christ Himself, who delights not in the judgement of the wicked. Just as the Father does, the Son also laments the judgement of the impenitent, but takes utmost joy in the mercy shown His children. Do not marvel that the Lord has that authority of judgement, for He's spent thousands of years trying to tell us.

Those who hide their eyes from the Lord often portray Him as a cruel and spiteful God, but that's only because they can't see past their fingers. The truth is, the Lord does not want anyone to perish. Righteous justice requires that the unrighteous suffer the penalty of sin, but the mercy and grace of God sacrificed His very own to settle the debt. All we must do is turn to that Savior. Instead, too many will keep their eyes covered, believing they can't be seen, but time will run out. Eventually God will have to fulfill the righteous requirement of justice, and that will not be something in which He takes joy.

"Therefore I will weep bitterly for Jazer, the vine of Sibmah; I will water you with my tears, O Heshbon and Elealeh... Therefore my heart shall sound like a harp for Moab, and my inward parts for Kir Hareseth." - Isaiah 16:9, 11 MEV

Even in the declaration of more temporal judgements God reveals His heart. For an example we look to Moab. Here was a nation spawned by deceitful incest; related by blood to Israel, but so often her bitter enemy. It was a nation that so boasted of herself that God tells us, through Isaiah, that Moab was proud even of her pride. But even when pronouncing judgement upon such a wicked people as Moab, He sends multiple messengers calling them to repent. Isaiah, Jeremiah, Ezekiel, and more, provide many witnesses, offering these people every chance to pull their hands off their eyes. It's in Isaiah though that the God of all righteousness expresses how He feels about it. The righteous God of justice mourns for the judgement of these wicked people.

Regardless of what picture the inside of your fingers shows, the Lord is not some ornery, trigger-happy God, eager to execute a good ol' fashioned smiting. Peel back those hands and look to Jesus, and you will see the God who is long-suffering, grieving over all our self-indulgent, destructive ways. You will see the God that was patient enough to wait for you to peek, when by all rights, He should have lit the fires long ago. This is the God who loves.

Notes

Notes

Day 150

"After several days, when Felix arrived with his wife Drusilla, who was a Jewess, he sent for Paul and heard him speak concerning faith in Christ. As he lectured about righteousness, self-control, and the coming judgment, Felix was afraid and answered, "For now, leave! When time permits, I will send for you." At the same time he hoped that money would be given him by Paul, that he might release him. So he sent for him more often and conversed with him." - Acts 24:24-26 MEV

The courtroom has just found Paul before Felix, but as Felix and Drusilla now inquire of the Apostle "concerning faith in Christ," Alexander McLaren dubs it "Felix before Paul." If you regularly read along, you may remember Felix "practiced all cruelty and lust in his government" (Tacitus), and now his sin is on trial by Spirit. It's at this point another character enters the scene, and we're introduced to his wife Drusilla.

This Drusilla was the daughter of Herod Agrippa (who we remember was eaten by worms when she was only 6), and thereby both a Jewess, and sister of Agrippa II who now reigned. At a young age she was betrothed to Epiphanes, the heir to the throne of Commagene, or what remained of the Seleucid empire. The young prince would not proselytize and submit to Jewish custom, so the engagement was cast off, and Drusilla instead married king Azizus, of Emesa, who did submit to circumcision and became a proselyte Jew.

Yet these appearances of religious and lawful adherence did not last long for the young queen, widely regarded the most beautiful in all the land. Felix, becoming enamored with her beauty, employed a certain Simon the magician (possibly the same Simon Magus from Acts 8), to "prevail upon her" with the impression to abandon her marriage and marry Felix, the inhumane and wicked gentile, instead. We now find she joins Felix in this inquiry of the sect of her father's religion which Paul preached.

Quite notably, there's a distinct difference in what we're told of Paul's preaching before these two, and his typical lectures which have been recorded throughout Luke's history. The preacher of the only Righteous

One, by whom everyone who believes is justified, now lectures on righteousness. The preacher of Christian liberty now lectures on self-control. The preacher of the forgiveness of sins, now lectures on the coming judgement.

"To persons so unjust, lewd, and otherwise wicked, Paul very properly discoursed on the virtues here mentioned, against which they had both so highly offended; for he knew that it would be to little purpose to address them on other subjects of Christianity, such as those of redemption and salvation through Christ, till they forsook these sins." - Joseph Benson

When it comes down to it, the gospel is not complete in any supposed believer, if they not repent of sin. That's not to say that Felix and Drusilla must cleanse themselves of sin before coming to faith. Such a feat is not possible. But turning to Christ inherently requires turning from sin. Let me rephrase that. It's not possible to truly believe in Christ and the salvation which He purchased for us, if we don't recognize our need of redemption, because of our shortcomings in sin, and forsake those lusts. Belief in Jesus is dependent on denial of self.

"Then [Jesus] said to them all, 'If anyone will come after Me, let him deny himself, and take up his cross daily, and follow Me.' " - Luke 9:23 MEV

We don't find Paul, as some would suggest, in contradiction to the epistle of James. To those who had missed their Messiah, he preached Jesus as the Messiah, and to those who might be incapable of feeling loved by the God of Israel, he preached the free gift of unconditional forgiveness in Christ; But to those who might latch on to the idea of reconciliation to God, while harboring no desire to abandon worldly sin, he preaches "righteousness, temperance, and judgement to come" (KJV).

We can be saved through faith by grace alone, but faith without works is dead. The two lessons are not mutually exclusive. When we recognize the despicable end of sin, and desire instead the restoration to God, He will not leave us in the muck where we were found. The Good Shepherd didn't leave the 99 to go sit satisfied in the brambles with the one. He came to rescue us out of them.

We don't find Paul preaching a partial gospel, like the Jews who would cross every distance or sea to make a proselyte at any cost. Instead, we see a man who would not dare welcome Felix and Drusilla into false faith which might keep them comfortably in the grip of the devil. What we find today can often be a different story.

More and more we're seeing an increase of preachers who will gloss over the need of repentance, or worse yet, justify what God calls sin as not so, because "we're in the 21st century now, after all, and that stuff was all just cultural." Beyond that we're even seeing pastors raised up to the pulpits, themselves impenitent, and even vocally proud of their open sin. That is not true belief in Christ. It is the work of the deceiver, to lull potential believers back to sleep.

Felix and Drusilla started to spiritually awaken with a yawn, and they asked to hear of faith in Christ. Hearing the part of that faith which tells of the judgement to come, Felix trembled with fear. The Spirit clearly convicted the procurator of all his sin, but when these two heard of the inconveniences of denying oneself, and giving up the firm grasp of sin they so loved, they procrastinated. They hit the snooze button, and consequently missed their flight.

"he shows a certain measure of respect for him, but he postpones acting "till a more convenient season," and so becomes the type of the millions whose spiritual life is ruined by a like procrastination. Nothing that we know of him gives us any ground for thinking that the 'convenient season' ever came." - Charles Ellicott

Sending Paul away, Felix makes a fatal mistake, saying "When I have a convenient time, I will call for you" (NKJV). My friends, there is no gain in waiting when the Spirit of God knocks on the door of your heart. Whether that knock be to embrace the first step of repentance and belief, or the invitation to take the next step in the maturing of our faith walk, let us run with excitement to answer that door.

If you find yourself in a false gospel where salvation and sin dance hand in hand, wake up; The enemy's flute is playing you a lullaby, but God will not fail to carry you out of the bunkhouse and give you a big cup of coffee, if you merely ask.

If you find yourself, yawning at the dawning of curiosity about all this Jesus stuff, please don't hit that snooze button. Our flight leaves soon, and if you sleep through this alarm, you'll be more apt to sleep through the next. There's no telling how much more time you have.

"Do we expect that as we advance in life our hearts will grow softer, or that the influence of the world will decline? Are we not at this moment in danger of being lost for ever? Now is the day of salvation; tomorrow may be too late." - Matthew Henry

Notes

Day 151

Inevitable Failure of Human Governance

"Desiring to do the Jews a favor, Festus answered, 'Are you willing to go up to Jerusalem to be judged concerning these charges before me?' " - Acts 25:9 MEV

Finally, relief! The wicked governor Antonius Felix has been deposed, and we now have a new man in charge. With all the negative accounts of history which we've heard of Felix over the past few days, we now come to a vastly different sort of ruler. The annals of Rome are largely quite positive about the short, two-year term of this Porcius Festus, deeming him fair and reasonable. For the most part the only negative accounts of him are that the Jews remained bitter against him because of the handling of the situation in Caesarea - this situation with Paul.

From the time that Felix left Paul imprisoned, to Festus now taking office two years later, we see little except that from within the guard of what is essentially both the governor's mansion and the military barracks, Paul is given both safety and freedom. Now Felix is off to Rome, many Jews of Caesarea chasing after him to bring charges of insufferable crimes, and Festus inherits the Paul problem.

While Festus does appear to be a gentler and more just ruler, there's still a human limitation to that justice. The case of Paul is not the only source of information we have of this procurator, but it is one of the chief sources of information which history gives us on his execution of leadership, and it doesn't paint a perfect picture.

It's evident from this record that Festus had received some degree of briefing on Paul's situation. Upon their first request to bring Paul to Jerusalem, Festus rightly says that Paul should remain in Caesarea for trial, and those who would bring a charge against him can travel to that judgement seat to speak. The Jews do just that and pile into the courtroom in such numbers that it's said they surrounded him. They're given their chance to plea, and bring many various accusations, all of which fall flat. It's clearly such a disaster that all Paul needs to respond in his own defense is, "Neither against the law of the Jews, nor against the temple, nor against Caesar have I sinned at all" (Acts 25:8 MEV).

It is at this point where we're told Festus, "desiring to do the Jews a favor," endeavors to hand him over into their grip. Again, it can be noted that there's considerable reason to believe he's been informed of what's gone on, up to and including their previous plot to kill him. We'll come back to that, but Paul again speaks, making it clear the evidence is extensive that he has in no way harmed the Jews. He says it so plainly that it is accompanied by the statement, "as you know very well" (vs 10 MEV). Then Paul lays forth the ultimatum, essentially giving the choice, if you hand me over to them, you know well that I will die, and you will be guilty, but if not, since you won't rule in favor of clear justice, send my case up to the supreme court.

By his own mouth Festus had testified to the Jews, "It is not the custom of the Romans to deliver any man to die before he who is accused meets the accusers face to face and has the opportunity to make his defense concerning the charge brought against him" (Acts 25:16 MEV).

By his own mouth he soon tells king Agrippa, "I found that he had committed nothing worthy of death" (Acts 25:25a MEV). Festus becomes to Paul, much like Pilate was to Jesus.

Despite the judgement of innocence, Festus is willing to send the man to his certain death merely to gain political favor with his new subjects. Surely, he's got plausible deniability, right? He didn't himself order the execution of this innocent man. He even pitched the journey as a question so that it could be said to be Paul's own choice. Even so, I honestly doubt there would be many who would justify his action as faultless here. The man who knowingly guides a traveler down a dark alley is just as guilty as the man who plunges the stiletto.

Study political history, and you'll find we've never seen any form of human government that wasn't without disastrous and even fatal flaws. Eventually pitchforks rise, and if you're lucky you're told you've got, "a republic ma'am if you can keep it," but if you're not so lucky the Bolsheviks or Chinese Communist Party move in and your victory leads to tens of millions dying of starvation and persecution. But even the U.S.

Constitution was rightly forecasted to be only fit for a moral people. More and more each day, we don't fit that qualification, and I'd suggest that's both by design, and by flesh nature. Election seasons roll around, and it doesn't matter whether you're hoping for a red wave or a blue wave; Things may get a little better or a little worse for a while, but there are no real, lasting solutions.

We can talk all day about ideas - "you know what we need is," "what would really fix this is," or, "such and such has to happen or else we're doomed," - but brothers and sisters, follow any of those ideas through to all their collateral damage, corruptibility by evil men, and logical conclusions, and you'll realize that God was right to be disheartened when Israel demanded a king. There is no human government that will ever solve the sin problem, and thousands of years of attempts can prove it. The government we need is to submit to the one true King, Jesus Christ. Nothing less will fix this.

Notes

Notes

Day 152

With All Pomp

"Then Agrippa said to Festus, 'I would like to hear the man myself.' He said, 'Tomorrow you shall hear him.' The next day Agrippa and Bernice came with great pomp, and they entered the hall with the commanders and the leading men of the city. When Festus gave the order, Paul was brought in." - Acts 25:22-23 MEV

For two years now, Paul has found himself unable to continue his mission. From these loose bonds he's not been allowed to evangelize the gentile nor Jewish world. His friends are allowed to attend upon him, and surely they come for weekly fellowship and learning at least, but aside from the soldiers and servants in Herod's praetorium to which he can possibly minister, neglect of the evangelical passion of Paul which Luke has expressed so vividly must, by now, be leading him to a deep depression. The man is washed up, locked down, and no longer of use to His Savior. Or so it seemed.

For some years now Agrippa II has been king of Galilee, having not been allowed, at 17 years old, to inherit his father's throne of Jerusalem, but, first receiving the inheritance of his uncles' territories, he had gained increasing authority to where he now ruled. The statement he makes, here translated "I would like to hear the man myself," was, in the original Greek, found in the imperfect tense. That could be read as if the king was just softening his tone, so as to present the request with respect to the new procurator, Festus. John Calvin, on the other hand, among others, reasoned that what was being said was that Agrippa had longed for some time to hear Paul speak. Possibly we shall never know.

"Festus said, 'King Agrippa, and all the men who are present with us, you see this man, concerning whom the whole assembly of the Jews petitioned me, both at Jerusalem and here, shouting that he ought not to live any longer. I found that he had committed nothing worthy of death. But when he himself appealed to Caesar, I decided to send him. But I have nothing to write to His Majesty concerning him. Therefore I have brought him before you, and especially before you, King Agrippa, so that upon examination, I might have something to write. For it seems unreasonable to me to send a prisoner without signifying the charges against him.' " - Acts 25:24-27 MEV

Paul and Agrippa need wait no longer. The royal procession rolls in with all the pomp of his errant father, though rather than keeping all the glory for himself and persecuting the church, this Agrippa lends his curiosity to the Lord. Finally, Paul gets his chance to testify of Christ before Kings. Finally, Agrippa gets to hear the testimony of Paul.

Remember when God prophesied to the Jewish exiles in Babylon through Jeremiah? In chapter 29, verse 13, God gave the exiles a promise that echoes to all lost sheep through the ages. "You shall seek Me and find Me, when you shall search for Me with all your heart" (MEV). What about this Agrippa though? Doesn't he now seek? The king admits he desires to hear Paul, then, in the midst of all the who's who of Judea "said to Paul 'you are permitted to speak for yourself' " (Acts 26:1 MEV)

"The king, before whom I also speak freely, knows about these things. For I am persuaded that none of this is hidden from him, for this was not done in a corner. King Agrippa, do you believe the prophets? I know that you believe.' " - Acts 26:26-27 MEV

Even Paul recognizes some esteem of the Lord in last of the house of Herod. So, was God's promise not true? After all, Agrippa says, "You almost persuade me to be a Christian" (Vs 28 MEV). There is no such thing as almost a Christian. Nearly persuaded is not a statement of faith, and living for almost 40 more years, there is no historical evidence the last Herodian ever came to Christ, just as the rest of his ancestors. But did Agrippa II really search with all his heart?

He certainly searched with curiosity, though not with humility, coming to the testimony with great pomp. He certainly searched for the truth about Paul, but only partially the truth of God. The end goal of Festus, Agrippa, and Bernice was, after all, laid out definitively and repeatedly; Festus had to send a prisoner to Caesar, but had no charge of any crime to excuse the chains. These men and women didn't listen fully with intent of finding God, but rather with hope of finding something with which they could at least give a shadow of a doubt of innocence.

"Here was a noble assembly brought together to hear the truths of the gospel, though they only meant to gratify their curiosity by attending to the defence of a prisoner. Many, even now, attend at the places of hearing the word of God with great pomp, and too often with no better motive than curiosity." - Matthew Henry

There's no promise of God which has ever shown unfaithful, and neither has this one been. Truly, if you search for God, not halfheartedly, you will find Him in Christ. Let not mere curiosity, nor impressions before men lead you to come idly into the fellowship to hear any preacher. Come with a heart seeking God, and find His salvation you shall.

Notes

Notes

Day 153

Almost Persuaded

"Then Agrippa said to Paul, 'You are permitted to speak for yourself.' So Paul stretched out his hand and made his defense: 'King Agrippa, I consider myself fortunate that today I shall make my defense before you against all the accusations of the Jews, especially because you are an expert in all customs and controversies of the Jews. Therefore I beg you to patiently listen to me.' " - Acts 26:1-3 MEV

Take a moment to inquire, "why does Paul count himself fortunate to make his defense before the king?" Certainly, it pertains not to his release. He's been repeatedly ruled innocent, yet not set free, and due to his appeal to Caesar, nothing he said this day would attain his freedom by the hand of Agrippa II. Yet Paul says he's fortunate to make his defense against the accusations of the Jews, because the king was well informed on the things of which he'd speak, and then he begs solemn attention. It sure seems like the man wants to argue for his freedom, except that when we look toward the end of this encounter, we see whose freedom he actually fights for.

"Paul said, 'I pray to God that not only you, but all who hear me this day, might become not only almost, but thoroughly and altogether, what I am, except for these chains.' " - Acts 26:29 MEV

Indeed, Paul entered this room full of the rich and powerful, with no delusions of making his own case. Rather, he makes the case for the Gospel, his only defense the apologia of Christ. With a chain hanging from his wrist, Paul extends his right hand, in the common manner of ancient orators, and begins to speak on the hope that his hearers - those who were bound in slavery to sin - might be set free. But if that's the case, why so much about his self-righteous upbringing?

"My manner of life from my youth, spent from the beginning in my own nation and at Jerusalem, is known by all the Jews. They knew me from the beginning and could testify, if they wished, how according to the strictest sect of our religion I lived as a Pharisee." - Acts 26:4-5 MEV

Even the royal and honorable ones knew the Pharisees for what they were. These men were the strictest, and most adherent to the law by which their forefathers had hoped to awake in the resurrection. If anyone could earn their way in by works, even his accusers "if they wished," had every evidence to say that this Pharisee of Pharisees, personally taught under the most honorable Rabbi, Gamaliel, and zealous for the law like no other; certainly he would be the one. His defense starts out sounding rather like the man is doing an awful lot of boasting.

"I, too, thought that I must do many things contrary to the name of Jesus of Nazareth, which I indeed did in Jerusalem and locked up many of the saints in prison by authority from the chief priests. And when they were killed, I cast my vote against them. I punished them often in every synagogue and compelled them to blaspheme. And being extremely enraged against them, I persecuted them even to foreign cities. So I went to Damascus with authority and a commission from the chief priests." - Acts 26:9-12 MEV

"Look, I was every bit as zealous and opposed to this sect as any of them," he entreats of the king, "but then something happened; Then the resurrected Jesus of Nazareth showed Himself to me. Now 'I have forfeited the loss of all things and count them as rubbish that I may gain Christ' (Philippians 3:8b MEV)." Paul boasts not of his youth nor his zeal for personal gain, but that he could use that testimony before these great ones, to turn hearts to their Savior.

"Then Agrippa said to Paul, 'You almost persuade me to be a Christian.' " - Acts 26:28 MEV

Can you imagine any more disheartening a reply? You almost persuade me? What is that? That is nothing - no gain, no coming to Christ, nor freedom for this last of the line of Herod. Having had perfect opportunity to change the end of the story of that great yet terrible house, Paul's apologia comes up short. I believe his response shows what state of mind such a disappointment put him in. With his spirit downcast, Paul fixed his eyes on Jesus, the last (and only) hope in this room. We can take his example in that prayer was all he had left.

"Paul said, 'I pray to God that not only you, but all who hear me this day, might become not only almost, but thoroughly and altogether, what I am, except for these chains.' " - Acts 26:29 MEV

Have you ever ministered to someone who refused to turn? Have you given your all, only to be left feeling you've failed them... failed Christ? They remain on the road to destruction, and your season of sowing seed has come to an end. Do you know, their refusal is not your failure?

Brothers and sisters, we cannot do an ounce of work to change the hearts of men. We can't bring about belief and repentance in the soul of a single person. Children of God take this to heart: we are not the ones to save sinners! Only the Spirit of God can soften the hearts that will be softened. Only the choice of each individual can take that step of belief. Only Jesus Christ can save a sinner. That's not our job. Our task is merely to bring the good news, and once that seed is planted, to pray that it might sprout and grow a healthy head of wheat.

Paul had given his best, and all that was left, in the face of failure, was to pray to God that everyone in that room would come to Jesus. Not only was that a prayer for the salvation of their souls, but it was a prayer for the peace and well-being of his own spirit, in the knowledge that God would multiply the offering as He would, and that the word of God would not return void.

Surely, in some, the word would pass right through, never taking root, as we have reason to believe happened with Agrippa, but there's no reason for us to believe that none of the others who heard Paul that day ever repented. Even if none of these ever did come to faith, Luke writes this as one who witnessed the speech first hand. Surely, he and others who were on Paul's side that day would be built up in the maturing of their faith by what transpired. Surely some of us reading this day will be as well.

We must trust, in the face of worldly evidence to the contrary, that God's word does not return void, and that our earnest works for His glory will be used by Him, as He wills. Trust in Christ is the greatest tool we have, both for the hearts of others, and for our own hearts as well.

Notes

Day 154

Why is it Thought Incredible

"Why is it thought incredible by any of you that God raises the dead?" - Acts 26:8 ESV

If you've been reading along with us, you may remember from chapter 25, and Festus' letter to Agrippa, the procurator wrote that he was particularly at a loss as to how to investigate the questions of "a certain Jesus, who was dead, but whom Paul asserted to be alive" (Acts 25:19b ESV). Here in chapter 26, in the original Greek record of Paul's question - "Why is it judged incredible by you that God raises the dead" (Acts 26:8 MEV) - the noun "you" is plural, making his statement a question, not just to Agrippa, but to many, possibly all the listeners, and most certainly to Festus. Why y'all actin' a foo'?

During Paul's discourse Festus is driven to loudly exclaim Paul's insanity saying, "much learning is turning you to madness" (Acts 26:24 MEV). There's not much in Paul's recorded speech to cause such fervent exclamation though, and so we can reasonably assume that Luke has merely recorded the outline of the entire dialogue. There's no need to fret though, as we have the entire rest of scripture from which to find these arguments. With King Agrippa, for example, Paul could reason from the royal annals, which we find in 1 and 2 Kings, where through Elijah and Elisha, God had resurrected the dead. But what about Felix and the other esteemed Roman guests to this inquiry? They didn't have reason to know or believe those scriptures.

"For what can be known about God is plain to them, because God has shown it to them. For his invisible attributes, namely, his eternal power and divine nature, have been clearly perceived, ever since the creation of the world, in the things that have been made. So they are without excuse." - Romans 1:19-20 ESV

From the beginning of time, all of creation has sung the song of God, testifying of His greatness. Look to the wonders of creation and it takes a certain amount of hardheadedness to not see the necessity of intelligent design in it all. The implication of Paul's question to those in his hearing that day, was that if God could create such wonder as the human life, what reason would any have to doubt that he could resurrect that same life? More than ever, we today can look at the wonder of creation and see the testimony of God. Look at just one example:

"DNA the size of a pinhead contains as much information as 25 trillion 189-page paperback books. A pile of these books would stretch 920 times the distance from the earth to the moon. If you were to stretch out one milligram of a double helix strand of DNA material, it would almost stretch from the earth to the moon" - Dr Werner Gitt

Over the past several decades, what we know of DNA has grown exponentially. The more we learn, the more impossible it becomes for it to have been formed by chaos and chance. Dean H. Kenyan is a biology professor at San Francisco State University. At one point in his career, many decades ago, he published a book defending and explaining Darwinian Evolution. Not long after, when confronting the issue of DNA, he found no option but to repudiate his former work, in favor of Creationism, making the following statement:

"This new realm of molecular genetics [is] where we see the most compelling evidence of design on the Earth."

The understanding of DNA was only just beginning at that point, but as knowledge of this immense code has grown, he has held firm to the stance. Even the simplest single cell organism has one fifth of the data in its DNA as the human DNA has. Yet for that single cell to function (to live) and come into being without a creator, the vast majority of those data points would have had to have, by pure chance, all happened in the same place at the same time, and just as it would need to be to form life. If any number of them were not, the cell would not replicate, and could thereby not "evolve" from not life into life.

"The chance that higher forms have emerged in this way is comparable with the chance that a tornado sweeping through a junk yard might assemble a Boeing 747 from the materials therein" - Sir Fred Hoyle

The education system has for some time now taught, as fact, a myth, which even they can only call a theory, but which the vast majority of scientific evidence testifies against. On the other hand, they have tried extensively to explain away the fact of history which is more extensively and indisputably recorded than most any other - that Jesus of Nazareth lived and died on the cross, after which many of his followers held fast to the claim of having seen him alive.

There's not enough belief in the world to convince me that this complex thing called life spawned purely from chaos. On the other hand, if God could create the life of this certain Jesus (the manifest Son of God), why is it thought incredible that He could rise from the dead?

But what about for those of us who already believe? We're still in this broken world full of suffering and death; We are still burying loved ones. I'd ask you to consider for a moment that concerning those we've lost who knew the saving grace of Christ, there is no shred of reason for us to think it incredible that the Risen Savior, who went up to glory, can and will resurrect them as well.

If we but overcome in faith to the end, and they did also, there is no more reason for us to mourn those we've buried, than there is those who have taken an extended journey across the globe. For a time, we will not see them, but that time shall come to an end, and we will be reunited in a land with no more pain, no more suffering, no more disease, nor mental decay.

Notes

Notes

Day 155

Works Worthy of Repentance

"Therefore, King Agrippa, I was not disobedient to the heavenly vision, but declared first to those at Damascus, then at Jerusalem and throughout all the region of Judea, and also to the Gentiles, that they should repent and turn to God and do works proving their repentance. For these reasons the Jews seized me in the temple and tried to kill me." - Acts 26:19-21 MEV

There's a narrow fence upon which the faithful Christians balance, and if you follow along with these devotionals, you've possibly grown tired of hearing the same exhortation again and again. Yet the inspired word of God saw fit to emphasize this truth in great repetition, and so again we come to it. Repetition not only denotes importance, but it also assists in the implantation of memory.

Getting to it, we see Paul summarize his work, declaring "that they should repent and turn to God and do works proving their repentance." If that sounds familiar, think back to John the Baptist and his statement, "Therefore, bear fruit worthy of repentance" (Matthew 3:8 MEV). The CSB actually translates Paul's statement here in Acts in the same language - "and do works worthy of repentance" - and with good cause. Matthew and Luke both used the same word, "Axios," translated most directly by language we don't much use these days, "meets." Works in meeting with repentance. That is, works that are worthy of, or prove repentance.

This brings us to that balancing act, the fence off of which it is so easy to tumble. Off one side, the rejection of any necessity for works. Paul was, after all, a greater evangelist than James, and he contradicted James' statement that faith without works is dead, right? If any still holds to that sort of argument, I must ask, what do you make of his words here? Paul says flat out that he told them to do works in keeping with repentance. Faith is not true, nor is repentance, if there is no change in the thoughts, emotions, and actions of the one claiming them.

"To say we are grieved for sin, and we hate sin, and yet to live in it, is but to deceive ourselves, and to mock God." - Matthew Poole

Yet how often do we find the Christian falling off the other side of that fence as well? We must take note that Paul lays out a specific order. Repent, turn to God, then do good works. Good works exercised without first having come to saving faith in Christ, are nothing more than trash ready for the compactor. Repent, that is change your mind from sin to Christ, and turn from the grip of Satan to the love of God and belief in Jesus, then do good works, as Paul tells the Colossians, "In the name of the Lord Jesus, giving thanks to God the Father through Him" (Colossians 3:17b MEV).

Where we find it easy to fall is when we make salvation dependent upon those works. Look back again at that previously referenced verse and dwell a moment on what Paul says we accomplish with our works done in the name of the Lord Jesus Christ. We give thanks to God the Father. Works never were, and never will be capable of saving our souls or "outdoing" our sin. Thank God for that, because I am confident that you know as well as I do that we're not very good at being faithful to good works. We stumble, we fall, and well, I'll let the lyrics of Micah Tyler speak for us:

"I still hurt
Fall short of what You say I'm worth
And that devil says I don't deserve
What You did on the cross
And he's right 'cause I don't
But You did it anyway" - I See Grace

I listened to that song on repeat the other day, tears of gratitude welling up, somewhat blurring the road as I drove. Can you imagine a greater God than this? That the Lion would humble Himself to become the Lamb, as one silent before it's shearers, not opening His mouth, but submitting to death on the cross so that we - sinners who would continue to fall short even after redemption - could have life and have it to the full? That's a good God, worthy of all my praise, all my gratitude, and every work of my hand. So how do we "do works worthy of repentance?"

While the 18th century theologian John Gill's staunch Calvinist lean may not mesh with my meager understanding of the Word, once he gets past that, his bullet list of what defines these works is rather suited to the question. What makes works worthy of repentance?

First, they are, "According to the will of God in His word." It could hardly be argued that anything done could be in the name of the Lord Jesus, if we don't submit all our works to His word and His will. We can't do bad things in the name of the Lord Jesus and consider that thanksgiving. What did Jesus say? “If you love Me, keep My commandments" (John 14:15 MEV).

Second, works that prove repentance are "such as spring from love to God, for if they are done through fear of punishment, or for sinister and selfish ends, they show repentance to be a mere legal one." It is when we love God, and gratefully submit ourselves to His will, that the mind-change of repentance is shown true. Merely fearing consequences is no change of mind.

Finally, "they are such as are done in faith, in the name and strength of Christ, and to the glory of God by him." Works worthy of repentance are not those done in our own strength, but by the strength of God, with all glory given to him. Go back to our selected passage today (Paul's apologia before Agrippa), and look at the very next sentence. "Therefore, having obtained help from God, I continue to this day, testifying both to small and great" (Acts 26:22a MEV).

Just as Tyler sings, we still hurt and fall short of what God says we're worth. We deserve neither what Christ did on the cross, nor what the King does now from the throne, and by the Holy Spirit inside us. But He did it anyway. What unfathomable grace! How could we ever deny the necessity of good works to give Him thanks, and yet still think we truly believe in and understand what He's done for us?

On the other side of that fence, how could we ever think our good works are necessary for our atonement, and yet not realize that such a stance means we're believing the finished work of Jesus wasn't enough? To trust in our own works is to neuter our vision of the Lord.

Notes

Day 156

Having Obtained Help From God

"When it was decided that we should sail into Italy, they handed Paul and some other prisoners over to a centurion of the Augustan Regiment, named Julius. Boarding a ship from Adramyttium, we put out to sea, meaning to sail along the coasts of Asia. Aristarchus, a Macedonian of Thessalonica, was with us. The next day we landed at Sidon. And Julius treated Paul kindly and gave him leave to go to his friends and be given care." - Acts 27:1-3 MEV

I hope you'll forgive me as our story jumps all around this chapter for the next couple of days. Festus, Bernice, and Agrippa pass judgement of innocence over Paul, and they determine he must be sent to Rome to fulfill his appeal. We find Paul now passed into the care of one centurion (and his hundred soldiers) of the imperial personal guard. Possibly they're in Caesarea having accompanied Festus to his new seat of power, and are themselves ready to return to the Capital. In this centurion, as in Lysias, Felix, Festus, and Agrippa before him, we see a certain level of favor and respect for Paul.

Look at the evidence as recorded by Luke. He's allowed travelling companions, consisting of at least the beloved physician, and Aristarchus, though whether they traveled on their own dime, or Rome's is not specified. He's allowed to freely speak to and among the centurion and his soldiers, and further into the storm, even to give orders. Later, all the prisoners are protected from mass execution, merely for the sake of defending Paul's life.

One of the first examples though, shown near the beginning of the journey, this prisoner of Rome is extended an unusual favor, being allowed leave of the ship to go be refreshed spiritually and temporally by his fellow Christians in Sidon. Surely for the coming journey, and after 2 years of imprisonment, the Apostle needed care. Before this treacherous journey, it could easily be assumed the man could stand some fresh garments and other necessities.

Look to the opposite end the journey, in chapter 28, and Paul and the rest of the shipwrecked crew were shown, "extraordinary kindness" by the local Islanders, and even housed in the estate of the chief man of the island. Then, at the end of the final leg of the aquatic portion of their travels, Paul, Luke, and Aristarchus are all given privilege to stay in the homes of their fellow Christians for 7 days. When they reach Rome, Paul's imprisonment is about as tame and favorable as any accused man could ever hope for.

So, what of it? Look at the rest of Paul's encounters with "the lawman." How many times previously to this was he bound in shackles and thrown inside dark cells? How many times has he now been beaten with rods, or received the forty lashes minus one? How many times has he unjustly seen the long arm of the law? Or what about his final stint in prison? The man is thrown into the dankest cell which is essentially the sewer pit, charged with fires he had nothing to do with, by the very man who caused them, and eventually loses his head for the false charge.

In all those times, through his words and actions which Luke recorded, and through the letters written by his own hand, we see the utmost faith, courage, and strength, and surely those were provided by God. Yet in these 4 years of awaiting justice, we see a somewhat different Paul. He's a little meeker, and a little more reserved, possibly a little more depressed, and with a little more doubt. Yet Paul knew a great truth, which we have just read past. "Therefore having obtained help from God, I continue to this day..." (Acts 26:22a MEV)

"For He has said: 'I will never leave you, nor forsake you.' So we may boldly say: 'The Lord is my helper; I will not fear. What can man do to me?' " - Hebrews 13:5-6 MEV

When Paul's faith stood firm, God let him pass through the fire so that by it both he and those who saw might be built up. When, on the other hand, Paul might be tempted to utterly despair, God was faithful, not letting the Apostle be tempted beyond what he could bear, but providing an escape that he may endure the temptation.

I could cry, "woe is me," but look at the favor God has planted in the hearts of these men with charge over me. I could give up hope, but look how God has provided for my care. I could consider myself abandoned, but look how God has blessed me with the fellowship of His servants. I could sink into the Mediterranean Sea and die, but look how God has rescued me. I could sulk in sorrow that I've lost my ministry, but look how God has ordained me to preach even from house arrest.

Have you ever escaped into a book, movie, or game? You could really use a break from the world, and so you sink deep into the pages of your favorite fantasy or thriller? There is an escape even better, in the darkest of sorrows, trials, and temptations, and that is to sink ourselves deep into the recognition of the blessings of God. There is no doubt in my mind that if each of us would devote ourselves to fix our eyes on Christ, we will see blessings upon blessings, which the eternally reigning King has abundantly rained upon our temporal lives. When we fix our focus firmly on what God has done for us, we tend to see how small our giant troubles really are. Oh Paul, you knew well what it was like to be tempted, and yet be shown the escape in the faithfulness of the Lord Jesus Christ.

O God, teach us this sort of unbreakable faith. Teach us to see Your faithfulness in our lives. Teach us to fix our eyes on Your Light, even in the darkest valleys, and carry us when we cannot see. In the precious name of Your Son Jesus Christ we pray, Amen.

Notes

Notes

Day 157

Four Anchors

"From there we put out to sea and sailed under the lee of Cyprus, because the winds were against us. Sailing across the sea off of Cilicia and Pamphylia, we came to Myra, a city of Lycia. There the centurion found a ship of Alexandria sailing to Italy, and he put us on board." - Acts 27:4-6 MEV

Today, we look at some of the distinguishing details of Luke's history. The doctor lays out time, place, weather, conditions, and characters, not to mention the tense excitement which we'll look closer at tomorrow. After narrating Paul's kindly care in Sidon, he draws our attention to the sailing ships.

"We sailed slowly for many days, and arrived with difficulty off Cnidus, and as the wind did not allow us to proceed, we sailed under the lee of Crete off Salmone. Sailing past it with difficulty, we came to a place called Fair Havens, near the city of Lasea." - Acts 27:7-8 MEV

Recording their path along the coast he explains why they stuck so close to the shore, and why they turned south to travel around the island of Crete. The winds of which Luke speaks are called Etesian winds, and they blow annually from mid-May to mid-September (the end of which we'll soon find approaches). The Etesians are described by the encyclopedia Britannica as a "remarkably steady southbound drift of the atmosphere over the eastern Mediterranean." If a ship at this time of year were to attempt to sail from modern Turkey toward Rome, and not make the loop south around Crete, the wind would smash them right into the north side of the island, if not another of many small islands in the vicinity.

"As much time had been lost and as the voyage was now dangerous, because the Day of Atonement was already over, Paul advised them, saying, 'Men, I perceive that this voyage will be with injury and much loss, not only of the cargo and ship, but also of our lives.' But the centurion was persuaded more by the captain and the owner of the ship than by what Paul said." - Acts 27:9-11 MEV

So, the sailors attempt to pass around the south side of Crete. They find a port of Crete called fair haven which is still known by the same name (in Greek) today. But against Paul's better judgement, the sailors and centurion decide to push off again, hoping to get to a more suitable port on the western side of the island.

"When a south wind blew gently, supposing that they had obtained the necessary conditions, they weighed anchor and sailed along the shore of Crete. But soon afterward a tempestuous wind swept through, called the Euroclydon." - Acts 27:13-14 MEV

The Euroclydon (or Northeaster depending on your translation) is also a recordable weather event still known to this day, now by the name of Levanter. Remember that Luke has given us the time of year as well, saying the Day of Atonement had passed. Yom Kippur happens (by our Gregorian calendar) toward the end of September or early October. That is one of two times of year when these Levanters are known to become gale force, and are often described by sailors as tempestuous or even typhonic. The Alexandrian ship will never again see the coast of Crete.

"When the ship was overpowered and could not head into the wind, we let her drift. Drifting under the lee of an island called Cauda, we could scarcely secure the rowboat. When they had hoisted it aboard, they used ropes to undergird the ship. And fearing that they might run aground on the sand of Syrtis, they let down the mast, and so were driven." - Acts 27:15-17 MEV

The Egyptian merchant sailors rightly fear the quicksands of Syrtis. The northern coast of Africa had two bays of sands known for swallowing entire ships, and overwhelming the men aboard. Throughout this record, Luke tells us neither sun nor stars appeared through the clouds for many days. They're afloat traveling vaguely southwest and have passed Cauda, approaching Libya, but have no idea specifically how close they are, so they take evasive action and drift, by the grace of God, toward Rome.

"They took soundings and found the water to be one hundred and twenty feet deep. When they had gone a little farther, they took soundings again and found it to be ninety feet deep. Fearing that we might run aground on the rocks, they dropped four anchors from the stern and prayed for day to come." - Acts 27:28-29 MEV

For two weeks these sailors desperately attempt to save their ship and their lives, but then they recognize the sound of land and drop anchor. Here is where it gets interesting. For several centuries now, tradition and the residents of Malta have claimed that the ship came aground in what's known today as St Paul's Bay. The trouble is, there has been a distinct lack of archaeological evidence there of Luke's account.

Recently though, the Bible Archaeology, Search & Exploration (BASE) Institute, took special note that Luke says the sailors "did not recognize the land." The traditional claim to Paul's shipwreck location was quite close to the bustling seaport of Valletta, the vicinity of which would be well known to any first century sailor. The BASE institute went back to the scripture, and using computer models, they implanted the information of Luke's record into weather and water patterns, coming to the conclusion that the ship must have run aground on the south side of the island.

"Casting off the anchors, they left them in the sea while loosening the ropes that secured the rudders. Then they hoisted the mainsail to the wind and made for shore." - Acts 27:40 MEV

Two bays became the potential locations, one of which perfectly fit both the weather pattern of the Euroclydon, and the description Luke gave, even down to the depth soundings of the approach. BASE arrived to find a story of two local divers who, some 50 years prior, had found 4 anchors, at precisely 90 feet deep, all within 40 yards of each other. The natives didn't know what they possessed, and had long ago melted down two of the anchors for the scrap metal value. A third anchor was lost to time, but the fourth anchor was left to the widow of one of the divers.

The head of Malta's department of classics and Archaeology, Dr Anthony Bonano, having examined the anchor, confirmed to BASE that this was indeed a first century Roman style anchor, the kind of which ships from either Rome or Alexandria (the main granary of Rome) would carry several. The radius of separation between the anchors is even confirmed to be a fitting distance for a first century freighter which could carry 276 people.

Over the centuries, thousands of Archaeological discoveries have confirmed the accounts of the Bible, but now, within our lifetimes, we have what is possibly the first artifact discovered which is a specific item spoken of in the New Testament. The God of heaven and earth, ordained the safe-ish path of the Alexandrian ship, so that Paul could testify in Rome, just as promised, but He also inspired the Physician to what is among the most perfectly accurate historical records of all time. This Bible we read is not just a story book. It is both a history lesson and the living word of God.

Notes

Day 158

Never Abandoned in any Storm

"We sailed slowly for many days, and arrived with difficulty off Cnidus, and as the wind did not allow us to proceed, we sailed under the lee of Crete off Salmone. Sailing past it with difficulty, we came to a place called Fair Havens, near the city of Lasea." - Acts 27:7-8 MEV

The 27th chapter of Acts is easy to read speedily through. A few hundred men are on a ship, bound for Rome, yet as they're beset by unfavorable winds, they eventually become shipwrecked on Malta. "Ok, Luke, I'm here for the Acts of Jesus Christ through His Apostles. Why spend so much time on one little voyage? What can we learn from it?" Surely this chapter emerged from the physician's quill because of the emotion of it all. Read through the chapter again, but as one of the men on the ship.

"But soon afterward a tempestuous wind swept through, called the Euroclydon. When the ship was overpowered and could not head into the wind, we let her drift. Drifting under the lee of an island called Cauda, we could scarcely secure the rowboat." - Acts 27:14-16 MEV

Up to this point they've already fought the winds for a large portion of the journey, barely managing to make port at Cnidus, and have lost exceeding amounts of time. Surely, they've heard talk from sailors, as well as the locals in the ports, about the risks they face if their journey continues this late in the year. They argued in Fair Haven about the dangers that lay ahead, and for days watched the sea until the sailors felt confident they had good wind, but no sooner had they embarked than the winds changed to that dreaded Northeaster which had, no doubt, been discussed in detail.

"We were violently tossed by the storm. The next day they threw cargo overboard. On the third day we threw the tackle of the ship overboard with our own hands. When neither sun nor stars appeared for many days, and no small storm was upon us, all hope that we should be saved was lost." - Acts 27:18-20 MEV

Drifting, because the winds overpowered them with sails deployed, they were barely even able to secure the rowboat (vs 16). Sailing with much difficulty at the mercy of the winds because they were drifting toward the quicksands of Libya, they were violently tossed by the storm, and lightened the ship of any and all extra weight. The seasoned sailors are so overwhelmed they even recruit the passengers in the fight. In sheer darkness they fight, for days on end, in the desperate fight of their lives, until all hope is lost.

Of course Luke wrote extensively about this experience. He's been watching for days as career sailors feared for their lives. He's been hearing their voices tremble, as they most certainly argued among themselves about the best course of action, just as most in such stressful circumstances would. He essentially tells us even the professionals were now exclaiming, "we're all going to die." If you have any doubt about how tense this was, consider that we're told they didn't eat anything for 14 days!

" 'For there stood by me this night the angel of God to whom I belong and whom I serve, saying, “Do not be afraid, Paul. You must stand before Caesar. And, look! God has given you all those who sail with you.” Therefore, men, take courage, for I believe God that it will be exactly as it was told to me. Nevertheless, we must be shipwrecked on a certain island.' " - Acts 27:23-26 MEV

But in the midst of all this trouble and fear, up stands a landlubbing prisoner, and he says "take courage." This was, after all, the man who had warned to delay the journey, but to the sailors that was like being told how to do your job by someone who's only read the book. Now, at the end of all hope, God interjects hope, and through Paul sends a message that "your lives will not be lost."

Look back to verse 20, and Luke tells us "all hope that we would be saved was finally given up" (NKJV). The seafaring men traversed the storm and tried everything they could by their own hands, until they finally realized their self-confidence came to nothing, and they could not rescue themselves. It was at this very point that Luke now records God sending a messenger to report that "God has granted" the saving of these lives. I don't doubt that the Gospel writer recognized the metaphor in all of this.

"When he had said this, he took some bread and gave thanks to God in the presence of them all. And when he had broken it he began to eat. Then they were all encouraged, and they also ate food themselves." - Acts 27:35-36 MEV

The ship drifts on, and we're shown a slightly different attitude on the ship. Some, having been offered good news, still trusted in their own knowledge and "fearing that we would be dashed against the rocks," put their hands back to the work before trying to abandon the ship at the expense of the lives of hundreds of passengers onboard. Others, having received hope, listened with respect to the servant of God, even to the point of cutting away the rowboat; that which seemed the only earthly hope of survival. The prisoner becomes the leader.

"Whilst they sailed with a prosperous gale, neither God, nor his poor prisoner and chained apostle, is thought upon; but in a storm or tempest they are glad to believe and follow his direction." - Matthew Poole

Yes, this is a strange chapter in Luke's account of the early Church, but it doesn't lack gospel instruction. Aside from the clear metaphor, we can take hope in the outcome of this storm. Whether or not you were led to believe life would be sunshine and rainbows after coming to Christ, if that turn didn't occur yesterday, you have no doubt weathered storms, as Paul, Aristarchus, and Luke did.

But see in this historic storm the evident truth that God's will prevails, and that even by the most treacherous tempest, He works all things to the good for those who love Him. See in this dramatic chapter the evidence of how typhonic gales may lend to the ministry of the evangelist, soften the hardest Roman soldier's heart to God's word, and even provide a testimonial seed which may later sprout in the impenitent sailor. See how God has never abandoned his children in any storm. This is, after all, the fourth man in the super-heated fiery furnace.

Notes

Day 159

Cast Off all Anchors

"Casting off the anchors, they left them in the sea while loosening the ropes that secured the rudders. Then they hoisted the mainsail to the wind and made for shore." - Acts 27:40 MEV

Before we move on from the story of the sea, let's take another look at those anchors. Several Roman style anchor stocks have been found in the depths around Malta over the last century. Some, several hundred pounds, and others measured in tons. Examples of these finds can be seen at the Malta Maritime Museum. One such find, discovered in the early 2000s, had very clear inscriptions of two Egyptian gods on them; Isis and Sarapis. It is said such inscriptions were not uncommon, much like the two carvings which adorn the hull of the next Alexandrian ship Paul finds himself on (Acts 28).

Sailors throughout the centuries have often been very superstitious men, and while Luke didn't see the anchors, or record anything about any inscriptions, it wouldn't be unexpected for the four anchors the Egyptian freighter dropped to be labeled with the names of these false gods. If the 1960s discovery of the four anchors which we recently discussed were indeed those specific anchors, we still don't know, because only the lead stock survived the millennia. So then what does Luke tells us of these four anchors? They were abandoned at sea.

If you're a KJV only reader, you will find this as "when they had taken up the anchors," and that variation is because of the root of the Greek word Luke used, "periaireō." The root "haireō" indeed means "to take," but I believe, as do most translators now, periaireō is best translated "take away." The word is only used 4 times in the New Testament, but can be found 52 times in the Septuagint, and it is in that Greek translation of the Old Testament we see sufficient evidence that the people of the ancient world understood this word as one indicating removal.

Having mentioned the four NT uses, it is worth note that two of the four occur in this chapter. Before the sailors removed the anchors, probably inscribed with the names of Egyptian gods for protection, Luke told us "all hope that we should be saved was then [periaireō] taken away" (vs 20 KJV). But now, having no hope left in their false gods, those anchors were cut away, and the promise of God given to Paul was all they had left to hope in. It's a good thing for them His promises never fail.

"Now fear the Lord, and serve Him with sincerity and faithfulness. [periaireō] Put away the gods your fathers served beyond the River and in Egypt. Serve the Lord." - Joshua 24:14 MEV

Malta remains, to this day, the most Christian nation in all of Europe. But where did that start? The abandonment of gods, by which God's promise, given through his servant, could be received. 276 men survived this shipwreck, and it could not have been possible if they hadn't cut away the idols made by human hands. 276 men made it safely to shore, and seeing miraculous things happen to and through Paul, the natives poured in from all directions in a new belief that they could be healed. The veil was lifted for many, and it was all because four anchors were cut away.

"But their minds were blinded. For until this day the same veil remains unlifted in the reading of the Old Testament, because the veil is taken away in Christ. But even to this day, when Moses is read, a veil lies on their heart. Nevertheless when one turns to the Lord, the veil is [periaireō] taken away." - II Corinthians 3:14-16 NKJV

Forget Egyptian gods for a moment though. There are many even to this day who can't see the forest for the trees, because they don't read the Bible in faith. The most dedicated biblical scholar could spend a lifetime searching these scriptures without Christ and only be left with questions and doubts, eventually "deconstructing his faith." God was not unclear about that. It is when one repents (changes his/her mind) and truly believes in the name and finished work of the Lord Jesus Christ that the veil is removed and the answers are revealed to have been right under our noses all along.

"But every priest stands daily ministering and repetitively offering the same sacrifices, which can never [periaireō] take away sins." - Hebrews 10:11 MEV

Whether a man follows Egyptian, Babylonian, Persian, Greek, Asian, or Norse gods, or whether in unbelief of the Messianic Fulfillment he follows the old covenant law, there is no salvation in any of it. There is no other name by which a man must be saved. The deconstructionist will often blaspheme God saying David was a wicked man called "a man after God's own heart," and thereby God can't be good. That's the veil, my friends.

"So David said to God, 'I have sinned greatly in doing this thing. Now, please, [periaireō] take away the iniquity of your servant, for I have acted very foolishly.' " - 1 Chronicles 21:8 MEV

David was not a man after God's own heart because he was good. None is good but God. David was a man after God's own heart because he cast off the anchors that held him down. He was humbly repentant. That is the heart which God loves; that which can know in faith that God takes away the iniquity of his servants. That is the sort of hope which can never be taken away from the faithful. That is the hope that we have in Jesus Christ. Cut away the anchors of your soul, release the rudders and raise the sail for shipwreck on the sandy beach of salvation. All the goods will be lost regardless, but your life shall be saved in the Lord's finished work.

Notes

Notes

Day 160

With our own Hands

"When they had escaped, they learned that the island was called Malta. The natives showed extraordinary kindness, for they kindled a fire and welcomed us all, because of the rain and the cold. When Paul had gathered a bundle of sticks and put them on the fire, a viper driven out by the heat fastened on his hand." - Acts 28:1-3 MEV

I imagine quite the sigh of frustration here. Years of imprisonment, weeks of certain death at sea, and now finally on land, a viper bites the man. But there's none of that shown in scripture. He shakes the thing off and continues with his day. Let's rewind though. 276 men were shipwrecked, and against all probability 276 men survived. Just a few years before this the Jewish historian Josephus was also on a freighter to Rome, and that ship also sank in the same region. Of the 500 men on board Josephus' ship, he wrote that only 80 survived.

Now though, just as the Lord had promised, none of their lives would be lost. That means they made it to Malta, they weren't dashed on the rocks, they managed to drive the ship right up onto the reef, those who could swim did, and those who couldn't were carried by the debris of the ship. They all make landfall, but remember it is winter in Malta. We now have 276 men, soaked to the bone, with no provisions, on a beach at first light, when the average morning temperature is around 50°F/10°C. Oh, and it's raining!

The danger has not passed. They could easily have lost the more weakened members of their gang to hypothermia, but God sends the natives out, not to plunder the ship. Instead they start a fire large enough to warm almost 300 men! With the fire started, the danger still has not passed, and a viper latches on to the hand of one of the prisoners. Even so, not a word God has spoken is shown unfaithful.

It is notable though, as we traverse this fallen world holding on to the promises of God, that we find Paul gathering sticks. The man has literally been the sole voice of reason, when all the sailors and soldiers decided to embark. He was the one who told them they would live, and look at how they did. He was the one who told them to eat, and they were encouraged. He was the one who saved all the soldiers and prisoners by ordering the sailors to not be allowed to leave. Clearly Julius the centurion had learned a lot of respect for this man, ordering that the typical Roman custom be thrown aside, and the risk of prisoners escaping be accepted for the sake of Paul's life.

Seriously, this Apostle could have sat by the fire like a king. I have no doubt the centurion would have allowed it, maybe even encouraged it. He could have sat there comfortable in the knowledge that God had promised his safe passage, and had no need to put his hand to the work. I mean, by the way we sometimes tend to handle the promises of God, he could have, but that's not where we find Paul.

Though the angel of the Lord told him he would testify in Rome, we find him compelled to appeal to Caesar (Acts 25:11, 28:19). We find him throwing the ship's tackle overboard, "with our own hands" (Acts 27:19 MEV). We find him gathering sticks for the fire. Not just a few twigs either. The man has a bundle of sticks so large that he doesn't even notice there's a viper within! God's servant is never shown to sit idly in the promises of God. He puts his hand to the work before him, confident in the faithfulness of God.

Listen, if you were to be exploring a cave when it collapsed, and if in the distress of darkness an angel came, illuminated the cavern, and told you that God had ordained that you would not die down there, and if, as the angel faded, you saw in his place a pickaxe leaned against the pile of rubble, would you sit there and stare at the darkness where the axe lay, waiting for it to dig you out? You'd have to be a fool, right? So why do we sometimes treat God's promises like this?

Brothers and sisters, there are times where the fulfillments of God's promises are entirely miraculous, or even naturally beyond the reach of our conduct, but those tend to be the exception, rather than the rule. If you don't utilize the provision that God puts within your reach, don't think He failed to provide. The Lord is Faithful and True. We, on the other hand, tend not to be.

Day 161

Not as Man Sees

"When the natives saw the creature hanging from his hand, they said to one another, 'Surely this man is a murderer. Though he has escaped from the sea, justice does not allow him to live.' But he shook off the creature into the fire and suffered no harm. They expected him to swell up or suddenly fall down dead. But while they waited and saw no harm befall him, they changed their minds and said that he was a god." - Acts 28:4-6 MEV

There's no real record of what gods the natives of Malta worshipped. They had been populated by Phoenicians several centuries before, but had since been visited by many seafaring men of various nations; Grecians, Romans, Egyptians, and more. What we do know is they were now visited by a man of God. Much like those in Lystra, it didn't take more than an unexplainable miracle to instantly make them decide he was a god.

One moment they thought him worthy of death, and the next, they thought him a god, much like the Lycaonians, one minute preparing a sacrifice to him, and the next preparing to stone him. Again though, what specific god they imagined him to be was unstated. Maybe Asclepius, whom Greek and Roman mythology considered the God of medicine, associated with vipers, and whom they believed was the son of their god Apollo. But this was no God, nor son of a god; This was a man who believed in the only begotten Son of God (who was with God and who was God), and through him, Jesus' prophetic promise was fulfilled.

"He said to them, 'Go into all the world, and preach the gospel to every creature. He who believes and is baptized will be saved. But he who does not believe will be condemned. These signs will accompany those who believe: In My name they will cast out demons; they will speak with new tongues; they will take up serpents; if they drink any deadly thing, it will not hurt them; they will lay hands on the sick, and they will recover.' " - Mark 16:15-18 MEV

The thing about Christ's final words in Mark, is that all of the promised signs of his followers were shown true in the building of His Church. They cast out demons. They spoke in various tongues which they did not know so that all present heard in their own language. They laid hands on the sick who were miraculously healed. Paul takes up the serpent but is kept from harm. All of these were fulfilled in the book of Acts, save one, and that one is the only one which wasn't "they will." Take note that the only one not fulfilled in this record is the one which Christ had said, "If they drink any deadly thing, it will not hurt them."

All of the miracles that were shown in these followers of Christ were used as signs to point the superstitious gentiles and hard-hearted Jews to the truth of Christ just as He had foretold. All of those miracles were the supernatural work of God, not the strength of men.

There is, actually, one vague tradition about the worship on this island, and it supposes they thought him to be Hercules. From what we've discovered of Paul's stature, that's rather difficult to believe, but there is also another old story that has persisted through the generations.

While Luke was clear the natives saw this viper and instantly recognized it as a poisonous beast, there are no poisonous snakes on the island today. Even within a couple hundred years after Paul's shipwreck, ancients recorded that there were no vipers left native to the island, but they recorded another strange phenomenon as well. Scorpions (poisonous throughout the world), were harmless on the island of Malta, even being eaten by the local children. Vipers, if imported from other regions, supposedly held no danger when on the island. The locals attributed it to the miracle of God shown through Paul. Whether or not any of that is true or not is really of no concern to us. I don't know about you, but I'm not planning to go eat scorpions in Malta anytime soon.

What we can make pertinent to our daily lives though, from this passage, is a truth we so easily forget. It is in our nature to associate good fortune with righteousness, and adversity with justice, but the reality is not so black and white. Indeed, all sin will be met with justice in the end, save that which has already been paid by the Lamb of God, and indeed God can sometimes use blessings to build us up in our faith, but that's not always the way it is.

Just because you see a person who always seems to succeed in everything he or she does, it does not necessarily mean that they are in the good graces of God. Often the devil pads our beds and tucks us in tight and cozy, so that we may not awake until the final judgement. Similarly, the man who is facing trial after trial - one misfortune after another - is not necessarily facing the judgement of divine justice. Often, these tribulations are nothing more than the troubles of the world which God allows so that through them He may work our sanctification. We cannot look at outward things and see if a person is a man of God or not, any more than those of Malta or Lystra could gaze at the prisoner and see if the man was a god or not.

" 'For the Lord sees not as man sees. For man looks on the outward appearance, but the Lord looks on the heart.' " - 1 Samuel 16:7b MEV

Notes

Notes

Day 162

Ambassadors in Foreign Lands

"When this happened, the rest on the island who had diseases also came and were healed. They honored us in many ways. And when we sailed, they provided us with necessary supplies. After three months we sailed in an Alexandrian ship whose figurehead was the Twin Brothers, which had wintered at the island." - Acts 28:9-11 MEV

We quickly approach the end of the writings of the beloved physician, and the beginning of nearly 2000 years of Christian history. The end of Luke's record is not the end of Paul's ministry, and we'll soon see a rather strange and abrupt end to the book, but these last few passages are not without important truths. Take this ship for example. Rather, let's remember where we are.

Paul had found favor in the eyes of all his Roman judges, as well as the Centurion with charge over the soldier accompanying the prisoners to Rome. He has found special favor in the eyes of 275 men, having been the sole conduit for God's hope in a hopeless situation, and the voice of reason in life and death decisions. He has found favor with the villagers, shaking off the bite of a viper in their sight and receiving no harm. He has found favor in the sight of the chief, or first man, of the island (the governor of Rome's rule), by miraculously healing his father, and he's found favor with the residents of the entire island who, having heard of the miracles, send their sick and dying to also be healed.

It is of special note that Luke points out that the figurehead of this second Alexandrian ship was "the twin brothers." You'll probably recognize this better as the star constellation "Gemini." The two Roman-Greco demi-gods were believed the patrons of the sailing man. When the constellation was visible, it was believed their favor shined on the seas. Essentially, the ship had on either its hull or bow, a carved idol, which the sailors invoked for safety on the mighty seas. Yet we don't see Paul shrink back from climbing aboard the ship.

Surely, with the acclaim this man has garnered among everyone here, he'd have some say, even as a prisoner. After all, he was the man who had both argued against the previous voyage, and been God's tool for rescue of every single soul on board. He has shown at every turn that he is indeed a man of God. Surely Julius would have given some ear if Paul had refused to board the ship adorned with false gods.

Whether the ship eagerly took on the wage of transporting hundreds of otherwise stranded travelers, or whether the Roman empire exerted their dominion and required compliance is unstated, but if Paul had taken a stand against the figurehead, there is a high probability something would have been done about it. At the very minimum, Luke would have written about it. At Fair Haven, Luke had recorded Paul's contention, but here he merely records the facts of this ship, and says nothing more. Clearly Paul wasn't concerned.

It's an interesting thing, for we're told to "flee from idolatry" (1 Corinthians 10:14), and to "abstain from all appearances of evil" (1 Thessalonians 5:22). We are also told "bad company corrupts good morals" (1 Corinthians 15:33). There's something else relevant which Paul wrote to the Corinthian Church though.

"I wrote to you in my letter not to keep company with sexually immoral people. Yet I did not mean the sexually immoral people of this world, or the covetous and extortioners, or the idolaters, since you would then need to go out of the world. But I have written to you not to keep company with any man who is called a brother, who is sexually immoral, or covetous, or an idolater, or a reviler, or a drunkard, or an extortioner. Do not even eat with such a person. For what have I to do with judging those also who are outside? Do you not judge those who are inside? But God judges those who are outside. Therefore 'put away from among yourselves that wicked person.' " -1 Corinthians 5:9-13 MEV

Though we are no longer of this world, we are still in it. We are still called to be a light in the darkness. We are still here as Christ's hands and feet, and His ambassadors. Ambassadors don't reach foreign people by sitting securely in an office in the homeland. As Paul said, if we tried to isolate ourselves from all unbelievers for their sin, we would not only be completely unable to fulfill the great commission, but we would find it rather impossible to even open our eyes in the morning.

Jesus didn't sin with the sinners, but He did eat with them, and it was by this manner - as One who was in our world yet entirely holy - that He made disciples. What Paul describes in the fifth chapter of 1 Corinthians is the difference between becoming "all things to all people so that by all means some may be saved," and failing to edify, exhort, and encourage our fellow brethren to come into the conformity of Christ.

It is tempting, when abstaining from idolatries and every form of sin, to place that burden on unbelievers. True it is that we must not be afraid to call sin what it is, regardless of company (else they could never recognize their need for the Savior), and we find it evident in the word of God that, removing the plank from our own eye we ought also sharpen one another within the Church, judging with righteous judgement, but even so, it is not our place to judge those who are outside.

Don't get this wrong. Not judging doesn't mean we don't speak truth. If I fail to tell even my enemy the cliff toward which he approaches, I am not loving as Christ loved. See what it says that, "God judges those who are outside." They will be judged, regardless of whether we preach Christ or shrink in political correctness. God won't shrink from the justice that is required for all righteousness to be fulfilled. He is faithful and that means He is also faithful to visit the iniquities of the transgressor. When such a wonderful, free gift as grace is offered unto all who believe, how could we keep that good news amongst ourselves?

If we refuse to board that ship because those who carved it were ignorant of Christ, how could we ever hope to carry His testimony to all the world? If we board ourselves up like monks from all the wickedness of the lost around us, how could we ever make a single disciple of any nation much less find a single morsel of bread? The old saying "we are in the world but not of it" is only faithful to Christ if we not neglect either half.

In the world and just like it avails not our souls.

Not like the world but neither in it avails not any souls.

Notes

Day 163

Faithful Fellowship, Great God

"From there we circled around and sailed to Rhegium. After one day the south wind blew, and the next day we arrived at Puteoli. There we found brothers, and were invited to remain with them for seven days. And so we went to Rome. From there, when the brothers heard of us, they traveled as far as the Forum of Appius and the Three Taverns to meet us. When Paul saw them, he thanked God and took courage." -Acts 28:13-15 MEV

After much trouble, the sailing is complete, and this weary band of travelers finds itself no more than 175 miles from Rome in Puteoli. Up until just a few years before this, Puteoli was the primary port by which Rome received grains and goods from Egypt. This was no small city. Just a few years after Paul passed through, the third largest amphitheater in all of Italy was constructed here, able to hold 60,000 people. The ship lands and Julius, his soldiers, Paul, Luke, and Aristarchus (as well as the rest of the prisoners) find themselves in a bustling port full of vim and vigor.

Luke tells us in the midst of all this life "we found brethren" (KJV). As we've previously discovered, "brethren" was one of the primary terms Christians used for one another. It is of particular note here though that they found "brethren" not "the brethren." That breaks from the standard we've seen previously in his writing, and even in the very next verse.

In Acts 21:7, for example, at Ptolemais "we greeted the brothers and stayed with them for one day" (MEV). Leaving there and arriving at Jerusalem, "the brothers received us gladly" (Acts 21:17 MEV). After Paul's week here in Puteoli, "when the brothers [from Rome] heard of us, they traveled as far as the Forum of Appius." The lack of definite article in this sentence is telling, and matches the fact we have no prior record of knowledge of a Christian community in this port. Rome, for example, has been well known by Paul for its church, many members of which he addressed by name in the Epistle to the Romans; That letter he has already, at this point, written.

Therefore, we find that along with his traveling companions, Paul steps off the ship chained to a Roman soldier, yet somehow comes into contact with Christians he didn't know to exist. Did he enter port preaching the Gospel and a local believer happened by to hear? Or did he enter port and find a local disciple preaching that Only Name? However it happened it becomes evident that faith was on display, and by it, God brought His children together.

The Greek word used for, "invited" (us to stay), was a word with more emphasis than we typically give it. It implied a strong desire. It is the same word used when all the sick of Gennesaret "begged" Jesus to let them touch His garment. The KJV translates that Paul and Luke "were desired to tarry with them for seven days." The local Christians, coming into contact with this traveling prisoner of the Lord Jesus Christ - maybe recognizing who he was, and maybe not - beg him and his friends to stay and eat the Lord's supper with them. Apparently, they also sent a messenger to their sister church in Rome, because the Christians there became aware of Paul's arrival.

As for those Roman brethren, they travel 43 miles to the Forum of Appius and spend the night waiting to greet Paul. The approach to this layover post on the way to Rome from Puteoli could be made by two routes, and was typically done by night. As for the post itself, the previous century had seen the poet Horace describe the place as, "an unsavory place crammed with boatmen, innkeepers, and wayfarers, who cheat, carouse, and quarrel."

Imagine, then, the overnight presence of this gang of Christ followers, joyously celebrating the arrival of a brother who they had long desired to meet, and who had so long harbored the same sentiment. Amidst the rabble-rousers and cheats, we have a strange group of the Holy priesthood, singing praises to the Lord, and telling of His faithfulness and grace. Is there any doubt that seeds were planted in this otherwise barren place?

It's a glorious work of God that when His servants faithfully preach Christ, His grace brings them into fellowship with their brothers and sisters; and likewise, that when His children joyfully gather in fellowship, His light is shined into dark places. Brothers and sisters, stand mightily in who you are in the family of Christ. We may be weak, but He is strong, and because of His faithfulness, our simple acts of faith produce much fruit.

Notes

Notes

Day 164

Jesus Christ, Our Sabbath

"For this reason I have asked to see you and speak with you, because I am bound with this chain for the hope of Israel." - Acts 28:20 MEV

At long last we come to Paul's final recorded speech, and it points to things that have always been, things that are in his present circumstance, and things yet to come even in our generation. Before quoting the foretold hardness of heart of the people of his nation, and telling them in the absence of their hearing, salvation has been sent to the gentiles, he speaks of the Hope of Israel. Surely the pharisee of pharisees recognized that he quoted Jeremiah. The hope of Israel was their Lord and Messiah. This man bound repeatedly by chains is, "Paul, an old man, and now also a prisoner of Jesus Christ" (Philemon 1:9 MEV).

"O the Hope of Israel, its Savior in time of trouble, why should You be as a stranger in the land, and as a wayfaring man who turns aside to pitch his tent for a night?" - Jeremiah 14:8 MEV

The Hope of Israel is twice used as the name of the Lord in Jeremiah's prophecy of discipline and rebuke against Judah. As the prophet pleads for mercy on behalf of the people of Israel - and on behalf of himself, caught as a faithful minister in the crossfire - the Lord declares his judgement which would soon come in the Babylonian captivity. Yet while this prophecy was primarily fulfilled in the sixth century BC, it also foretold of greater things. Through Jeremiah, God declares the four judgements he would bring on Judah (Jeremiah 15:2), and they're a perfect match for those four horsemen that Jesus Christ told John would come in the end days (Revelation 6:1-8).

"O Lord, the Hope of Israel, all who forsake You will be ashamed. 'Those who depart from Me in the earth will be written down, because they have forsaken the Lord, the fountain of living waters.' " - Jeremiah 17:13 MEV

We now know who the Fountain of Living Waters is, and so we can see who is the Hope of Israel. The Lord, Jesus Christ, is the same Lord and Word of God who spoke to the prophets. As Jeremiah continues to plead,

God declares his unrelenting wrath, and says it is because they have rejected the Sabbath. He goes on to promise that if they would sanctify the Sabbath in their hearts, "this city will be inhabited forever" (Jeremiah 17:25 MEV), and so we see again that this immediate prophecy had a factor that is yet to be fulfilled. New Jerusalem is yet to come. But the Orthodox Jews still practice the Sabbath keeping, right?

"For we who have believed have entered this rest... Since therefore it remains for some to enter it, and they to whom it was first preached did not enter due to unbelief, again He establishes a certain day, 'Today,' saying through David, after so long a time, as it has been said: 'Today, if you will hear His voice, do not harden your hearts'... Therefore a rest remains for the people of God. For whoever enters His rest will also cease from his own works, as God did from His. Let us labor therefore to enter that rest, lest anyone fall by the same pattern of unbelief." - excerpts from Hebrews 4:3-11 MEV

The Sabbath of the Old Covenant was indeed a day of the week, but Jesus came and became our Sabbath, for he said, "come to me all who labor and are heavily burdened, and I will give you rest" (Matthew 11:28 MEV). The works of Sabbath day keeping are not sufficient to save any from sin, but the grace granted to us in Jesus Christ is sufficient. The Lord Jesus is our Sabbath now, the Hope of Israel, and all who come to Him in belief enter into that rest.

Back to Paul though, we find him in chains because he was determined to go preach Christ to his fellow Jews, but the Jews rejected their Messiah, and the messenger of His good news. "They did not enter due to unbelief." Truly Paul was bound with that chain for the Hope of Israel. And yet, He continued, even in Rome, to make an attempt for their lives, so that death would be defeated.

It is interesting that we can look to the letter he had previously written to the believers in this city, and find the Apostle's take on that hope. Why was he so determined to reach these people? He pressed on because he knew from scripture that the Lord would at some point remove the veil from their eyes and the Jews would be saved. Like us, Paul didn't know specifically what "soon" meant, but he knew that his countrymen would eventually turn to Christ, their rest. Can you blame him for trying so hard to be a tool in the hand of God during that glorious chiseling?

"For I am speaking to you Gentiles. Inasmuch as I am the apostle to the Gentiles, I magnify my ministry, if somehow I may make my kinsmen jealous and may save some of them." - Romans 11:13-14 MEV

It's in that letter that Paul defines for us why we've seen this pattern of him always going "to the Jew first and then to the gentile." He was ordered by God to preach to the gentiles, and God told him the Jews would largely not listen to his words, but still the man loved his people. There's absolutely nothing wrong with that, granted he didn't elevate them above God in his heart. Look at the greatest two commandments, and we see he was right to love God first, and love the people next.

Yet the unbelieving Jews remained resistant to grace. Even to this day we see that resistance. A pew research study from 2021 found that among US Jews, 21% consider religion important, compared to 41% of the general public. Only 26% believe in the Judeo-Christian God, as opposed to 58% of the US overall. 22% of Jews say they don't believe in any form of higher power, as opposed to 9% of the overall population. The Orthodox Jews which make up 9% of US Jews are actually highly religious, skewing those numbers to look better than they really are, but they are by and large just as firmly opposed to Christ as anyone could endeavor to be.

"For I do not want you to be ignorant of this mystery, brothers, lest you be wise in your own estimation, for a partial hardening has come upon Israel until the fullness of the Gentiles has come in. And so all Israel will be saved, as it is written: 'The Deliverer will come out of Zion, and He will remove ungodliness from Jacob'; 'for this is My covenant with them, when I shall take away their sins.' " - Romans 11:25-27 MEV

Don't get this wrong though! We are those who should pray for Israel. We are those who know God keeps His remnant. We are the gentiles who benefited because of their temporary hardening. When the last of us is saved (the fullness of the gentiles), the Lord will revisit His people and there will be great revival in the sons and daughters of Abraham.

No, don't get this wrong. The servant brought into the field at the first hour is often jealous of the wage of the servant brought in at the last hour, but as He taught, that jealousy is not in the Spirit of Christ, my friends. If indeed we know Him and love Him, our joy is in every soul that comes into His rest, regardless of how late the hour is, or what they did while we were working the field. Whether the last hour servant is the murderer who finds Christ on death row, or the blaspheming Jew who finds Christ in the final revival, we are all equally unworthy of this mercy.

These are, in the eternal perspective, our brothers and sisters! Salvation is ours only because of them. It belongs first to Israel, and that day when they come into the Sabbath rest that is Jesus Christ will be a blessing beyond our wildest dreams. That day all will be fulfilled and we will be ready for harvest. Maranatha.

"I say then, have they stumbled that they should fall? God forbid! But through their transgression salvation has come to the Gentiles, to make them jealous. Now if their transgression means riches for the world, and their failure means riches for the Gentiles, how much more will their fullness mean?" - Romans 11:11-12 MEV

Brothers and sisters, we approach the end of our study of the word of God penned by the inspired hand of the beloved physician, but this end is only a beginning. The best is yet to come, as they say. I don't know about you, but this promise - that our fullness will mean riches for them, the likes of which riches we inherited from them - this promise inspires me all the more to share the gospel far and wide. Like Paul, we can press on with the knowledge that God's word is true, and that none of His children shall be lost. Every single member of our Christ family will be there when we praise Him in Heaven. Let's be God's tools to sculpt such a day. Let's submit to His plan and will in every moment.

Notes

Day 165

Christ's Church Continues!

"Paul remained two whole years in his own rented house. He welcomed all who came to him, boldly and freely preaching the kingdom of God and teaching those things which concern the Lord Jesus Christ." - Acts 28:30-31 MEV

It's been said that Luke's record doesn't so much as end, but rather just stops. After Paul's release, there are competing theories to the assumption of whether he went to Spain or back to Jerusalem before returning to Rome and being executed. As for Luke though, there's very little we can know of what happened to him after this except that it is widely believed he no longer accompanied the Apostle in his journeys. What happened with the rest of Luke's earthly life and body is a mystery, but the spirit of Luke is well known to us; The Lord inspired the pen of our beloved physician to the completion of the works that were prepared for him, sometime after which he awakes in the glorious presence of our Savior.

Luke began this second treatise by rehashing the things Jesus began to do and to teach and the Kingdom of God which he preached, and now he ends with Paul preaching the Kingdom of God, and teaching the things of the Lord Jesus Christ. Truly this was the Acts of the Lord Jesus Christ.

"How convenient if Luke had told us a little more! But Paul's history is unfinished, like Peter's and John's. This book's treatment of all the Apostles teaches, as we have often had to remark, that Christ and His acts are its true subject. We are wise if we learn the lesson of keeping all human teachers, even a Paul, in their inferior place, and if we say of each of them: 'He was not the Light, but came that he might bear witness of the Light.' " - Alexander McLaren

And so, we come to the completion of Luke's history, with Paul preaching, and teaching boldly from house arrest. It is believed that while chained to a soldier for 2 years in Rome the Apostle authored the epistles of Ephesians, 2 Timothy, Philippians, Colossians, and Philemon - most likely in that order. In the opening of Philippians, he dwells on the blessing that his sufferings have brought. Trying to share Christ with his countrymen, they had attempted and then demanded his immediate execution, but through his imprisonments many, even in the imperial house, came to the saving knowledge of Christ.

"But I want you to know, brothers, that the things which happened to me have resulted in advancing the gospel, so that my imprisonments in Christ have become known throughout the entire palace guard and to all the rest. And a great many of the brothers in the Lord, having become confident because of my incarcerations, have dared to speak the word without fear." - Philippians 1:12-14 MEV

Not only did he preach Christ to those lost sheep among the gentiles, submitting fully to his temporary role as the Shepherd's crook, but he tirelessly taught God's children the grace and knowledge of the Lord Jesus. We've studied through Paul's imprisonments and seen the truth that although the world threw the book at him, Jesus, the Author and Founder of our faith, protected the man as long as his good works were yet to be done. The Church was born, her reach was spread, and the children were given instruction to spiritual maturity.

During his time in chains Paul was able to fix his eyes on Christ and see the working of all things to the good. He was able to see how even imprisonment was useful that Christ be known. He was able to see, even then, that "a great many brothers in the Lord" became confident to speak the word without fear, "because of my incarcerations." Oh, but Paul, if you only knew how great a many that truly was throughout the millennia!

From this rented villa, as he wrote to the church at Philippi, Paul's soul cried out "maranatha," pleading to be in the presence of the Lord, yet dwelling on the sanctifying work that was still to be done in Christ's church. One of his most famous scriptures came about in this internal struggle, and it is the inward cry of all who suffer for the Name. "For to me to live is Christ, and to die is gain" (Philippians 1:21 ESV). The Apostle exposes the conflict within his heart, saying he is hard pressed between the fruitful labor and the presence of Christ.

"Having this confidence, I know that I shall remain and continue with you all for your joyful advancement of the faith," - Philippians 1:25 MEV

Yet for a time, the Lord ordained the man to live in the flesh, to continue so that we all could benefit by our joyful advancement of the faith. One small Benjamite in chains sent ripples through the pond of time, and our boats are still rocked to this day. Even to this day men are made confident to boldly preach the Kingdom of God and teach the things of Christ by the reading of Paul's incarcerations.

So it has been through all of church history. One parent trains up a child in the way he should go, and he serves the Lord for decades to come. One faithful servant brings a sinner to Christ and that sinner becomes a great teacher. One teacher instructs a single brother in Christ, and that brother becomes the tool through which God raises up one of his greatest evangelists. And on, and on it goes, that our seemingly inconsequential acts of faith are used greatly by God, leaving a mark on history the likes of which dwarf any other legacy we could hope to build. All glory and power and honor are His.

Sure, Stephen was bludgeoned with stones, Paul lost his head, and Peter was crucified, but as we read of their lives, can there be any doubt of the joy they have in eternal life? Nothing any faithful Christian has suffered for that Only Name will be forgotten, and nothing God works through us is fruitless.

"For this corruptible will put on incorruption, and this mortal will put on immortality. When this corruptible will have put on incorruption, and this mortal will have put on immortality, then the saying that is written shall come to pass: 'Death is swallowed up in victory.' " - 1 Corinthians 15:53-54 MEV

There are lots of questions as to what happened after Luke closed his scroll. Where their bodies were laid to rest, we do not know, but, "where did their souls find rest," is a question the answer to which we can be fully confident of. The question, and its answer, are that which can encourage every maturing child of God to serve the Lord, fearless of anything the world can bring against us. "What shall we then say to these things? If God be for us, who can be against us?" (Romans 8:31 KJV)

"To Paul now, what are all his sorrows, and persecutions, and toils in the cause of his Master? What but a source of thanksgiving that he was permitted thus to labor to spread the gospel through the world? So may we live - imitating his life of zeal, and self-denial, and faithfulness, that when we rise from the dead we may participate with him in the glories of the resurrection of the just." - Albert Barnes

And so we come to the end of our study. I pray that you've been as blessed and built up as I have been, in exploring the record of nearly 70 years of God's work, divided between two volumes, written through the doctor's pen; A prescription for life everlasting - the cure for death - as it were. What will you study next?

Notes

Works Cited

Barnes, Albert. *Barnes' Notes on the Whole Bible*. 1870. https://www.studylight.org/commentaries/eng/bnb.html

Battistelli, Francesca. *He Knows My Name* © 2014 Capitol Christian Music Group, Inc. https://www.youtube.com/watch?v=jYpBgJHmGmw

Bengel, Johann Albrecht. *Johann Albrecht Bengel's Gnomon of the New Testament*. 1897. https://www.studylight.org/commentaries/eng/jab.html.

Benson, Joseph. *Benson's Commentary.* 1857 https://www.studylight.org/commentaries/eng/rbc.html.

Beza, Theodore. *The 1599 Geneva Study Bible*. 1599-1645. https://www.studylight.org/commentaries/eng/gsb.html.

Casting Crowns. *Nobody* © 2019 Provident Label Group LLC, a division of Sony Music Entertainment https://www.youtube.com/watch?v=1yBzIt_z8oY

Clarke, Adam. *The Adam Clarke Commentary*. 1832. https://www.studylight.org/commentaries/eng/acc.html.

Exell, Joseph S; Spence-Jones, Henry Donald Maurice. The Pulpit Commentary. 1897 https://www.studylight.org/commentaries/eng/tpc.html.

Ellicott, Charles John. *Ellicott's Commentary for English Readers*. 1905. https://www.studylight.org/commentaries/eng/ebc.html.

Gill, John. *Gill's Exposition of the Entire Bible.* 1999. https://www.studylight.org/commentaries/eng/geb.html.

Gitt, Werner; Compton, Bob; Fernandez, Fernandez. *Without Excuse.* Powder Springs, Georgia. Creation Book Publishers. 1 January 2011

Henry, Matthew. *Matthew Henry's Concise commentary on the whole Bible.* Accessed 22 January 2023 https://www.biblegateway.com/resources/Matthew-Henry/Luke

Jamieson, Robert, D.D.; Fausset, A. R.; Brown, David. 1871-8 *Commentary Critical and Explanatory on the Whole Bible - Unabridged.* https://www.studylight.org/commentaries/eng/jfu.html.

"Jewish Americans in 2020." Pew Research Center, Washington, D.C. (11 May, 2021) https://www.pewresearch.org/religion/2021/05/11/jewish-americans-in-2020/

Josephus, Flavius. *Wars of the Jews book II,* http://data.perseus.org/citations/urn:cts:greekLit:tlg0526.tlg004.perseus-eng1:2

Lumby J.R. Commentary on Acts. *Cambridge Bible for Schools and Colleges.* Cambridge University Press. 1891.

MacLaren, Alexander. *MacLaren's Expositions of Holy Scripture.* https://www.studylight.org/commentaries/eng/mac.html.

Mowery, Paul. *Acts 21:15-40.* Leo, Indiana: November 30, 2014 Harvest Fellowship.

"Jürgen Moltmann Quotes." Quoteslyfe.com, 2023. Fri. 27 Jan. 2023. https://www.quoteslyfe.com/quote/Jesus-healings-are-not-supernatural-miracles-in-773082

Nave, Orville. "Repentance - Nave's Topical Bible." Blue Letter Bible. 24 Jun, 1996. https://www.blueletterbible.org/search/Dictionary/viewTopic.cfm.

Ortlund, Dane C. *Gentle and Lowly. Wheaton, Illinois. Crossway,* 2020.

Paul's Shipwreck, Bible Archaeology Search & Rescue Institute, 2019. https://baseinstitute.org/pages/pauls-shipwreck

Piper, John. *The Pleasures of God, Meditations on God's Delight in Being God.* Colorado Springs, Colorado. Multnomah, 2000.

Poole, Matthew. *Poole's English Annotations on the Holy Bible.* 1685 https://www.studylight.org/commentaries/eng/mpc/luke-16.html.

Ramsay, W.M. *St. Paul the Traveller and the Roman Citizen*, 1908, Hatchette, UK, Hodder and Stoughton.

Ryle, J.C. *Expository thoughts on the Gospels.* 1857

Spurgeon, Charles H. *CSB Spurgeon Study Bible*. Nashville, Tennessee: Holman Bible Publishers, 2017

Spurgeon, Charles Haddon. *Spurgeon's Verse Expositions of the Bible.* https://www.studylight.org/commentaries/eng/spe.html. 2011.

Tyler, Micah. *I See Grace* © 2022 Fair Trade Services. https://www.youtube.com/watch?v=p6bjAk3EGQw.

Wickham, Phil *Where I'm Standing Now (Official Audio) ft. Brandon Lake.* © 2021 Fair Trade Services. https://www.youtube.com/watch?v=IMPAfIdXi98.

www.ingramcontent.com/pod-product-compliance
Lightning Source LLC
LaVergne TN
LVHW010553100826
845148LV00014B/2693
9798988132837